Theocritus

Theocritus
Space, Absence, and Desire

―――❖―――

WILLIAM G. THALMANN

OXFORD
UNIVERSITY PRESS

OXFORD
UNIVERSITY PRESS

Oxford University Press is a department of the University of Oxford. It furthers
the University's objective of excellence in research, scholarship, and education
by publishing worldwide. Oxford is a registered trade mark of Oxford University
Press in the UK and certain other countries.

Published in the United States of America by Oxford University Press
198 Madison Avenue, New York, NY 10016, United States of America.

© Oxford University Press 2023

All rights reserved. No part of this publication may be reproduced, stored in
a retrieval system, or transmitted, in any form or by any means, without the
prior permission in writing of Oxford University Press, or as expressly permitted
by law, by license, or under terms agreed with the appropriate reproduction
rights organization. Inquiries concerning reproduction outside the scope of the
above should be sent to the Rights Department, Oxford University Press, at the
address above.

You must not circulate this work in any other form
and you must impose this same condition on any acquirer.

Library of Congress Cataloging-in-Publication Data
Title: Theocritus : space, absence, and desire / William G. Thalmann.
Description: New York, NY : Oxford University Press, [2023] |
Includes bibliographical references and index.
Identifiers: LCCN 2022027414 (print) | LCCN 2022027415 (ebook) |
ISBN 9780197636558 (hardback) | ISBN 9780197636572 |
ISBN 9780197636589 | ISBN 9780197636565
Subjects: LCSH: Theocritus—Criticism and interpretation. |
Space in literature. | LCGFT: Literary criticism.
Classification: LCC PA4444 .T38 2022 (print) | LCC PA4444 (ebook) |
DDC 884/.01—dc23/eng/20220711
LC record available at https://lccn.loc.gov/2022027414
LC ebook record available at https://lccn.loc.gov/2022027415

DOI: 10.1093/oso/9780197636558.001.0001

1 3 5 7 9 8 6 4 2

Printed by Integrated Books International, United States of America

Contents

Preface — vii
Introduction — xi
Note on Text and Transliteration — xxi

1. Theocritean Spaces 1: The Bucolic and Urban Poems — 1
    Fictional Space 1
    Bucolic Space 4
        General Description of Bucolic Space 4
        Spatial Relations in *Idyll* 5 16
        Spatial Relations in *Idyll* 1.1–23 25
        Spatial Relations in *Idyll* 7 27
    The "Urban Mimes" 32
        Idyll 15 32
        Idyll 2 40

2. Theocritean Spaces 2: Mythological and Encomiastic Space — 44
    Mythological Space 44
        Idyll 13 45
        Idyll 22 53
        Idyll 24 63
    Encomiastic Space 73
        Idyll 16 73
        Idyll 17 85
        Idyll 14 89

3. The Poetics of Absence   93
   Absence, Desire, and Song   93
       Idyll 1: A Version of Bucolic Origins   101
       Idyll 7: Lykidas's Song   121
       Idyll 6: Breaking the Frame   129
       Idyll 2: Desire in Town   140
       Idyll 13: Herakles in Love   147

4. On the Margins of Bucolic   154
   Poems Concerning Margins   154
       Idyll 4: The Waning of Bucolic   155
       Idyll 10: The World of Labor   169
       Idyll 21: The Dream of a Fisherman   181

5. Conclusion   192

References   203
Index of Passages Cited   215
Subject Index   225

Preface

I FIRST READ Theocritus's bucolic poems as a college sophomore, in a course taught by Gilbert Lawall, whose book about them was then in press and who let the class read it in proof. I would like to thank Professor Lawall for introducing me to this wonderful poet and for offering me some ways of approaching him. Unfortunately, despite his best efforts, I failed to appreciate the riches of this poetry. It seemed to me too labored, too bookish, trivial by comparison with the great questions raised by Homer and Greek tragedy, which enthralled me then and still do. This response, or lack of it, had nothing to do with Professor Lawall's teaching but was due to the callowness of my nineteen-year-old self. Still, I left Theocritus with a vague intuition that there was something interesting in those poems, if I only knew how to come to grips with them. In graduate school I read through all of Theocritus because he was on the reading list, this time with more engagement but with a certain amount of bewilderment at what seemed to me a very miscellaneous collection. Over the years I taught a few of the *Idylls* now and then to graduate students, usually in Greek literature survey courses, and often with the thought that I should come back to Theocritus someday; but I was busy with other projects. While I was working on my book on Apollonius's *Argonautika*, I gave a graduate seminar several times in Alexandrian poetry that began with Theocritus. I worried at first that the students would be left cold by him, more or less as I was as a student, but was delighted when, each time, the opposite proved to be the case. Their enthusiastic engagement with the texts, their animated discussions of tantalizingly puzzling lines (what does "all invented for the purpose of truth," *Id.* 7.44, mean?), and their intellectual energy inspired me. I thank all of those students for our discussions.

I would like to thank in particular two alumni of that seminar. As I was forming and clarifying my ideas about Theocritus, I had the benefit of many hours of discussion with Matthew Chaldekas while he was working on his dissertation on vision in the *Idylls*. After this lapse of time I do not recall specifics of the conversations, and I am not aware of particular debts, though there may be some. In any case, these discussions were very valuable to me. Later, he read and commented generously on a first draft of what is now chapter 3. More recently, John Kelleher took time from his dissertation on Plato and fourth-century intellectual history to read a penultimate draft of the whole book. His comments on its overall arguments came at a critical time and helped me keep them in focus.

Because of administrative and other responsibilities, work on this book had to proceed in fits and starts and took a long time. I would like to thank the University of Southern California and the USC Dornsife College of Letters, Arts and Sciences for leaves in the spring semesters of 2017 and 2020 that enabled me to concentrate on research and writing.

The second leave coincided with the beginning of the Covid-19 pandemic, which led to fifteen months of isolation at home. This involuntary leisure gave me time to concentrate on further reading of books and articles and to write and rewrite most of the book. This work gave me a focus during an otherwise miserable time. It would be facile and wrong to call what I was doing escapism into Theocritus's green world, but immersing myself in the *Idylls*' complexity and the challenge of writing about it did much to offset the constant feeling of oppression caused by awareness of so much suffering and death and by appalling political events.

Because of these circumstances, I had no direct access to a library. So I am especially grateful to the staff of the USC libraries, who, working behind the scenes and anonymous to me, provided electronic copies of innumerable articles and book chapters that I badly needed. It is no exaggeration to say that without their help, I would have made no progress on the book during this difficult period and could not have completed it.

Chapters 1 and 2 are a revised and greatly expanded version of my chapter, "Theocritus and the Poetics of Space," in *Brill's Companion to Theocritus*, edited by Poulheria Kyriakou, Evina Sistakou, and Antonios Rengakos. I thank the editors for inviting me to contribute to this fine collection while I was developing my ideas on Theocritean space.

Once again, the staff of Oxford University Press has been a pleasure to work with and has made the process of submission, review, and production smooth. I thank in particular Stefan Vranka for his support of the book and Project Editor Sean Decker for his constant helpfulness. Jubilee James at Newgen Knowledge Works kept everything on schedule and inspired me with her efficiency. I am extremely grateful to Wendy Keebler for her meticulous and wise copyediting. Warm thanks as well to the anonymous readers for the press.

Over the years, my colleagues in the USC classics department have created an atmosphere of warmth, generosity, and intellectual energy in which it has been a pleasure, and an education, to work and teach. They have played no small part, though an intangible one, in the writing of this book.

Finally, I thank my family—my sisters, my wife, our son and daughter, their spouses, and our grandchildren—for being an inexhaustible source of joy even during the dark times when we could communicate only by phone and FaceTime.

Introduction

IN ADDITION TO a number of epigrams, thirty complete or mostly complete poems have come down to us under the name of Theocritus, a poet evidently active in the 280s and 270s BCE. He probably spent at least part of that time in Alexandria, where he seems to have enjoyed the patronage of Ptolemy Philadelphus. Not all of the collection is certainly by Theocritus; some poems are fairly clearly of later date, although they are in his manner, and the authorship of others is uncertain. This book is concerned with many of the Theocritean poems and a few whose authorship has been questioned. The poems in the collection are conventionally, and more or less appropriately, called *Idylls* (from εἰδύλλια, "little pictures, vignettes," or else "short poems of different types").[1] As the diminutive term suggests, they are brief poems; the longest (*Id.* 22) is not much more than two hundred lines, and most are considerably shorter. Although Theocritus is best known for his bucolic *Idylls*, the collection is surprisingly—and for many first-time readers, bewilderingly—diverse. One might expect that such a slender group of short texts hardly provides material for a book. In fact, Theocritus is an extraordinarily rich, suggestive, and rewarding poet. Each poem, every line almost, can take the reader's thoughts in many directions at once. There is no way to read these poems casually. To read them and reread them and to write about them has been challenging and a joy. Their very complexity is what has kept me fascinated.

Because of the nature of the poetry and the variety of the collection, much of the scholarship has tended to consist of articles focusing on single *Idylls*, although there have been excellent books as well. These careful, deep readings have been extremely valuable, but they have tended to atomize the collection, to obscure what many of the poems have in common, such as themes that crop up in very different poems. Following a recent trend in scholarship, I have attempted here to consider each *Idyll* in its individual nature—and every one of these poems is

---

1. The latter translation is from Gutzwiller 1996, 132.

Theocritus. William G. Thalmann, Oxford University Press. © Oxford University Press 2023.
DOI: 10.1093/oso/9780197636558.001.0001

distinctive—and in relation to the corpus as a whole, or as much of it as I could appropriately discuss in a single book. And so I have picked out certain topics that especially interest me and that cut across individual differences among poems. I want to make it clear at the outset that these choices make no pretense at somehow exhausting the possibilities of this poetry, as if such a thing were ever possible. There are many different ways of approaching Theocritus and thinking about his poems, and I often indicate in footnotes alternatives to the views I express. I have simply selected a few perspectives on the poems that I think might be useful. My hope is to contribute somewhat to a continuing conversation about Theocritus and Alexandrian poetry, one that should accommodate a variety of voices.

This book continues and extends my interest in space in literature that I explored in an earlier work on Apollonius of Rhodes (Thalmann 2011). Space and spatial readings are the core of my discussions here as well, but I have taken a rather different approach, one better suited to the nature of Theocritean poetry. These poems are less obviously spatial texts than the *Argonautika* is, with its linear journey and its concern with places and their associated narratives, but I hope to show in the end how fruitful spatial readings of Theocritus also can be. The special challenge here is that, with some important exceptions such as those explicitly set on Kos or in Alexandria, space in these poems is largely fictional; despite obvious mimetic aspects, these spaces are in important ways products of the imagination. For reasons I give at the beginning of chapter 1, the fictionality of space is not really a problem or any bar to a spatial approach.

The first two chapters treat space directly as it is constructed by the poems. The *Idylls* I discuss can be grouped into four categories: bucolic, urban, mythological (the so-called epyllia or "small-scale epics"), and encomiastic. These are more than rough-and-ready groupings for the convenience of discussion; the poems within them seem to cohere in significant ways, and those within each group configure space in their own way. In the end, however, these groups taken together, even including the mythological poems, as I shall argue, create an overarching space in which the bucolic and urban worlds are placed within the Ptolemaic empire as their wider context. This is obviously true in regard to *Idyll* 15, which is set in Alexandria, but the town in which the conversation between Thyonikhos and Aiskhinas is set in *Idyll* 14 is, by the end of the poem, placed in relation to Alexandria as margin to periphery. The bucolic poems generally focus on their own space, which readers experience as almost autonomous, but they, too, as we shall see, are located within imperial space. *Idylls* 4 and 5 are exceptional in that they are explicitly located near cities in South Italy in a region that was, by Theocritus's era, suffering hard times. This area contrasts implicitly with the Ptolemaic empire, within which, we may infer, the bucolic world can flourish in its abundance.

Space is partly constituted by the objects and people within it, but in Theocritus it also is defined by what is not there, by absence. Chapter 3 examines the constitutive role of absence in the bucolic poems especially but also in some others, and in particular the way it motivates, and indeed generates, both internal songs and the *Idylls* themselves through arousing desire that, crucially, can never be satisfied because its objects cannot be attained. Bucolic space especially is thus constructed as a space of desire and therefore depends upon absence. The bucolic *Idylls* bring the reader closer to the bucolic world, but because that world is fictional—as the poems often remind us—they keep it forever out of reach. The readers' desire for it mirrors the desire of the characters within the poem; it is what keeps them reading.

In keeping with its fictional nature, Theocritus constitutes bucolic space not through detailed descriptions but with a selective and stylized repertoire of elements: mountains, hills, and caves; trees and bushes; animals, especially sheep and cattle; and herders. He refers to this space consistently as "the mountain" (τὸ ὄρος), even though it seems actually to be in foothills, so that it cannot be placed within a literal topography. He also defines it through what is on its margins, and that is the subject of chapter 4. There I discuss *Idyll* 4, which I argue is marginal although it is set in the bucolic world, because it depicts that world, and the conventions of its poetry that Theocritus constructs in other *Idylls*, in the process of disintegration. I then turn to *Idyll* 10, which concerns reapers and is not bucolic and which, I argue, confronts bucolic leisure and erotic desire with the realities of agricultural labor. I end with the questionably Theocritean *Idyll* 21, which similarly depicts the labor and grinding poverty of fishermen, who appear on the edges of attention in the bucolic poems.

Chapter 5, the concluding chapter, attempts to take stock of the discussions in the earlier chapters and then come to grips with the question of what the stakes are for the reader, particularly in the bucolic *Idylls*. I discuss this problem from the perspective of the dynamics of absence and desire described above.

Theocritus is especially memorable for his bucolic poetry, partly because of its qualities and partly because, thanks to Vergil, it is the precursor of the European pastoral tradition. The temptation is to concentrate on those poems. The foregoing summary might suggest that I have succumbed to that temptation, and it is true that I have written especially with an eye on them. But in fact, the book contains sometimes lengthy discussions of non-bucolic poems as well. I do give prominence to the bucolic poems, but Theocritus himself is partly responsible for that. As I argue at several points, bucolic thinking pervades even some of the other *Idylls*, as can be seen, for example, in the vision of a restored Sicily in *Idyll* 16, in the description of the surroundings that Amykos enjoys in *Idyll* 22, and even in the tableau of Aphrodite and Adonis in the royal palace at Alexandria in *Idyll* 15. Bucolic is thus central to my discussion because it is important in the Theocritean corpus,[2] but I should emphasize that I discuss many other aspects of the non-bucolic *Idylls* as well and consider them just as interesting and important.

Even though each poem has distinctive individual qualities, and even though one can justifiably divide many (though not all) of the *Idylls* into groups, there is an overall coherence in the Theocritean corpus—not a rigid unity but a coherence that arises in the first instance from the remarkable number of connections that readers can draw between very different poems. But it amounts to more than that. Many poems seem in one way or another to respond to the new mobility of the Greek world in the wake of Alexander's conquests and to both the excitement and the anxieties it seems to have produced.[3] Along with that, they respond indirectly, I think, to the experience of living outside the Greek world as traditionally defined and in closer contact with non-Greeks, especially in multicultural Alexandria, an experience that could raise questions about definitions of the self and the fluidity of boundaries. We can see such anxieties reflected indirectly, for instance, in *Idyll* 17's attempt to depict the Ptolemaic empire as producing spatial clarity, a comprehensive order for a large part of the world under Greek rule, where every component has a defined place.[4] Or we might think of Aiskhinas dislodged from home in *Idyll* 14 through his own fault in an unhappy love affair. As a mercenary, he will be deracinated perhaps, but his movement will have a goal and a purpose: Alexandria and service to Ptolemy. *Idyll* 15 is another obvious example, with the women's encounters in the streets of Alexandria with Greeks from other parts of the homeland and Praxinoa's notorious disparagement of Egyptians.

Theocritus's creation of the bucolic world can be considered a similar, though perhaps more submerged, response to the same conditions. It might have offered, in imagination, a vantage point from which to think about movement and

---

2. To say this is not to claim that Theocritus's poetry as a whole, or whatever collection of it was made in antiquity, was "governed by the bucolic concept" (Gutzwiller 1996, 119, arguing against this notion), only that the bucolic concept exerts an influence in poems outside the bucolic *Idylls*. Stephens (2006, 92) also shows "how deeply the values associated with pastoral are embedded in all of Theocritus' poetry"—a view subtly different from the one Gutzwiller rejects.

3. On this deracination and literary responses to it, see especially Selden 1998.

4. Stephens's argument (2003, 147–170) that the praise of Ptolemy is couched in both Greek and Egyptian cultural idioms adds a further important dimension.

placelessness—Michel Foucault's "heterotopia."[5] Such a world, with its intense localism, offered a vision of stability, timelessness, and rest, where everything and everyone seemed to have a proper place and to fit. The attractions of such a refuge must have been strong, but readers who expected only that might have been surprised. One of the questions that the bucolic *Idylls* implicitly raise (for example, spatially at the beginning of the programmatic *Idyll* 1, as I will show) is the relation of human culture to nature and whether human beings can ever truly fit into nature. One prominent manifestation of this question is the contrast between the elaborate and usually frustrated human quests for love and the easily satisfied lust of goats. And bucolic leisure only allows time for restless desire, which issues in song. In addition, *Idyll* 7, as I will argue, is from one perspective about being out of place. Lykidas is a bucolic figure who shows up in the lowlands, displaced from "the mountain," and Simikhidas and his friends are on a day's jaunt from the town that is their home. They meet in an apparently featureless place, and the question of their identities is very much in play, as modern scholarly discussion shows. Is Lykidas goatherd or god? Is Simikhidas a mask for Theocritus? What kind of poet will he be? Will he be worthy of "the mountain"? At the end of the poem, Lykidas abruptly departs, and Simikhidas ends up on a farm, in a beautiful (but not bucolic) place where all his senses are gratified, enjoying a festival to Demeter that commemorates the completion of farm labor. But he has done no work. Does he belong here? And so I suggest that the bucolic *Idylls*, along with the others, raised questions posed by the new conditions of their readers' world and offered them a distanced perspective on issues that they were confronting in their actual lives.

To speak of groupings of the *Idylls* and of an "overarching coherence" among them does not imply that I think that we have the remains of an ancient poetry book in any way like some we know of from the early third century BCE, such as the Milan Posidippus, with texts grouped by subject and placed in a way that invites reading a given poem both in itself and in relation to adjacent poems. We do not know whether Theocritus himself collected his poetry and published it together or if someone else did so after his death, or what form such a collection might have taken in either case. The earliest collection we know of was compiled by Artemidorus in the first half of the first century BCE, and subsequent ancient editions arranged the poems in different orders, although all put the bucolic poems first and began with *Idyll* 1.[6] The corpus we have seems to derive from those editions, with accretions of post-Theocritean poems that already had begun

---

5. Foucault 1986.

6. These statements are all based on Gutzwiller 1996.

to be added in antiquity, notably *Idylls* 8 and 9. The unity I speak of, then, is the result of recurrent themes, concerns, and outlook in what we have of Theocritus's poetic production.[7]

It is reasonably safe to think that Theocritus was born in Sicily; that was the prevailing belief in antiquity, although we have no idea what it was based on. Beyond that, we know virtually nothing of his life. In particular, there is no evidence independent of the poems themselves as to where Theocritus wrote his poetry.[8] What has been considered internal evidence is not strong. *Idyll* 16, addressed in part to Hieron II of Syracuse and containing a wish for Sicily's restored prosperity, has often been read as a plea for Hieron's patronage, and that has led to the assumption that Theocritus must have been living in Sicily when he wrote it. That is far from a necessary conclusion, and it rests on a reading of the poem that I would question. I try to show in chapter 2 how many interesting aspects of *Idyll* 16 can emerge if we do not make patronage in itself the center of our reading. *Idylls* 1 and 11 are clearly set in Sicily, but that does not mean that Theocritus wrote them there. *Idyll* 7 has been thought to show him living and working on the island of Kos, but that is based on the notion that the poem's narrator, Simikhidas, straightforwardly *is* Theocritus. Theocritus's poetry could have been written anywhere. Nevertheless, like many others, I think it likely that he worked at least for some time in Alexandria, under the patronage of Ptolemy Philadelphus and with the resources of the Library, and that he came there into creatively productive contact with Callimachus and Apollonius of Rhodes, who we know were there. There is no evidence for this. Having cast doubt on biographical readings of other *Idylls*, I would not point to the tributes to Ptolemy and his patronage in *Idylls* 14 and 17, although the importance of Alexandria in the spatial configuration of the poetry, as discussed in chapter 2, is suggestive. Theocritus's connection with Alexandria is just a heuristic belief advanced for the sake of discussion, and nothing in this book depends on it. I do (usually tentatively) refer to readers in Alexandria in describing the possible effects of the poems, and I have this much justification at least: that even if Theocritus's poetry was not written in Alexandria, it was certainly read there. The skeptical reader can understand "Alexandria" in such contexts as shorthand for "any city in the Hellenistic Greek world," since it is clear from their nature that the poems

---

7. Cf. Stephens 2006, 92, who argues for "treat[ing] the idylls as a whole—not as a poetry book, but as a group of texts with internal dynamics and intertextual play that transcend generic boundaries." Stephens 2018, 57–83, shows what a reading of the corpus from this perspective looks like. On the limits imposed on our understanding by the tendency to separate the bucolic poems from the rest of the *Idylls*, see also Krevans 2006.

8. On this question, see the concise discussion in Hunter 1999, 1–2.

appealed especially, although probably not only, to a sophisticated and very well-read audience that significantly included urban elites.

Idylls 13 and 22 bear a strongly marked relation to Apollonius's *Argonautika*, but which poet influenced the other is a much-discussed question that has never been resolved. I find Richard Hunter's various arguments that Theocritus used and responded to Apollonius quite compelling, particularly his point that these two interconnected *Idylls* treat episodes (of Amykos and Hylas) that straddle the division between *Argonautika* 1 and 2.[9] It is also tempting to take, as some scholars have done, the eagle simile at *Id.* 13.25 as a reference to the eagle that the Argonauts see returning from its feast on Prometheus's liver when they get to the mouth of the Phasis River at the end of *Argonautika* 2. In general, the more I have worked with *Idylls* 13 and 22, the more they have seemed to me responses to Apollonius, and in particular I would like to think of Theocritus's treatment of space in *Idyll* 13 as self-consciously in contrast to that of Apollonius. However, Murray's recent arguments,[10] on the basis of astronomical references in the poem, for dating the *Argonautika* to 238 BCE, would put the finished version of the poem later than Theocritus and pose a significant difficulty for this view. Significant but not insurmountable. Since Apollonius must have worked on his epic over many years, it is possible, as others have suggested,[11] that the poets were in communication with each other as their works evolved and that they responded simultaneously to each other—a process that would have been facilitated by, although it would not have required, Theocritus's presence in Alexandria. However that may be, in my discussions of *Idylls* 13 and 22 in chapter 2, I leave questions of priority aside. My references to Apollonius there are meant only to point to alternative ways of shaping narratives about the same myths that set in relief the choices that Theocritus made.

I have not tried to cover all the *Idylls*, not even all that are certainly by Theocritus, but I have discussed most of the latter. A few just would not fit well into the topics that were my focus. Furthermore, I have made no attempt to offer a "complete reading" (whatever that would be) of any one poem. Instead, I concentrate on aspects of each that seem relevant. In some cases, this has meant that I discuss different parts of the same poem in separate chapters, and this approach in turn has necessitated a certain amount of repetition. I apologize to the reader for any awkwardness this method entails, and I hope it will be offset by clear movement of the argument.

---

9. Hunter 1996, 59–63; 1999, 264–265.

10. Murray 2014.

11. E.g., Foster 2016, 128–129: "Theocritus has read some version of Apollonius' *Argonautica*."

My use of the term "bucolic" rather than "pastoral" is in line with current scholarly usage that seeks to distinguish Theocritus's poems from the later pastoral tradition, of which they were the forerunner, and should occasion no controversy.[12] What is more unusual and may invite criticism is my restriction of the term "bucolic" to poems about livestock herders (that is, among genuine Theocritus, *Idylls* 1, 3–7, and 11, although, as I have said, there are distinctively bucolic passages in other poems).[13] The consequence of this narrowing of the term by comparison with other writers' usage is that I do not consider every rural scene in Theocritus bucolic, and in particular I distinguish carefully between the bucolic and the agricultural. I think it is a mistake to call the scene at the end of *Idyll* 7 bucolic or to consider *Idyll* 10 bucolic even though it concerns reapers. I make this distinction because I think Theocritus consistently does so, and I think that it can lead to fruitful results. At the same time, the reader should be aware that my use of "bucolic" may not be entirely consistent with ancient usage. Kathryn Gutzwiller has argued, to my mind quite persuasively, that what made poems "bucolic" were thematic concerns related to one or another of the meanings that "to bucolicize" (βουκολεῖν) had acquired in Greek by Theocritus's time.[14] The reader should feel free to understand "bucolic" in this book as a term of convenience to designate a distinctive and highly influential subset of Theocritus's *Idylls*.

I have tried, in any case, to avoid getting bogged down in questions of genre, although some of these are unavoidable. Whether bucolic may be said to be a genre and what its relation to later pastoral may be are matters that have been well handled by others and that I have not touched. There is another aspect of genre that I do discuss, with some mild skepticism. One tendency among scholars is to suggest that in one or another *Idyll*, Theocritus is using but also implicitly criticizing earlier genres, such as epic poetry. I think that this can be important, and certainly one of the pleasures of his poetry is his manipulation of the conventions and values of several genres at once into new and surprising combinations.

---

12. For strong arguments from two different perspectives, see Halperin 1983 and Gutzwiller 1991, 3–13.

13. Some would omit *Idyll* 11 from this category, but Polyphemos is a herdsman, and his values are those of the bucolic world (see especially *Id.* 11.34–49). Spatially and in other respects, *Idyll* 7 differs significantly from the other bucolics, and what is described at the end is an *agricultural*, as distinct from bucolic, pleasance. But Lykidas, at least, is a bucolic figure even if Simikhidas is not, despite his claim at *Id.* 7.91–93; and Tityros's song, embedded within the song of Lykidas, takes us into the bucolic world.

14. By this criterion, however, *Idylls* 10 and 21 would be bucolic (Gutzwiller 2006, 398), whereas I think there are advantages to the distinctions I make. Perhaps the difference is between semantic and spatial approaches, and each in its own way can be productive.

But I doubt that generic play or critique was ever his sole aim. As I say at several points, I think of genre as being like a language through which he was expressing other concerns. If that involved critique of epic or tragic values, so much the more interesting; but I do not think that our reading of any poem should end there.

I can bring together these remarks about genre and my groupings of Theocritus's poems by responding briefly to David Halperin's *Before Pastoral* (1983). Halperin makes a powerful case for understanding the *Idylls* as a kind of *epos* that renews for contemporary Hellenistic tastes traditional Greek *epos*; presumably the term *epos* is meant to include Hesiod, the *Homeric Hymns*, and other hexameter poetry as well as heroic epic. There are considerable advantages to this view. It places Theocritus in the context of the Greek literary and cultural tradition, and it helps us avoid the temptation to read him anachronistically with expectations formed by later pastoral poetry. It also helps us appreciate how original his poetry is. And it provides a basis for stressing what the various poems have in common. On the other hand, it tends to play down, or might unintentionally lead the reader to play down, the very important presence in the *Idylls* of other strands of the tradition, particularly lyric poetry and drama. In a formal sense, Halperin may be right to identify the bucolics and other *Idylls* as *epos*—after all, they were written in dactylic hexameters—but that is one view of them that should be supplemented with attention to the way they incorporate other poetic types as well, which all had their own history that becomes part of the new poems' fabric. The point is not the formalist "crossing of genres" but the combination of older poetic types in new and striking ways that does for them what Halperin says Theocritus does for *epos*: reinvigorate them for a new age.

In the second place, bringing all the hexameter poems by Theocritus in the corpus together, although it has the advantage of calling attention to their common formal and thematic elements, works against the kind of division of them into groups (bucolic, urban, mythological, and encomiastic) that I have made. I do think these categories have a real basis in the poetry; they are something more than an arbitrary way of organizing the poems for discussion and far less than formal subgenres of what could be called Theocritean *epos*. I would not agree with Halperin, for example, that grouping the bucolic poems together is necessarily the result of the fallacy of viewing them through expectations formed by later pastoral. I have been guided principally by the way they work together thematically and play off one another, and especially by the way they cumulatively construct a bucolic space, the margins of which Theocritus explores in certain other *Idylls*. I would make much the same claim in regard to the mythological, urban, and encomiastic poems. I hope that the first two chapters will show the bases for these statements. Ultimately, nothing of what I say here seems incompatible with Halperin's arguments.

Note on Text and Transliteration

For the Greek text of Theocritus, I have used A. S. F. Gow's 1952 edition and have quoted from that, indicating in the footnotes where I would hesitate to accept his readings in particular passages or would be open to other readings. Like everyone else who has written on Theocritus, I am greatly indebted to his commentary in the same edition. After seventy years, it remains fundamental, even when one does not fully agree with Gow's conclusions.

Translations from the Greek of Theocritus and other poets are my own except where indicated. They are fairly literal and intended merely as an aid to the reader. They do not do anything like justice to the richly suggestive language of the original, toward which I hope my discussions will help point.

How to transliterate Greek words and especially proper names into the English alphabet is a problem to which there is no perfect solution. There are only two ways to be completely consistent. One is simply to Latinize everything, but that misrepresents the sounds of the Greek words, even though a reader might at first be more comfortable with those familiar forms. Or one might transliterate exactly and represent the sounds of Greek as accurately as possible in English. That would preserve an important sense of unfamiliarity: the Greeks were not "just like us," and their words, like the rest of their culture, were not the same as our own. But complete consistency verges on pedantry and risks distracting and confusing the reader with names such as Aiskhulos rather than Aeschylus. Compromise is the only recourse, but where to draw the line is largely a matter of taste. I have generally transliterated Greek words and many proper nouns fairly exactly, including the use of *-k-* rather than *-c-* for Greek kappa (so Herakles instead of the hybrid Heracles) and *-kh-* for Greek chi. My only departure is transliterating Greek upsilon with *-y-* instead of the more strictly correct *-u-*. With personal and place names, I have been more flexible. I have used Latinate or English forms for the most familiar names: for example, Theocritus rather than Theokritos, Homer not Homeros, Syracuse instead of Syrakousai. For less common names, I have stuck to more precise transliteration (Simikhidas, Lykidas, Simaitha, and so on), and in borderline cases, I have sided with Greek rather than Latin, as with Olympos. I apologize to any reader who finds this method of transliteration an obstacle. In my experience, one can get used to it easily and quickly.

1

Theocritean Spaces I

THE BUCOLIC AND URBAN POEMS

Fictional Space

The poems of Theocritus, like those of Apollonius of Rhodes and Callimachus, are markedly spatial in their emphasis, for reasons that might have to do with the expansion of the Greek world in the wake of Alexander's conquests and in particular with the Ptolemaic empire. But Apollonius's *Argonautika* led the *Argo* through a space consisting of places that his readers could, or thought they could, identify as real, and the stories in Callimachus's *Aetia*, not to mention those in his hymns, are firmly tied to actual cities, regions, and islands. Some of Theocritus's *Idylls* are similarly associated with real places; but it may seem perverse, or at least futile, to consider space in the bucolic poems, a subgroup of his poetry that constructs a fictional world and self-consciously puts its fictionality on display. What can space mean in such a context?

The question is a natural one to ask, but as I hope this chapter will show, the problem is trivial or nonexistent. The spaces depicted in all three poets, including bucolic space, bear some relation to actual spaces within which people lived and went about their activities: cities and, within them, houses and palaces; hillsides, sometimes with names of actual landmarks and towns; and the Ptolemaic empire. The real challenge is how to talk about space in literature, in contrast to the real, material spaces and places that are described and studied by anthropologists and geographers. In order to do that, we have to give up any assumption we might be tempted to make that literary spaces are necessarily mimetic—a faithful and neutral portrayal of regions and places as they actually are. Instead, depictions of space are part of the world-building that literary texts perform.[1] They are, then,

---

1. On world-building as opposed to mimesis, see Doležel 1988.

representations of space—space conceived and presented in particular ways that fit the modes of seeing things adopted by the text. They may bear some relation to actual spaces and places that often have the same names, but they are not identical to them. Literary depictions of space are never exhaustive and always purposeful. "Representations of space" is, in fact, the term Henri Lefebvre uses for the second of his three "moments" in the "production" of space.[2] By this he means conceptualizations of space as reflected in maps, diagrams, measurements, and so on—practices that link space to power and control. Literary representations, as discursive constructions of space, would evidently fit into this category as well, although he never makes this explicit.

But literary representations of space are seldom abstract the way a map is. Within them are constructed what Lefebvre calls "spaces of representation," his third "moment," or what David Harvey calls "relational space."[3] This is space as people "live" it and invest natural features and human artifacts with meaning. "[A space of representation] is alive: it speaks. It has an affective kernel or center: Ego, bed, bedroom, dwelling, house; or: square, church, graveyard."[4] For Harvey, in relational space, human relations produce their own space and time, of ideas, memories, dreams, myths, and fantasies. As he also says, human identities in relational space are not fixed and static, as the Cartesian notion of the subject would suggest, but constantly formed and re-formed through social processes and interactions with nature. I suggest not only that literary texts construct space discursively but also that within those discursive formations, they often show people forming spaces of representation through their various activities and interactions. Within Theocritus's poetry, we can see this occurring most obviously in the bucolic *Idylls*, but we will also find it in many other poems of this diverse corpus.

In this light, it appears that there is little essential difference between our actual spatial practices and what we read about in literature. Unless we are looking at a map, and sometimes even when we are,[5] our experience of space is

---

2. Lefebvre 1991, 38–39.

3. I prefer the literal translation of Lefebvre's "les espaces de représentation" to the 1991 English translation's somewhat confusing "representational space." The most convenient discussion of Harvey's own triad—abstract, relative, and relational space—is in Harvey 2006. In briefly describing his and Lefebvre's ideas, I have drawn on my fuller discussion in Thalmann 2011, 15–17, 22–23.

4. Lefebvre 1991, 42.

5. I have in mind times when we look at a map and see marked on it some place where we have been. We see that it is between other places—north of one, south of the other—and how many miles it is from each of them: relative space in Harvey's term. But we might also start to visualize buildings and landmarks within that place and recall experiences we had there, including encounters with others: relational space.

subjective. For one thing, we experience it and orient ourselves within it from the body outward: here, there; up, down; left, right; east, west; and so on. This is what Harvey calls relative space. But it is also part of our lives as humans, and especially as humans in culture, that we turn certain spaces and places into relational space or spaces of representation in the sense described above. Literature shows us this essential aspect of ourselves in heightened form. It depicts our customary ways of experiencing and representing space to ourselves, which we are usually scarcely aware of, and makes them the object of attention and conscious thought, just as literary language is marked and so becomes a focus of awareness in writer and reader.

It should be clear from the foregoing that, especially in the case of spaces of representation or relational space, human societies and human cultures bear a reciprocal relation to space: their practices at once shape space and are shaped (both enabled and constrained) by it. It follows that space is not merely a setting for what goes on within it; it is not inert but a process. For this reason, I think that Paul Alpers, who is very attentive to space in pastoral, with reference to *Idyll* 1 of Theocritus and Vergil's first *Eclogue* distinguishes too sharply between foreground and background when he says (using Kenneth Burke's concept) that the "representative anecdote" of pastoral is "herdsmen and their lives" rather than landscape.[6] I would say instead that herdsmen and pastoral space, like all people and their spaces, are mutually implicated.[7] Furthermore, space is composed not just of its physical features but also of people, animals, and objects—human-made and natural (rocks, trees, plants)—that help define it along with those other features. And finally, space is defined also by absences, by what never was present or is no longer. This will be the subject of chapter 3.

The first two chapters seek to give an overview of space in Theocritus's poetry. Each of the different groups into which many of his surviving poems can be placed—bucolics, "urban mimes," mythological narratives, and encomia—constructs space differently, according to its own requirements.[8] Given the

---

6. Alpers 1996, 22–24. I should make it clear that what I am disagreeing with is giving priority to one over the other—perhaps an inevitable result if one is looking for *a* representative anecdote.

7. This mutual implication is, I think, implicit in Segal's discussion (1981, 189–190) of a "gradation of landscapes" according to a "scale of bucolic values" in Theocritus's bucolic poems. Segal's essays are exemplary for the way they conceive Theocritus's poetry in spatial terms.

8. For another discussion of space in Theocritus, see Klooster 2012. Her approach to space is informed by narratology, mine by spatial theory drawn from the social sciences, but there are welcome convergences between our discussions. Worman 2015, 185–121, offers a very interesting discussion of spatial features in Alexandrian poetry, including prominently Theocritean

reciprocal relations between actors and space, we would naturally expect to find particular kinds of people engaging in characteristic activities in certain spaces. At the same time, space in each of these groups can be read in relation to the spatial configurations of the other groups, so that reading with attention to space will allow us to draw connections of similarity and contrast between poems across the Theocritean corpus. To do so is to find signs of an overarching coherence in Theocritus's poetry. Taken together, many of the *Idylls* construct a spatial system in which country and city, herding, heroic myth, and the Ptolemaic empire both construct their own spaces and are brought into relation with one another. My aim will be to discuss space in each category of poem both in itself and within this larger framework.

Bucolic Space
General Description of Bucolic Space

Except for the ending of *Idyll* 7 (131–157), which is not bucolic, there is no comprehensive description of the spatial setting by a narrative voice in any of the bucolic poems.[9] Instead, Theocritus builds up an impression of bucolic space through comments on natural features or animal and human inhabitants delivered by characters more often than by a narrator. The reader learns about these elements of the landscape as they obtrude on a character's attention and become associated with that person's experiences and feelings. Within the poems, space is experienced subjectively, in ways that tell the reader much about the characters and convey an emotional response to the bucolic world.[10] This world may be recognizable, but it is constructed piecemeal and selectively (it is a "reality effect" rather than reality), and it always comes to us refracted through a character's

---

bucolic, as "metonyms" for a light, graceful, refined style. For example, the scene at the opening of *Idyll* 1 "serves as a trope for bucolic poetry," and "the *Idyll* as a whole thus does not just set forth a programmatic instance of bucolic poetry; it also articulates a signature style ('naturally' sweet and melodious) that is made up of the very setting itself" (197). The bucolic world thus provides a "heterotopia" for representing urban cultural hierarchies. My own view of space and its significance is less abstract, but I see it as complementary to Worman's.

9. For my use of the term "bucolic" to refer to those *Idylls* concerned with herdsmen (1, 3–7, and 11), see the introduction.

10. Klooster 2012, 106–110, sees characterization as a major function of space in the "mimetic" *Idylls*; I would extend this to the bucolic poems generally, although it will not be a focus of my discussion. For landscape as an expression of emotion in *Idylls* 7 and 11, see Elliger 1975, 331–333, 348–349.

or a narrator's consciousness.[11] In part, this subjective approach to space can be related to the *Idylls*' self-consciousness about their own fictionality, or it might be chalked up to their fondness for the "pathetic fallacy" (a notion that, as will emerge in chapter 3, I do not find very useful)—but only in part. It is also significant that the bucolic *Idylls* in this way call attention to the ways in which we habitually put ourselves in a reciprocal relation to space and interact with others (humans or animals) in ways inflected by that space.

Nevertheless, it is possible to derive from these scattered references a cumulative picture of landscape and space, as the reader does in going from poem to poem. Bucolic space is highly stylized, composed of relatively few recurring features.[12] Trees and bushes are a constant presence: pine, elm, oak, tamarisk. Among smaller plants are galingale and brush for fodder or couches for the herders' rest. Less congenial are brambles and thorns. Bucolic scenes tend to take place at springs, at which the herders water their animals and find relief from the afternoon heat and leisure for song. Rivers divide up the landscape and connect land and sea. River meadows can be used for cattle pasture (*Id.* 4.17–25). Alongside what can be seen, sounds help make up this space: the whispering of pines and the plash of water on rocks (*Id.* 1.1–2, 7–8), the hum of bees and the song of cicadas, and the herders' singing and piping, for which those other sounds provide a natural analogue. Thus, an imaginary bucolic space is constructed for human activity.

These few elements are often enough by themselves to suggest a bountiful natural setting. At times, Theocritus fills in a far richer background, at least in botanical terms. For example, according to Alice Lindsell, he mentions eighty-seven different plants and trees, mostly in the bucolic poems and with considerable botanical accuracy.[13] That number is somewhat high because she includes post-Theocritean poems in the corpus, but it is still impressive. But even here, there is a limit to mimetic realism; she points out that the plants and trees that are referred to in the *Idylls* set in Sicily do not actually grow there but are at home in the Aegean, like those mentioned in the other poems—another sign of stylization. Additional trees, plants, insects, and animals are mentioned mainly where they are relevant, as in the dying Daphnis's vision of the natural order confused (*Id.* 1.132–136). The various references to the elements of their world in the amoebean

---

11. See the neat formulation by Daspet 2017, 91–92: the place of bucolic singing orients the song in space and at the same time is constructed differently in each poem by the singer's voice. (I regret that I saw this paper too late to take it more fully into account.)

12. Legrand 1898, 197–198; Elliger 1975, 325. Seeck 1975, 202, speaks of "die typisierende Reduktion" in descriptions of the *locus amoenus*.

13. Lindsell 1937.

song contest between Lakon and Komatas in *Idyll* 5 can be read as a construction of bucolic space, but despite the richness of detail (to be discussed later in this chapter), they do not amount to a methodical description; the selection of details seems arbitrary, and they come up in random order. They are conjured up for the purpose of the contest, not for their own sake.

In *Idyll* 6 (3, 45), by contrast,[14] the only markers of the setting are the spring at which Daphnis and Damoitas exchange songs and the equally conventional soft grass in which their calves frolic. That is apparently because in their songs, the emphasis is on the relation between the sea, Galateia's home, and the land, scene of Polyphemos's herding, rather than on the land itself. And yet, because of our experience of the other poems, spring and grass function as signifiers of a whole bucolic world, and the spring's centripetal force creates the archetypal scene of bucolic singing: the meeting of two herdsmen.[15] In *Idyll* 3 there is a similar economy in the creation of space: a hillside (ὄρος, *Id.* 3.2) where the goatherd has left his goats to graze, the mouth of Amaryllis's cave, covered by fern and spatially distinct,[16] which is established as the place where the goatherd performs his *kômos* by the demonstrative in τοῦτο κατ' ἄντρον ("from the mouth of *this* cave," *Id.* 3.6) and the pine tree under which he then reclines to sing of mythic lovers (*Id.* 3.38). The goatherd mentions only two other places, both marginal to the bucolic world: the place (orchard?) from which Amaryllis told him to bring her apples (*Id.* 3.10–11) and the rock or cliff from which the fisherman watches for tunny (*Id.* 3.25–26; cf. 1.39–40). A few props suggest a scene, and yet the spatial relations set up in this way are significant: the contrast between the inside and outside of the cave—a boundary never to be crossed that casts in physical form the goatherd's whole problem of unfulfilled desire—and between the scene of his singing and the hillside, where bucolic life goes on, viewed from the perspective of one who has been drawn out of it by his erotic dilemma: "Tityros, my well-loved friend, pasture the goats and take them to the spring...." The bucolic world is distanced from the "here" of the goatherd's monologue—a spatial effect that is analogous to the narrative distancing effect that inset songs often have in other

---

14. This contrast has now been noted also by Daspet 2017, 103.

15. See Alpers 1996, 81, and below.

16. Gow 1952, II, 66, unnecessarily posits a change of scene between lines 5 and 6, as does Elliger 1975, 351. Against this see Hunter 1999, 110. As we will see below, "the mountain" (ὄρος) acts as a shorthand for bucolic space in these *Idylls*. What matters is that the goatherd is outside that space—where does not matter. On this spatial indefiniteness, see Payne 2007, 61. For a somewhat different view of the spatial dynamics in this poem, see Daspet 2017, 98–100.

Idylls.[17] Bucolic life goes on at a safe remove, cloistered from and impervious to the drama of frustrated wooing unfolding in the forefront of our attention.[18]

As the example of the fisherman's rock in *Idyll* 3 shows, bucolic space is defined by its margins and boundaries as well as by what occupies it or happens in it.[19] One boundary is that between land and sea, which fishermen, "whose prey is from the sea" (*Id.* 7.60), cross, but herdsmen never do.[20] It is on the shore that Polyphemos, neglectful of his sheep, wastes away in love for Galateia (*Id.* 11.13–16), and sitting on a high rock like the fisherman's, gazing out over the sea (*Id.* 11.17–18), he pleads with her in song to leave her watery home and join him on land. He cannot cross the boundary and come to her because he lacks gills and cannot swim (*Id.* 11.54, 60). The division between bucolic land and sea appears more permeable at first in *Idyll* 6, but when Galateia seems about to emerge from the water, the barking dog on the beach ends up seeing not her but its own reflection (*Id.* 6.10–12), as though the barrier between land and sea were absolute. Against the sea's fluidity, bucolic space takes on solidity and definition, fictional though it is. There is another important—even defining—contrast as well: between the fishermen's hard labor across this boundary and the leisure of the herdsmen enclosed in bucolic space (this contrast will be explored more fully in chapter 4).

Agricultural fields and orchards are adjacent to bucolic space, and there is contact between herdsmen and farmworkers; but although the boundary can be porous, these spaces and the activities within them are kept distinct, with (as we shall also see in chapter 4) a similar contrast between labor and leisure.[21] The

---

17. In his interesting discussion of the opening of *Idyll* 3, Cusset 2021, 288, suggests that this spatial separation "is symbolic of the transformation of the goatherd into a singer." I would hesitate to go that far, because his identity as a goatherd is basic to his portrayal throughout the poem and gives his song its special character. The bucolic *Idylls* do not separate herding from singing but join them together instead.

18. For a possible further contrast here (which would also be emphasized spatially), see Hunter 1999, 111–112: Tityros's name suggests that he could be a he-goat, and the verbs in lines 2 and 4 may contain sexual double entendres, so that "such an earthy opening would stand in obvious counterpoint to the pathetic emotion and frustrated desire of the rest of the poem."

19. On margins, with an excellent discussion of non-bucolic characters, see Myers 2016, 28–30. On boundaries and the inside and outside of bucolic space in Vergil's *Eclogues*, see Jones 2011, 43–65.

20. Cf. Jones 2011, 76, on the sea as boundary in Vergil's *Eclogues*. He adds, curiously, "in this regard there is a clear difference from the Theocritean world, where one finds both the sea and fishing." But fishermen in Theocritus are outside the bucolic world; they belong to the world of labor, as *Idyll* 21, even if it is not by Theocritus, shows (see chapter 4).

21. On this leisure and what it entails, see Edquist 1975. In her discussions of *Idylls* 1 and 7, however, she runs together the bucolic and agricultural worlds and ignores the way the labor necessary in the one sets off the leisure characteristic of the other. Her remark at the beginning (101)

non-bucolic *Idyll* 25, possibly by Theocritus, contains the only full description of rural agricultural space in the corpus (*Id.* 25.7–33), the farm of Augeias, who lives in the city but visits his country estate to inspect it. It consists of pasturage for his flocks near streams and marshes and in water meadows for his cattle, fields for growing grain, and, at the borders, orchards and, it seems, olive groves and vineyards.[22] Human habitation fits harmoniously into this landscape. Livestock steadings and huts for the workers stand side by side near a stream amid plane trees and wild olives, with a shrine of Apollo Nomios ("of the pasture") nearby. The farm extends over the entire plain, "right up to the edge of Akroreia with its many springs" (*Id.* 25.31); the name and its epithet, πολυπίδακος (regularly used of Mount Ida in Homer), suggest a mountain. This "edge" might consist of wild, unworked land, the "groves and thickets" referred to in other *Idylls* where wild beasts have their lairs. Within this boundary, all is peace, order, and spectacular prosperity, where livestock and workers go about their regular daily and seasonal rounds.

In this picture, time and space are unified as both medium and expression of harmonious order, which has its social aspect as well. For it is one of Augeias's slaves who describes the estate to Herakles, so that we envision it through his sensibilities. He speaks with obvious pride in his master's wealth and in his own and the other slaves' contributions to it (*Id.* 25.23–26):

εὐθὺς δὲ σταθμοὶ περιμήκεες ἀγροιώταις
δέδμηνθ', οἳ βασιλῆι πολὺν καὶ ἀθέσφατον ὄλβον
ῥύομεθ' ἐνδυκέως, τριπόλοις σπόρον ἐν νειοῖσιν
ἔσθ' ὅτι βάλλοντες καὶ τετραπόλοισιν ὁμοίως.

Right next door the extensive quarters for the laborers
are built, we who industriously maintain his unspeakably great wealth
for our master, casting seed in fallow-land
plowed now three times and now four.

---

that "Theocritus' bucolics are ... as much to do with the non-realisability of *otium* [leisure] as with its attainment" is suggestive, but she does not develop the idea.

22. Φυτοσκάφοι (line 27) could mean those who dig around the roots of fruit and olive trees, and the ληνοί or wine vats of line 28 imply vineyards. See Gow 1952, II, 446, on lines 28 and 32. The references are indirect because the emphasis in these lines is on the slaves and their labor (οἱ πολύεργοι, literally "those with much work," line 27). Vineyards are explicitly mentioned toward the end of the poem (line 157), evidently at the edge of the estate: on their way to the city, Herakles and Phyleus walk on a small, obscure footpath that leads from the centrally located steadings through a vineyard to the main road. The relation of this vineyard to the "green vegetation" of line 158 is unclear; see Gow 1952, II, 458–459.

Juxtaposed to the spatial location of the laborers' quarters, the references to sowing and plowing conjure up the seasonal rhythm of the agricultural year. Although there is an acknowledgment here of the importance of slaves' labor that is rare in Greek literature, this voice of the slave who is content with his station in life and proud of the fruits of his labor is part of an idealizing picture of agricultural wealth that may have had some connection with reality in the early Hellenistic period[23] but is surely exaggerated.

According to *Idyll* 25, then, on an elite man's country estate, which is worked by slaves (οἰκήων, δμώων, 33, 36) while he lives in the city (ἄστυ, 45, 153), herding is part of an agricultural system, and each kind of labor has its place. In the bucolic poems, the focus is on herding, and other activities are mentioned only as they impinge on herdsmen's interests. They are thus made to seem on the margins of the bucolic world, whatever the realities of early Hellenistic farming may have been, and references to them serve mainly to highlight that world by means of what it is not. The bucolic world is not sealed off, of course; there is contact with agriculture, but mainly when it suits the purposes of a given poem. Reapers need music, as do herders, but to accompany their work, not to fill pauses in work as is the case with herdsmen. The goatherd Lykidas is considered best at playing the *syrinx* ("panpipe") "among both herdsmen and reapers" (*Id.* 7.32–34).[24] Bombyka, who recently played the *aulos* (a pipe sounded with a reed, like the oboe) for the reapers "at Hippokion's," is the daughter, more likely the slave, of Polybotas, "man of many cattle" (*Id.* 10.16–17).[25] He may be a wealthy proprietor rather than a bucolic figure.

The bucolic *Idylls* also refer to orchards and vineyards, but in their world apples are love tokens, not produce (*Id.* 3.10–11, 5.88–89, 6.6–7, etc.). A section of the amoebean contest between Lakon and Komatas in *Idyll* 5 (108–115) mentions fruit trees, reapers, and vineyards (Komatas has, or claims to have, grapevines); the foxes that are commanded there not to leap the fence and harvest the grapes on Mikon's farm recall the third scene on the cup in *Idyll* 1 (45–54).

---

23. Hunter 2008, 302, who cites Alcock 1993, 87–88. Cf. Scholl 1989, 23–24.

24. Gow 1952, II, 139, suggests that Lykidas "may be called in to help with the harvest." The meaning may just be that there are *syrinx* players among both herders and reapers and Lykidas excels them all, but in favor of Gow's idea are the facts that the *syrinx* is the bucolic instrument par excellence and that Bombyka, by contrast, plays the *aulos* for the reapers. If Lykidas plays his *syrinx* in both settings, his music surely serves different, even opposing functions in each: the enjoyment of leisure as opposed to relieving the monotony of work.

25. "At Hippokion's" (παρ'Ἱπποκίωνι) might suggest an independent farmer, a smallholder who calls in seasonal labor to reap, in contrast to Augeias, and whose farm has nothing to do with herding.

Curiously—because that cup has often been seen as an analogue for bucolic poetry—the three scenes depicted on it are all non-bucolic: the two men quarreling on either side of a woman could be anywhere, and the fisherman and vineyard are on the edges of the bucolic world. And that fits with the cup's provenance (*Id.* 1.57–58). It is an import from the wider world; the goatherd bought it from the Kalydnian ferryman, who represents movement of people between places in that larger world as opposed to bucolic localism. He traded a goat and a cheese for it—bucolic items in exchange for an object with non-bucolic scenes. In addition to whatever metapoetic significance its carvings may hold, they also provide a defining spatial contrast to the bucolic world that has been so beautifully sketched in the poem's opening lines and that will be a central concern of Thyrsis's song to follow.[26]

The bucolic poems, then, give little impression of interconnected activities in the countryside but rather emphasize herding as separate from the rest. Perhaps herding really was distinct from the other occupations. But in view of the example of Augeias in *Idyll* 25 and the fact that the herdsmen in *Idyll* 5 are dependents of similar absentee, city-dwelling proprietors (together with the possible hint in Polybotas's name in *Idyll* 10), it seems to me more likely that the poems' intense concentration on herding relegates all else to the margins. That is, we seem to be dealing with Theocritus's imaginative creation of a bucolic world that is by and large sufficient to itself.

Towns and cities for the most part are similarly glimpsed by the inhabitants of the bucolic world out of the corner of the eye—and that only occasionally and evidently when it suits a given poem's concerns. Theocritean bucolic therefore lacks, and seems not interested in, a marked opposition between country and city, which is fundamental to later pastoral. In general, cities are at best a shadowy presence in Theocritus's bucolics.[27] *Idylls* 3 and 6 could take place anywhere. Without Thyrsis's reference to the Anapos River (*Id.* 1.68) and a few other rural landmarks, we would never know that he imagines Daphnis's death as occurring

---

26. It is interesting, therefore, that when the cup is first mentioned (*Id.* 1.27), the goatherd calls it a κισσύβιον—a word that occurs three times in the *Odyssey* in rustic settings: Polyphemos's cave and Eumaios's hut (*Od.* 9.346, 14.78, 16.52). If Theocritus is invoking its Homeric associations (and the word was evidently much discussed in the Hellenistic period: Athen. 476f–477e), it might represent the appropriation of this foreign object to the bucolic world. Or, better, it might reflect the goatherd's rustic perspective: it is what a bucolic person might naturally call a cup. The usage here appears marked, because at the end of the poem, the cup is referred to by more common words for "cup": σκύφος (*Id.* 1.143) and δέπας (*Id.* 1.149).

27. On the weakness in Theocritus of the city/country antithesis, see Elliger 1975, 363, and Klooster 2012, 100. By contrast, see Kloft 1989: 50–51 on Longus's depiction of city and country as economically interdependent partners in *Daphnis and Chloe*.

in the vicinity of one of the most important cities of the Greek world, for Syracuse is never named.[28] The text ignores it because, I suggest, what is at stake in that poem is the survival and integrity, after Daphnis's death, of the bucolic world seen in and for itself. The frame dialogue between Thyrsis and the goatherd might be set on Kos, but the only hint is the reference to the "Kalydnian ferryman" in line 57—that is, to someone outside the world they inhabit. By Hellenistic times, any poem involving the Cyclops had to be set in Sicily, but the only firm indication of this in the text of *Idyll* 11 is the reference to Mount Aitna in line 47[29]—again, a natural feature rather than a city or town. In *Idyll* 7, by contrast, which contains elements of bucolic—Lykidas's song—but (as we shall see later in this chapter) is not set in the bucolic world, the landmarks mentioned are clearly those of Kos, and there is an unnamed city nearby. Although it is important to our view of Simikhidas that he lives there, this city is only a shadowy presence at the beginning of the poem. Bucolic poetry's general indefiniteness as to place gives a sense of completeness and integrity to bucolic space, although at the same time an aura of unreality, and even if the larger world can impinge on it at times, it is not affected in any fundamental way.

Idylls 4 and 5 are exceptions in that they do specify their settings near cities in southern Italy, and those cities are somewhat more prominent, although they are viewed from within the bucolic world. *Idyll* 4 is set in the vicinity of Kroton, whose shrine to Hera Lakinia figures in Korydon's specimen song (*Id.* 4.32), and Battos pronounces a malediction on "the people [or sons] of Lampriadas," evidently a deme or a prominent family within it (*Id.* 4.21).[30] We thus hear an expression of hostility toward a more organized civic group, or some of its citizens, which we can interpret in two ways. Either Battos, who does not seem to be a bucolic figure, is assuming hostility to cities in (what he takes to be) a bucolic attitude or he is importing urban tensions into the bucolic environment. The greater attention paid to a city than in the other bucolic *Idylls* may be one of a number of signs (to be discussed in chapter 4) that this poem depicts the bucolic world on the wane. *Idyll* 5 is also set in southern Italy, in the neighborhood of Sybaris and Thurii. The only connection Komatas and Lakon have to those cities is that each of their masters is a citizen of one of them and absent from the bucolic scene. The woodcutter Morson, whom they summon to judge their singing contest, evidently lives

---

28. Calame's suggestion (2005, 186) that the scene is immediately outside Syracuse's walls presses too hard on *Id.* 1.117–118.

29. We can add ὁ παρ' ἁμῖν in line 7 if the phrase means "our countryman," and on the assumption that Theocritus was born in Sicily.

30. Deme: Gow 1952, II, 80–81; Hunter 1999, 135. Sons of Lampriadas: Dover 1971, 122–123.

in one of these cities (πόλις) and has come to the countryside to gather tree heath (ἐρείκη), which was burned for fuel,[31] to take back to town (*Id.* 5.63–65, 78–79). He is, then, part of the city's exploitation of the countryside, whereas the bucolic ideal is that herders fit into it comfortably and belong in it. Although the herders clearly know him, Morson is twice referred to as ξένος, "stranger" or "visitor" (*Id.* 5.66, 78), a temporary presence; in the second occurrence, Lakon urges Komatas to begin the contest, saying, "let the stranger get back to the city while he is alive." Morson is only second choice as judge; the herders call on him because the cowherd Lykopas, one of their own, is absent (*Id.* 5.62).[32] Morson's proximity may suggest that the boundaries of the bucolic world are porous, but the text of this poem finds all these ways to assert its self-sufficiency.[33]

Another boundary of bucolic space is the untamed land beyond it, the woods (ὕλη), thickets (δρυμοί), and groves (ἄλσεα) that are the haunts of wild animals. From there, jackals, wolves, and lions howl in grief for Daphnis, whereas his tamer bovines grieve at his feet (*Id.* 1.71–75). There is a similar distinction between these types of animals and an explicit contrast between the wild spaces and the "here" (ὧδε) that has been the scene of Daphnis's herding activities, at *Id.* 1.115–121. Bucolic space may have its brambles and thorns (*Id.* 4.57), but it is tamer and seems kinder than the wilds. It is thus intermediate between urban spaces and that remote region.[34] In it, humans live free of the confinements of the city and on intimate terms with domesticated animals and the landscape.

In a few other ways as well, the poems show an awareness of the larger world. In *Idyll* 4, Olympia is a rival site that has attracted Aigon, who has left his cows bereft. Battos himself may be only a visitor to bucolic space: he is not wearing sandals and runs a thorn into his foot, and Korydon has to admonish him about conditions on "the mountain" (*Id.* 4.56–57). In *Idyll* 1, the lists of where the Nymphs (66–69) and Pan (123–126) might be instead of at the scene of Daphnis's death reflect alternative spaces but serve as devices for focusing on *this* place, where, it is implied, they ought to be. Since Daphnis's death inaugurates bucolic poetry, the places of his activity become constructed as bucolic space even as he leaves it, as distinct from those other places, although the idea that they exist and are worthy haunts of the Nymphs is in significant tension with the uniqueness of this scene. In Lykidas's song in *Idyll* 7, Daphnis wastes away in love just as the snow

---

31. Lindsell 1937, 87.

32. On Morson and the minor role of cities in Theocritus's bucolics, see now Hunter 2021, 240.

33. The South Italian location of *Idylls* 4 and 5 seems due to particular reasons, which will be discussed in chapter 4.

34. See Calame 2005, 175–178, for discussion of "liminality" in *Idyll* 1.

melts on high northern mountains (*Id.* 7.76–77). And in Simikhidas's song, Pan is threatened, unless he helps Aratos in love, with exposure on the mountains of the Edonians in midwinter and among the remote Aithiopians in the extremes of summer (*Id.* 7.111–114). These places contrast with the bucolic world, where it is usually late spring or a more temperate summer.[35]

Where, then, are we to locate the scene of bucolic herding and singing itself? In contrast to the spatial precision of *Idyll* 25, and with the exception of Thyrsis's song in *Idyll* 1, with its several geographical markers, the bucolic setting is vaguely "the mountain" (ὄρος),[36] and this word serves as shorthand for that setting. "Mountain" here is probably not to be taken literally, although sheep and especially goats might be herded on mountainsides. To judge from the shrubs mentioned in the bucolic *Idylls*, the setting Theocritus had in mind was the maquis or foothills.[37] For example, in *Idyll* 4, Korydon's calves have descended too low and are eating shoots of (cultivated) olive trees. Battos tells him to drive them up "from below" (κάτωθε), and Korydon calls to them to go "to the hill [λόφος]" (*Id.* 4.44–46). That might accurately describe the maquis, but then, not many lines later (*Id.* 4.56), after Korydon removes the thorn from Battos's foot, he admonishes Battos not to go barefoot to "the mountain" (ὄρος). Theocritus clearly knew the difference between a hill (λόφος, γεώλοφος) and a mountain, and so he must have had a reason for using "mountain" as he does. The line would make perfect sense if "mountain" here meant generally "bucolic space," even though "hill" might be more literally accurate. I suggest Theocritus uses "the mountain" as he does because it makes the bucolic world seem more remote and autonomous as a "place apart," especially for an urban reader, and as a result, the herders, though lowly, seem freer from social structures than Augeias's slaves. So the term shows how stylized is this world that he invents (or elaborates).

Another aspect of this stylization may be that Theocritus has cattle, as well as sheep and goats, grazing on "the mountain." The best fodder for cattle would be

---

[35]. Cf. Jones 2011, 44–45, commenting on similar "places beyond" in Vergil's *Eclogues*: "A sense builds up that Eclogue-land is contained in a temperate zone, bounded and closed in on itself by a ring of climatic and geographical extremes (but also that poetry can reach out from within it to a larger imaginative world)."

[36]. E.g., *Id.* 3.2, 4.56–57, 7.51, 7.92, [8].2. See van Sickle 1969, 136–137, who translates the word, perhaps more appropriately, as "the hill." My reason for using the more literal "mountain" is given in the text. See also Segal 1981, 129–132 (on *Idyll* 7).

[37]. Lindsell 1937, 83: "surely the most obvious botanical fact about the pastoral idylls is that they are staged, almost all, in maquis." Note that at *Theog.* 23, the passage that clearly inspired Simikhidas's claim that the Nymphs taught him his song as he herded cows "along" or "among" (ἀνά) the mountains (*Id.* 7.91–95), Hesiod says that the Muses appeared to him while he pastured his sheep "below" (ὑπό) Mount Helikon—at its foot or in the foothills.

found in low-lying river meadows, such as the ones referred to at *Id.* 25.13–17, with their sweet grass that flourishes throughout the year beside the marsh of the River Menios.[38] That poem may not be by Theocritus, but in *Idyll* 4 (17–19), Korydon pastures Aigon's calf beside a river and "around/in the vicinity of Latymnos"— the preposition could imply maquis if the scholiast is correct that Latymnos is a mountain. He pastures Aigon's bull near "the salt marsh" at "Physkos's place," probably a low-lying farm (*Id.* 4.23–25), and also beside a river; the plants said to grow there are in fact water-loving.[39] These are places where we would expect cattle to be pastured, but interestingly, at line 56 it turns out that Battos, Korydon, and the cattle are on "the mountain." Perhaps when Korydon claims to be giving his charges only the best fodder, the reality of herding takes over, but for the rest of the poem we are back in the fictionalized bucolic world, which is difficult to locate physically in relation to those low-lying pasturelands.

On the other hand, only certain areas in the Greek world enjoyed abundant water and lush grass; as it happens, Elis and the area around Kroton, the settings of *Idylls* 25 and 4, respectively, were among them.[40] In other places, transhumance may have been an option: cattle and other livestock were kept at lower elevations and along the coast during the winter, when rainfall was relatively plentiful, and pastured during the dry summer and fall in the mountains, where heavier winter rains fed springs and produced more abundant fodder.[41] It might be possible to argue that other poems by Theocritus assume transhumant herding. The bucolic *Idylls* are set in late spring or summer, so that "the mountain" could be taken literally as the kind of place where livestock and their herders would appropriately be. Angelos Chaniotis makes the point that transhumance implies "specialized pastoralism" carried out by people, often slaves, whose sole task is herding,[42] and that might seem to describe Theocritus's herdsmen. But it also involves large herds, and Theocritus's poems give the impression of herds of modest size. Moreover, our evidence for most of the Greek world is very limited, and we do not know how widespread transhumance was, either in the Hellenistic or earlier periods. It was practiced in some places,[43] but we cannot be sure that it was so common that Theocritus and his original readers would have taken it for granted. For the

---

38. Bakker 2013, 49: "Bovines . . . need grassy, humid meadows."

39. Lindsell 1937, 81–82.

40. Isager and Skydsgaard 1992, 98–99.

41. For a succinct description of transhumance, see Isager and Skydsgaard 1992, 99–101.

42. Chaniotis 1995, 51–53.

43. See, e.g., Soph. *OT* 1133–1139.

Hellenistic period, transhumance is relatively well documented for the island of Crete, the subject of Chaniotis's study; but as he stresses, transhumance there was intertwined with Crete's particular form of social, economic, and political organization, so that it is impossible to generalize from this case to the rest of the Greek world or any part of it.[44] On balance, there are serious difficulties with explaining Theocritus's references to "the mountain" through transhumance, and we are led back to the notion of a privileged, bounded, separate fictional world. Any suggestion that his herders are there for only half the year would seriously undermine that image created in our minds.

The composer of the post-Theocritean *Idyll* 9 does seem to have taken Theocritus's "mountain" literally but with quite improbable consequences that tend to support my point. There (*Id.* 9.7–13), Daphnis leads off a kind of singing contest with Menalkas by boasting of the *locus amoenus* he enjoys, with a fourfold repetition of the bucolic keyword "sweet" (ἁδύς). One of its amenities is a couch piled high with the skins of white heifers that were blown off a mountain peak (ἀπὸ σκοπιᾶς) by a southwest wind as they fed on arbutus. Upland meadows may be one thing, but cattle do not belong on mountain peaks (Gow dryly comments, "the animals . . . seem to have been behaving more like goats than cows").[45] In addition, cattle can graze on the shoots of the arbutus, a small tree or shrub with large, bright red berries that birds feed on (Ar. *Av.* 240, 620; the kind common in Greece is the arbutus unedo), but it is at home in the maquis, not in the mountains.[46] So this poet gets the food right but the location wrong. But he is, I think, responding to what Theocritus does. Theocritus brings all three forms of herding together for the sake of the self-enclosure of the bucolic world. We may identify that world with the maquis or foothills, but it is essentially an imaginary space, a "space of representation"—"the mountain."[47]

---

44. Chaniotis 1995, 42–51, 70–72. He points to epigrams by Callimachus and Leonidas of Tarentum that concern herders on mountains that are either explicitly or by implication located on Crete (his further reference to Theocritus's Lykidas in the Kos of *Idyll* 7 does not seem especially pertinent). He comments that "the Hellenistic poets would not have 'staged' their bucolic poems in Cretan landscapes, had Crete not been known for its pastoralism." If Crete was distinctive in this way, that would suggest that specialized pastoralism and transhumance were not to be found in many other regions, or at least not on the same scale.

45. Gow 1952, II, 187.

46. Chriyaa 2004; Lindsell 1937, 83.

47. I should also point out that Menalkas's song puts to rest any thought of transhumance that Daphnis's song might prompt. He caps Daphnis's picture of coolness amid summer heat with the claim that he has many goatskins to keep him warm in his cave in winter (*Id.* 9.15–21), when, if he were a transhumant goatherd, he would have abandoned the mountains for the lowlands.

Within that space, the herdsmen perform their tasks of caring for their animals, fall in (usually unrequited) love, and sing about that love or about their bucolic surroundings. Other inhabitants of this world who do not take part in the narrative action are mentioned: Mermnon's servant girl (a slave?), "the dark-skinned one" (*Id.* 3.35–36); Agroio the old sieve diviner (*Id.* 3.31); Kotyttaris, the old woman who taught Polyphemos how to avoid the evil eye (*Id.* 6.40); the absent Aigon, whose cattle Korydon is herding; and an old man who seems to own the herd, either Aigon's father as a scholiast suggests (but he is clearly just guessing)[48] or his employer (*Id.* 4.4); the girls who flirt with Polyphemos (*Id.* 11.77–78); and Nymphs (Amaryllis, Galateia)—these examples will give some idea of the background characters. Again indirectly and through casual references as needed, the individual herders who play major roles appear to be part of rudimentary social networks rather than isolated rustics. Women take no part in herding except in the post-Theocritean *Idyll* 27, but they figure as absent love objects or servants. The herdsmen's status is for the most part unclear. Lakon certainly is a slave, and Komatas possibly is one[49] (*Id.* 5.5, 8), and their herds are owned by men who live in Sybaris and Thurii (5.72–73). Their herding could possibly be part of a farming economy on relatively large farms, though probably not on the scale of Augeias's estate in *Idyll* 25. But if so, there is only this hint, such is the concentration on the bucolic world. As for the herdsmen of other poems, if they are slaves, in the bucolic world their status does not matter, so tenuous are their links to external society.[50]

So runs a general account of bucolic space and humans' interactions with one another and with nature that are conditioned by and in turn constitute that space. I end this section by looking at three different examples of such interactions and their spatial dimensions, in *Idylls* 5, 1, and 7, in that order.

Spatial Relations in *Idyll* 5

All the bucolic idylls are, I believe, interconnected, but *Idyll* 5 has points of contact especially with *Idylls* 1, 4, and 6. Contrasts with *Idylls* 1 and 6, which also involve

---

48. ὁ δὲ γέρων οὗτος τάχα ἂν εἴη ⟨ὁ⟩ πατὴρ τοῦ Αἴγωνος ("this old man would perhaps be Aigon's father").

49. If we take ὤλεύθερε ("O Mr. Freeman") in line 8 as a sarcastic retort to Komatas's taunt that Lakon is a slave—a possibility reinforced by τῷ δεσπότᾳ ("your master") in line 10. If we take it literally, he might be a freedman, even though the term for that is ἀπελεύθερος, in view of the same reference to his master, which is difficult to explain if Komatas is freeborn. See Scholl 1989, 20.

50. On the possibility that they are slaves, cf. Levi 1993, 115–116, 120–121; Cusset 2021, 274.

herdsmen meeting at a spring with song the result, offer a good way of approaching *Idyll* 5 from a spatial perspective. "Pastoral poems," Alpers has written, "make explicit the dependence of their conventions on the idea of coming together."⁵¹ *Idyll* 5 enacts this coming together as an occasion for song, but this meeting between a shepherd and a goatherd sparks quarreling that will lead to a rancorous singing contest. And no sooner do they come together than they fly apart (*Id.* 5.1–4):

ΚΟΜΑΤΑΣ αἶγες ἐμαί, τῆνον τὸν ποιμένα, τὸν Συβαρίταν,
φεύγετε, τὸν Λάκωνα· τό μευ νάκος ἐχθὲς ἔκλεψεν.

ΛΑΚΩΝ οὐκ ἀπὸ τᾶς κράνας; σίττ' ἀμνίδες· οὐκ ἐσορῆτε
τόν μευ τὸν σύριγγα πρόαν κλέψαντα Κομάταν;

KOMATAS Run, my goats! That shepherd, the one from Sybaris,
flee him—Lakon! Yesterday he stole my goatskin.

LAKON Ssst, lambs! Get away from the spring! Don't you see
the one who stole my *syrinx* the other day, Komatas?

In *Idyll* 6 (1–4), Daphnis and Damoitas drive their herd of cattle together "to one place" (εἰς ἕνα χῶρον), also a spring, and sit down together to exchange songs. Their songs complement one another rather than seriously compete; those of Lakon and Komatas are sharply antagonistic, often bitter in tone. The narrative frame of *Idyll* 6 does use the verb ἐρίζειν ("compete," line 5) to describe the cowherds' reciprocal singing, but any element of rivalry has been reduced to a vanishing point. There is no wager in the "contest" and no winner, just an exchange of kisses and gifts at the end (*Id.* 6.42–46), whereas *Idyll* 5 begins with mutual accusations of theft ("negative reciprocity"), there is a wager, and in the end there is a definite winner. *Idyll* 1 also shows Thyrsis and the goatherd coming together and engaging in reciprocal exchange (cup for Thyrsis's song), and it ends with the goatherd's admiring comments on Thyrsis's singing.⁵² In *Idyll* 5, by contrast, ἐρίζειν has a strong force of "rivalry," verging into "quarrel" (*Id.* 5.60, 67, 136). Morson declares Komatas the winner and awards him Lakon's stake, a lamb, as prize, and Komatas gloats unabashedly over Lakon (*Id.* 5.142–144). So, as the contrasts with these other *Idylls* emphasize, the initial coming together at the

---

51. Alpers 1996, 81.

52. For a different view, *Idyll* 1 as "an unusual bucolic *agon*" see Frangeskou 1996. This characterization involves understanding the goatherd's description of the cup as his "performance" and Thyrsis's song, the medium of competition, as, at the same time, the goatherd's prize for his successful description. It also necessitates seeing the goatherd and Thyrsis as the judges of each other's performance. All of this stretches the meaning of the term *agon* very far.

spring only to move apart embodies in spatial movement the discord that is the organizing principle of *Idyll* 5.[53]

In fact, *Idylls* 5 and 6 seem systematic inversions of each other. A keynote of *Idyll* 6 is similarity and complementarity, and a keynote of *Idyll* 5 is difference and opposition. This contrast is enacted in the differing character of the song exchanges—amoebean verses in which Lakon seeks to cap those of Komatas as opposed to the way Damoitas's response completes Daphnis's song, so that the two together create a situation and a story.[54] As we will see in more detail in chapter 3, *Idyll* 6 depicts Daphnis and Damoitas as equals and as nearly identical but not quite. Damoitas seems slightly older than Daphnis, a difference that might make room for an *erastês-erômenos* relation between them, just as the kisses that they exchange after their songs (*Id.* 6.42) may or may not be a decorous sign of a sexual relationship. *Idyll* 5 allows no such delicate hints or ambiguity. Komatas is distinctly older than Lakon (ἐόντα παῖδ' ἔτι, "when you were still a boy," *Id.* 5.36–37), and he states his claim of a pederastic relationship with Lakon in unvarnished detail. Daphnis and Damoitas are both cowherds, Komatas and Lakon goatherd and shepherd, respectively. The gifts that Damoitas and Daphnis trade, *syrinx* and *aulos* or pipe, are treated as of equal value (*Id.* 6.43). Reciprocity (χάρις) is just what Komatas complains is missing from his relationship with Lakon (*Id.* 5.37). Lakon accuses Komatas of having stolen his *syrinx*, and Komatas's reply suggests that the *aulos* is an inferior instrument (*Id.* 5.3–7). When Damoitas and Daphnis proceed to play the *aulos* and *syrinx* together, the harmony in which their poem ends extends to the cows, which dance (ὠρχεῦντο, *Id.* 6.45). Not only does *Idyll* 5 end with the disharmony of Komatas's victory over Lakon and his gloating, but he also exhorts his goats to snort unmusically (φριμάσσεο, *Id.* 5.141).[55] This moment in turn recalls his earlier alleged act of dominance over Lakon, when, he says, he penetrated the boy while the she-goats bleated and the ram mounted them (*Id.* 5.41–42).

---

53. For antithesis and contrast as structuring the language and the overall conception of *Idyll* 5, see Ott 1969, 14–43. On the spring as the locus of moving apart, particularly by contrast with *Idylls* 1 and 7, see Segal 1981, 185–186 (especially the contrast with the "one road" of *Id.* 7.35 as the setting for song exchange there), and his further spatially informed remarks on *Idyll* 5 on 186–188. For general contrasts between *Idylls* 5 and 6, see Lawall 1967, 67. Damon 1995, 121–122, also draws detailed contrasts, which she attributes to the underlying difference between mimetic (*Id.* 5) and narrative (*Id.* 6) modes.

54. Damoitas's song could be seen as capping, and therefore trying to outdo, that of Daphnis so that there could be an element of competition, but any rivalry, if it exists at all, is muted. In *Idyll* 5, it is the essence of the whole poem.

55. Ott 1969, 39, briefly connects the two passages.

The mutual repulsion between Komatas and Lakon that is expressed physically and spatially is thus carried through in all these ways that invert the unity and affection between Daphnis and Damoitas. And it recurs in spatial terms when they dispute about where they will sing (*Id.* 5.31–34, 45–59). A similar question is raised in *Idyll* 1 (12–23), and Thyrsis and the goatherd end up sitting together in "the shepherd's seat." It is in keeping with the emphasis on unity in *Idyll* 6 that Daphnis and Damoitas simply go to "a single place" without needing to discuss the matter. In *Idyll* 5, by contrast, there is no question of a shared bucolic space. Lakon and Komatas are apart by this time. Each seeks to persuade the other to come and sing in his place, and deictics heighten the sense of separation and distance: τεῖδε, ὧδε, τουτεί,[56] and ἔνθα ("here"), used multiple times by both speakers as each describes the beauty and comfort of his own place.[57] These descriptions detail lush, typical bucolic *loci amoeni*, as many have said, but here aspects of bucolic beauty are used not to create a space where herdsmen might hope to be at home in the natural world but as counters in a competitive game as each tries to outdo the other by proving that his place is superior to the other's. Komatas and Lakon construct agonistic space that is shaped by the hostile relations between them and that, because each finally remains in his own place and sings from there, structures their competition. This exchange thus lays the essential groundwork for their singing contest, in which each again tries to prove his own superiority by outperforming, and several times denigrating, the other in a display of masculine competitiveness that has been very well described by Gutzwiller.[58] It is no accident that embedded within this contest of venues, and in parallel with it, is Komatas's claim to have penetrated Lakon sexually, perhaps the most aggressive way of asserting dominance over another man in Greek culture.[59]

---

56. For the conjectural reading of this word at *Id.* 5.33, see Gow 1952, II, 100–101.

57. On these deictics, see Segal 1981, 186: "the 'here' or 'there' (τεῖδε, τηνεί) which attends the coming together of the bucolic characters into friendship, song, the sharing of festivity or beauty... here points to division rather than accord."

58. Gutzwiller 1991, 139–142.

59. I refer to Komatas's *alleged* penetration of Lakon because we have no way of knowing whether the act occurred. Lakon denies it (*Id.* 5.43, 118). If it did happen, then Komatas is shaming Lakon by reminding him of a time when he was dominated, and Lakon has to parry the blow by false denial. But I think an alternative is just as likely—and more interesting: Komatas's words are in themselves an act of verbal aggression, a speech act analogous to actual penetration. When Catullus wrote to the hapless Furius and Aurelius "paedicabo vos et irrumabo," he surely had no intention of carrying out those acts. The words themselves sufficed for abjection of his enemies. And so maybe here. Lakon's reply at *Id.* 5.43 has often been taken as an admission that the incident happened. Hubbard 1998, 33: "An event Lakon is here unable to deny" (similar is Stanzel 1995, 91). Rinkevich 1977, 300: "Lakon parries the blow with criticism of the longitudinal deficiency of Komatas' weaponry... and a curse of burial

The two opposed places may also figure in the singing contest by implication. During the contest, Komatas repeats his story of penetrating Lakon, whom he depicts as having held on to "that oak tree" (καὶ τᾶς δρυὸς εἴχεο τήνας, *Id.* 5.117). Since oak trees were one of the charms of his place (*Id.* 5.45, cf. 61), the oak in question may have been there. This supposition is strengthened by the fact that in his answering couplet, Lakon charges that Komatas's master, Eumaras, tied him up and beat him "here" (τεῖδε)—that is, in Lakon's place. Given the parallels between Lakon's answering couplets and Komatas's challenging couplets throughout the singing contest, "here" surely answers "that oak tree." Earlier in the contest, in a sequence that repeats the opening four lines of the poem, Komatas calls on his goats to get away from the wild olive (σίττ' ἀπὸ τᾶς κοτίνω) and to graze "here" (ὧδε)—that is, where he is (*Id.* 5.100). Lakon earlier mentioned the wild olive as one of the amenities of his place. In response, Lakon now orders his sheep away from "the oak tree" and tells them to graze "here [τουτεί], toward the east."[60] Thus, the spatial opposition between Lakon and Komatas remains alive during the contest, underpinning the parallels and contrasts between their opposing couplets. The contest is spatialized; this is an excellent example of the way space both is structured by and helps structure human cultural activity.

And yet, through the medium of this acrimonious competition, Komatas and Lakon collaborate in the same world-building that occurs in the internal songs of other bucolic poems, which corresponds to Theocritus's own world-building and thus constitutes an internal parallel to his poetic activity.[61] Their descriptions of their places even before the contest begins are part of this process: the details work together to build a picture of natural abundance. Each couplet in the contest mentions people, animals, plants, trees, and objects that gradually come into alignment in the reader's mind as constituents of this world, which is given shape by its extremes. On the one hand, there are animal pests: foxes and locusts that damage vineyards, beetles that eat the figs. On the other hand, there are wish-fulfilling images of abundance: rivers and springs flowing with milk, wine, and honey, pastures full of the right plants for goats and sheep to graze on. Because the pests are agricultural and the images of plenty are bucolic, we may have again, in this embedded singing, an idealizing depiction of the bucolic by contrast with

---

commensurate with it" (cf. Kyriakou 2018, 38). But surely "may you be buried no deeper than that penetration" means "may you not be buried at all (because you never penetrated me)." For a Greek, lack of burial was an effective curse, not shallow burial.

60. The importance of the trees in these passages is also noted by Lawall 1967, 63–64, who gives them a different significance.

61. We know of poetic contests in Alexandria, and if *Idyll* 5 were performed at one, the fit between poem and occasion would be close.

what is on its margins, as well as an integrated picture of the countryside and life within it.

Together all these elements create an impression of comprehensiveness that is partly an illusion but succeeds because the reader's imagination can work on them to build a whole.[62] Human relations are in place in this world: slavery and labor, love (heterosexual and pederastic, fulfilled or unsuccessful), hostility and competition. The rivalry and hostility between Komatas and Lakon are not a matter of this one meeting but seem to be habitual, in view of the mutual accusations of theft at the beginning of the poem. The bucolic world encompasses agonistic relations between men as well as moments of convergence and harmony, as in *Idylls* 1 and 6, and naturally so in view of the importance of competition in Greek culture. Lakon's and Komatas's competitiveness, in fact, is a bucolic version at the lowest level of society of the competition that is at the heart of elite society in epic poetry, just as Komatas's claim to have "taught" Lakon by penetrating him is a debased version, a parody, really, of the sympotic notion of pederasty as instruction of a youth by an older man in elite values and modes of conduct that is reflected in the relation between Herakles and Hylas (*Id.* 13.8–9).[63]

To appreciate how *Idyll* 5 builds a bucolic world through an accumulation of specific details, it is important to notice that this poem contains more proper names of humans, gods, and places; references to other places; and names of trees and shrubs, animals, and objects than any of the other bucolic poems, and to recall that people, animals, and things are part of space, not just located in it. Table 1.1 gives an idea of the richness of *Idyll* 5's inventory of bucolic detail—in contrast, again, to *Idyll* 6, for example, which relies on the bare mention of a spring to conjure up an entire world.

This table is useful because it shows in outline how many features Theocritus crowds into a mere 150 lines and how diverse they are: plants, animals, gods and Nymphs, people, and various places, including a nearby city. Because there is no particular order or system, when one reads the poem, it is not always easy to keep in focus how, from this accumulation of details, the poem constructs a picture of rural space that encompasses both herding and agriculture (vineyards, orchards, reapers) as contiguous, and somewhat contrasting, activities in relation to the landscape and both wild and domestic animals. Thus, the table also shows a widening of focus by comparison to other *Idylls'* concentration on bucolic space, a broadening that makes that space seem less

---

62. Cf. Daspet 2017, 93.

63. See the discussion of *Idyll* 13 in chapter 2.

Table 1.1. Constituents of space in *Idyll* 5

Places	People	Gods	Plants and shrubs	Animals	Objects
Sybaris (city) (1, 73)	Siburtas (1, 73)	Pan (14, 58, 141)	Wild olive (cf. 100), grove, [spring], grass, στιβάς (31–34)	Komatas's goats (1 etc.)	Goatskin (2)
Spring (3)	Korydon (6; cf. *Id.* 4)	Nymphs of the lake (17)	Oaks (cf.102, 117), galingale, [two springs], shade, pine (45–49)	Lakon's sheep (3 etc.)	*Syrinx* (4)
Krathis (river) and rock above it (16, 124)	Lykon (8)	Nymphs (54, 70, 139, 148)	Fern, pennyroyal (55–56)	Goat (sacrificed) (12)	Lambskins, goatskins (50–53, 56–57)
Lakon's place (31–34)	Eumaras (10, 73, 119)	Muses (80)	Oaks (61)	Kid, lamb, goat as wagers (21, 24, 30)	*Krateres* (54–55)
Komatas's place (45–49, 55–56)	Krokylos (11)	Apollo (82–83)	Tree heath (64–65)	Bee vs. cicada (metaphor) (29)	Milk pails, bowls of honey (58–59)
Thurii (72)	Kalaithis (15)		Briar, anemone, roses (92–93)	Grasshoppers (34)	Cheese baskets (86)
Polis (= Thurii?) (78)	Daphnis (20, 80–81)		Wild apples, acorns (94–95)	Wolf cubs, puppies (metaphor) (38)	Fleece for a cloak (98)
Rosebed beside wall (93)	Lykopas (62)		Juniper (97)	She-goats, ram (41–42)	Cypresswood pail, *Krater* by Praxiteles

Hill (101 = *Id.* 1.113)	Morson (63–65)	Tamarisks (101)	Pitcher (127)
Vineyard, fence (108–109)	ἁ παῖς = Klearista = παρθένος? (85, 88, 96, 105)	Grapevines (109; cf. 112–113)	Bees, birds (46, 48)
Mikon's vineyard (ῥαγίζοντι) (113)	Boy = Kratidas = boy? (87, 90, 99, 107)	Figs (115)	Goats sacrificed to Muses (81) *Syrinx* (135)
Old woman's grave (121)	Reapers (111)	Squills (121)	Ram raised for Apollo (82–83)
Haleis (river or lake?) (123)	Mikon (112)	Cyclamen (123)	Ring dove (96, 133)
Himera (spring? see Gow)	Philondas (114)	Marsh plants (σία) (125)	Konaros, Kinaitha (sheep) (102)
Sybaris lake (126, 146; cf. 17)	ἁ παῖς (slave girl?) (127)	Moon clover, goatwort (128)	Phalaros (goat? dog?) (103)
	Alkippe (132)	Mastich, arbutus (129)	Dog that throttles wolves (106)
	Eumedes (134)	Balm (130)	Locusts (108)
	Melanthios (150)	Cistus (rock rose) (131)	Cicadas (110)
			Foxes (112)
			Beetles (114)
			Jays, nightingale, hoopoe, swans (metaphor) (136–137)

self-contained but still special and distinct. The agonistic relations between Lakon and Komatas are part of this bucolic world; during the contest, we are never allowed to forget that each of them hurls these details at the other in an attempt to prevail; note especially how the mutual taunting in lines 120–123 is followed immediately by visions of springs and rivers flowing with milk, wine, and honey in the next lines. This kind of juxtaposition shows the extremes in Theocritus's bucolic conception that help bring that world into focus for us, just as its margins help define this world spatially. And here is a final and perhaps the most all-encompassing difference between this poem and *Idyll* 6 that shows how the two poems are complementary within the Theocritean corpus. Formally, as in other respects, they are inversions of each other. In *Idyll* 6, an idealizing bucolic frame encloses the dramatization of a scene, set on the edge of the bucolic world, the seashore, in which a relationship, between Polyphemos and Galateia, is amiss. In the frame of *Idyll* 5, an acrimonious relationship between slaves set amid the grittiest realities of a herdsman's life is the frame for the creation, through agonistic collaboration, of a finer version of the bucolic world, though one not free of reminders of its basis in harsher modes of being.[64] That such a vision can spring from two men mired in those realities shows, once again, something important about the power of the imagination. Lakon and Komatas are in this sense parallel to Theocritus: a poet living amid the realities of urban life who imagines both them and the world they project.

From the coarse to the idealizing, then, *Idyll* 5 explores extremes in the possibilities for the bucolic world and for bucolic as a poetic type, both internally and in its relations with other poems. The name of Komatas evokes those same extremes. The Komatas of Lykidas's song in *Idyll* 7 (82–89), addressed there as "most blessed" and "divine," was a goatherd of an earlier generation who was fed on honeycomb by bees and whose now silent voice is an object of longing by the singer. But the Komatas we encounter in *Idyll* 5 is a far earthier version of a goatherd: smelly (*Id.* 5.51–52), sexually aggressive, uninhibited in describing his exploits, and of explicitly low status. He is his archetypal namesake stripped of the mystique. And yet he, too, is a talented singer. Perhaps the solution to the much-discussed puzzle of why Morson awards him the prize in his contest with Lakon when the text gives no indication of his superiority is simply that the name Komatas is a signifier in Theocritus for "divinely talented singer-goatherd."

---

64. For detailed discussion, see Crane 1988, 113–117, especially: "If the poor slaves of poor masters frame their contest with squabbling and scurrilous abuse, their contest allows them, if only briefly and in limited degree, to recast their own world in a gentler and more refined form" (115).

Someone with that name has to win the contest.[65] In any case, the two figures named Komatas (perhaps the same figure) incorporate opposing possibilities, each of which expresses a truth about the bucolic world and about its poetry, which also can range from the heights to the depths.

Spatial Relations in *Idyll* 1.1–23

Idyll 1, unlike *Idyll* 5, begins by describing a seamlessly harmonious bucolic setting, and common elements between the two poems[66] point up the contrast. If Thyrsis's song in *Idyll* 1 represents the constitution of bucolic space as well as of bucolic poetry, it is fitting that the beginning of this programmatic poem shows two herders, in some way heirs to this space, enjoying it (1.1–23). It is this opening scene that I would like to discuss here, with other aspects of the poem reserved for chapter 3. The setting is an archetypal bucolic pleasance, but there are three distinct places within it, demarcated by deictics: the knoll with tamarisks where Thyrsis and the goatherd initially converse (τεῖδε, "here," 12), the whispering pine and plashing spring a little apart from them ("*that* pine," "*that* water," τήνα/τῆν[ο], 1, 8), and the place where they eventually sit beneath an elm while Daphnis sings, with oaks and a seat for shepherds facing statues of Priapus and water Nymphs (δεῦρο, "over here," 21).[67] They conceive of space according to their perspective; deictics locate the different places with reference to their position. In Harvey's terminology, this is "relative space." By contrast, Thyrsis and the goatherd describe three examples of "relational space," one of which they finally enter in preparation for Thyrsis's song, which takes us into the mythic time and space of Daphnis's death.

Lines 1–11 imply a vision of relational space that never materializes, a fusion of humans with nature, so that the goatherd's piping equals the whispering of the pine tree, and Thyrsis's voice outdoes the plash of water on the rocks, and the herders will be second only to Pan and the Muses, who might appear to

---

65. And yet etymologically, the name ought to mean "hairy, shaggy," like a goat. Between its literal sense and what it signifies, then, the name compresses in itself the dual possibilities embodied by the two men who bear it. Cf. Kossaifi 2002, 356–357.

66. References to Daphnis at *Id.* 5.20, 80–81, the identical 5.101 and 1.13, and the similarity between 5.45–46 and 1.106–107 and between the endings of the two poems (5.147–150 and 1.131–132).

67. I follow Hunter 1999, 75, in taking κρανίδων (22) as statues rather than the Nymphs themselves (Gow 1952, II, 5). On the deictics and the different spaces in this passage, see also Calame 2005, 183–184. Cf. Elliger 1975, 326–327, and Klooster 2012, 105–106. Payne 2007, 26–28, also discusses the deictics but considers the landscape a single space in which the herdsmen are fully integrated.

claim their prizes. The herders are to find their places in the hierarchies of the natural world. Here is a picture of full presence of the bucolic world to humans that contrasts with the story of loss and absence that Thyrsis will sing. It is possible, it seems, at least sometimes, to touch that fullness and to hear its music. It seems—but the herdsmen never enter that place, and that merging remains an ideal to which bucolic song can only aspire. Thyrsis's proposal that the goatherd play the *syrinx* where they are evokes in response a harsher aspect of nature: the risk of Pan's anger if his noontime sleep is interrupted. So if the elusive Pan does appear, it will be not to take pleasure in music but to punish mortals for it. From this perspective, human music does not wholly fit into the natural world, which contains powers far beyond the human. Thyrsis and the goatherd finally go to a place that is more appropriate for them, one that has been altered by human culture (*Id.* 1.21–23).[68] With the shepherd's seat it has been turned from a completely natural scene to a place with a human use: culturally constructed space. The statues and the seat have presumably been made by people who used this place. And it is here that a basic institution of human culture is activated that differs from the awarding of prizes in musical competitions: reciprocal exchange, Thyrsis's song for the she-goat and the cup (itself the object of an earlier exchange). Yet the place and the gods represented by the statues are rustic. In bucolic space, human culture locates itself in nature but remains distinct from it, and bucolic poetry, rather than resting on identity between the human and natural worlds, constructs, in Gutzwiller's term, "analogies."[69] This third space is thus paradigmatic for bucolic poetry and a fitting scene for the performance of Thyrsis's song.

This place is relational, then, in two ways. It makes possible, and in its cultural aspect is a projection of, human relations such as the exchange between Thyrsis and the goatherd (which stands, I take it, for the relation between song and its audience within bucolic poetry and externally between Theocritus and his audience). And it constructs, and is constructed by, a particular relation between humans and nature that bucolic poetry explores. Thyrsis's song that follows portrays the bucolic world as relational—when the animals mourn for Daphnis, for example, and gods appear to him. This is the kind of fusion suggested in the first lines of the poem (1–11): humanity, in the person of Daphnis before his death, is as fully in place in nature as it can be. But with Daphnis's death this near-identity is lost, and Thyrsis and the goatherd must sit in a more humanly inflected place.

---

68. In line 21, δεῦρο ("here") implies movement, in contrast to τεῖδε of line 12: "come over here," as opposed to "here, where we are now standing."

69. Gutzwiller 1991.

The link with nature is still strong in *Idyll* 1, as we can see when the goatherd addresses his goats in the closing lines (151–152), but the distinction between places at the beginning of the poem gives a sense of both closeness to nature and difference from it in a bucolic world without Daphnis. We can even say, with Mark Payne and Evina Sistakou, that in the opening lines, human song is projected onto nature, that "it is nature that sings humanly, not vice versa."[70] So it is possible to connect with nature not in itself but only through human categories. In chapter 3, when we focus more directly on the significance of absence in Theocritus's poetry, we will see how Thyrsis's narrative gives signs of a disjunction from nature that comes about as Daphnis dies.

Spatial Relations in *Idyll* 7

How far *Idyll* 7 should be considered bucolic is uncertain. It has bucolic elements, such as Lykidas and his song, which he "labored to complete on the mountain" (7.51). But the narrative is set in the lowlands, not in bucolic space, and the goatherd Lykidas is out of his element. For their part, Simikhidas and his friends are on their way from the city, where they seem at home, to the agricultural, not bucolic,[71] *locus amoenus* where the poem ends. If the city and the farm are the endpoints of Simikhidas's journey, Lykidas does not belong on this itinerary, and he appropriately diverges from it before Simikhidas reaches the farm. Lykidas sings a consummate bucolic song, but its artful embedding of the bucolic world within successive frames (to be explored in chapter 3) makes that world seem remote, a product of wish-fulfilling imagination, its reality opened to question all the more by his own distance from "the mountain."[72] Inside the bucolic world, Lykidas's appearance would be unremarkable, probably no different from that of other herdsmen. In the lowlands, seen through the eyes of the city dweller Simikhidas, he stands out, and that

---

70. Payne 2007, 25–27; Sistakou 2021, 325n6 (the source of the quotation).

71. I think this distinction is important, and as we see several times in this chapter, Theocritus consistently maintains it, even if the agricultural and bucolic worlds sometimes interpenetrate. On *Idyll* 7 as mediating between the more markedly bucolic poems and other types such as *Idyll* 22, see Thomas 1996, 238. A welcome exception to the usual tendency to assume that the setting at the end of *Idyll* 7 is bucolic is Bowie 1985, 80. Note his comment there: "Most societies, and that of ancient Greece is no exception, are marked by substantial differences between the pastoral and arable-farming communities and ways of life."

72. On embedded spaces in Lykidas's song, see Klooster 2012, 102–103. She makes the interesting point that precise geographical references disappear as the song moves into an idealized bucolic world—another sign of its doubtful reality.

is why we get in *Idyll* 7, and nowhere in any of the poems set in the bucolic world,[73] a detailed description of this goatherd's appearance and smell (13–19). Simikhidas, on the other hand, has pretensions toward both the bucolic and the agricultural worlds. He sings a song that he claims—improbably—to have learned from the Nymphs as he tended his herd "on the mountains" (7.92), but it ends with the urban convention of the *paraclausithyron* (7.122–125). His song fails to be bucolic, and so I read his claim to have been taught by the Nymphs, with its echo of Hesiod, as a bookish affectation.[74] His address to Pan (*Id.* 7.103–114), with its reference to a ritual conducted by Arkadian boys, seems to be a nod in the direction of bucolic, but the allusion to an obscure cult practice has few if any parallels in the internal songs of Theocritus's other bucolic poems (Daphnis's apostrophe of Pan in *Id.* 1.123–126 may come close, but "the ridge of Helike" and "the tomb of Lykaon's son" were probably not obscure to ancient readers). At the same time, Simikhidas is only a visitor to the farm; his prayer to plant his winnowing fan in a heap of grain "again" (7.155–158)—a sign of completed labor—rings hollow because he has done no work. He belongs in the world of the polis, from which he started out and to which he obviously will return.[75]

This sense of being out of place is expressed spatially and temporally. Despite the geographical precision, with mention of specific place names, that puts this poem on the island of Kos, the location of Simikhidas's meeting with Lykidas is strikingly indefinite: "we had not yet reached the midpoint of the way, and the tomb [σῆμα] of Brasilas had not yet come into our sight, when we encountered a certain wayfarer . . ." (*Id.* 7.10-11). The word for "tomb" means "sign," and here it might carry the implication of "landmark" beyond the literal meaning "tomb." There is nothing in sight to give this space definition or make it a place. And the meeting occurs at an in-between time of day, in the noontime lull between

---

73. Except for the reference to the goatherd Komatas's smell in *Id.* 5.52.

74. Hes. *Theog.* 22–23. On Simikhidas's "velléités pseudo-pastorales," see Legrand 1898, 152. Hunter 2021, 240, puts the contrast between him and Lykidas nicely: "Simichidas is a '*polis*-dweller*,* for whom 'bucolic song' is a poetic mode to be adopted, not—as it is for Lycidas—a mode of life."

75. Worman 2015, 207–209, takes a very different view: that the songs of Lykidas and Simikhidas represent older and newer strata "of what Theocritus took to constitute the bucolic mode" and that *Idyll* 7 as a whole demonstrates the range of what bucolic can encompass, including the agricultural setting at the end. I think that this is inconsistent with Theocritus's representation of bucolic space in other *Idylls* and with features of *Idyll* 7 that I discuss here. I also think that for him, "bucolic," though flexible to a degree, has more specificity than Worman's reading would give it.

morning and afternoon activity: "Simikhidas," Lykidas asks, "where are you directing your feet at midday, when even the lizard is asleep in the wall and the crested larks do not flit about?" (*Id.* 7.21–23). This indefiniteness is the essence of a journey, of movement from one place to another. Here, in this in-between space and time, people who are normally kept socially and spatially separate encounter one another, different life trajectories converge, and identities, usually solidified when people are in their particular places, become open and more fluid, so that, for example, the urban Simikhidas can try out being a cowherd and a bucolic poet.[76] If place helps shape identity and social behavior, movement and being out of place even temporarily promote fluidity. Simikhidas and Lykidas could not belong to more different social contexts, but in this transient here and now, their identities come into contact and enter into a dialogue that takes the form of an exchange of songs.

This open and—to judge from the description—featureless space through which Simikhidas, his friends, and Lykidas move contrasts sharply with bucolic space as it is depicted in Lykidas's song. As Alberto Borgogno points out, that space is characterized by enclosure, rest or lack of movement, and reduction in scale.[77] The goatherd and Komatas imprisoned in chests and Lykidas lying on a rustic couch and enjoying Tityros's singing, perhaps within a hut or some other structure, have counterparts in the formal properties of the poem, as Borgogno emphasizes: the embedding of song within song and the way the description of the goatherd in the chest in lines 78–79 is enclosed at the mathematical center of the poem. I would add that this bounded space is also full and lush, with natural features, trees, bushes, flowers, and bees, a sheltered springtime place as opposed to the barren, snow-covered mountains mentioned in lines 76–77. The contrast between lowland and bucolic space has an analogy in Ageanax's voyage over the dangerous, featureless sea to arrive safely, so it is hoped, in the harbor of Mytilene (*Id.* 7.60–61)—another enclosed and sheltering place, though part of a city and not bucolic. The journey of Simikhidas and his friends ends in a delightful natural place on Phrasidamos's farm that is also enclosed, by trees.[78] There they lie on couches of reeds and vine leaves that recall Lykidas's

---

76. Cf. Bakhtin 1981, 243–245, a passage cited by Burton 1995, 10, in connection with *Idyll* 15, to be discussed later in this chapter.

77. Borgogno 2002, 16–18, 24–25. He notices, without making any particular point of it, the contrast with the space of Simikhidas's journey, which he calls "uno spazio privo di valore" (16). I would say that it does have a certain kind of value, as a place where identities are open to question and can be explored, whereas in bucolic space they seem fixed.

78. Borgogno 2002, 18–19.

couch (*Id.* 7.132–134, 67–68). But the setting is a farm, and this place is one of rest after the work that, as we shall see in chapter 4 in connection with *Idyll* 10, characterizes agricultural space in contrast to bucolic leisure.

Perhaps we can infer that this kind of pleasance is what lowlanders like Simikhidas can attain but not the bucolic world of "the mountain." It shares certain features with the bucolic environment, such as bees, but it is not the thing itself. Perhaps the emphasis on reduction of scale and enclosure in this poem's conception of bucolic has to do with a Hellenistic aesthetic of short poems, as Borgogno argues, or with Epicurean philosophy, or with the individual in this age turning inward on the self—possibilities that he also mentions. But I am interested here in the way the construction of space in *Idyll* 7 sets bucolic space apart from other kinds and makes it seem self-enclosed and remote—the effect as well of Lykidas's successively embedded songs—and partly for that very reason highly desirable. But at the same time, it raises the question of how real that world can be. Is it any more than a possibility raised in Lykidas's wish-fulfilling song? Lykidas himself, a figure who has stepped out of it, an authentic goatherd, would seem to guarantee its existence in some sense, but who is he? He appears suddenly as though out of nowhere and leaves as abruptly, turning in the opposite direction from Phrasidamos's farm. What is he doing in the lowlands in the first place?

These questions return us to the fluidity of identities on the road and the condition of being out of place. It is not without reason that so many scholars have not taken the identity of either Simikhidas or Lykidas at face value. It has often been thought that Lykidas is a god in disguise. His sudden appearance gives him an enigmatic air, and the narrator's insistence that he was a goatherd because he looked just like one (*Id.* 7.13–14) seems to raise the question of the relation between appearance and reality. His gift to Simikhidas of a shepherd's club in return for the latter's song is reminiscent of a poetic investiture of a mortal by a divinity in the manner of Hesiod and Archilochus. As for Simikhidas, many scholars have taken it for granted that he is a stand-in for Theocritus. I would like to take a somewhat different approach, especially with regard to Simikhidas, since I am skeptical of a one-to-one autobiographical reading of the poem. I would suggest instead that Simikhidas, as narrator, represents not the historical Theocritus but a possible persona of him, one way in which he could be viewed: as a city dweller claiming to be able to bucolicize, an urban sophisticate writing about simple herders. From this perspective he might seem like Theocritean self-caricature. Lykidas might then represent another potentiality in Theocritus, or in any successful bucolic poet: the ability, through the imagination, to write with some authenticity (or its appearance) about herdsmen and their world.[79] This view would not rule out the idea of a disguised epiphany; that would add a further dimension of possibility in this mysterious figure. Between them, these two figures would be one manifestation of the paradox created by an urban poet writing on rustic themes, which produces in turn the fine balance in Theocritus's bucolic poetry between his creation of a world and the simultaneous acknowledgment, implied in many of these poems, of its fictionality. Thus, this encounter in the placeless place of "the road" raises fundamental questions about bucolic poetry. Why would a poet of the city write about the countryside? Of what use could such a subject be to him or his readers? What degree of authenticity can he, or should he try to, attain? If Simikhidas and Lykidas are both out of place, what would it mean to be in place? Lykidas, on the other hand, opens to question the relation of the bucolic world to that of the city and its countryside. His song offers a vision of a world where people are fully in place, where a goatherd in a chest can be sustained by bees. But that vision is so distanced and so contingent on the fulfillment of wishes (as we shall see in chapter 3) that its reality is questionable. We have seen something similar in the relation between places at the beginning of *Idyll* 1. Bucolic space is, then, an imaginative projection—but a projection of what?

One answer to these questions might be that bucolic space represents for the Greek poet and his Greek readers a response to the dislocations in the wake of Alexander's conquests, when being in and out of place was an issue to many and especially to Greeks living in Alexandria and other cities outside the traditional Greek world.[80] From this perspective, fictionality and stylization are part of the point. Bucolic space offered readers a "heterotopia"[81] through which to examine from an imaginary distance questions they encountered living among non-Greeks outside the Greek world as traditionally defined and to address consequent feelings of displacement. Through their exploration of the relations between humans and nature (a matter of interest to urban readers especially), the bucolic *Idylls* offered a picture of humans belonging to a place but qualified it at the same time,

---

79. For a different, but despite differences not, I think, ultimately incompatible, reading of Simikhidas as a persona of Theocritus, see Payne 2007, 20, 130–141: Simikhidas's song is "immature" rather than "spurious" bucolic because he represents Theocritus at an earlier stage of his career, while he is still developing as a bucolic poet and encountering in Lykidas a character out of his own fictions.

80. On Theocritus and Alexandria, see the introduction. As I say there, wherever he wrote his poems, they were certainly read in Alexandria.

81. Foucault 1986.

as we saw in the opening scene of *Idyll* 1, by a recognition of the ways human culture operates on nature and can only be in place by not quite being part of it. The fictionality of the bucolic world also showed how provisional even the most idealizing vision of "fitting in" was. The question of spatial boundaries and interest in margins might draw attention to analogous distinctions: between humans and animals, self and other. It is not much of a leap from this to the fluidity of ethnic and cultural distinctions in the lives of the poems' first readers. Much was at stake, therefore, in the relation between, let us say, Alexandria and this other space constructed in the imagination.

Idyll 7 has often been considered a poetic statement by Theocritus, "a conscious showpiece of his art and a manifesto of his poetic ideals as they are embodied in bucolic poetry."[82] And so I think it is, but not quite in the way others have considered it. Theocritus removes bucolic poetry, along with Lykidas, from "the mountain" to "the road," where definitions are open to question, and brings it into contact with other poetic styles: not only Simikhidas's essentially urban, or at least urbane, song but also the description of the bountiful place of rest on Phrasidamos's farm at the end of the poem (*Id.* 7.131–157). Simikhidas may not amount to much as a bucolic poet, but he does a beautiful job of turning this agricultural setting into poetry. The appreciation of natural bounty through sight, smell, and hearing may seem to bring this passage close to bucolic, but it lacks basic bucolic values: it represents leisure that can be earned only by work. With Lykidas's abrupt disappearance, we may imagine that he and bucolic song return to "the mountain," but now the nature of bucolic and what sets it apart have been clarified by this experience of blurred boundaries and the resulting drawing of contrasts with other poetic styles, which can occur only on "the road."

The "Urban Mimes"
Idyll 15

Like *Idyll* 7, *Idyll* 15 involves a journey and encounters "on the road" that call into question, or provoke the affirmation of, various kinds of identity, here especially gender and ethnic identity. Joan Burton has given an excellent account of the "motif of the road" in this poem and of the complementary theme of thresholds. She connects this journey and its boundary crossings with conditions created by mobility and immigration as discussed above, so that we can see an underlying affinity in this respect between *Idyll* 7 and the urban poems. By leaving home, Gorgo and Praxinoa are forced to negotiate situations they would not

---

82. Halperin 1983, 120.

have encountered in their houses and to deal with strangers, each of whom has his or her own perspective and goals in this diverse city of Alexandria. "Insofar as chance meetings on a road," says Burton, "can offer opportunities to learn to adjust to the requirements of new social arenas, by representing such encounters the poet can explore social rituals, rites of passage for moving from one space to another."[83]

In addition, *Idyll* 15 is a fine illustration of Michel de Certeau's description of walking through a city as a "pedestrian speech act": "The act of walking is to the urban system what the speech act is to language."[84] The pedestrian, he goes on to say, appropriates the topography of the city by finding her own path, out of many possible routes, from one place to another, spatially "acts out" the place by instantiating a spatial system, and comes into relation with other people who are also in movement along their own paths. Movement between places also aligns the starting place of a journey with its end and brings them into relation with each other.[85] Here the feminine space of the ordinary[86] house's interior contrasts with the female-dominated ceremonial space of the Adonis festival inside the royal palace, private contrasts with public, the prosaic details of daily life (the cat sleeping on spun wool) in linear time contrast with an occasion marking Adonis's annual return in circular ritual time.[87] Along with these contrasts, as John Whitehorne suggests, connections between the women in the house and in the palace are created through women's work.[88] The fine, soft wool of the coverlets in the Adonis tableau (*Id.* 15.125) evokes the filthy wool that Gorgo's husband bought (*Id.* 15.18–20), and the tapestries (*Id.* 15.80–86) outdo the fine dress that Praxinoa wove for herself (*Id.* 15.34–38). That the palace far outshines the house in magnificence adds to the royal mystique ("everything's rich in a rich man's house," *Id.* 15.24), but there is an analogy between them because women, not men, create and are connoisseurs of fine wool and

---

83. Burton 1995, 10.

84. De Certeau 1984, 97.

85. See especially Tilley 1994, 29–31.

86. Or perhaps not so ordinary, though far short of the palace's opulence. Whitehorne 1995, 67, has argued plausibly that Gorgo and Praxinoa live in an affluent suburb of Alexandria. Their complaints about their husbands are indirect boasts about the latters' prosperity, which is the result of opportunities afforded to Greeks in Egypt by Ptolemy's power (66–70).

87. Burton 1995, 17–18, notes how the women's leaving the house is coordinated with their crossing the palace threshold when they arrive by the repetition of words for "inside" and "lock" (*Id.* 15.1, 43, 77). Davies 1995 makes the contrast between the festival and ordinary life the basis for his reading of *Idyll* 15.

88. Whitehorne 1995, 70–72.

weaving.[89] Whitehorne further argues that there is a correlation between the women's husbands and Ptolemy: just as the husbands' prosperity underwrites their wives' material surroundings and their work, so the Adonis festival created by Arsinoe and her women workers (*Id.* 15.80) is a display of Philadelphus's wealth and imperial power.[90] To Whitehorne's discussion I would add that the poem spatializes these relationships by aligning house and palace by means of the women's journey through Alexandria from one to the other and back. The picture that emerges from this reading of *Idyll* 15 is of a close-knit Greek community within the multicultural environment of Alexandria, in which prosperity radiates outward from the palace and the palace draws its members to itself for self-display that promotes unity—a microcosm within the city, perhaps, of Ptolemaic imperial rule. This affirmation seems all the stronger and more necessary against the background of the hazards to identity posed by being "on the road," where Greek women might be exposed to allegedly treacherous Egyptians but for the order imposed by Ptolemy (*Id.* 15.46–50).[91]

In travel from home and back, the journeys outward and homeward are not necessarily the same, even though they may traverse exactly the same space (considered abstractly, as on a map). They are experienced differently. Space

---

89. Cf. especially Skinner 2001, 213–214. This point is made humorously by Praxinoa's story (*Id.* 15.15–17) that when she sent her husband to buy materials for cleaning and dyeing wool, he came back with expensive salt instead (Whitehorne 1995, 64–66).

90. Whitehorne 1995, 72–74. It seems to me that his reading is not as incompatible with the feminist reading of Griffiths 1981 as he suggests (Whitehorne 1995, 73). Even if Gorgo and Praxinoa are rivals of each other rather than of their husbands, that could be the result of their situation as women. For a different view of *Idyll* 15 that is explicitly opposed to the readings of Griffiths and of Burton 1995, see Lambert 2001, 100, who argues that Theocritus "presents us with a male perspective of [*sic*] women's perspectives on a women's festival, with a comic literary pedigree, which would not have been unfamiliar to his cultured audience." Skinner 2001, 213, although she allows for some irony on Theocritus's part, takes the opposite view to Lambert's, that in Gorgo's and Praxinoa's admiration of the tapestries he gives voice to women's perspective following a movement set by female epigrammatists that helped shape Hellenistic aesthetics. Davies 1995 traces the portrayal of the women to the influence of comedy and mime instead, whereas for Skinner mime is relevant mainly with Herodas's *Mimiamb* 4, which she sees as an attack on the movement that she traces. Perhaps, then, the question is where one locates the influences on Theocritus in *Idyll* 15. A more interesting possibility is that he leaves several opposed subject positions open to his audience, so that a gendered response to art within the text evokes gendered responses in modern readers. On the importance of weaving and gender in the poem, and of other objects, see also Noel and Remond 2017, 79–89.

91. This is only part of the picture. Any notion of a seamless Greek identity in this poem is complicated by evident tensions among Greeks (see below). And Foster 2006 argues that allusions to Homer and Greek historiography suggest that Philadelphus and Arsinoe are at once Greek and Egyptian rulers, in line with Stephens's arguments about Alexandrian poetry (Stephens 2003).

appears in its relative aspect, as one moves through it. The trip outward feels like movement into the unknown, to new experiences, into the future; travel homeward has the quality of return to the familiar, the already experienced, the past.[92] It is a restoration of security—or dullness? The women's walk to the palace through crushes of people in the streets and in the palace doorway is filled with incident. It is an adventure. Their return is not even narrated and is unremarkable. And we know what they will come home to: husbands surly if a meal does not appear on time.

The women walk from a house possibly on the outskirts of the city through urban space to the palace. Perhaps we are to imagine them making their way along one of the wide avenues that ran through Alexandria from east to west, because this would be the most likely place to encounter a contingent of royal cavalry (*Id.* 15.51–52). But we can only guess, because there is not a word in the text about the physical city itself. Instead, in a technique like that of the bucolics, the experience of the streets comes to us filtered through Praxinoa's fearful reactions to the horses, and we have Gorgo's earlier comments on her struggle to get from her house to Praxinoa's through all the chariots and the booted and cloaked soldiers (*Id.* 15.4–7).[93] This is relative space again: space as perceived from the body outward and from a particular point of view. We get no sense of what an Alexandrian street looked like, but we get a vivid picture of what it was like for a woman of a certain (middling) class to walk through one on a festival day. Gorgo's remark to Praxinoa, "you live farther away all the time" (*Id.* 15.7), gives another example of relative space. It does not have to be taken literally, as though Praxinoa's husband keeps moving to more and more remote houses to keep the two women apart. It more likely means that the trip between houses seems to get longer and to take more time, even though the physical distance has not changed at all.[94]

The crowd at the palace door, considered from the perspective of relative space, is significant as an illustration of Ptolemaic power. It shows the centripetal effect of the palace in drawing people to itself. Space is not neutral, and people's movements through it are not random; both are inflected by relations of power. The palace has this effect not only within Alexandria. Goods also flow into it from the sphere of Ptolemaic influence and control in the Aegean and Asia Minor (the

---

92. Tuan 1977, 12.

93. In fact, "everywhere boots, everywhere cloaked men" (*Id.* 15.6) can refer to either soldiers or civilians. Burton 1995, 11, says that "the text's indeterminacy reflects Gorgo's alienation in the public space." I would add that the reduction of men to boots and cloaks reflects fears of the street's strangeness on the part of a woman accustomed to being indoors.

94. A possibility noted by Gow 1952, II, 268.

movement of goods is another aspect of relative space), as two often-overlooked lines suggest (*Id.* 15.126–127):

ἁ Μίλατος ἐρεῖ χὠ τὰν Σαμίαν καταβόσκων,
'ἔστρωται κλίνα τὠδώνιδι τῷ καλῷ ἄμμιν.'

Miletos will say, and he who pastures his flocks on Samos,
"a couch has been spread for the beautiful Adonis by us."

It is uncertain whether the lines refer to fine wool produced in both Miletos and Samos or to the couch, manufactured in Miletos, and Samian wool.[95] On balance I think the reference is to the wool of the coverlets on which Aphrodite and Adonis lie, but the question does not matter to my point, which is the movement of expensive goods to Alexandria and the palace. Miletos was famous for the excellence of the wool raised there and for its textile industry, and Samos, just off the coast from Miletos, would have been in the same sphere of production. The whole coast of Asia Minor, in fact, was well known for its wool production.[96] So the reference to wool (or possibly wool and furniture) from this region works with the other opulent details of the tableau as an offering to the dying god and his bereft lover but also, intertwined with this sign of religious devotion, as a display of the Ptolemies' wealth—and of the basis of that wealth: Ptolemaic imperial power. These lines depict a city within the imperial sphere and even the lowliest island shepherds expressing pride in their contributions to it. Everyone has a role to play in creating and sustaining this economic and imperial system, at the apex of which sit Philadelphus and his wife Arsinoe.[97]

These lines, then, are spatial in their reach. They link people and places in the empire to Alexandria and the royal palace in economic as well as political

---

95. In line 127, the last word quoted, ἄμμιν, is Gow's conjecture for ἄλλα of the manuscripts; for discussion, see Gow 1952, II, 298–299. Gow says that his reading implies that Samos and Miletos supply the coverlets and not the couch, inclusion of which would require Ahrens's ἁμά. I am not sure that either reading necessarily implies what Gow says it does, but the advantage of ἄμμιν, I think, is that it stresses the agency of Miletos and the shepherd and so expresses their pride in participating in the economic and religious processes of the empire. Dover 1971, 213, keeps the manuscripts' ἄλλα ("*Another* couch"), which he says "[implies] pride that the magnificent object is produced year after year." Gow had already dismissed this interpretation as "a desperate expedient," but I think it might have the advantage of adding chronological depth to the spatial extent of the empire implied by mention of Samos and Miletos.

96. Kloft 1989, 50. On Milesian wool and textiles, see Papadopoulou 2017, 165.

97. For further discussion of the connection between the festival of Adonis and Ptolemaic imperialism and self-legitimation, see Reed 2000.

terms. Maria Papadopoulou has discussed the importance of wool in Theocritus, especially in regard to the "chain of production," the process by which wool is obtained and turned into finished textiles: the raising and shearing of sheep, the dyeing of raw wool and spinning it into thread, and the weaving of textiles such as the coverlets on Adonis's couch or the (allegedly) expensive dress that Gorgo puts on (*Id.* 15.34–37). Theocritus, she argues, creates spatial distinctions by means of wool and specifically dress.[98] In the bucolic *Idylls*, in which the bucolic world is seen in and for itself and where the herdsmen wear animal skins, there is no mention of what will be done with the animals' wool when it is sheared or of the production of textiles. In the urban poems, the emphasis is on the textiles themselves, especially the dresses that the women wear, so that clothing articulates the spatial distinction between the city and the countryside. I would add to this argument that in *Idyll* 15, with its urban perspective, the two lines we have been looking at place the bucolic world in the wider perspective of the Ptolemaic empire. Here that world is seen not as a place apart but as part of an imperial system.[99] Wool, then, is not solely a marker of gender distinctions, although it is importantly that as well. With this glimpse from the city outward to its place of origin, wool stands as a paradigm for the ingathering into Alexandria of material objects and wealth from other places in the empire.

It may seem that I am wringing too much significance from a mere two lines that simply give a small detail in the singer's description of the tableau. But these lines stand out if we think of Theocritus in spatial terms, because they give us an urbanized and imperial view of the bucolic world that we have seen only from the inside in the bucolic *Idylls*. And as we shall see shortly, the whole tableau represents the city's appropriation of the bucolic into itself. These lines show the same thing in a more material form.

Corresponding to this movement to Alexandria and into the palace, a reciprocal movement outward may be implied by Gorgo's comment that the cavalry has gone ἐς χώραν (*Id.* 15.57). A. S. F. Gow understands the phrase to mean that they have gone to the starting post for races in the hippodrome,[100] but it could also mean "to the countryside." If so, it would imply the Ptolemies' control, exerted outward from Alexandria, over the rest of Egypt.

---

98. Papadopoulou 2017. On the thematic importance of textiles in *Idyll* 15, see Foster 2016, 206–209.

99. On these lines, see also Whitehorne 1995, 73, and Foster's reference to the wool "gotten from Samian sheep herded at the edges of a realm all too ready to dedicate its resources and efforts to the aggrandizement of the house of Ptolemy" (Foster 2006, 143).

100. Gow, 1952, II, 282.

As wool flows to Alexandria, so the people within the city converge on the palace. They participate in the same centripetal pattern of movement, and all of them in this way relate the palace to their places of origin and define Alexandrian space in a hierarchical way. Praxinoa and Gorgo see themselves as singular and the crowd as an undifferentiated mass, like ants (*Id.* 15.45) or pigs (*Id.* 15.73). This scene of movement and arrival makes of the palace a place in the sense described by Doreen Massey: a locus of convergence of various people's lives with their trajectories and stories, and of the formation or enactment of relations of power, and in this case relations of gender also.[101] From this perspective, space in *Idyll* 15 is also relational. There are, first, the prickly relations between the women and their husbands, centered on their houses. In the palace, by contrast, Arsinoe's association with Aphrodite (*Id.* 15.106–111) emphasizes the erotic relations between her and Philadelphus. There is the division whereby the effect of Philadelphus's authority is felt in public (the cavalry is his, *Id.* 15.51–52, and he has made the streets safe for Greeks, *Id.* 15.46–50), whereas the festival in the palace is dominated by females, and identity is defined matrilineally.[102] Thus, the conventional Greek arrangement of private houses (men outside, women inside) is projected onto the public organization of Ptolemaic Alexandria. The women's encounters with an oracular old woman and two men, one helpful, the other annoyed and ridiculing, enact various other aspects of gender relations. Praxinoa gives her version of Egyptian–Greek relations in Alexandria and expresses her fear and distrust of Egyptians (*Id.* 15.46–50). Later, she and Gorgo are the object of ridicule for their broad-voweled Doric (*Id.* 15.87–88), and we see something of the possible tensions among Greeks who have come together in Alexandria, as they would have been less likely to do in the traditional Greek world. Praxinoa's retort, expressing pride in her Syracusan and ultimately Corinthian descent, shows how it was necessary, in the diversity of Alexandria, to maintain identity by insisting on local identifications.[103] And once again we see the centripetal force exerted by Alexandria, on population this time and not only on goods.

---

101. Massey 2005.

102. Burton 1995, 75.

103. Hinge 2009 makes the opposite argument. Noting that in the Hellenistic period, Greek dialectal differences were leveled in favor of koine, he sees the stranger's taunt as a sign that the women's clinging to their Syracusan Doric is obsolete and sees Praxinoa's pride in Syracuse's Corinthian roots as anachronistic: "the new identity as an Alexandrian cosmopolitan required the abandonment of the old epichoric dialects and the adoption of Koine since in the multiethnic milieu of Alexandria, the old local affinities have lost their meaning" (p. 74). But I think it just as likely that under these conditions of deracination, asserting a local identity would have been felt all the more important. One might be (for example) Syracusan with regard to other Greeks and Greek with regard to Egyptians; both aspects of identity are depicted in *Idyll* 15.

The space of the women's journey is presented as relational in another way as well: it is given a mythic coloring through allusions to Homer. "By trying the Akhaians came into Troy," says the old woman in answer to Gorgo's question about whether it is easy to get into the palace. "By trying all things are accomplished" (*Id.* 15.61–62). Walking into the palace is as formidable a task and as great an accomplishment as the ten-year assault on Troy! The incongruity is humorous, of course, and marks the distance between mime and epic. But the epic allusion may also express how women whose lives were spent mainly at home might feel about braving the urban bustle, and perhaps the awe they might feel at the door of their rulers' home. Burton, who discusses the old woman as a helper figure often encountered on epic journeys, also points out other Homeric type scenes realized in this poem,[104] so that the journey through the streets of Alexandria resembles an epic quest. Once the women are in the house, Gorgo points to the tapestries, which she calls "fine and graceful" (λεπτὰ καὶ . . . χαρίεντα, *Id.* 15.79)—an allusion to *Od.* 10.223, which describes Kirke's weaving. The allusion is reinforced by Praxinoa's comparing the pushing crowd to pigs just a few lines before (*Id.* 15.73)—the animals into which Kirke transformed Odysseus's men.[105] At least momentarily, being in this hall, seen through the lens of mythic narrative, takes on an aura of magic and danger, and this may reflect the women's feelings about the unfamiliar space they have entered.[106]

Once inside the palace, Praxinoa and Gorgo are confronted with a tableau of Adonis in the arms of Aphrodite in a scene that Nita Krevans has argued is "pastoral" in nature (see especially *Id.* 15.118–122). A connection is surely suggested by the fact that Adonis was a shepherd or cowherd and is referred to as such at *Id.* 1.105 and *Id.* 3.46. This is an enchanted, ritual space, however artificial, that provides a temporary refuge from the urban space that encloses it. Krevans also suggests a metapoetic effect: "By emphatically (and comically) evoking the contrast between 'real' city and 'ideal' retreat, Theocritus invites us to see pastoral in its full context, as the product of an urban court, and to see the pastoral poet

---

A similar need for an identity rooted in place of origin, and not just antiquarianism, may lie behind Callimachus's interest in local myths in his *Aetia* or Theocritus's apparently gratuitous use of Laconic and Thessalian words for "lover" and "beloved," respectively in *Idyll* 12.13–14.

104. Burton 1995, 15–16. For further discussion of Homeric echoes, see Griffiths 1979, 121–123. For the significance of allusions to Homeric scenes of hospitality, particularly those involving Arete, Helen, and Kirke, who help characterize Arsinoe as "a dominant woman to be admired—and feared," see Foster 2016, 194–196, 210–214 (quotation from 196).

105. Foster 2006, 138, sees these allusions to Kirke as part of the depiction of Arsinoe: "casting Arsinoe in Kirke's part cleverly underscores Arsinoe's hybrid identity as a Macedonian/Greek queen and Egyptian royal consort who treads the boundary between human and divine." See also Foster 2016, 217–218.

106. For a more "ironic" reading of the Homeric allusions, see Griffiths 2021, 590.

in *his* full context, as a resident of Alexandria."[107] Here is another link between the bucolic and the urban poems. I would like to build on Krevans's ideas and suggest that the importance of bucolic poetry to a contemporary Greek audience, outlined at the end of the preceding section, is enacted spatially in this *Idyll*. After a linear journey through the streets of Alexandria, where Praxinoa can best assert her Greek identity by scorning Egyptians (*Id.* 15.46–50) but where another Greek derides the women's flat vowels and calls them turtledoves, provoking an angry assertion of her Hellenism from Praxinoa (*Id.* 15.87–95), she and Gorgo arrive at a place within the palace where a rustic tableau is part of the celebration of Adonis's recurrent return and departure, in a ritual that might be thought to give Greeks a common focus of identification (as subjects of Ptolemy, of course). But just as in bucolic poetry, the myth and its ritual only work because boundaries are fluid. Adonis crosses the line between the underworld and this world and goes back again (*Id.* 15.136–137). In an opposite movement, Aphrodite has made Berenike immortal (*Id.* 15.106–108). In this privileged quasi-bucolic space at the heart of this huge, diverse city, the same questions about movement and identity are raised that the women experience in its streets, but also the same ones as in bucolic poetry. That is, in yet another centripetal move, the city and the palace draw into themselves what poetry projects outward, onto "the mountain."

Idyll 2

In *Idyll* 2, a woman walking from her house to a religious festival has an encounter on the road; the basic situation is the same as in *Idylls* 7 and 15, but here eros is an issue as well as gender and ethnic identity (Delphis is a Myndian), as in *Idyll* 15.[108] In contrast to that poem, however, the urban setting here[109] is not very important: the most prominent location throughout the poem is the interior of Simaitha's house—the spatial analogue of her interior feelings[110]—and probably (during her address to the moon) the area in front of the door.[111]

---

107. Krevans 2006, 145–146. On the relations between *Idylls* 15 and 1, see the suggestive discussion of Griffiths 1979, 124–128.

108. Burton 1995, 19–20. Burton 1995 and Segal 1985 have discussed space in *Idyll* 2 extensively, and so I can be brief here. I treat the themes of absence and desire in *Idyll* 2 more fully in chapter 3.

109. Simaitha lives in a polis (*Id.* 2.35), she has neighbors, and there is a *palaistra*, as was common in Hellenistic cities. Otherwise, there is little trace of the city.

110. Segal 1985, 108.

111. White 1979, 17–20, argues that the whole poem takes place indoors.

Even though the setting in the "now" of the poem is static, *Idyll* 2 is a markedly spatial text. For much of the poem, Simaitha's house is the center and other places are brought into alignment with it by movement from them to it, and vice versa. For example, Delphis comes to it from the *palaistra* (a building consisting of an open wrestling ground surrounded by rooms for washing and so on) when the slave woman goes there from Simaitha's house to invite him, with the result that he and Simaitha begin their short-lived affair; and Delphis's movement toward the house is balanced by the slave's second departure from it, this time to Delphis's house in order to sprinkle magic herbs over the threshold to compel him back to her mistress.[112] The text leaves it doubtful that he will complete the pattern and come back.

A different kind of double movement occurs when Simaitha first sees Delphis. She is on her way with a female neighbor[113] to a festival of Artemis when they encounter Delphis coming with male friends from the *palaistra*—feminine and masculine spaces juxtaposed. Both Delphis and Simaitha are at this moment outside their "proper" spaces; being "on the road" here may be a sign that their love affair will be unhappy. One spatial relationship is between Simaitha's house and Artemis's grove—both female spaces. Simaitha sees Delphis when she is in the middle of the way (*Id.* 2.76); this detail may remind us of Simikhidas's meeting with Lykidas (*Id.* 7.10). As there, a movement between two places intersects with someone else's movement from a third place (the mountain, the *palaistra*). But here the journey is interrupted. Simaitha forgets about the procession and never reaches Artemis's grove. The circuit of movement between two sheltered places considered "safe" for women by Greek culture—house to grove and back to house—is disrupted by illicit love. Simaitha's interrupted movement corresponds to the sudden onrush of eros. "How I got back home I didn't know" (*Id.* 2.83–85); the return journey pales by comparison with the momentous event that has occurred "on the road." She may be returning to security and the past like the Syracusan women going home, but unlike them, she has been changed by the experience, and her relation to domestic space has been altered. She lies lovesick on her bed for ten days and visits the houses of other women to seek advice

---

112. Cf. Segal 1985, 105, on the complementary centrifugal and centripetal movements to and from Simaitha's house.

113. The account of the festival gives the impression of a female community that balances the male society of the *palaistra*: Anaxo, a basket bearer in the procession, the Thracian nurse who accompanies Simaitha, and Klearista, whose wrap she has borrowed (*Id.* 2.66–74). To this list are added the mother of Philista, "our flute girl," and of Melixo (*Id.* 2.145–146). And of course there is Simaitha's relationship with her slave Thestylis.

(apparently) and magic charms (*Id.* 2.86, 91–92). The house is no longer a shelter for her virginity.

Two other places figure in the poem: the implied house in which the symposium occurs, at which Delphis reveals that he is in love with someone else, and that other person's house, which he goes off to wreathe with garlands (*Id.* 2.151–153). Neither bears any relation to Simaitha's house, and that is significant: she has lost him.

Spatially, the house and *palaistra* are at first aligned in a relation of contrast: between male and female, elite and lower class.[114] But there is a mutual interference between these places that shows in the end how inappropriate this erotic union is. Delphis often left his oil flask with Simaitha (*Id.* 2.156)—a token of the *palaistra* in this female space—and Simaitha intends "tomorrow" to go to the *palaistra* and bawl Delphis out for his treatment of her. Whether or not she actually will do so is left uncertain, but the reader is invited to imagine the incongruous spectacle of an angry woman bursting into this quintessentially male space. This blurring of distinctions between distinctively male and female spaces is part of a larger pattern of the inversion of gender roles that is also enacted spatially and once again marks this relationship as doomed.

Doors and thresholds play a prominent role in *Idyll* 2 (59–60, 104–106, 160),[115] and the theme of liminality, which unsettles the distinction between inside and outside, stresses the uncertainty of social roles and categories. The sexually ambiguous Delphis crosses Simaitha's threshold (*Id.* 2.104–106) instead of performing what he recognizes as the expected *kômos* (*Id.* 2.118–122) that normally acknowledges the distinction between the outside and the feminine inside. The *kômos* might, as he claims, have resulted in either her allowing him inside after his request or his forcing his way in (*Id.* 2.124–128), but in either case he would have been taking the initiative. As it is, she has invited him to the house and inside and so has taken the active role. So the male enters the bedchamber that the female would usually leave, for marriage if a virgin (like Simaitha) or adultery if married (*Id.* 2.136–138). In this female-dominated space, Simaitha controls their physical union.[116] As for Delphis, he eventually gets things right

---

114. Burton 1995, 19.

115. For discussion, see Segal 1985, 106–107; Burton 1995, 19–20, 46.

116. For details, see chapter 3. For other gender inversions in the poem, see Burton 1995, 43–44. Burton's suggestion (20) that Delphis crossing her threshold represents a transition in Simaitha's life would be stronger if the act had been hers; compare Apollonius's Medea, *Arg.* 4.26–42. Andrews 1996, 32–34, suggests that the message Simaitha gives to Thestylis for Delphis, Σιμαίθα τυ καλεῖ ("Simaitha calls you," *Id.* 2.101), alludes to *Il.* 3.390, Ἀλέξανδρός σε καλεῖ οἶκόνδε νέεσθαι ("Alexander calls you to come to his chamber"), Aphrodite's words

and follows the conventional pattern of the distracted lover's behavior (in literature, at least) by giving himself away at a symposium, rushing out to cover the beloved's door with wreaths, and presumably staying outside all night in a state of desire[117]—but only later and with a different love object.

If bucolic space seems to a great extent (though not entirely) self-contained and occupied mainly by herders, space in towns and cities is more open, and using it results in encounters with various types of people, their characteristic ways of being, and their different values. In this built environment, space involves structures such as houses and palaces, and it both reflects and determines the relations between the people within them. But it is just as importantly constituted by movement between various places and buildings that relates them to each other and integrates them into larger spaces (such as the city of Alexandria). In the course of this movement, strangers form momentary or longer-lasting relationships: love, cooperation, hostility. In the bucolic world, herders come together, but they seem already to know one another, and their relations are not affected by these encounters. Nor are their identities, whereas in urban spaces, movement opens identities to question even if they are in the end affirmed. To use bucolic space is to be at rest, enjoying leisure and its pursuits. *Idyll* 7 combines these different concepts of space and of what being in them means. To live in or move through the more hectic urban space is to risk chance encounters that put identity at risk, for better or worse, and can change lives. It changes Simaitha's life for the worse, and we are left uncertain how she will fare. It does not seem to affect life permanently for Gorgo and Praxinoa, whose return to their own social and familial niche from the "great world" of the royal palace provides closure on this episode with a resumption of their ordinary lives.

---

to Helen; this puts Delphis in the position of Helen and Simaitha in the position of Paris. Andrews also well describes the spatial dislocations highlighted by the poem's play with the topos of the *paraclausithyron*: "in a wry inversion of the most conventional behavior for an *excluded* lover, Simaitha articulates the pain of *her* exclusion from Delphis' affections from her position *inside* the house; meanwhile, the beloved, Delphis, who should be the excluded lover, must be summoned from *outside* of the house!" (44; emphases in original).

117. This, rather than gaining access to the house by force or permission, is the usual pattern in the literary *kômos*. When Delphis mentions the two other possibilities, he is either showing that he does not understand the (literally) proper behavior for a lover or engaging in overstatement in order to feign an infatuation that he does not feel.

2

Theocritean Spaces 2

MYTHOLOGICAL AND ENCOMIASTIC SPACE

Mythological Space

Idylls 13 on Herakles and Hylas, 22 on the Dioskouroi, and 24 on the infant Herakles's strangling the snakes sent by Hera are difficult to classify. They bear clear affinities with epic poetry. Herakles had been a figure in epic, and *Idyll* 13 and the Amykos episode of *Idyll* 22 treat stories from the Argonautic saga, which had been a subject of epic since before the *Odyssey*. Closer to home, Theocritus's contemporary Apollonius of Rhodes narrated both stories on either side of the division between Books 1 and 2 of his *Argonautika*. But Pindar is an important presence in the Polydeukes section of *Idyll* 22 and, along with Simonides, in *Idyll* 24. And so in what follows I avoid the term "epyllion," which would imply that Theocritus was only experimenting with small-scale epics when he was clearly doing other things as well.[1] I considered "epicizing" as a description but rejected that as similarly limiting, although it describes an important aspect of these texts. I have adopted instead the term "mythological space" as at least noncommittal

---

1. On the history of this term with a case for its continued usefulness, see Gutzwiller 1981, 2–9. She sees these and other similar Hellenistic poems as combining epic with Callimachus's "leptotic" style, with the result that "the epyllion is epic which is not epic, epic which is at odds with epic, epic which is in contrast with grand epic and old epic values" (5). I am going to take a somewhat different approach while taking it for granted that many of the effects Gutzwiller describes so well are undoubtedly there. On the other hand, Acosta-Hughes 2012a, 156–157, expresses well-founded skepticism about the underlying assumption that poems of this nature arose as a response to an alleged opposition between small-scale narrative works and traditional large-scale epic. He suggests instead that hexameter and elegiac poetry spread in the Hellenistic period "into the space occupied earlier by other metrical forms" and that "one might prefer to see the proliferation of the shorter hexameter poem as a result of metrical expansion rather than generic reaction."

regarding generic affinities but still preserving distinctions from the bucolic and urban poems.[2]

The label hardly matters for my purposes, however. There is no single characteristic and distinctive space that these *Idylls* share. *Idyll* 24 is set mainly within domestic space. In the other two poems, Theocritus creates lush natural settings. In *Idyll* 13, this setting partially reworks certain elements of bucolic space but is not properly bucolic. In *Idyll* 22, it is bucolic but becomes the stakes in a non-bucolic boxing match. Springs figure conspicuously in both, but springs now are not places where herdsmen come together and sing; they are places of more dangerous kinds of convergence. Charles Segal assimilates *Idylls* 13 and 22 to the bucolic poems in regard to their treatment of water.[3] I suggest that there are important points of overlap but equally important distinctions to be made. Callimachus's Epigram 22, which Segal quotes, illustrates both. A Nymph snatches the Cretan goatherd Astakides "from the mountain"—that is, if "the mountain" has the same significance here as it does in Theocritus, she makes him vanish from bucolic space. Like Hylas, Astakides is now divine (ἱερός—the sound play with ὄρεος, "[from] the mountain," emphasizes the separation). In the second couplet, we are back in the bucolic world, beneath the oaks of Mount Dikte, where "we" will no longer sing of Daphnis but always of Astakides.[4] In good bucolic fashion, an absence provokes songs (see chapter 3). The epigram strikes a balance between the inside and the outside of bucolic space, but in *Idyll* 13 there is no bucolic space from which Hylas disappears.

Idyll 13

In *Idyll* 13, Theocritus makes a display of *not* creating a space that we could identify with epic poetry, either. When the heroes mustered at Iolkos for the voyage in quest of the Golden Fleece, Herakles brought Hylas with him (*Id.* 13.19–24):

ἵκετο χὠ ταλαεργὸς ἀνὴρ ἐς ἀφνειὸν Ἰωλκόν,
Ἀλκμήνας υἱὸς Μιδεάτιδος ἡρωίνας,

---

2. *Idyll* 26, on the story of Pentheus's dismemberment by his mother and her sisters, offers very little of interest in regard to space and will not be discussed here.

3. Segal 1981, 54–63.

4. This replacement of one archetypal bucolic "hero" by another as subject for commemoration perhaps suggests that Callimachus was responding to Theocritean bucolic, perhaps playfully "correcting" it. If so, "the mountain" in the epigram is likely to signify bucolic space. The word's occurrence in the first couplet would tip off the canny reader about this poem's relation to Theocritus.

σὺν δ' αὐτῷ κατέβαινεν Ὕλας εὔεδρον ἐς Ἀργώ,
ἅτις κυανεᾶν οὐχ ἅψατο συνδρομάδων ναῦς,
ἀλλὰ διεξάιξε βαθὺν δ' εἰσέδραμε Φᾶσιν
αἰετὸς ὥς μέγα λαῖτμα, ἀφ' οὗ τότε χοιράδες ἔσταν.

> There came also to wealthy Iolkos that workhorse of a man,
> the son of Alkmene, the heroine from Midea,
> and with him Hylas went down to the strong-thwarted *Argo*,
> the ship that did not touch the dark Clashing Rocks,
> but darted through and sped to deep Phasis
> like an eagle, a great expanse of sea [to cross], from which time then
> the rocks stood still.

In a spectacular ellipsis, the *Argo*'s entire voyage outward, from its origin at Iolkos through the Bosporos strait to Phasis, is implied, not narrated, by reference to these three points—all in one breathless sentence (*Id.* 13.16–24), of which I have quoted only part. The journey across the Aegean Sea to the Bosporos gets no mention whatever, and the passage along the whole length of the Black Sea is summarized as "a great expanse."[5] That is, in this poem, in glaring contrast, at least to us, with Apollonius's *Argonautika*, the Argonauts speed through undifferentiated space that is worth mentioning only as an obstacle between them and their destination.[6] Then, after mentioning the *Argo* reaching the end of its voyage, the

---

5. Lines 23–24 are problematic (on the difficulties, see Hunter 1999, 272–273), especially the construction of μέγα λαῖτμα. To avoid forcing an interpretation, I have omitted the commas after Φᾶσιν and ὥς printed by both Gow and Hunter. In my translation I have followed the suggestion of White 1979, 80–82, that the phrase is in apposition to the second half of line 23. I find Hunter's "as an eagle [soars] over a vast expanse" also tempting. Either interpretation makes my point possible: that the Black Sea is just something to be sped over, abstract rather than constructed space. Both have the advantage of giving μέγα λαῖτμα the sense it must have: an expanse of open sea. For that reason, understanding the phrase as referring to the Bosporos (Dover 1971, 184) or to the mouth of the Phasis River (Gow 1952, II, 236–237) is unpersuasive. Griffiths's Πόντον for Φᾶσιν is unnecessary (1996, 107–108), since the name of the river can be explained as I am doing. A more serious problem is ἀφ' οὗ τότε ... ἔσταν (the collocation of both τότε and an aorist verb with ἀφ' οὗ, as Griffiths points out) in line 24. Possibly ἀφ' οὗ is corrupt and the rest of the line can be retained. Excision of line 24 would not affect my point about the telescoping of the Black Sea voyage, as long as Φᾶσιν is retained in line 23.

6. This narrative selectivity is mentioned briefly by Elliger 1975, 352–353, as characteristic of the opposition in this poem between the epic and bucolic worlds. As will emerge, I see something more complex than this straightforward opposition.

narrative goes back to the beginning, the *Argo*'s departure from Iolkos, which begins an equally long sentence that similarly traverses a long expanse of space without mentioning it (*Id.* 13.25–31):

Ἆμος δ' ἀντέλλοντι Πελειάδες, ἐσχατιαὶ δὲ
ἄρνα νέον βόσκοντι, τετραμμένου εἴαρος ἤδη,
τᾶμος ναυτιλίας μιμνάσκετο θεῖος ἄωτος
ἡρώων, κοίλαν δὲ καθιδρυθέντες ἐς Ἀργὼ
Ἑλλάσποντον ἵκοντο νότῳ τρίτον ἆμαρ ἀέντι,
εἴσω δ' ὅρμον ἔθεντο Προποντίδος, ἔνθα Κιανῶν
αὔλακας εὐρύνοντι βόες τρίβοντες ἄροτρα.

> When the Pleiades rise, and the farthest meadows
> pasture the newborn lamb, with spring now turning into summer,
> Then the godlike flower of heroes turned their attention to
> sailing, and sitting down in the hollow *Argo*
> they came to the Hellespont, aided by the south wind that blew for
>   three days,
> and they put to shore within the Propontis, where the Kianians'
> cattle cut wide furrows as they wear out the plowshares.

No sooner do the Argonauts take their seats on the rowing benches at the *Argo*'s first launch than they reach the Hellespont in the next clause and then moor the ship at Kios in the Propontis, where the main part of the narrative, the loss of Hylas, is set. There is no mention of crossing the Aegean from Iolkos or of sailing up the Hellespont or of anything that happened along the way. At the end of the poem, yet another dramatic elision occurs. The narrative leaves Herakles rushing through mountain thickets, while his companions wait for him on the shore so that they can set sail, and appends these lines (*Id.* 13.72–75):

οὕτω μὲν κάλλιστος Ὕλας μακάρων ἀριθμεῖται·
Ἡρακλέην δ' ἥρωες ἐκερτόμεον λιπαναύταν,
οὕνεκεν ἠρώησε τριακοντάζυγον Ἀργώ,
πεζᾷ δ' ἐς Κόλχους τε καὶ ἄξενον ἵκετο Φᾶσιν.

> So the most beautiful Hylas is numbered among the blessed gods.
> But as for Herakles, the heroes taunted him as a ship deserter,
> because he left the thirty-benched *Argo*
> and came to the Colchians and inhospitable Phasis on foot.

There is a lot going on in these lines, but here I just want to mention that we are not even told of the Argonauts sailing through the Bosporos and crossing the Black Sea to the Phasis River. If Herakles got there on foot and they are there to taunt him, they must have completed the voyage, but the text does not bother to say so. An obvious point, perhaps, but once again a long and—according to other sources—eventful voyage is simply left out, in a third example in this short poem of a radical telescoping of space and time. It is true, of course, that we have already been told of the arrival at the Phasis in line 23, in what may be an anticipation of the inexplicitness here. In fact, lines 23 and 75 form a ring, with ἵκετο Φᾶσιν recalling the earlier εἰσέδραμε Φᾶσιν. References to the arrival at the goal of the quest thus enclose the narrative proper, as if to signal both that this episode at Kios is part of a larger story and, at the same time, that the frame narrative is not what *this* poem is interested in telling. Theocritus does manage to get the entire voyage to Colchis into his poem, but he does so by leaving out all the struggles and adversity that made the Argonautic myth the story of a heroic quest. And he offers even the skeleton of that larger story almost flamboyantly out of order: mustering at Iolkos, passage through the Clashing Rocks, arrival at the Phasis, departure from Iolkos, arrival at the Hellespont, putting to shore at Kios, the Hylas episode, Herakles's arrival at the Phasis (to find the other Argonauts already there).

This convoluted order stands in strong contrast to the linear structure of Apollonius's *Argonautika*, and the difference shows clearly that Theocritus suppresses what Apollonius so beautifully portrays: the *Argo*'s progress along the south coast of the Black Sea as a process of constructing a network of places that in historical times were sites of Greek colonies, with the voyage thus forming the eastward segment of a great loop that by the end of the poem takes in the Adriatic Sea and the western Mediterranean and has mainland Greece as its center.[7] Whatever the relation between the two texts, they show alternative ways of handling the same mythic material. The contrast shows all the more clearly that the narrative dislocations and ellipses in *Idyll* 13 are a device to focus attention on *this* place, Kios, and *this* story, Herakles's loss of Hylas. In the *Argonautika*, the episode is subordinate to the main narrative and a diversion from the Argonauts' heroic purpose—a permanent diversion in the case of Herakles, who is lost from the expedition. *Idyll* 13's emphasis is not on heroic achievement but on the power of eros, which subdues both the mighty Herakles and the divine Nymphs. Apollonius, by contrast, never makes it explicit that Herakles feels eros for Hylas.

---

7. See Thalmann 2011. On the question of the priority of Apollonius or Theocritus, see the introduction to the present book. The contrasts I am drawing here imply no position on that.

We can infer from the narrative that he does, but there is no need to; Apollonius's emphases lie elsewhere.

Theocritus is interested in space but in one place, not in the grand sweep of the Argonautic voyage. Kios is the place where the desires of Herakles and the Nymphs for Hylas clash. At Kios, two locations are described in detail: the beach where the Argonauts land, with the adjacent meadow from which they collect brush for couches on which to eat dinner, and the spring whose Nymphs pull Hylas into the water (*Id.* 13.32–35, 39–45). These two settings have been discussed in particular by Donald Mastronarde and by Einfried Elliger, who map onto them the oppositions they see as structuring the poem: that between eros, along with "realism (especially rusticism) and pastoral imagery," and heroism for Mastronarde and that between bucolic and epic for Elliger.[8] Mastronarde considers the scene at the meadow pastoral, or at least rustic, in nature, so that the Argonauts, pulled away from epic in the direction of bucolic, are transformed "into simple herdsmen in a Theocritean idyll." The spring is if anything more intensely bucolic ("the pastoral fantasy-world") and so the place of anti-heroic eros.[9] Elliger essentially agrees, noting differences between the Argonauts' preparations for the meal and the corresponding Homeric type scene. For him as well, the spring remains within the bucolic framework but shows nature in a darker, more sinister aspect than does the meadow.

As for the meadow, not every natural setting is bucolic, and at least in connection with Theocritus, it can be misleading to identify the countryside as a whole with pastoralism. Theocritus always provides certain markers of the bucolic when he wants us to think of a scene in that way, and most—but not quite all—are missing here. In fact, he has identified Kios as an *agricultural* place (*Id.* 13.30–31), and this low-lying meadow fits into that context, as with Augeias's estate in *Idyll* 25, even though meadows can also be part of the landscape of the bucolic poems. These meadows are not distinctively bucolic. There are indeed two details of the description that appear as appurtenances of the bucolic world: galingale (κύπειρος; cf. *Id.* 1.106, 5.45) and couches of brush, στιβάδες, on which herdsmen take their ease and enjoy song (cf. *Id.* 5.34, 7.67).[10] These are not enough to make this setting bucolic, but I do not consider them insignificant, either. They

---

8. Mastronarde 1968 (quotation from 279); Elliger 1975, 351–356.

9. Mastronarde 1968, 284, 285. I give a different view of *Idyll* 13, but I do so with great respect for the quality of this deservedly influential article.

10. The other words that Mastronarde lists (1968, 284n25) seem to me to have far less specific connection to the bucolic world: χαμεύναν, a bed on the ground, occurs in an agricultural pleasance at *Id.* 7.133; the meadow (λειμών) I have already discussed; and στόρνυμι appears also at *Id.* 6.33 but can be used of making up a bed in almost any context (including epic).

show Theocritus reusing elements of his bucolic poetry in a new context that still retains some contact with the bucolic world.[11] Perhaps we could say that he is conceiving this agricultural meadow scene to some extent through the lens of the bucolic imagination. I will return to this point below.

No spring in the bucolic poems is given anything like the description lavished on this one, although, as Elliger notes, the emphasis is on the plants that border it (*Id.* 13.39–42), none of which appears anywhere else in Theocritus, with one exception.[12] We learn little else, beyond the location in a "low-lying place," the darkness of the water, and of course, the three Nymphs dancing in its midst (*Id.* 13.40, 49, 43–45). The impression is one of natural lushness, but the atmosphere is uncanny. This is not a bucolic place. Unlike bucolic springs, which are places of leisure and relaxation, "this place does not invite one to tarry."[13] If it has any affinities outside this poem, they are with Kalypso's cave in the *Odyssey* (5.63–75), and, like that place, it has strong associations with female sexuality.[14]

This spring needs to be seen in relation to the meadow by the shore. The meadow is a place of spatial clarity, a scene of pause in a linear journey (even if that is not directly narrated), where nature furnishes the necessities of human comfort, where human sociability finds expression, and where the social order that prevails aboard the *Argo* is preserved: the Argonauts disembark κατὰ ζυγά, in the order in which they sit in pairs on board ship,[15] and Herakles and Telamon intend to share a meal just as they always have shared the same table (*Id.* 13.32, 37–38). At the spring, a human social relationship is severed, and the boundary between human and divine is blurred, when Hylas is made immortal. The Nymphs, as sexual aggressors, invert normative Greek gender relationships, and Hylas, instead of being guided into manhood by Herakles, is reduced to childishness, sitting in tears on the Nymphs' laps as they try to comfort him (*Id.* 13.53–54). So the inland spring, unlike the shore, is a place where normal human categories are disordered and where mortals are up against powers beyond their control. Accordingly, spatial categories—near and far—are also confused. Three times,

---

11. On more general affinities between *Idylls* 13 and 11, see Sens 2021, 180, and 178–181 on "the porousness of the boundaries between the mimetic and narrative poems." I fully agree with his argument, but as he implies, even porous boundaries still exist.

12. The exception is celery, σέλινον; cf. *Id.* 3.23, 7.68. On the idiosyncrasies of this description, see Elliger 1975, 354–355. See also Foster 2016, 129–135, who gives an ingenious explanation of why celandine is here said to be "dark-hued," an apparent botanical impossibility.

13. Elliger 1975, 355.

14. Hunter 1999, 277.

15. I do not find the problems raised by Gow (1952 II, 238) and Hunter (1999, 275) serious obstacles to understanding the phrase in this way.

"with all the power of his deep throat" (Gow's translation), Herakles bellows for Hylas; "and three times the boy responded, but his voice came thin from [below] the water, and although he was very nearby he seemed far off" (*Id.* 13.59–60). Immediately afterward, like a lion charging after a fawn, Herakles rushes randomly and without direction in search of Hylas (*Id.* 13.62–67). His spatial disorientation reflects his mental derangement and therefore dramatizes the power of eros that is the poem's main theme. "In longing for the boy," he "whirl[s][16] among untrodden [hence, pathless] brambles" and "cover[s] much ground . . . over mountains and through thickets." As with the Argonauts' voyage to Colchis but for very different reasons, space is something to be passed through, and its only features worth mentioning are the obstacles—mountains and thickets—to Herakles's mad flight. And these mountains (plural) are very different from "the mountain" of bucolic poetry, which is constructed as benevolent and nurturing according to human needs and desires. They are featureless except for their thickets, devoid of cultural significance. Thickets (δρυμοί) do figure in bucolic poetry, but they are on the margins of the bucolic world and help to define it by contrast. Finally, and in sharp opposition to the scene in the wilds, the focus shifts back to the shore, where the Argonauts wait in vain for Herakles so that they can resume their purposeful journey to the Phasis River.

What, then, of the opposition between epic and bucolic as the structural basis of *Idyll* 13? As we have seen, bucolic is not much in evidence in this poem; a few of its elements are there, but they are just traces. For that reason, I doubt that this opposition plays a role here, although I would agree with Mastronarde that Theocritus places eros in strong contrast to traditional epic values. And questions of literary genre certainly play a role in the poem. To leave Apollonius to one side for a moment, in addition to echoes of Homeric and Hesiodic epic and perhaps the *Homeric Hymn to Demeter*,[17] the opening lines display "clear affinities with sympotic elegy and lyric,"[18] in keeping with the theme of eros. But I would suggest that genres are not the main issue in the poem or its central focus but instead that Theocritus uses them as a literary tool. That is, by reconfiguring conventional elements of epic and lyric, he creates a novel text that escapes traditional generic categories, something that is neither epic nor lyric—nor bucolic, either: a poem

---

16. δεδόνητο: "this unusual passive . . . combines the whirl of Herakles' emotions with the rapid movement of his legs" (Hunter 1999, 285). This verb expresses the effect of erotic passion in Sappho and Pindar (passages cited by Hunter).

17. Gutzwiller 1981, 22–27. On Homeric allusions, see also Foster 2016: 122–128.

18. Hunter 1999, 262. On the lyric (as well as epic) affinities of the simile in *Id.* 13.62–63, see Kampakoglou 2021, 251–252. On "the sympotic Herakles," see Foster 2016, 144–146.

in hexameters that uses a mythic episode to demonstrate the sweeping powers of eros.[19]

It would still be possible to claim that this poem takes an anti-epic stance or shows the incompatibility of eros with heroism.[20] Even so, these are in service to the poem's main program, the depiction of eros's effect, not that program itself. David Halperin, however, offers a more complex view, in accordance with his argument that the *Idylls* represent a Hellenistic form of "epos." Through his twin techniques of "epic inversion" and "epic subversion," Halperin suggests, Theocritus tries not to *expose* the obsolescence of traditional epic but to *forestall* it by "[remaking] the genre of *epos* into a suitable vehicle for 'modern' (Alexandrian) aesthetic ideals and themes" and therefore by creating continuity with earlier epic even when he took an "anti-heroic" stance: "genuine continuity with the past could be achieved only by the most radical departures from tradition."[21] A strength of this perspective, I think, is that Theocritus's poetic project appears more constructive than polemical, but as I have said in the introduction, we need to take account of the strong elements from lyric poetry as well. Alexander Sens's recent description of Theocritus's relation to the epic tradition seems partly to dovetail with Halperin's view:

> Broadly speaking, Theocritus' mythological poems appropriate (a refined version of) the language and meter of the epic tradition to explore a range of alternative perspectives on heroic and divine behavior. In this sense they are not hostile to epic but rather call into question the privileged authority of that genre in the tradition.[22]

The common ground with Halperin here is the idea of opening up alternative perspectives. Doing so can result in exposing to question the traditional authority of epic, but that would not be the main effect of these poems or the most interesting one.

---

19. This will be discussed further in chapter 3.

20. Gutzwiller 1981, 19–29, and Mastronarde 1968, respectively.

21. Halperin 1983, 217–248 (quotations from 228 and 237, respectively). By "epic subversion" Halperin means "the transferral of a traditional mythological subject to a mundane, anti-heroic situation," and by "epic inversion" he means portraying "low mimetic subjects in roles previously assigned to heroes" (237). On Halperin's argument about *epos*, see my introduction.

22. Sens 2021, 177. He elaborates this view in connection with each of the mythological poems in the final section of his essay (188–195).

I approach the mythological poems in a similar spirit. Here I would like to propose a way of looking at *Idyll* 13's relation to epic that is suggested by the few bucolic elements it does contain and that is consistent with the views of Halperin and Sens. Theocritus took the Argonautic myth, which lent itself well to epic treatment, and showed what else might be done with it by one whose imagination was capable of producing bucolic poetry. One signal of this new approach early on in the poem might be the time marker for the launch of the *Argo* in lines 25–26, which is thoroughly, and in the context somewhat jarringly, bucolic: "when the farthest meadows pasture the newborn lamb" (quoted earlier). This could be read as a polemical appropriation of epic to bucolic, or vice versa, but it can be understood also as a sign that a characteristic story of the epic repertoire is about to be told not *as* bucolic but from the perspective of a bucolic sensibility. From this point of view, one might say that constructing continuities with tradition, especially when such claims call attention to their constructed nature by deliberately reading contemporary preoccupations back into it, was as much in the spirit of Alexandrian poets' dealing with the past as irony was.

An element of this reimagining of the story as one of eros was to play with vast distances and shrink them to insignificance in the treatment of the voyage to Colchis, to condense the spatial and temporal scope of the myth to one sole incident of a few hours in a single place. Conversely, in the scene at the spring in which eros's power was played out, Theocritus took a small distance and expanded it: Hylas is close to Herakles, but his cry seems to come from far away. Another move was to counterbalance the spatial clarity of shore and meadow with the spatial confusion of the spring. In this way, Theocritus created an environment in which the greatest hero of the Greeks, the killer of the Nemean lion, rushed lion-like in yearning for his lost love.

Idyll 22

In *Idyll* 22, two Argonauts, the Dioskouroi Kastor and Polydeukes, again leave camp on the shore and go inland, where they, too, find a spring in possession of a formidable inhabitant, not Nymphs this time but the monstrously huge Amykos, who challenges Polydeukes to a boxing match. Now eros is not at issue but almost its opposite, male competition as opposed to hospitality. The underlying issue is the respective claims on a place by a native and a newcomer or guest—a question of more than casual interest to Greek readers in the wake of Alexander's conquests or the long process of Greek colonization more generally.

Whatever is the relation between this poem and *Idyll* 13 on the one hand and Apollonius's treatment of the same stories on the other, the two Theocritean

Idylls implicitly invite us to read them alongside each other.[23] After a hymnic proem, the Amykos section of *Idyll* 22 begins like this (*Id.* 22.27–29):

ἡ μὲν ἄρα προφυγοῦσα πέτρας εἰς ἓν ξυνιούσας
Ἀργὼ καὶ νιφόεντος ἀταρτηρὸν στόμα Πόντου,
Βέβρυκας εἰσαφίκανε θεῶν φίλα τέκνα φέρουσα.

> Well, the *Argo*, escaping the rocks that clash together
> and the forbidding maw of the snowy Pontos [Black Sea],
> arrived at the territory of the Bebrukes, carrying the gods' dear sons.

Once again, the passage through the Bosporos is passed over with a quick summary in favor of a narrative focus on the place that will be the setting of the incident to be recounted. Theocritus locates the Amykos episode on the coast of the Black Sea, after the *Argo* escaped the Clashing Rocks, whereas Apollonius put it, like the Hylas episode, in the Propontis, before that point.[24] Spatially and narratively, then, the two *Idylls* bracket the Clashing Rocks, and the effect is to make all the more conspicuous the ellipsis of the passage through them, which in the myth was a major exploit of the Argonauts and an important heroic achievement that—as Apollonius's account of it shows—offered an epic poet the opportunity for bravura treatment. The emphasis is thrown all the more strongly on the major themes of these two accounts, which are in some ways opposites: Herakles's mad dash through the spatially indeterminate wilds under the compulsion of eros, as opposed to the reclaiming of a natural space for the civilized institution of ξενία ("hospitality") through the overcoming of Amykos, who considers this place his alone and tries to enforce that claim violently. In short, in the two poems, respectively, we see the limits of the greatest mortal hero as opposed to the civilizing triumph of a god in the guise of a hero.

Polydeukes overcomes Amykos through brute force (whereas in Apollonius, the struggle is between physical might and crafty intelligence), and the same is later true of Kastor's victory over Lynkeus, which carries a very different moral valence. In both duels, it is easy to forget, at least temporarily and despite the

---

23. On the relation between the two *Idylls*, with 22 possibly "a kind of narrative completion" of 13, see Hunter 1996, 59–61.

24. Cf. Sens 1994, 71–72, who argues that Theocritus has already alluded to Apollonius's account of the passage through the Bosporos in the proem when he described ships in distress rescued by the Dioskouroi (*Id.* 13.10–12) and calls Theocritus's placement of the Amykos episode a "correction" of Apollonius. If this should be right—and again, it may involve a chronological difficulty—it would sharpen the point I am making. Cf. Sens 1997, 28–29.

poem's "hymnic" opening, that (as Theocritus implies) these brothers are divine, and so we are tempted to see the episodes as combats between mortal heroes. This possibility is reflected in the ambiguity of the phrase "the dear sons of the gods" in line 29. Conventionally, in epic this refers to the race of heroes, but in the case of the Dioskouroi, it turns out to be literally true as they triumph in what are, after all, unequal fights.

In both *Idylls* 13 and 22, arrival on the shore is followed by a scene of disembarkation (*Id.* 13.32–35, *Id.* 22.30–33). The two descriptions have much in common, including verbal similarities.[25] But the similarities, by inviting us to compare the two scenes, accentuate a major difference. *Idyll* 13, as we have seen, constructs the encampment on the shore and the nearby meadow as a place that is aligned with and opposed to another place, the spring where Hylas disappears. In *Idyll* 22, no such process occurs. We learn only that the beach was "deep" and sheltered from the wind. What might have been a description of a meadow is replaced by the summary phrase "they strewed couches" (εὐνάς τ' ἐστόρνυντο); this is followed, in the same line, by preparations for dinner, which are reduced to a mention of the Argonauts twirling fire sticks. Clearly the interest in this account is not in the shore and activities there, or in aligning two different places, but in the spring itself.[26]

Whereas spring and shore are contrasting places in *Idyll* 13, then, they have nothing to do with each other in this poem. The spring is a separate, self-contained space. A hint of this can be seen in the Dioskouroi's departure from the camp (*Id.* 22.34–36):

Κάστωρ δ' αἰολόπωλος ὅ τ' οἰνωπὸς Πολυδεύκης
ἄμφω ἐρημάζεσκον ἀποπλαγθέντες ἑταίρων,
παντοίην ἐν ὄρει θηεύμενοι ἄγριον ὕλην.

Kastor of the swift horse and dark-faced Polydeukes
both went off alone, wandering away from their companions,
observing the wild variegated wood on the mountain.

Whereas Hylas had a purpose in leaving the encampment—to fetch water for the meal—and a destination, the brothers simply "wander away" from their companions and "are solitary"; both verb forms in line 35 are highly significant. They are in a deserted place (the overtone of ἐρημάζεσκον), cut off from the human society

---

25. On these, see Matthews 1985, 68.
26. Elliger 1975, 357, makes several of these points but with little discussion.

of their companions. And they are "wandering away" without fixed path or destination. This compound verb occurs in the *Odyssey* to indicate being destitute of a safe or known place as well as uncertainty as to direction (it is also a favorite of Apollonius).[27] Like Odysseus, they are entering unknown places but, unlike him, with no particular purpose. They are just looking at the natural scenery. But as the sequel shows, they are "on the mountain," not just as a place very different from the flat seashore but in the specific sense Theocritus gives the phrase: they are entering bucolic space. The Dioskouroi's entry into what is virtually another world seems all the more marked by contrast with Apollonius, who has Amykos come to the shore to challenge the Argonauts (*Arg.* 2.8). And whereas in *Idyll* 13 the Argonauts wait on the shore for Herakles to reappear, here all the Argonauts come to witness the boxing match when Kastor returns to the ship to lead them into this other space. The Bebrukes seem to have been there already, since they gather "swiftly" (θοῶς) in response to Amykos's signal with the conch shell (*Id.* 22.75–79).

Unlike the one in *Idyll* 13, this spring is part of a bucolic landscape (*Id.* 22.37–43). The abundant clear water beneath the smooth rock recalls the spring plashing down from a rock at *Id.* 1.7–8, except that there the sound is stressed, whereas here the description is visual. Two of the four nearby trees—firs and cypresses—appear in Theocritus's bucolic poems,[28] unlike those that surround the spring in *Idyll* 13. The meadow with fragrant flowers offering "work dear to bees" might remind us of the bees feeding the mythical goatherd and Komatas on honey gathered from meadow flowers in *Idyll* 7 (78–85). These flowers are "such as grow in abundance throughout the meadows when spring is ending"—*the* bucolic season, as we have seen. This time marker appeared in *Idyll* 13 (26), though not in the identical phrase, not to describe a stylized timeless setting (where it seems always to be spring) but to mark the particular time of the *Argo*'s launching. There it signaled the difference between what starts as a heroic narrative and the bucolic world; this narrative has moved into that world. All of this comes to us as observed by the Dioskouroi: "they found it" (εὗρον, *Id.* 13.37, the initial word of the description). They are outsiders who gaze upon the fullness of this bucolic space.

---

27. *Od.* 8.573, 9.259, 12.285, 15.382. It is hard not to think of the uncompounded verb at the beginning of the second line of the *Odyssey*. In view of the associations of Amykos with Polyphemos, it may be significant that the instance in Book 9 occurs when Odysseus is identifying himself and his men as wanderers from Troy and in the same position in the line as in *Id.* 13.35. On Apollonius's use of the verb, see Thalmann 2011, 61.

28. πεῦκαι: *Id.* 7.88; κυπάρισσοι: *Id.* 11.45, *Ep.* 4.7 Gow (cf. *Id.* 5.104). On the relation between *Idyll* 22 and bucolic, see Sens 1997, 40–41, 95.

But as we follow the Dioskouroi's gaze, we become aware of a figure who seems—at least at first—incongruously out of place in this peaceful scene: "there a prodigious [ὑπέροπλος] man sat sunning himself [ἐνδιάασκε], terrible to look upon." With his cauliflower ears, his swelling chest and broad back, and his muscles like boulders washed down by a winter torrent (an epic comparison) in contrast to the pebbles visible at the bottom of the spring,[29] Amykos seems like a figure out of epic and—at least initially—alien to this bucolic space.[30] The lion skin he wears associates him with Herakles, now absent from the Argonautic expedition, but this Herakles figure will be outclassed by Polydeukes. Theocritus, in fact, combines a number of poetic strands in his narrative and his depiction of Amykos. Apollonius's treatment of the episode, even if Theocritus was not responding to it, shows how this boxing match can be encompassed in epic poetry. The boxing match in Book 23 of the *Iliad* (653–699) lies behind the narrative here, as does Odysseus's encounter with Melanthios at a spring (*Od.* 17.204–253). Amykos himself combines traits of both Polyphemos and Iros in the *Odyssey*.[31] Some have seen the influence of comedy on the narrative and give "ironizing" readings of the whole episode.[32] There is furthermore, as I have been suggesting, Theocritean bucolic. And the poem begins by identifying itself as a hymn.

It is difficult to know what to make of this mixture. Many have seen in the poem a commentary of one kind or another on traditional (i.e., epic) notions of heroism, so that "the hero" no longer fits with the conditions and values of the Alexandrian world (this view resembles Mastronarde's influential reading of *Idyll* 13).[33] In a welcome move that goes beyond the notion of "die Kreuzung der Gattungen" (intersection of genres), Richard Thomas has discussed *Idyll* 22 as an example of generic "multiplicity" or "indeterminacy," which he suggests, following Todorov, can lead to the transformation of existing genres and the formation of new ones.[34] I think all these various readings can reasonably be elicited from

---

29. Noted by Hunter 1996, 62.

30. On the contrast, see Elliger 1975, 357–358.

31. See especially Laursen 1992, 77–81; Sens 1997, 96. That hospitality is also an issue in the Polyphemos episode of the *Odyssey* is, as Sens points out, an important link between it and *Idyll* 22.

32. See Elliger 1975, 358, and sources cited there; Effe 1978, 64–71, who understands an ironized distance between the poet and his subject as the hallmark of Theocritean poetry.

33. E.g., Griffiths 1976, 361; Laursen 1992: 92–93. Cf. Sens 1994: 349 (on the Lynkeus episode).

34. Thomas 1996, 232–238. I would not want to push this notion of "indeterminacy" too far, however. Generic distinctions remain important in Theocritus; it would be hard otherwise to recognize the way he recombines the features of various genres. As I hope this chapter and chapter 1 have shown, despite Thomas's reservations, such distinctions do not necessarily

the text, but I would like to ask specifically why this scene is set in a bucolic space. Given the prominence of bucolic in Theocritus's poetic production, it does not seem just one in an indeterminate mix of types, but it is especially marked. Those who see the poem as a critique of epic or its ideas of the hero could answer that displacing a duel set in mythic times into a bucolic environment while preserving epic overtones is a way of launching a critique of that tradition by appropriating it to a new context and, perhaps, diminishing it. I think this view is defensible, but I would prefer to say more neutrally, as with *Idyll* 13, that the poem views epic anew through a bucolic lens and shows what it would look like then, because again I think that Theocritus uses genres and generic expectations as a language rather than making them his main point. Something more than generic play may be going on in this case.

Polyphemos is a memorable figure in an epic poem, the *Odyssey*, but even there he is a herdsman and lives in a proto-bucolic world. There is a richly suggestive incongruity between his monstrous appearance and behavior and the natural bounty amid which he lives. But this Polyphemos is also capable of tenderness toward his pet ram, in contrast to his ferocity toward Odysseus (*Od.* 9.447–460). It was perhaps not a great leap for Theocritus (following Philoxenus, of course) to depict him as both grotesque and vulnerable in his love for Galateia (*Idyll*s 11 and 6). As the *Odyssey* and Theocritus's own poems show, then, such a figure is not entirely out of keeping with the bucolic world, even though we may also smile at the thought of a Cyclops as a cheese-eating shepherd. I suggest that the same is true of Amykos. Let us look again at the line that introduces him, *Id.* 22.44 (quoted above). He is called ὑπέροπλος, "prodigious"—probably a description at once of his size and his arrogance. It looks like a Homeric epithet, and it is a Homeric word; but it never is used of persons in either Homer or Hesiod. In view of the prominence of Homer in this episode, Theocritus's usage may be a hint that Amykos is an epic-style figure with a difference: not a warrior but an Iros figure, as it turns out, a weak boaster.[35] And in fact, when the Dioskouroi come upon him, he is enjoying the leisure and pleasant surroundings of the bucolic world: ἐνδιάασκε, "he was sunning himself." This rare word occurs one other time

---

prevent us from drawing connections among poems in the corpus that belong to different types (bucolics, urban mimes, and so on).

35. Apollonius does use the adjective for people, and he calls Amykos ὑπεροπληέστατος ἀνδρῶν, "most prodigious of men" (*Arg.* 2.4; cf. Hunter 1996, 62; on the epithet, see also Campbell 1974, 40–41, and Sens 1997, 29–30, 113). If Theocritus should be responding to Apollonius, his use of the adjective would signal that he is taking the Apollonian figure away from the shore into the bucolic world and making the issue not a simple challenge by an overweening ruler but the rights of hospitality.

in Theocritus, again in a bucolic context (*Id.* 16.38), of shepherds pasturing their flocks in the sunlight.[36] He seems at home in this bucolic space, and from this perspective the Dioskouroi are intruders who disrupt his peace. Of course, this is not to deny his monstrosity or to claim that he is in the right vis-à-vis Polydeukes. It is only to say that he, like Polyphemos, has his gentler moments. Book 9 of the *Odyssey* shows the same ambivalence, although Odysseus-as-narrator seems unaware of this. There is a sense in which Odysseus and his men intrude on the Golden Age conditions that the Cyclopes enjoy (*Od.* 9.107–111) and disturb the closeness between the herdsman and his animals, the innocence of this proto-bucolic setting. This is only a countermovement to the main thrust of the episode, but I would argue that the scene the Dioskouroi come upon also seems to have a certain wholeness and innocence, in the sense that it is untouched by human culture and its demands. Again a contrast with Apollonius may set this point in relief. In the *Argonautika*, it is Amykos who comes down to the shore and interferes with the Argonauts' setting sail with his challenge to a boxing match, which is unmotivated except by the fact that he challenges everyone who passes by.

What I am suggesting is that the line between epic and bucolic may not be as sharp as many writers seem to suggest, that in Theocritus's hands each form can be accommodated to the other. By reconfiguring epic elements, he may be putting them in a new context but not, from his point of view, perhaps, a wholly alien one. We may, if we like, want to find in this process a critique of epic or perhaps the creation of a new and rather ironic type of heroic poetry. But I think that Theocritus is commenting on bucolic as well. With the figure of Amykos, he is showing us, as he did in *Idylls* 11 and 6, that the bucolic world can contain the grotesque and make it at home. Understanding this gives us an added sense of the complexity and richness of his bucolic imagination.

This reconfiguration of epic, along with the different ways it can be read, is perfectly encapsulated by lines 105–106. Polydeukes delivers the first of two knockdown blows:

αὐτὰρ ὃ πληγεὶς
ὕπτιος ἐν φύλλοισι τεθηλόσιν ἐξετανύσθη.

But he [Amykos], when struck,
fell sprawling on his back among the luxuriant leaves.

---

36. There is in addition ἐνδίους at *Id.* 16.95, also of shepherds in sunlight.

The epithet "luxuriant" especially invites us to visualize this ugly and now battered colossus against the background of natural abundance in a brief reprise of the earlier description of the spring and his appearance. Once again, is the effect simple incongruity, or might we also, without denying the incongruity, see monstrosity and its overcoming by a hero drawn into the bucolic world and given a place in it? Would this effect not be heightened by the fact that Amykos falls among leaves, whereas in epic poetry defeated heroes fall in the dust,[37] or should this be understood only, or even principally, as a diminishing of epic and heroism?

In fact, one way to read the relation between the setting and the action of this part of the poem goes in the same direction. The episode ends with remarkable self-restraint on Polydeukes's part and an oath by Amykos that he would cease being a plague to strangers—that is, with a vindication of the Greek norm of hospitality and so of civility (*Id.* 22.131–134). Usually we would expect that a hero who conquers a monster would kill him, as the form of expression in line 131 suggests: "*although* he won, [Polydeukes] did nothing extreme to him." Polydeukes does kill Amykos in Apollonius, and if Theocritus were writing in response, the contrast would be calculated to make the result as he contrives it all the more striking. In any case, given the traditional heroic emphasis on competitive honor, this outcome is unexpected.[38] But it fits well into the bucolic nature of this place. At its best, the bucolic world is a welcoming place, one that promotes reciprocities such as those in *Idylls* 1 and 6 or those at the heart of hospitality. The real incongruity all along has been Amykos claiming this place solely for himself. Now its bounty is open to all who come in need of it.

With the sparing of Amykos and the introduction of the Greek institution of hospitality to a non-Greek place that lacked it, this episode might well stand as "an idealized version of Hellenization."[39] It seems to present an ideal resolution of the issue I pointed to earlier of the respective claims on a place by newcomers and the indigenous inhabitants—with, of course, Greeks dominant. Through the mechanism of hospitality, newcomers are to be welcomed and are to share in the local resources peaceably and without friction. This solution might bear on the question of the relations of the Greeks in Alexandria to Egypt in particular or the situation of Greek settlers in non-Greek lands anywhere else. The appropriation of territory through colonization or by other means and the

---

37. Laursen 1992, 86; Sens 1997, 149.

38. Odysseus, at a similar moment, considers killing Iros but then restrains himself—and breaks his jaw instead (*Od.* 18.90–99)! He holds back only to keep the suitors from recognizing him (line 94); his self-restraint is strategic (κέρδιον).

39. Sens 2021, 183.

hierarchical relations created in this way are presented in the guise of hospitality and reciprocity.[40] From this perspective, it seems fitting that this mystification of intercultural relations occurs in, and has as its object, an idealized, virtually enchanted, bucolic space.

Very different from the treatment of space in the Amykos episode is the almost total lack of any landscape or spatial description in the third section of the poem, which narrates the quarrel between the sons of Aphareus, Idas and Lynkeus, and the Dioskouroi over their prospective brides, the daughters of Leukippos, whom the Dioskouroi have abducted. The emphasis in the story as Theocritus has shaped it is on kinship and the family, whereas in Pindar's treatment of the same myth (*Nemean* 10), the quarrel is over cattle. In Pindar, the sons of Aphareus attack the Dioskouroi and kill Kastor. Polydeukes then pursues them to their father's tomb, they hit him with the stele, he stabs Lynkeus, and Zeus incinerates Idas. Polydeukes is thus taking revenge for his brother's death in reaction to an attack by the sons of Aphareus. In Theocritus, on the other hand, Lynkeus's speech (*Id.* 22.145–180) makes it clear that it is the Dioskouroi who are bent on violence rather than a peaceful settlement.

Idas and Lynkeus have been pursuing their rivals and catch up with them at the tomb of Aphareus, where Lynkeus and Kastor fight a duel, Lynkeus is killed, and Idas, who tears off the stone marker on top of his father's grave in order to throw it at Kastor, is struck by Zeus's thunderbolt. That tomb, with its stele, is the only landmark mentioned. It figures already as "an adornment of Hades" in Pindar (*N.* 10.65–68). Here it fits with the narrative's emphasis on the family; it represents intergenerational kinship, which supplements the horizontal kinship among the Dioskouroi, the Aphareidai, and the Leukippides: all three sibling pairs are cousins. Theocritus makes the tomb a physical emblem of the dubious morality of this episode, for Idas sits on it to watch the "battle within the family" (μάχην ἐμφύλιον) taking place between Kastor and Lynkeus (*Id.* 22.199–200). Other than the tomb, however, there are no spatial markers of any sort.[41] The contrast with the spatial detail of the Amykos episode is stark, and by comparison with the lushness of the spring there, silence about the setting creates the impression of a featureless landscape where the problematical destruction of Lynkeus and Idas is all too much at home. This spatial difference works together with all the other contrasts between these two sections of the poem. Both present

---

40. Here Theocritus seems to come close to Apollonius's representation of colonization, especially in connection with the site of Heraclea Pontica. See Thalmann 2011, 101–111.

41. For comments on the lack of setting of this section of the poem, see Gow 1942b, 15; Griffiths 1976, 362; Kurz 1991, 294; Laursen 1992, 87. Legrand 1898, 90–91, gives a good general discussion of the relation between the two mythic narratives in *Idyll* 22.

masculine competition that involves basic social institutions: in one, rights to a place and hospitality and in the other, a contest over women that fits into a larger mythic-heroic background of marriage contests.[42] Polydeukes clearly champions justice and the rights of strangers, whereas Kastor is, along with his brother, just as clearly in the wrong. Both sections involve duels as a means of trying to limit violence, successful in the first case, in vain in the second.[43] In the earlier episode, the moral and social issues are debated in a passage of stichomythia (*Id.* 22.54–74) that is surprising in a hexameter hymn or other narrative poem and that has affinities with tragic dialogue;[44] in this episode, they are laid out in a long speech by Lynkeus.[45] There is also a marked stylistic difference. Frederick Griffiths speaks of a reversal "between the gracefully variegated narrative of the Polydeuces episode and the oppressive Iliadic style of what follows."[46]

With the combination of heroic and bucolic themes in the Amykos episode, through the relation of opposition between it and the third section of the poem, and in the closing address to the twin gods (*Id.* 22.214–222),[47] Theocritus seems to be engaging in a complex experiment in writing heroic poetry through

---

42. Sens 1992 shows in detail how the duel between Paris and Menelaus in Book 3 of the *Iliad* is in the background of this narrative. That in turn is a realization of the more general pattern. See Thalmann 1998, 153–170, 193–206.

43. Sens 1997, 15, makes a related point: "whereas in the first narrative a boxing match between strangers ends without mortal violence, in the second φίλοι ['friends, relatives'] fight each other with the weapons of war, and with terrible results."

44. The stichomythia could also be another touch that creates affinities with Theocritus's bucolic poetry, in which several poems contain or consist of dialogue constructed as exchanges of speeches that have the same number of lines. See Thomas 1996, 233–236; Sens 1997, 40–41.

45. It will be obvious that I do not agree with Wilamowitz's postulate of a lacuna after line 170 and his assignment of lines 170–180 to Kastor. The question has been much discussed, but I find the arguments of Moulton 1973 and Griffiths 1976 especially persuasive. See also Sens 1997, 190–191.

46. Griffiths 1976, 362. On the contrast in styles, see also Gow 1952, II, 383; and Moulton 1973, 45–46, who argues that "Theocritus has deliberately accompanied his stylistic contrast between the two major sections of the poem with a moral contrast." Sens, on the other hand, offers a positive appreciation of the style of the Lynkeus episode and, although he leaves open the possibility that "the episode can be read with profit as a subversion of the heroic tradition," is skeptical of claims that both narratives are critiques of epic poetry (Sens 1997, 41–42, 19, 20–21, respectively). I would prefer to speak neutrally of the poem as a rewriting of the heroic or epic tradition. On the differences between the two narratives more generally, see also Kurz 1991, 243–244; Laursen 1992, 87–88; Sens 1997, 15. I would not follow Laursen in finding a gradual transition in the character of the Dioskouroi; I think that the contrasts are intended to be sharp and sudden.

47. On this final passage, see Sens 1992, especially 348–349; Sens 1997, 22–23.

an Alexandrian sensibility[48] by manipulating traditional forms. But this is not just a formal experiment. He is also trying out a new way of writing a hymn: by manipulating inherited stories and forms to explore both the beneficent and the destructive power of the gods.[49] His striking treatment of space in this poem is an essential medium for carrying out this project.

Idyll 24

Herakles makes recurring appearances in Theocritus's poetry, in keeping with his importance to the Ptolemies, who claimed him as an ancestor.[50] In *Idyll* 13 and the possibly Theocritean *Idyll* 25, he is a man and engaged in the exploits that established his heroic fame. In the Olympos scene near the beginning of *Idyll* 17, he is immortal, living among the gods, and married to Hebe, goddess of youth, as Teiresias prophesies in the poem to be discussed now, *Idyll* 24. There Herakles is a ten-month-old baby who performs the prodigious exploit of throttling two huge snakes sent by Hera to kill him, and the poem's first two parts are set not in the wider arena of heroic action but within the house of Alkmene and Amphitryon. This location is, of course, entailed by Herakles's infancy, and it naturally appears in Theocritus's two most important models for *Idyll* 24, Pindar's *Nemean* 1 and *Paean* 20. It has epic precedent in the second half of the *Odyssey*. But Theocritus seems to emphasize the unheroic and mundane in, for example, the ineffectualness of Amphitryon. Roused from sleep by his wife, he takes time to strap on his sword and rushes to where the babies are lying, shouting for the slaves to bring torches, only to find that Herakles has already strangled the snakes. Thereupon he wraps Herakles back up in his blanket while Alkmene comforts the terrified Iphikles and goes back to bed like any sleep-deprived parent. Is the poem therefore a comedy set against epic models? Does it exploit the tension between the outlooks of epic and lyric in order finally to undercut the heroic tradition?[51] Does

---

48. Another dimension of that sensibility is the importance of the Dioskouroi to the Ptolemies' self-presentation, on which, especially as it is reflected in Alexandrian poetry, see Acosta-Hughes 2012b. For how the Lynkeus episode might have fit into that program, see the quotation from Clayman in the next note.

49. See Hunter 1996, 72–73. Clayman 2021, 570, has recently pointed out the political implications of the diverging portrayals of the divine brothers: "The contrast suggests the double nature of Ptolemy, both a human who is expected to behave as a gallant aristocrat and an immortal being with absolute power and no need for scruples."

50. For a helpful discussion of Herakles's various portrayals in Theocritus, see Acosta-Hughes 2012a.

51. Gutzwiller 1981, 10–18.

it instead, or in addition, recast the heroic and mythic traditions in order to make them accessible to the Hellenistic age, giving the old heroes "room to breathe"?[52] Does it, in its main narrative and in many details, juxtapose the mortality and immortality that are Herakles's fate, showing the prevalence of the latter over the former?[53]

Of course, there is deft humor in the poem, but it is mixed with the serious theme of death and immortality that is central to earlier epic and tragedy, in keeping with the heroic and comic potential in Herakles's nature and story, and so a focus on comedy and trivialization is not very helpful. As for the matter of genre, *Idyll* 24 mixes in an interesting solution a large number of literary models even for Theocritus, only some of which I will discuss here, but I am skeptical that the point is entirely the overcoming of epic in a Callimachean rejection of large-scale poetry. I prefer to understand the poem as a renewal of the tradition and its literary forms to suit the interests and sensibilities of a new age. In this spirit, I would like to draw attention to the poem's central spatial feature, which is often overlooked in this poem, perhaps because it is so obviously there: the house.

It is not easy to visualize this house, because Theocritus gives only piecemeal and cryptic references to parts of it as they suit the narrative. On the basis of what clues we have, perhaps we should imagine the parents asleep in one room while the infants sleep in another.[54] While Herakles is strangling the serpents, an unearthly light fills the house, but when Amphitryon is ready to go investigate its source, it suddenly disappears, and the "spacious παστάς [*pastas*]" is plunged again into darkness (*Id.* 24.46). The *pastas* could be the parents' bedchamber,[55] but the word could equally well refer to a colonnade connecting the doors of various rooms and fronting on an inner courtyard—a known arrangement in Hellenistic houses.[56] This meaning suits the context better, since the point should be that darkness fills the whole house, not just a single room. This prepares for the

---

52. Griffiths 1979, 98. Acosta-Hughes 2012a, 255, tends in a similar direction: "Theocritus' Heracles is recognizably the Archaic hero, but seen from a perspective that is not Archaic, and this results in an object of attention at once familiar and novel."

53. Stern 1974.

54. This rather than the infants in an alcove in the parents' bedroom; see Gow 1942a, 109.

55. Gow 1942a, 109; 1952, II, 423.

56. Nevett 1999, 22–25, and discussions of houses found at various sites, particularly Olynthos. That modern archaeologists refer to this type as a *pastas* house, of course, says nothing about the ancient usage of the word. The epithet "spacious" (ἀμφιλαφής) could suit the bedchamber as a reminder that we are reading about a house of heroic proportions, but in its literal meaning, "spreading on both sides," it seems especially apt for a portico viewed from the courtyard; Herodotus (4.172) and Plato (*Phdr.* 232b) use it to describe the spreading canopies of trees.

hubbub that follows. Amphitryon shouts to his snoring slaves to bring torches and unbar the doors, and his order is seconded by a slave woman who has been sleeping at her mill, perhaps in the inner courtyard (she recalls the slave in *Od.* 20.98–121, just as the light evokes Athena lighting the way for Odysseus and Telemakhos at *Od.* 19.33–40). The slaves obey, and the whole house is filled with people rushing here and there (*Id.* 24.47–53). In the next line, all are in the children's room, shouting in amazement at the sight of the nursling Herakles holding the two serpents in his soft fists (*Id.* 24.54–56), but it is easy to infer that the slaves have unbarred the door to the room[57] and have crowded inside with Amphitryon and Alkmene holding torches to light up the scene.

This is a possible reconstruction that might help us visualize the scene, but it is far from certain. Gow attributes the lack of explicit description to Theocritus's failure to imagine clearly the circumstances of his own narrative,[58] but I would suggest instead that the layout of the physical house matters far less than its significance to the narrative. The idea of the house helps create an emphasis on boundaries and enclosure that underlies whatever meanings we give the story as a whole.[59]

The infants are inside a room within a house. Inside that room, they lie in another enclosure, a bronze shield, and they are wrapped in swaddling blankets. Within all these nesting enclosures, they seem protected and secure. The shield is a highly significant object. It is a war trophy; Amphitryon took it in battle from the corpse of his enemy Pterelaos. As many have noted, it is a subtle reminder of Herakles's and Iphikles's conception by two different fathers, Zeus and Amphitryon, on the night of the latter's return from the war; and as a destructive weapon, a καλὸν ὅπλον (*Id.* 24.5), put to new, peaceful use, it represents the domestication of martial, heroic violence and of Amphitryon himself, who is now in the role of a peacetime father. This is domestication in the literal sense of "placed within the house." In the *Odyssey*, weapons are locked in a storeroom or hung on the walls of the hall or *megaron*, inert but kept ready for violent use;

---

57. I think that the door referred to in Amphitryon's command (*Id.* 24.49) is that of the children's room rather than the one leading to the slaves' quarters (possible) or the door of Amphitryon's room (a fainter possibility) or the outer door of the house (surely inappropriate here). See Gow 1942a, 109–110. The plural could be a poetic usage or a reference, as often elsewhere, to the two leaves of a single door.

58. Gow 1942a, 109.

59. Difficult though it is to reconstruct the house as a whole, we are given an idea of its various parts. In Pindar's account (*Nemean* 1), by contrast, the action is confined to a single room, the one in which Alkmene has just given birth to the twins. See Foster 2016, 168–169. The difference shows the greater thematic importance that Theocritus gives the house.

a shield is not repurposed as a cradle. The Homeric phrase used to describe the shield when Alkmene rocks the babies in it, σάκος μέγα ("the great shield," *Id.* 24.10), seems incongruous,[60] but it also stresses the weapon's diversion to nurture rather than destruction.

Alkmene's prayer for the children as she is rocking the shield, with its repeated εὕδετε ... εὕδετε at the beginning of successive lines (*Id.* 24.7–8), recalls Danae's words to the infant Perseus in Simonides's "Danae Fragment" (*PMG* 543) as they are tossed at sea inside a "well-wrought chest" (λάρνακι ... δαιδαλέᾳ), of which the shield is the counterpart. The echo is well known but is usually discussed in connection with Theocritus's reworking of earlier Greek poetry.[61] But the allusion adds significantly to the scene, because it imports into it the wider context of Danae's prayer. She and her baby are in great danger; the wind is blowing, and the sea is rough. These are her words to him before her prayer (lines 8–20):

> σὺ δ' ἀωτεῖς, γαλαθηνῷ
> δ' ἤθεϊ κνοώσσεις
> ἐν ἀτερπέι δούρατι χαλκεογόμφῳ
> ⟨τῷ⟩δε νυκτιλαμπεῖ
> κυανέῳ δνόφῳ ταθείς.
> ἅλμαν δ' ὕπερθε τεᾶν κομᾶν
> βαθεῖαν παριόντος
> κύματος οὐκ ἀλέγεις, οὐδ' ἀνέμου
> φθόγγον, πορφυρέᾳ
> κείμενος ἐν χλανίδι, πρόσωπον καλόν.
> εἰ δέ τοι δεινὸν τό γε δεινὸν ἦν,
> καί κεν ἐμῶν ῥημάτων
> λεπτὸν ὑπεῖχες οὔας.

> But you sleep, and in a nursling's
> way you slumber
> in this joyless vessel with brazen bolts
> night-shining [?]
> stretched out in the murky dark.
> You have no care for the deep salt water above your head
> as the wave passes by, nor of the wind's
> howling, lying in your purple

---

60. Gutzwiller 1981, 11.

61. Hunter's discussion (1996, 26–27) is especially suggestive.

> robe, lovely face.
> If what is frightful were frightful to you,
> you would lend your tender ear to my words.

Sea and wind outside all around them, but inside the chest a precarious but protecting shelter, in which Perseus can sleep with a baby's obliviousness to the danger surrounding him. In the same way, Herakles and Iphikles sleep in the shield within the protection of the house, unaware of the danger threatened by Hera's machinations.

But unlike Perseus's chest, the house proves inadequate against this divine malice. Sent by "much-contriving" Hera (πολυμήχανος, like Odysseus), two enormous snakes, "bristling with dark coils," reach the broad threshold between the posts of the house's outer door (*Id.* 24.13–16).[62] The narrative emphasizes this threshold and doorway, the boundary between outside and inside, and therefore the moment when the serpents pass it. Pindar's account, by contrast, hurries by the passage through a doorway with a genitive absolute, οἰχθεισᾶν πυλᾶν ("when the door had been opened, *Nem.* 1.41), and the door in question seems to be that of the chamber in which Alkmene has just given birth to the twins (no sooner are the doors opened than the snakes go into the innermost part of the room). Theocritus dwells on the description of the serpents slithering through the house, uncoiling their "blood-devouring" bellies and spitting out venom, their eyes flashing fire, until they reach the children (*Id.* 24.17–20).

Unlike Perseus, Herakles is far from helpless but mighty, even as an infant. His strangling of the serpents restores the integrity of the house's boundary. That the reassertion of boundaries is at issue here is suggested when Teiresias tells Alkmene the next day to burn the snakes on spits and to order a slave woman to collect the ashes and throw them across the river, beyond the territory's boundary (ὑπερούριον, *Id.* 24.95). As Jacob Stern has argued, this ritual casting out reinforces another distinction that runs parallel to the spatial drawing of boundaries, between mortal and immortal. That the serpents are to be burned at midnight, the same hour at which they would have killed Herakles, suggests that they are a substitute for him. The fire that flashed from their eyes becomes the fire that reduces them to ash and annihilates them. That fire contrasts with the fire of Herakles's funeral pyre, which will, years later, burn away his mortal parts and release him

---

62. The door is identified as such by the genitive οἴκου, "of the house." See Gow 1942a, 109. The force of the adjective in the phrase "the hollow posts of the door" is unclear. It may suggest an aperture beside the posts or, on the analogy of κοιλόσταθμος, latticework or paneling in the leaves of the door themselves (Gow 1942a, 108)—some opening that the snakes can squeeze through, at any rate.

immortal to Olympos, where he will become son-in-law to "the immortals who set on these monsters that live in a lair to destroy the child" (*Id.* 24.79–85).[63] The underground nest that is their home contrasts with the house, where their presence is polluting. The house itself enters into the pattern of association created by fire. After the snakes' ashes are ejected, it is to be purified with sulfur; the word for "fumigate" has at its base the word for "fire": πυρώσατε (*Id.* 24.96). As fire will burn off the impurity of mortality from Herakles, so the house will be cleansed of the impurity introduced by the serpents' invasion, its wholeness restored.[64]

The house is a feminine space, and this explains why Amphitryon, who has performed heroic deeds outside it and indeed beyond the boundaries of his territory, plays such a peripheral role in the action and why Alkmene is the dominant figure.[65] Not only does she give orders to Amphitryon and he obeys her (*Id.* 24.41: ἀλόχῳ ... πιθήσας), not only does she send for Teiresias, who prophesies to her in private, whereas in Pindar, Amphitryon sends for him and he speaks publicly (*Nem.* 1.60–61: παντὶ στρατῷ, "to the whole host") in a masculine setting, and not only does she arrange for Herakles's education when he reaches boyhood (*Id.* 24.134: φίλα παιδεύσατο μάτηρ, "his dear mother had him taught"). What is less often remarked on is that Teiresias's prophecy depicts Herakles's future glory from a markedly female perspective. Pindar's Teiresias goes into some detail about Herakles's future exploits, and his speech culminates in the apotheosis as recompense for those labors (*Nem.* 1.62–72). In Theocritus, Teiresias gives only a quick summary of the labors as demonstration of Herakles's superiority to all other men and beasts (*Id.* 24.81–83), and that is enfolded in the prophecy of the hero's immortalization, which gets the main emphasis in the account of Herakles's fate. But the apotheosis in turn is introduced as the reason for *Alkmene's* future glory and subordinated to it (*Id.* 24.75-80):

ναὶ γὰρ ἐμῶν γλυκὺ φέγγος ἀποιχόμενον πάλαι ὄσσων,
πολλαὶ Ἀχαιιάδων μαλακὸν περὶ γούνατα νῆμα
χειρὶ κατατρίψουσιν ἀκρέσπερον ἀείδοισαι

---

63. Stern 1974, 355–357; cf. Stephens 2003, 137–138, for Egyptian parallels, although the ritual can be explained in Greek terms as well.

64. There is an important parallel here with Odysseus's purification of his house with fire and sulfur after removal of the corpses of the suitors (*Od.* 22.481–482, 493–494). This act is "a remedy of evils" (κακῶν ἄκος), a cleansing of the impurity in the house caused by the killing, and an important step in the restoration of his house's integrity after he has gotten rid of the intruders.

65. On Alkmene in the story of the infant Herakles and her neglect by modern scholars, see Davidson 2000. On her central role see more recently Kyriakou 2018, 204–217, especially 215–216.

Ἀλκμήναν ὀνομαστί, σέβας δ' ἔσῃ Ἀργείαισι.
τοῖος ἀνὴρ ὅδε μέλλει ἐς οὐρανὸν ἄστρα φέροντα
ἀμβαίνειν τεὸς υἱός ...

> Yes, by the sweet light of my eyes lost long ago,
> Many Akhaian women, while they rub with the hand the wool
> on their knees to soften it, will sing toward dusk
> of Alkmene by name, and you will be revered by Argive women.
> Such a man will he be, and he will ascend to the starry heaven—
> your son.

Publicly performed epic and epinician poetry may celebrate men's achievements, but within the community of women, Alkmene's name will be kept alive in songs that accompany their work within the house. Of course, she will be celebrated for doing what women in Greece's patriarchal culture were supposed to do: produce mighty sons for aristocratic families or for gods, as in the catalogue of heroines seen by Odysseus in his visit to the dead.[66] But the emphasis here is on the contribution of Herakles's achievements to Alkmene's lasting fame. From the women's point of view, his glory is hers.

Thus, spatiality (the house as a feminine, protecting place) and gender (Alkmene's active role and future glory) are mutually implicated and reinforce each other. This intertwining is an essential part of the artistry of *Idyll* 24 and is not merely to be expected. Pindar, after all, had no difficulty giving Amphitryon control of the action after the killing of the snakes, even though that took place in Alkmene's bedchamber right after she gave birth. Theocritus's emphasis on the maternal also seems related to, though it is probably not completely explained by, the ambiguity regarding Herakles's father. He hints delicately at this when, relatively late in the poem, he describes Herakles as "called the son of Argive Amphitryon" (*Id.* 24.103–104)—his son in name only or known as his son because he was? Earlier, we are told that when the serpents entered their room, the children woke up "because [?] Zeus knew all" (*Id.* 24.21: Διὸς νοέοντος ἅπαντα). This genitive absolute strangely interrupts a straightforward statement of fact and so stands out. What is Zeus up to? Is he contriving that this baby, who is destined to be Greece's greatest hero, begin his career with a display of infantile might so prophetic of what is to come? Is he protecting his son from his stepmother's spite? Or both? Circumspection doubtless was necessary; questions

---

66. *Od.* 11.225–330. When Kleobis and Biton failed to awake the morning after their exploit, the Argive men gathered around and called them blessed (ἐμακάριζον) because of their strength, while the Argive women called their mother blessed for bearing such sons (Hdt. 1.31.3).

surrounding Philadelphus's legitimacy as Soter's heir may have made legitimacy a delicate subject.[67] These hints about Zeus's paternity—to which the shield (discussed earlier) should be added—would have been caught by any reader, but a more active role for Amphitryon would have thrown this question into relief.

I doubt that these considerations dictated Alkmene's prominence, but they work with it and with the setting inside the house. Theocritus seems to have developed the importance of the woman's perspective through the use of several mythic prototypes. The allusion to Danae and Perseus through Simonides is effective for several reasons in addition to the spatial point made earlier. Like Herakles, Perseus was also the son of Zeus, who gained access to both mothers by a shapeshifting ruse: he took on the likeness of Amphitryon in the one case and visited the imprisoned Danae as a shower of gold. Alkmene is, in addition, Perseus's granddaughter through her father, Elektryon, a fact made explicit when Teiresias addresses her as Περσήιον αἷμα ("blood of Perseus," *Id.* 24.73; cf. *Id.* 25.173). So the emphasis in *Idyll* 24, once again, is not on Zeus's paternity but on the matriline. Like his great-grandson Herakles, Perseus was a monster slayer (Medusa and the sea monster from which he rescued Andromeda). According to Apollonius, the poisonous snakes in the desert of Libya, which was next door to Alexandria and important to the Ptolemies, sprang from the blood dripping from Medusa's severed head as Perseus flew above.[68] But there are two important contrasts between the stories of these two heroes. Both died, but Herakles's immortal part survives on Olympos. An even more significant difference is that Perseus and Danae were set adrift in the chest by her father, Akrisios, in an attempt—ultimately vain—to avoid fulfillment of an oracle that warned of Akrisios's death at the hands of any son his daughter should beget. The prophecy about Herakles will also be fulfilled, but it involves not murder but immortality. Confined in an enclosure analogous to the chest, he performs an exploit from which Teiresias can read his entire future career. The strangling of the serpents is not just a display of Herakles's prodigious strength, but it embodies and condenses a future that, beginning with the systematic education his mother arranges for him, will unfold as a series of re-enactments of what is already enacted here.[69]

---

67. Gow 1942a, 107. This would have been especially true if, as some have thought, *Idyll* 24 was composed in honor of the Basileia of 285 BCE celebrating Philadelphus's co-regency with Soter, though delicacy would have been prudent at any time. There may have been other reasons as well to leave Herakles's paternity ambiguous; see Griffiths 1979, 96–97.

68. *Arg.* 4.1513–1517. Cf. Stephens 2003, 133, who shows that "Perseus . . . provides the Ptolemies with a Greco-Egyptian pedigree."

69. Cf. Cusset 1999, who interprets the killing of the snakes as a victory over death that will be repeated years later on the funeral pyre.

The light that fills the house in *Idyll* 24 evokes the light that shines throughout Keleos's house in the *Homeric Hymn to Demeter* when the goddess angrily reveals herself after her attempt to make Demophon immortal by putting him in the fire has been foiled by that child's mother, Metaneira (*h. Dem.* 275–280). The allusion reinforces *Idyll* 24's focus on the house along with maternity and childrearing. Demophon's mortality provides an obvious foil to Herakles's overcoming of death.

The line of *Idyll* 24 that reminds us of Herakles's descent from Danae and Perseus also refers to another mother–son pair, Thetis and Akhilleus (*Id.* 24.73, prominent by its position at the beginning of Teiresias's speech):

θάρσει, ἀριστοτόκεια γύναι, Περσήιον αἷμα

Take heart, woman who has borne the best son, blood of Perseus

The compound adjective that Teiresias uses to describe Alkmene, *aristotokeia*, "who has borne the best son," surely recalls one of the most moving passages in the *Iliad*, Thetis's lament for Akhilleus, who she knows will soon die (*Il.* 18.54–60):

ὤ μοι ἐγὼ δειλή, ὤ μοι δυσαριστοτόκεια,
ἥ τ' ἐπεὶ ἄρ τέκον υἱὸν ἀμύμονά τε κρατερόν τε,
ἔξοχον ἡρώων· ὁ δ' ἀνέδραμεν ἔρνεϊ ἶσος·
τὸν μὲν ἐγὼ θρέψασα, φυτὸν ὣς γουνῷ ἀλωῆς,
νηυσὶν ἐπιπροέηκα κορωνίσιν Ἴλιον εἴσω
Τρωσὶ μαχησόμενον· τὸν δ' οὐχ ὑποδέξομαι αὖτις
οἴκαδε νοστήσαντα δόμον Πηλήιον εἴσω.

Oh, my misery, bearer of the best son to my sorrow,
seeing that I bore a son blameless and mighty,
outstanding of all heroes. And he shot up like a young sapling.
I nurtured him, like a seedling in the rise of an orchard,
and then I sent him forth in the curving ships to Ilion
to fight the Trojans. I will not receive him back again,
returning home into the house of Peleus.

Thetis's long, unforgettable compound adjective, *dysaristotokeia*, which strikingly fills the entire metrical space between the fourth-foot caesura and the end of line 54, and which I have needed eight words to translate into English, is answered by Teiresias's *aristotokeia* to describe Alkmene—the same word without the ominous prefix *dys-* ("badly," "unluckily," or, as I have translated it, "to my sorrow").

Thetis fulfilled her maternal function by Greek standards, even though, in the myths about her, she married Peleus unwillingly. She produced a glorious son who achieved lasting fame because of the complex mixture in his story of outstanding success and outstanding failure. And—to step away from the *Iliad* momentarily—according to a later story told by Apollonius (*Arg.* 4.866–879) and closely resembling that of Demeter and Demophon, Thetis attempted to make the infant Akhilleus immortal by putting him in fire at night until she was interrupted by her husband. She would be remembered as the goddess who had to sorrow impotently at the death of that son. Alkmene will be celebrated as the mother of the hero who, by his labors, transcended mortality. As though to make these contrasts more emphatic, Theocritus again alludes to Thetis's words in lines that introduce the account of Herakles's education (*Id.* 24.103–104):

Ἡρακλέης δ' ὑπὸ ματρὶ νέον φυτὸν ὣς ἐν ἀλωᾷ
ἐτρέφετ', Ἀργείου κεκλημένος Ἀμφιτρύωνος.

Herakles was nurtured like a young sapling in an orchard
by his mother, in name the son of Argive Amphitryon.

In this allusion, the pathos of the flourishing child Thetis is about to lose, who "shot up like a young sapling," is replaced by the promise of the boy setting out on the path that will lead to Olympos.[70]

Thus, Theocritus uses references to three mothers and their sons—infants in the first two cases, in the third a warrior facing death whose begetting and childhood are recalled—to set off the splendid fates in store for Alkmene and Herakles. This concentration on the maternal and childrearing is of a piece with the house as the location of the action in *Idyll* 24, and vice versa. It acts as a reminder of something latent in earlier poetry and myth, as the three examples that the poem uses show, but not emphasized there: that however much the half-divine heroes accomplished, often seeking to equal or surpass their fathers, and however much they might thus serve as models of heroic masculinity, they began life in a nurturing bond with their mothers. The emphasis on motherhood may reflect the newly influential role of women in Ptolemaic Alexandrian culture that is also evident in the importance given to Berenike and Arsinoe in *Idylls* 15 and 17. If so, it finds a

---

70. Kyriakou 2018, 213–214; 2021, 642, 643, notes both allusions to Thetis but reads them differently. On the first, she comments that it "raises the specter of maternal loss and suffering." I think the main effect is to draw a contrast between the two heroes (and their mothers), but there could at the same time be an ominous undertone: with his struggles and terrible death, was Herakles's heroic career completely different from that of Akhilleus?

place among the many other features of *Idyll* 24 that have a bearing on the first two Ptolemies.[71]

Encomiastic Space
Idyll 16

Considered as an encomium, *Idyll* 16 is a peculiar poem. The many references to Homer, Pindar, and Simonides put it in some relation to the tradition of praise poetry. But the actual praise sets in only in the second major section of the poem (*Id.* 16.66–100), and its recipient, Hieron II of Syracuse, is only named twice. In the first main section (*Id.* 16.5–65), Theocritus deplores the present state of poetry: no one is willing to pay for it or, presumably, read it anymore. The actual praise of Hieron also takes an unusual form. He turns out to be the man prophesied (future indicative tense, *Id.* 16.73) as one who will need Theocritus as a singer by virtue of matching the accomplishments of Akhilleus and Aias at Troy. For already now (present indicative) the Carthaginians are trembling, already Hieron is arming himself in might. Then, beginning at line 82, all the verbs change to optatives of "wish": a prayer to Zeus that Hieron defeat the Carthaginians decisively and restore Sicily to fertility, peace, and prosperity.

So Theocritus has seemed to many to project the persona of a poet in search of a patron, possibly at the start of his career, praising a Syracusan ruler for a military victory, as Pindar and Bacchylides had praised Hieron I, from whom they had actual commissions. From this perspective, it would appear that Theocritus has had to find a way to praise a possible patron newly or recently come to power who has not actually done anything and who can only be celebrated for what he

---

71. The Ptolemies claimed Herakles and therefore Zeus, Perseus, Danae, and Alkmene as ancestors. Theocritus makes Herakles ten months old when he kills the snakes, whereas in Pindar he is a newborn baby; this, together with the astronomical indication in *Id.* 24.11–12, aligns his birthdate with that of Philadelphus (Gow 1942a, 107; 1952, II, 418). (For an important adjustment of the chronology, see Stephens 2003, 125–126.) Soter was reputed to have been exposed in a bronze shield as an infant and protected by an eagle (see especially Stephens 2003, 129–130). Herakles's education as outlined in the poem has been thought by many to resemble that of a Hellenistic prince, since it begins with him learning "letters" (γράμματα, *Id.* 24.105)—an un-Heraklean skill. Herakles's divinization might be thought linked to that of Soter, who appears with Alexander as one of Herakles's Olympian drinking companions in *Idyll* 17 (16–33), and his marriage to Hebe, his half-sibling, would naturally seem to reflect that of Philadelphus to his sister Arsinoe. These last two parallels must be treated with caution, however. They will not work if *Idyll* 24 dates from as early as the Basileia of 285 BCE (see note 67 above). Soter was, of course, still alive, and the marriage to Arsinoe was in the future. Still, these possibilities are worth keeping in mind, since the connection with the festival cannot be proven. If the early dating is correct, Theocritus was as prescient about his hero as Teiresias was about his.

might do. It is not even clear that Hieron was undertaking a campaign against the Carthaginians in Sicily.[72] Griffiths well describes the artfulness with which Theocritus negotiates this extraordinary task, with, he argues, inevitable inconcinnities between parts of the poem and an unusual mixture of genres as a result.[73] Perhaps, others suggest, we should not see this poem as actually an encomium at all. "It is [Theocritus's] way in this poem," writes Gutzwiller, "to give us an encomiastic mode but not encomium."[74]

Norman Austin sees the poem, and the prominence given within it to Simonides, as a response to the position of poetry in the early Hellenistic period.[75] José González also downplays the notion of an encomiastic program and extends Austin's view. The poem, he argues, is a plea for the restoration of the poet to his traditional function within the polis: to articulate and reinforce essential ethical, religious, and civic values.[76] A reading that might at first seem opposed to this view has recently been offered by Dee Clayman, who argues that *Idyll* 16 is satiric in the manner of traditional iambic poetry.[77] This perspective is not in principle incompatible with González's reading, however, although she suggests that it is. A poet concerned with problems in society and the displacement of poetry from a central protreptic role might well adopt a satiric stance. And in fact, the best evidence for Clayman's view is in the poem's first, critical section, where Hipponax and the Callimachus of the *Iambs* seem to be significant presences. Finally, Poulheria Kyriakou has offered a reading to which encomium and patronage are central. *Idyll* 16, she suggests, "sketches, among other things, a spiritual journey of

---

72. Hans 1985, who says, plausibly, that the poem may instead reflect anti-Carthaginian propaganda that Hieron had used to gain power. In fact, Hieron fought not the Carthaginians but the Mamertines and broke their hold on eastern Sicily (Bell 2011, 193–197).

73. Griffiths 1979, 9–50.

74. Gutzwiller 1983, 218. Her own interpretation, that the poem "is Theocritus' response to his own disinclination to write praise poetry" because of his "distaste for the grand" (213–214), risks taking a tendency in Hellenistic poetry and making it the interpretive key for this poem. It also begs the question of why he should have written it at all.

75. Austin 1967. Cf. Kyriakou 2004.

76. González 2010. Like Griffiths 1979, 30, he sees the poem as "promoting a restitution of poetry to its old role in society," but unlike Griffiths, he would presumably deny that Theocritus was simply ignoring all the changes that had taken place between the archaic period and his own time (Gutzwiller 1983, 24, also denies this, for different reasons). González depicts the first part of the poem as describing the unfortunate conditions that had resulted from such changes, the second half as showing how these ills might be cured. In his treatment, then, *Idyll* 16 is in some sense a politically engaged poem and more protreptic than encomium.

77. Clayman 2021, 573–580. I would not follow her in concluding from the satiric elements that the poem is an "anti-encomium."

the narrator in his quest for rewards," a movement on the part of the "narrator," in the course of the poem, from eagerness to praise anyone willing to pay for a poem to a project of needing "to praise men of means against a background of heroic and encomiastic poetry."[78] We might then see the poem not as straightforward encomium but as reflection on the function and purpose of encomium in the conditions of the early Hellenistic period. But this issue seems part of the larger question of the social and cultural position of the poet as set forth by González.[79]

I would like here to explore the spatial dimensions of the poem's program essentially as González describes it. At the same time, I take the encomiastic aspect of *Idyll* 16 more seriously than he seems to, even though it takes a peculiar form and even though in hindsight Hieron did not do much to fix what Theocritus implies is wrong with society. That is why I have included the poem in this section. On the other hand, I do not consider the poem a pitch for Hieron's patronage in particular. Encomium and patronage can be intertwined, as they are in this poem, but again they are part of the issue of poetry's purpose. The prospect of praising Hieron serves as an example that brings larger questions into focus.

One of several advantages of González's reading is that the apparent incoherence between the poem's two major sections disappears. They are complementary. The first uses the poet's plight to depict current social and political conditions, the dysfunction resulting from individual greed and self-interest on the part of the elite. The second offers a utopian vision of peace and harmony resulting from restored unity, which would be implicitly signaled by the poet's integration into society as celebrator of civic values through praise of Hieron. There are still differences between these sections on which the poem pivots, as Griffiths shows. Images of enclosure give way to global images, descent (for example, to the Underworld) gives way to return, money yields to herds as the pertinent measure of wealth, and time is replaced by space.[80] In regard to this last contrast, I would say instead that space-time is configured differently in the two parts. But all of these contrasting pairs—including the different measures of wealth, as we shall see—are represented spatially in the course of the poem.

In the first place, the poem is full of movement of various kinds;[81] I will center my discussion on movement (or its lack) involving houses. The first example, which is essential to the poem as a whole (*Id.* 16.6–12), is the return of the poet's

---

78. Kyriakou 2018, 278–279.

79. Kyriakou seems to come very close to this viewpoint in her concluding remarks about *Idyll* 16 (2018, 297–299).

80. Griffiths 1979, 33–35.

81. On the idea of the traveling poet in *Idyll* 16, see Hunter 1996, 92–94.

"Graces"—his poems as well as their divine patronesses—homeward (οἴκαδε) because the master of another house (οἶκος) has not spread wide its doors (πετάσας) to welcome them in but (by implication) has shut them out. The "Graces," now in the form of papyrus rolls, "sit in the bottom of the empty chest" with their heads on their knees—a posture of mourning as well as a sign of how cramped and oppressive this enclosing space is, unlike the protective enclosure of the shield in *Idyll* 24.[82] "There they always have their seat, whenever they come home unsuccessful." The frustrated journey of the "Graces" sets up a spatial relation: to the would-be patron's closed house correspond the poet's house and the chest within it. These images of enclosure and the frustration of movement that results in stasis encapsulate—in some sense are—the problem. The counterpart to the "Graces" shut within the chest is the money within the wealthy house (*Id.* 16.22–23). Neither circulates. And that means neither is used for good—or any—purposes. The poems are not read and do not spread their subjects' fame, and the money is not used for its owner's benefit or that of his kin, of others, of the gods (through sacrifices), or of guests—in a word, for the benefit of society. When the poet says that it should also be used to pay poets, he is not just being mercenary. Poetry, if it circulates, can promote social cohesion by celebrating "good men" (ἀγαθῶν ... ἀνδρῶν, *Id.* 16.2) and in this way reinforcing civic values held in common (and also hierarchical structures, since the phrase can also mean "aristocrats"). The closed house, by contrast, is an emblem of the isolated individual and thus of the fragmentation of the city.

The positive model is the house open to guests (*Id.* 16.27–28):

μηδὲ ξεινοδόκον κακὸν ἔμμεναι ἀλλὰ τραπέζῃ
μειλίξαντ' ἀποπέμψαι ἐπὴν ἐθέλωντι νέεσθαι.

And do not be a bad receiver of guests, but at the table
gratify them and send them on their way whenever they wish to leave.

That is, do not send visitors away by closing your doors before they have even been admitted, but give them hospitality and let them choose when to leave. Because of the contrast with the scene of the "Graces" turned back from the door, hospitality to guests, in addition to being an appropriate way to spend money, is parallel to the reception of poetry, which thus is assimilated to this important social ritual and has, or should have, the same crucial function of knitting people and households together. This analogy has precedent in earlier praise poetry.

---

82. Gow 1952, II, 309.

Consider, for example, the opening of Pindar's *Seventh Olympian* (1–4, 7–9; I am citing this passage as a parallel, not claiming for it direct influence on Theocritus):

> Φιάλαν ὡς εἴ τις ἀφνειᾶς ἀπὸ χειρὸς ἑλών
> ἔνδον ἀμπέλου καχλάζοισαν δρόσῳ
> δωρήσεται
> νεανίᾳ γαμβρῷ προπίνων
> οἴκοθεν οἴκαδε,
>
> ******************
>
> καὶ ἐγὼ νέκταρ χυτόν, Μοισᾶν δόσιν, ἀεθλοφόροις
> ἀνδράσιν πέμπων, γλυκὺν καρπὸν φρενός,
> ἱλάσκομαι ...

> Even as a man who takes a golden bowl,
> his best possession,
> brimming with the froth of wine inside it,
> and gives it
> with lavish hand to his new son-in-law,
> toasting him from home to home,
>
> **************
>
> So I, sending a stream of nectar,
> the gift of the Muses, the sweet yield of my mind,
> offer libation ...
>
> (translation by Nisetich 1980)

Here the institution that unites households and underpins society is marriage rather than hospitality, but the two are closely related. Pindar makes a very precise analogy between the wine that seals the marriage and the poem that he sends to its recipient, Diagoras of Rhodes. Both are media of exchange intended to create social relationships that are based on reciprocity, as hospitality is, too. The common noun that underlies Theocritus's "Graces," χάρις, in fact, implies reciprocity,[83] which is occluded by the closed door that sends the "Graces" home. That reciprocity is expressed materially and spatially in the Pindar passage by οἴκοθεν οἴκαδε, "from home to home." Pindar's poems travel and are intended to create a reciprocal relationship between poet and honorand, just as in *Idyll* 16 the poet

---

83. Gutzwiller 1983, 221; González 2010, 85–90, who discusses the rejection of the "Graces" as "the breakdown of the political order" (88).

hopes to create one with Hieron (poetry for money).[84] That is to say, praise and the poetry that encapsulates it have an important spatial dimension.

Thus, the opening vignette of the "Graces" repulsed at a rich man's door and crouching doubled over in the chest within the poet's house generates issues developed over the course of *Idyll* 16. And we are not done with it yet. For there is a striking contrast between their situation as papyrus rolls out of circulation fixed at a single point of space at the bottom (ἐν πυθμένι) of the chest and the poet's later prayer, "may singers carry Hieron's fame [κλέος] on high [ὑψηλόν], both across the Skythian sea and where Semiramis, who fitted the wide wall together with asphalt, reigned" (*Id.* 16.98–100). As Gow comments, Skythia and Babylon mark the northern and southern extremities of the eastern edge of the Greek world as conventionally understood, and Sicily is near the western limit.[85] So the phrase means "throughout the world." Spatially, then, the two passages set up a contrast between high and low, vertical descent and horizontal movement across the earth's surface, breadth and depth, fixity and mobility. It is tempting also to suggest that there is a contrast between written and oral,[86] between the poems stored on papyrus rolls and their wide dissemination in sung performance throughout the world, although that depends on how far one wants to press the implications of ἀοιδοί ("singers") in line 98. The phrase "carry Hieron's fame on high" may be a reminiscence of *Od.* 9.20 and 107: καὶ/ἣ γὰρ μευ/σευ κλέος οὐρανὸν ἵκει/ἱκάνει ("and my/your fame reaches heaven"). The first occurrence of the phrase comes when Odysseus identifies himself to the Phaiakians; the second is among the first words he speaks to Penelope and begins a passage that was probably in Theocritus's mind when he wrote the description of a newly flourishing Sicily (discussed below). The allusion to Odysseus is significant because elsewhere in the poem, Theocritus describes him as one who "wandered for 120 months throughout all of humankind, and went alive to farthest Hades [horizontal movement across the stream of Ocean, earth's

---

84. Critics have been troubled by the open plea for money in *Idyll* 16, which is underscored by the prominence in this poem of Simonides, who was notorious in antiquity for insisting on the importance of monetary payment (the image of the "Graces" in the chest here seems based on an anecdote about him that was supposed to illustrate this). But Pindar and Bacchylides also composed poems on commission. It is easy to forget this fact because Pindar is so successful at tricking out this economic relationship as gift exchange (cf. δωρήσεται, "will give," in the passage quoted), in line with contemporary aristocratic ideology that sought to disguise economic as personal relationships (Kurke 1999). *Idyll* 16 makes the same move by contrasting with each other the houses closed and open to guests and by moving from money to livestock as a measure of wealth, though it is more candid, finally, about the role of money. But Theocritus is not departing from encomiastic tradition even as that is embodied by Pindar.

85. Gow 1952, II, 322.

86. On this, see Griffiths 1979, 24–26.

boundary] and escaped the cave of the murderous Cyclops [vertical movement]" (*Id.* 16.51–53, almost at the center of the poem). Odysseus, who functions in the poem as a paradigm of return and restoration of homeland,[87] recapitulates in his journey the contrast between downward (immobility, possible death) and horizontal (movement, life, fame), which provide the axes of *Idyll* 16.

Finally, for a reader of Theocritus, poetic texts immobilized in a chest might recall the goatherd and Komatas imprisoned in chests and kept alive on honey brought by bees, the counterpart of the "sweet nectar" that the Muse poured into the goatherd's mouth and so an image of poetic inspiration (*Id.* 7.78–85). The goatherd's plight, like that of the "Graces," was a sign of social disruption; its cause was the "arrogant folly" of his master, or a king (κακαῖσιν ἀτασθαλίαισιν ἄνακτος). So right at the beginning of the poem, questions of poetry and its rightful place are implicitly framed from a bucolic perspective that anticipates the vision of a restored and peaceful Sicily toward the end.

That vision is as follows (*Id.* 16.88–97):

ἄστεα δὲ προτέροισι πάλιν ναίοιτο πολίταις,
δυσμενέων ὅσα χεῖρες ἐλωβήσαντο κατ' ἄκρας·
ἀγροὺς δ' ἐργάζοιντο τεθαλότας· αἱ δ' ἀνάριθμοι
μήλων χιλιάδες βοτάνᾳ διαπιανθεῖσαι
ἀμ' πεδίον βληχῷντο, βόες δ' ἀγεληδὸν ἐς αὖλιν
ἐρχόμεναι σκνιφαῖον ἐπισπεύδοιεν ὁδίταν·
νειοὶ δ' ἐκπονέοιντο ποτὶ σπόρον, ἁνίκα τέττιξ
ποιμένας ἐνδίους πεφυλαγμένος ὑψόθι δένδρων
ἀχεῖ ἐν ἀκρεμόνεσσιν· ἀράχνια δ' εἰς ὅπλ' ἀράχναι
λεπτὰ διαστήσαιντο, βοᾶς δ' ἔτι μηδ' ὄνομ' εἴη.

May cities be dwelt in by their former citizens,
all the cities that the enemies' hands devastated top to bottom.
May the citizens work teeming fields. And may countless
thousands of sheep, fattened on the fodder,
bleat throughout the plain, and cows returning in herds
to the steading urge the twilight traveler on his way.
May fallow fields be worked toward seed time, when the cicada
high in the trees watching shepherds in the sunlight
chirps on the boughs. May spiders weave their fine webs
in weapons, and not even the name of the war cry be heard.

---

87. Griffiths 1979, 41.

"After a long time," says Diodorus, describing Sicily in the late fourth century BCE, "because of internal dissension and civil wars, and also because of the multitude of tyrants who kept rising up, the cities were depopulated and the countryside had turned wild because it was not worked and the fields no longer bore cultivated produce."[88] It is striking how exactly Theocritus imagines the reversal of these conditions: cities repopulated by their original citizens and fields now worked productively, the wilds tamed and controlled, fields providing crops and fodder for domestic animals. The war cry will be replaced by the bleating of sheep and the chirping of cicadas (a well-known figure for poetry). This vision is spatial—city and countryside—and its mode, as many scholars comment, is bucolic. Even though the vista resembles that of the agricultural system of Augeias's farm in *Idyll* 25, which integrates farming and herding and is related to a town by the owner's visit from there, the emphasis here is on herding: livestock grazing and returning to the steadings at nightfall, their homecoming contrasting with the wayfarer's continued journey (bucolic leisure as opposed to purposeful travel). In this description, bucolic time dominates. Agricultural time is measured by the succession of seasons of the year that bring distinct tasks in annual rotation. Bucolic time is founded on the rhythm of the day: grazing and returning to steadings (this circularity provides another contrast with the traveler's linear journey).[89] The time marker in lines 94–95 is bucolic, the time of day, noon or the afternoon. It plays off against the season marker for the agricultural workers' task of preparing fields for sowing ("toward seed time"), and it is the shepherds, not the workers, whom the cicada watches.[90] The first major section of the poem presented a very different space-time: a present time of social fragmentation and closed houses in town or city (Syracuse?) when the poet looks to the past by alluding to earlier praise poets for a model of social integration. The second section is oriented toward a wished-for future of peace, leisure, and plenty described in the idiom of bucolic ease: bucolic space-time. The fact that this vision is contingent and expressed with optative verbs—it may or may not be attained—is thoroughly in keeping with bucolic poetry's awareness of its own fictionality.

---

88. Diod. Sic. 16.83.1, quoted by González 2010, 76.

89. Agricultural labor can also be measured by the time of day, as in *Id.* 10.48–51 (still tied to the seasons, however), but this is not mentioned in the present passage, which emphasizes the rhythm of the seasons in connection with plowing. In the bucolic *Idylls*, by contrast, it seems to be perpetually spring or summer.

90. Contrast *Id.* 5.111, where cicadas are said to irritate or provoke reapers to work. The contrast marks the difference between agricultural labor and bucolic leisure (see especially the discussion of *Idyll* 10 in chapter 4).

In certain ways, this picture of Sicilian peace and prosperity looks back to the earlier description of the wealth of Simonides's Thessalian patrons (*Id.* 16.34–49), which is also bucolic in character. But there are differences. In the earlier passage, there is a much more pronounced emphasis on quantity as a measure of riches—"many . . . and many . . . and ten thousand" (lines 34, 36, 38)—whereas in the Sicilian description, there is only one such reference, "countless thousands" (lines 90–91), and here it seems to imply fertility at least as much as wealth. And dependent workers are prominent in the earlier passage, right at the beginning: "many were the *penestai* [virtually, "serfs"] who measured out their monthly rations in the houses of Antiokhos and lord Aleuas" (lines 34–35; shepherds are also subject of the sentence in line 39). The number of dependents is as much an index of wealth as the number of animals, and the implied social and economic hierarchy is part of these rulers' prosperity and power. In the later passage, human workers are almost entirely effaced, as though the sheep fattened themselves on the fodder in the pastures and the cattle came back to their steadings by themselves. "May the fallow fields be worked toward seed time"—worked by whom the passive verb leaves unspecified. Shepherds are mentioned, but not as part of this picture itself; instead, they appear in the Hesiodic-style[91] time indication in lines 94–96, the object of the cicadas' watchfulness, and the emphasis is on the insects' chirping.[92] The passage thus gives an impression that this bucolic space is relatively independent of social and economic structures. In addition, whereas the earlier passage describes individual wealth as the basis of fame attained especially in racing contests (lines 66–67: more animals, horses, and mules), in Sicily we are given a picture of collective prosperity that is to be brought about and, it is implied, maintained by Hieron's military achievement, for which he is to get worldwide fame through poetry (lines 98–100 again, which cap the whole description). This bucolic space is constructed as a common good produced by an effective ruler.

Scholars often cite Hesiod's description of the just and unjust cities (*Works and Days* 225–247) as the inspiration for this passage.[93] The allusion emphasizes that the prosperity of the just city depends on the goodness of its rulers. But a

---

91. Cf. Hes. *Op.* 582–584.

92. It is true that people carry out the (agricultural) work in line 90: "may they work teeming fields." But the subject of the verb is the citizens of two lines before, and so the sentence does not affect my point about the effacement of subordinate labor.

93. See the excellent discussion in Hunter 1996, 87–89.

more direct statement of this idea appears in Odysseus's words to Penelope in *Odyssey* 19.107–114, which must also be in the background here:[94]

ὦ γύναι, οὐκ ἄν τίς σε βροτῶν ἐπ' ἀπείρονα γαῖαν
νεικέοι· ἦ γάρ σευ κλέος οὐρανὸν εὐρὺν ἱκάνει,
ὥς τέ τευ ἢ βασιλῆος ἀμύμονος, ὅς τε θεουδὴς
ἀνδράσιν ἐν πολλοῖσι καὶ ἰφθίμοισιν ἀνάσσων
εὐδικίας ἀνέχῃσι, φέρῃσι δὲ γαῖα μέλαινα
πυροὺς καὶ κριθάς, βρίθῃσι δὲ δένδρεα καρπῷ,
τίκτῃ δ' ἔμπεδα μῆλα, θάλασσα δὲ παρέχῃ ἰχθῦς
ἐξ εὐηγεσίας, ἀρετῶσι δὲ λαοὶ ὑπ' αὐτοῦ.

Lady, no mortal anywhere on the boundless earth
could find fault with you: for your fame reaches the wide heaven,
as of some blameless ruler, who reverently
holding sway among many noble men
upholds right judgments, and the dark earth brings forth
wheat and barley, and the trees are weighed down with fruit,
and the unfailing flocks bring forth young, and the sea provides fish,
as a result of good leadership, and the people flourish beneath his rule.

Just ruler, thriving people, and abundant nature form a coherent and interdependent complex. The final element of this picture, not mentioned in the Homeric passage but explicit in Theocritus (*Id.* 16.40–47, 98–100) is a poet to celebrate the ruler's achievements and the people's benefit. This unity is set against the opening picture of disunity (individual houses, not the city) of the opening lines, where the poet and his art are separated from the city. Right after the description of Sicily restored, an interesting thing happens, one that should give pause to those who see this poem as simply a pitch by Theocritus for Hieron's patronage (*Id.* 16.101–103):

εἷς μὲν ἐγώ, πολλοὺς δὲ Διὸς φιλέοντι καὶ ἄλλους
θυγατέρες, τοῖς πᾶσι μέλοι Σικελὴν Ἀρέθοισαν
ὑμνεῖν σὺν λαοῖσι καὶ αἰχμητὴν Ἱέρωνα.

I am one, but the daughters of Zeus cherish many others as well.
May they all be concerned to hymn
Sicilian Arethousa with its people, and spearman Hieron.

---

94. Cited also by Griffiths 1979, 41.

Pindar would never hide within "many," and he is not shy about criticizing rival poets. But Theocritus is not making a gesture of modesty, either. Along with the plural "singers" in line 98, these lines make it clear that at least by this point in the poem, the focus is on "the poet" as a type, any poet, and what his role in a properly structured and functioning polity should be.

This understanding of poetry, that it must be integrated into a unified city and is useless, even ignored, outside that context, of course looks back to the archaic and early classical periods. Is Theocritus therefore ignoring all the cultural and political changes that had taken place by the third century BCE? I would say that he seems very aware of them. All the optatives from line 82 to line 103, which express wishes and in fact a prayer to Zeus, make it clear that the whole passage is an idealizing vision, in the same way that bucolic, at its most idealizing, is utopian.[95] They are very different from the factual indicatives that earlier have described things as they are now. Like that of so much of Theocritean bucolic poetry, this vision is contingent, and it is no accident that it is couched in the bucolic idiom. A final sign that it is provisional comes in the immediately succeeding lines, which end the poem (*Id.* 16.104–109), where optatives of wish are replaced by potential optatives and the focus shifts from open bucolic space back to the enclosed space of the house, as in the poem's beginning:

ὦ Ἐτεόκλειοι Χάριτες θεαί, ὦ Μινύειον
Ὀρχομενὸν φιλέοισαι ἀπεχθόμενόν ποτε Θήβαις,
ἄκλητος μὲν ἔγωγε μένοιμί κεν, ἐς δὲ καλεύντων
θαρσήσας Μοίσαισι σὺν ἀμετέραισιν ἴοιμ' ἄν.
καλλείψω δ' οὐδ' ὔμμε· τί γὰρ Χαρίτων ἀγαπητὸν
ἀνθρώποις ἀπάνευθεν; ἀεὶ Χαρίτεσσιν ἅμ' εἴην.

Oh Eteioklean divine Graces, O you who love
Minyan Orkhomenos, once hateful to Thebes,
If I am not invited I would remain at home, but to the houses of
  those who invite me
I would go, taking heart, along with my Muses.
And I will not leave you behind, either; for without the Graces
  what loveliness is there for men? May I always be in the Graces'
  company.

---

95. In fact, Hieron's reign apparently did usher in a period of agrarian prosperity in eastern Sicily, perhaps as a result of his uniting cities there into a *koinon* and his organizing of agricultural administration (Bell 2011). But this is evidently in the future from the perspective of *Idyll* 16, which thus expresses a wished-for ideal.

If the poet is invited to others' houses, that would be a sign of social integration and the fulfillment of the wishes he has articulated. But the text leaves open the equal possibility that there will be no invitation. And so by the end of the poem, the initial picture of the poet in his house, his papyrus rolls lying cramped and rejected in the storage chest, has unfolded into a double image, one superimposed on the other: either a prolongation of that scene or the poet received in the houses of others along with his "Graces"—both the goddesses who personify loveliness and reciprocal social relations and the poems that are their individual manifestation.

Far from ignoring the differences between the archaic period and his own age, I think that Theocritus is using traditional ideas about poetry, civic virtue, and prosperity and refashioning them to fit a world in which the polis was still an important element but a world that was now shaped by the conditions of autocratic and imperial rule—a project facilitated by the fact that Pindar, Bacchylides, and Simonides had written for tyrants and oligarchic families as well as for citizen athletes. This means that he is retooling a traditional ideological complex to fit his own age. To observe him doing so is to recognize not only the politics, in a broad sense, of *Idyll* 16, along with those of *Idyll* 17 (discussed below), but also the ideology of his bucolic poetry in general, which, as we have seen, provides the idiom for the climactic passage of *Idyll* 16.

As regards that ideology, let us look back to the passage on the Thessalian rulers in that poem. In connection with lines 34–35 ("in the households of Antiokhos and lord Aleuas, many were the *penestai* who had their monthly ration measured out"), Gutzwiller speaks of the "contentment of the [*penestai*] who have generous masters."[96] This contentment on one side and generosity on the other are not to be found in the text, but it is not surprising that a reader might infer them because of the ideological allure of bucolic and pastoral poetry in general. As William Empson argues, pastoral makes social and economic inequalities seem natural and self-evidently right.[97] The *penestai* and shepherds are depicted as having their rightful, subordinate place in a structure of wealth enjoyed by Antiokhos and Aleuas. What they get from it is sustenance that enables them to do further work. Gutzwiller's account of lines 31–33 also seems to me to reverse their meaning: Theocritus "suggests to potential patrons that being forgotten in Hades is no worse than poverty on earth." I would say "just as bad as." Both poverty and being forgotten after death are the lot of people such as the *penestai*. Theocritus's

---

96. Gutzwiller 1983, 226–227.

97. Empson 1974, 3–23. Cf. Griffiths 1979, 40, who also cites Empson.

addressees enjoy wealth and, if they use it correctly, will be remembered through poetry. The traditional role of poetry that Theocritus implicitly evokes in this poem was to help maintain distinctions of wealth and standing as well as to transmit certain values, which themselves had class affiliations. The Thessalian passage carries out this same function in that it depicts dependent workers as part of elite households' wealth; the same can be said of *Idyll* 25.

The utopian vision of a restored Sicily produces a similar effect, though in a different way. Like the passage from *Odyssey* 19 quoted above,[98] with its focus on natural abundance produced by a good ruler, it disguises its hierarchical nature by eliding the labor on which it is based. The bucolic poems, by contrast, concentrate on herdsmen, but to similar effect. As we saw in chapter 1, they depict the bucolic world and its inhabitants as more or less autonomous, with generous opportunities for leisure amid natural abundance, and they leave vague or omit any references to cities and to the herdsmen's place in larger economic and social relations and to their actual labor.[99] *Idyll* 4, with its explicit setting near Kroton, and *Idyll* 5, with its references to servile status and the city of Sybaris, along with *Idyll* 25, whether or not it is by Theocritus, suggest what the other bucolic poems leave out: the position of the bucolic world within a hierarchical system that is taken for granted and therefore unquestioned.[100] As we saw in chapter 1, a few lines (126–127) in the urban *Idyll* 15 offer another perspective: the economic integration of the bucolic world into the Ptolemaic empire. There the shepherd's work is not glossed over, but we get instead his pride at contributing material for the Alexandrian Adonis festival. The implied picture of natural abundance and social harmony, with the shepherd happy in his subordinate role, supplements the praise of Ptolemy's rule in *Idyll* 17, to which we now turn.

Idyll 17

As Susan Stephens has suggested, the bucolic poems fit into the larger framework of Theocritus's *Idylls* in that the prosperity of the land is the standard by which a king should be judged, and as she further argues through reading *Idylls*

---

98. This passage has complex effects. For one thing, the beggar Odysseus attributes to Penelope the role of a male ruler. But it is also important that it occurs just before Odysseus's own restoration to his position of authority in his household and on Ithaka—that is, the restoration of hierarchy that is legitimated by this kind of idealizing vision.

99. On the realities of country life, including harsh toil and servile status, glossed over in Vergil's *Eclogues*, see Leigh 2016.

100. The exceptional nature of *Idylls* 4 and 5 in this respect will be discussed further in chapter 4.

16 and 17 together, the good king is not Hieron but Ptolemy.[101] Thus, when *Idyll* 17 is considered with *Idyll* 16, it emerges that Ptolemy and his empire represent the fulfillment of the vision of civic and natural peace and prosperity that can only be wished for in the case of Syracuse and Sicily. If so, then what Theocritus implies in *Idyll* 16 about the wished-for connection between poets and people of wealth and power is transferable to the (actual or desired) relation between himself and Ptolemy. As in the case of Hieron, it would be an oversimplification to say that Theocritus is staking a claim to Ptolemy's patronage. Relations of patronage are all but explicitly described in the poem, but once again as a way to integrate poetry into (what is ideally to be) a well-ordered state under an enlightened ruler.

In Ptolemy, according to *Idyll* 17 (especially lines 106–116), we have the reverse of the hoarder who withholds his patronage and closes his house to guests; his "wealthy" or "rich" house (*Id.* 17.96, 106) is very different from the house of the man who hoards his riches in *Id.* 16 (22–23). Ptolemy's wealth does not lie useless in his rich house but is depicted as a means to be generous. He contributes to the gods' temples, and he gives money to kings, cities, and his own companions. And—the climax to this list—to poets who flock to the poetic festivals of Dionysos, he gives worthy recompense for their art, in the kind of reciprocal exchange depicted as missing at the beginning of *Idyll* 16. He actually rewards the "mouthpieces of the Muses" (Μουσάων ὑποφῆται, *Id.* 17.115), the very ones the speaker in *Idyll* 16 (line 29) can only exhort the rich man to honor. In contrast to Ptolemy's productive use of wealth, all the riches that the sons of Atreus plundered from Troy molder in the darkness, "from which there is no return" (*Id.* 17.118–20). In their fate they would resemble the hoarder mourning "nameless" (ἀκλεής) in Hades (*Id.* 16.30–34) if not for one essential difference: the sons of Atreus had a poet to keep their name alive—Homer—like the other epic figures mentioned at *Id.* 16.48–57. But Ptolemy has the advantage even over them. He recirculates his wealth *and* he has a poet to spread his fame—the one whose poem is now in progress—and so on Theocritus's terms, he fulfills the model of kingship more completely than the sons of Atreus did.

---

101. Stephens 2018, 79–83. Developing an idea of Gutzwiller 1996, 141, Stephens also raises the intriguing possibility that *Idyll* 16 might have opened and *Idyll* 17 closed a papyrus roll of Theocritus's non-bucolic *Idylls*, so that the two poems would have been "read contrastively." (I would add that this is far from suggesting that Theocritus intended this arrangement; it could have been made, if at all, by any editor at any time.) I owe a more general debt to her discussion of these two poems and of the bucolic *Idylls*, which has been of great help to me in getting my own ideas in order. On imagery of peace and abundance used to legitimate the Ptolemaic and other empires, see Strootman 2014.

Ptolemy is a "spearman" (αἰχμητής), as is his father, Ptolemy Soter (*Id.* 17.56–57):

> σὲ δ' αἰχμητὰ Πτολεμαῖε,
> αἰχμητᾷ Πτολεμαίῳ ἀρίζηλος Βερενίκα.
>
> You, spearman Ptolemy [Philadelphus],
> to spearman Ptolemy [Soter] famous Berenike [bore].

For the Greeks, the son's resemblance to the father was highly desirable. It guaranteed the son's legitimacy, and it was part of the epic heroic ideal that the son should measure up to, and even surpass, the father.[102] But it was also part of the Egyptian ideal of kingship, which Ptolemy, as pharaoh, fittingly is shown to embody.[103] In addition, the spear played an important role in imperial self-fashioning from Alexander through Roman times, especially insofar as it implied the notion of δορίκτητος χώρα ("spear-won land").[104] And finally, Hieron is also called "spearman" in *Idyll* 16 (line 103). These are the only instances of the epithet in the entire Theocritean corpus, and the passages are surely connected. As André Looijenga points out,[105] Theocritus can call Ptolemy "king" (βασιλεύς) but not Hieron. Of course, Hieron was not a hereditary king, and Ptolemy was, or claimed to be, but the difference may be another sign that *Idyll* 16 wishfully points toward what is fully realized in *Idyll* 17.

Unlike Hieron, Philadelphus rules a land that is actually fertile and teeming (*Id.* 17.77–94). This is not just expressed as a wish, although the poem only suggests that his kingship is the cause of Egypt's prosperity without making it explicit; the emphasis is rather on his wealth and imperial power. But he does, according to Theocritus, protect Egypt and benefit it with his generosity, as Egyptian kings were traditionally expected to do.[106] As for Theocritus, the poet who in *Idyll* 16 depicted thriving cities and countryside in bucolic terms actually wrote bucolic poetry, likely at Ptolemy's court, where it provided a useful heterotopia for urban readers and reflected well on the order and natural bounty promoted by imperial

---

102. E.g., *Od.* 3.120–125; Hes. *Op.* 235 (cf. 182). There may be a specific epic prototype here in the spear of Akhilleus, which was given to him by his father, Peleus; see Kyriakou 2018, 287–288.

103. Stephens 2003, 155–158; cf. Hunter 2003, 141–142.

104. Looijenga 2014, 217–218, 226–229 (discussions of *Idylls* 16 and 17).

105. Looijenga 2014, 230.

106. Stephens 2003, 159–165.

rule. If we see *Idyll* 16 as background and context for *Idyll* 17, we can say that in both poems, taken together, Theocritus expresses some ideas about the possible relation of poetry to autocratic power and suggests an important role for the poet in providing Ptolemy with cultural, if not political, capital—as, in fact, we see him in the act of doing in *Idyll* 17. It would be a wild exaggeration to claim that Alexandrian poetry had a central place in the life of the city or empire; in that sense, the old model of praise poetry that Theocritus seems to evoke in *Idyll* 16 is perhaps a nostalgic way of speaking. But neither is Theocritus's poetry disengaged from its cultural and political world. In some sense, at least, poetry and other cultural productions were integrated into structures of authority, just as the Mouseion and Library were integrated into the court.

Idyll 17 thus seems to be an experiment in connecting poetry with royal and imperial power by explicit praise of Ptolemy, and its spatiality matches its encomiastic program. All of Theocritus's poems considered so far have been locally rooted. *Idyll* 17, by contrast, ranges far and wide in space, in keeping with its emphasis on empire, and it gains chronological depth by including the Ptolemies' alleged ancestor Herakles and their imperial prototype Alexander, as well as Soter and Berenike in the generation before Philadelphus and Arsinoe. So in this poem, as in *Idyll* 16, though in a different form, we have another example of encomiastic space-time.

Celebration of Ptolemy's parents, with emphasis on the locations of their immortality (Olympos for Soter, Aphrodite's temple for Berenike), is followed by Philadelphus's birth on Kos, with an analogy drawn to Apollo's birth on Delos. Next comes a list of the regions and countries subject to Ptolemy's encroachment or hegemony.[107] This is a kind of map of Ptolemy's power, and like a map, it is an abstraction of space, here as often for hegemonic purposes. At the same time, it brings these areas into relation to one another as elements of an empire. The wealth of its ruler, Ptolemy, and of its center, Alexandria, next becomes the focus. Vast riches flow daily "from all sides" (17.97) into Ptolemy's wealthy house, which exerts a centripetal force as in *Idyll* 15. At the same time, Ptolemy keeps enemies outside the borders of Egypt. Corresponding to the inflow of wealth is its redistribution outward by Ptolemy's generosity as described above. The poem's final section praises Ptolemy's relationships: his filial piety in instituting shrines and sacrifices to his parents and his marriage to Arsinoe, which corresponds to that of his parents, praised earlier.[108] The encomium proper ends, as it began, on Olympos,[109] this

---

107. On this catalogue, see Hunter 2003, 159–161.

108. On Arsinoe's eros for Philadelphus, see Hunter 2003, 191–192.

109. As Griffiths 1979, 73, points out, an elaborate pattern of reverse symmetry frames the poem: Hades (120), Olympos (131 ff.), Mount Ida (133 ff.) at the end, corresponding to Mount Ida (9 ff.), Olympos (14–33), Acheron (or Hades, 46–99) earlier. Mount Ida, Griffiths says,

time with the marriage of Zeus and Hera (also brother and sister) as an analogy to the relationship between the royal couple. Thus, in its construction of imperial space, the poem moves horizontally over a large area on the surface of the world and vertically from Olympos to the earth and then back again to Olympos. In this way it puts Alexandria in context, as hegemonic power exerting a centripetal force over much of the surface of the earth and with close connections, through its ruling dynasty and its ancestor Herakles, with Olympos and its gods.

Idyll 14

Considered from a spatial perspective, *Idyll* 14[110] takes a narrower view, with a focus on two places on the earth's surface, and suggests something of the dynamics of the relationship between Alexandria and the territories under its sway. In that poem, the space in which the conversation between Aiskhinas and Thyonikhos takes place is indefinite, and correspondingly the poem emphasizes mobility. Burton centers her discussions of the poem on the symposium, which she describes as one of those traditional institutions through which Greeks could retain their ethnic identity in a Hellenistic world characterized by mobility and fluidity of categories.[111] As others have remarked, when Aiskhinas tells Thyonikhos about the drinking party at his house at which the terrible episode occurred between himself and Kyniska and he punched her twice in a fit of jealousy, he lists as his fellow symposiasts an Argive, a Thessalian, and a mercenary soldier whose origin is not specified.[112] This gathering of people from various

---

serves as "a point of intersection between the divine and mortal spheres, a permeable boundary which suggests that certain privileged natures can pass from one realm to the other."

110. This poem might be considered a mime and combines town and country (Pretagostini 2006, 67). My reasons for discussing it here will, I hope, become clear.

111. Burton 1992; 1995, 24–28. See more recently Pausch 2011, 27–28, who suggests that this non-elite symposium, despite obvious contrasts, sets up a relationship between the place where it occurs and the Ptolemaic court at Alexandria, a relationship between center and periphery that is emphasized by the vagueness of the poem's setting. That relationship will be central to the point I want to make about *Idyll* 14.

112. Significantly, he does not include Kyniska in the list, even though she joins in the drinking and is expected to take part in the game of toasting one's love object (*Id.* 14.20–21). Similarly, having identified her as ἁ χαρίεσσα Κυνίσκα ("the lovely Kyniska") in line 8, he uses her name only one more time, at the climax of his story when she gives herself away by bursting into tears (line 31). Otherwise, Kyniska is simply "she" (ἅ, αὐτά, lines 21, 23) or "that woman" (τήνα, line 41). The reason for this mode of reference could be that the symposium was traditionally a men's club, and the only women present were hetairai, there for the men's sake and taken for granted as part of the normal furnishings for such an occasion, although Kyniska's status is indefinite. But it could also tell us a great deal about Aiskhinas's attitude to her, lovelorn though he now says he is, and so about Aiskhinas himself; this would be another of the signs of his insensitivity and lack of self-awareness that Stern 1975 discusses well.

places seems to be a sign of how much a fact of life mobility was. Then there is the pale and barefoot Pythagorist to whom Thyonikhos compares Aiskhinas in his lovelorn squalor. "He arrived the other day and said he was from Athens" and was in love—with food he could cadge (*Id.* 14.6–7). A true philosopher, who might fittingly be from Athens, or a charlatan posing as a philosopher? At any rate, he exemplifies another type of itinerant person who might show up anywhere in this itinerant world.

Aiskhinas says that the drinking party took place "in the country, at my house" (ἐν χώρῳ παρ' ἐμίν, *Id.* 14.14). He and Kyniska must have spent some time there for her to fall in love with the neighbor's son. By implication, the present meeting between Aiskhinas and Thyonikhos must be taking place in a town or city somewhere in the Ptolemaic sphere of influence. After enumerating the delicacies he served, Aiskhinas says, "ἧς πότος ἁδύς: the drinking party was sweet." "Sweet" is, of course, a key word of the bucolic *Idylls* that describes the beauty of bucolic space. This party would be, for a town dweller, the counterpart of bucolic leisure in a non-bucolic sympotic setting. But the drinking gets out of control and ends in chaos and with Kyniska's flight, a conclusion that presumably has sent Aiskhinas back to town. I would connect this result also with the theme of mobility because it reflects a failure to fit into a place, a χῶρος—a word that is used of the country in this poem but also means place. Aiskhinas has failed to use the pleasures of a house in the country, to enjoy the company of friends, and to love properly. As for the town that would normally be the opposite pole to the countryside, it is not explicitly mentioned, and we have no idea where it is supposed to be. "Since nothing in the poem points to the islands or to the West," says K. J. Dover, "we are perhaps meant to think of the Peloponnese."[113] But perhaps we are not to think of any region in particular; lack of definition is the point. Under these conditions of movement, places are often what people pass through or leave dissatisfied.

This indefiniteness as to place is matched by uncertainty about status. Is Kyniska a hetaira or higher on the social scale, her presence at the symposium a mark of the new relative freedom of women in the Hellenistic period, as Burton argues?[114] How can we tell? As for Aiskhinas, we have a few more hints. He is affluent enough that he has a country farm as well as (probably) a house in town. He would be the social equal of his drinking companions, two of whom are identified as a horse trainer and a soldier—of middling standing or perhaps a bit lower. The profession he now aspires to is commensurate with that: "your

---

113. Dover 1971, 189.

114. Burton 1992, 237–238; 1995, 25–26; cf. Pausch 2011, 21.

soldier is not the worst of men nor yet the first, maybe, but as good as another" (*Id.* 14.55–56, Gow's translation; the last phrase, ὁμαλὸς δέ τις, essentially means "just like everyone else"). No epic heroism for our Aiskhinas! By becoming a mercenary, he is proposing to join those itinerant soldiers who by definition had no fixed attachment to place but went wherever there was warfare and they could find employment, in a direction he only vaguely refers to as διαπόντιος, "across the sea" (*Id.* 14.55), like his friend Simos (*Id.* 14.53–54).[115] From this point of view, it is significant that Aiskhinas does not say where his drinking friend Kleunikos is from, only that he is a soldier. The omission seems to reflect how such a man was viewed: his profession mattered more than his birthplace as a marker of identity.[116]

But in the concluding section of the poem, everything changes. Thyonikhos gives Aiskhinas a definite destination for his career as a mercenary: Alexandria. There Ptolemy is such a generous paymaster, Thyonikhos implies, that men at loose ends flock to Alexandria to serve under him. As we saw with the movement of goods in *Idyll* 15, so it is with the movement of people: Ptolemaic imperial power, centered on its capital city, exerts a centripetal force on the rest of the Greek world and gives the space of the empire definition. Thyonikhos makes it sound as if Alexandria will provide a fixed point, as if the Greek world is in flux with a purpose, to feed into Alexandria, and as if Aiskhinas, though a common soldier, can share vicariously in Ptolemy's prosperity and will even have a personal relationship with the king ("Ptolemy is generous, but don't ask him for everything you need"—a paraphrase of *Id.* 14.63–65). So the emphasis on fluidity of place and social categories in most of the poem has a point: this is a structured mobility, flowing to the center of imperial power. We can appreciate the effect of this spatial refocusing all the more if we follow Jan Kwapisz's recent suggestion that this poem forms a "diptych" with *Idyll* 15: Aiskhinas's proposed journey from somewhere in the empire to Alexandria is matched by the women's expedition from a home within the city to the royal palace, so that "these are two stages of the same journey, or even two versions of the same journey."[117] Together, then, the two poems explore aspects of immigrants' experience in an empire dominated by

---

115. It is true that Simos returned home, cured of love, and Aiskhinas expects to do the same. But that does not affect the point made here about his deracination and placelessness while he is abroad.

116. Contrast Agis, the Thessalian horse trainer (*Id.* 14.12), whose profession and region go together, because Thessaly, with its wide, fertile plains, was famous for its horses, as we see already in the *Iliad*, where the Thessalian Eumelos has the best horses of all the Greeks at Troy (*Il.* 2.763–767).

117. Kwapisz 2021, 111–112. Cf. Pausch 2011, 28–30.

Alexandria and its rulers, and they show different ways in which men and women of middling standing might become involved with, benefit from, and (modestly) contribute to the power of Ptolemy and Arsinoe, through military service and cult, respectively. Writing poetry under royal patronage might well come into sight here as an implied third way.[118]

This portrait of Ptolemy and his power may be meant as flattery, but in carrying out this encomiastic program, *Idyll* 14, like the bucolic *Idylls* but more directly, speaks to the condition of uprootedness and the uncertainties of social and spatial definitions in its contemporary Greek world. Interestingly, and somewhat paradoxically, it offers Alexandria, the new, diverse city of immigrants, where old certainties were open to question as never before, as a center of stability. Perhaps this idealized view of Alexandria is a sign of how much Theocritus's readers needed such reassurance.

Everything comes back to Alexandria. The encomiastic poems may seem distinct from the other *Idylls* discussed in these first two chapters, but they are not. They provide a wide spatial and political context for the Alexandria through which housewives walk to the festival of Adonis, for the town that is the scene for Simaitha's erotic desperation, and for the hillsides on which herdsmen sing of love and loss.

---

118. For an interesting "metapoetic" reading of *Idyll* 14 along these lines, see Pausch 2011, although his suggestion that by narrating the story of the unfortunate dinner party to Thyonikhos, Aiskhinas engages in the same kind of "self-therapy" as Polyphemos does in *Idyll* 11 seems a bit of a stretch.

3

The Poetics of Absence

Absence, Desire, and Song

An unnamed goatherd stands before the mouth of a cave, pleading with "Amaryllis" just to look out at him, while one Tityros tends his herd. Pleas turn into futile exclamations of despair and a threat of suicide. Then, leaning or sitting against a pine tree, he serenades her with a song cataloguing examples from myth of goddesses or mortal women falling in love with men. When this performance produces no result beyond a headache for him, he resolves to lie on the ground and let wolves devour him, to her satisfaction, as he sarcastically hopes ("may this be sweet honey trickling down your throat").

The poem is the third *Idyll* of Theocritus, and it is a brilliant mime-like rustic version of the usually urban *kômos*; the poem's illocutionary first word (κωμάζω) sets it in relation to what was to be a popular situation in Hellenistic and Roman poetry: the lover pleading and singing at the barred house door of the beloved, who remains silent and aloof.[1] This poem beautifully exemplifies a pervasive element of Theocritean poetry, the interplay of presence and absence, and particularly the role of absence in generating and sustaining the poem. The importance of absence is especially marked in the bucolic poems; *Idyll* 1, I will argue, presents it as foundational for bucolic.[2] But it is not limited to those *Idylls*, and I will discuss several non-bucolic poems to suggest its importance for the whole Theocritean corpus.

---

1. For a helpful summary of the conventions of the *kômos*, see Hunter 1999, 107–108. See also Gow 1952, II, 64. The *kômos* is referred to in its characteristically city context in *Idylls* 2.118–128, 153; and 7.122–125.

2. Absence is central to Purchase's reading of *Idyll* 1 (2003–2005), which draws on Lacan and Winnicott. For Konstan's excellent remarks, see below.

Absence, loss, and discontinuity are a well-recognized condition of later pastoral poetry. Vergil's *Eclogues* begin with Meliboeus's departure from his country and "sweet fields," while Tityrus remains in possession of the pleasures of the pastoral world. The importance of absence in Theocritus's bucolic poems has occasionally been noted, but for the most part in passing, as though it were obvious and unremarkable. I hope that this chapter will show that it repays sustained attention across Theocritus's poetry. The discussion that follows will complement and fill out the consideration of space in the first two chapters. If many of his poems construct spaces and the natural features, objects, animals, and people and their social relations within them, what is absent is, perhaps somewhat paradoxically, part of that construction. Presence and absence are mutually implicated; as the example of Vergil shows, Tityrus's continued enjoyment of pastoral fullness is balanced, and made to seem more fortunate, by Meliboeus's loss of it.

A closer look at *Idyll* 3 will help bring out important aspects of this topic. The *kômos* presupposes absence—of the beloved—and expresses the anguish of the lover, who is present within the implied narrative of the poem. This separation is spatialized in the sharp opposition between the area in front of the door and the inaccessible interior of the house. The first is the space of desire, the second the space of desire's imagined but always deferred fulfillment. The absolute dividing line between them is the house door or the doorposts. It represents the minuscule distance that would have to be traversed in order for the absent one to become present, and, if the desire were mutual, as it presumably would be if entrance were granted, for the lovers to become fully present to each other. Generally, however, that distance remains insuperable. All the lover can do is either try to force entry (a dubious proposition) or—sing. That is, the beloved's absence and frustrated desire produce the song. That is clearly the case in *Idyll* 3, where the house is replaced by a cave and its door by a screen of ferns. The goatherd's situation seems to be summed up by the name of the plant whose leaf he uses to divine whether or not "Amaryllis"—the quotation marks will be explained presently—loves him: τηλέφιλον or "love in absence" (*Id.* 3.29).[3]

But the poem complicates this basic situation in interesting ways. The goatherd expresses this wish (*Id.* 3.12–14):

---

3. If the leaf that the goatherd smacked onto his arm withered and fell off—an indication that "Amaryllis" did not love him—that would be a physical sign, alongside the verbal one, of absence. For this interpretation and the difficulties of lines 29–30, see Gow 1952, II, 70–71, and Dover 1971, 116, accepted by Hunter 1999, 119.

αἴθε γενοίμαν
ἁ βομβεῦσα μέλισσα καὶ ἐς τεὸν ἄντρον ἱκοίμαν
τὸν κισσὸν διαδὺς καὶ τὰν πτέριν ἅ τυ πυκάσδει.

I wish I could become
that buzzing bee and come into your cave,
slipping through the ivy and the fern that covers you over.

A barred door is not the obstacle, as it is in the urban *kômos*; there is only a screen of foliage over the mouth of this cave. If a bee can fly inside, why can't the goatherd just walk in?[4] He cannot for two interrelated reasons. First, the bucolic poems show an awareness of the differences between animal and human sexuality. Animals can satisfy their sexual desire directly and simply, but humans cannot, because human eros is directed and limited by the conventions of culture, even (or perhaps especially) in a bucolic setting.[5] This distinction seems to be behind Priapos's taunt to Daphnis in *Idyll* 1 (85–88) that he is δύσερως (unfortunate or inept in love) and like a goatherd rather than the cowherd he is called. Perhaps goatherds were proverbially randy. But if a goatherd, seeing his animals copulating, can only weep in frustration because he was not born a he-goat, he at least acknowledges the differences and is bound by the constraints of culture that make of desire and its fulfillment a process, a game (in a non-frivolous sense) shaped by rules.[6] A contrasting passage that reverses the situation is *Id.* 5.41–42, where Komatas claims to recall his pederastic intercourse with Lakon, which was witnessed by the goats. The she-goats bleated (out of lust or in sympathy with Lakon's pain?), and "the he-goat drilled [ἐτρύπη] them." Here, unlike the goatherd of *Idyll* 3, the animals matter-of-factly satisfy their mimetic lust.

---

4. For further comments on the bee, see Isenberg and Konstan 1984, 305–306.

5. Cf. Gutzwiller 1991, 118, on *Idyll* 3: "that he [the goatherd] looks like his goats and yet leaves them to pursue Amaryllis suggests the basic paradox that love is both a product of our animal nature and a distinctly human emotion." On Hellenistic philosophical discussions about the relation of humans to nature, particularly regarding sexuality, see Samson 2013, 201–328.

6. Galateia's teasing of Polyphemos in *Id.* 6.7 by calling him δυσερώτα καὶ αἰπόλον ἄνδρα ("unfortunate [or inept] in love and a goatherd") seems to assume the same contrast. There the shepherd Polyphemos is tending his flocks and pretending to ignore the nymph. She in effect tells him that if he rejects her, he may as well resort to animals as goatherds are said to want to do. The irony is that he is playing, or trying to play, the human game of "hard to get." The probably post-Theocritean *Idyll* 27 shows a successful seduction in progress and ends in the mutual satisfaction of desire by Daphnis and Akrotime. As Bernsdorff (2006, 192–193) says, this contrasts strongly with the depiction of human and animal sexuality in Theocritus's bucolics and points in the direction of the romance novel. In Theocritus, there are no such moments of erotic fulfillment, *Idyll* 5 being hardly an exception. On Priapos's speech, see also Stanzel 1995, 88–90.

The description minimizes, if it does not efface, the difference between humans and animals, since Komatas is gratifying his lust just as straightforwardly (and the verb used, ἐπύγιζον, is not metaphorical but anatomically explicit). The he-goat's imitation of his human master comments on the latter's act, which is not accompanied by the usual choreography of inaccessibility and desire. The contrast with other poems in this respect helps us appreciate the way they depict the importance of absence in human sexuality. This effect is all the sharper if the incident Komatas boasts of is only a fiction invented as a move in his agonistic game with Lakon.

Second, if the goatherd simply entered the cave, there would be no song. As David Konstan has pointed out, pastoral song is elicited by a sense of loss, distance, frustration, and loneliness—the very conditions of desire. Thus, the song "always has something of the plaintive strains of a lament for a lost wholeness, an irrecoverable moment of oneness with others in a garden universe. The feeling of desire and loss is constitutive of the pastoral lover's subjectivity."[7] Bucolic song is therefore both a complaint about absence and distance and an attempt to overcome that distance that is always doomed to failure, except, occasionally, through imagination, for example, by recourse to the mythical, as in *Idyll* 3. These repeated failures are what keep song going. The conventions of the *kômos* and of the bucolic poetry that incorporates it are a counterpart to, or more precisely an expression of, the cultural conventions that complicate human as opposed to animal sexuality. Human culture is separate from nature, and bucolic poetry, which depicts humans in a natural setting, in a liminal area where domestic meets wild space, and in close contact with domesticated animals, is an especially pointed medium for exploring that distinction and its implications through the extremes of proximity and distance.

Desire caused by a sense of loss understandably gives rise to an impulse toward idealization. "What seems specific to pastoral poetry," Konstan writes, "is the extraordinary magnification or exaltation of the object of desire in the mind of the lover. Thus the beloved is frequently represented as remote and unattainable, separated by an uncrossable divide that suggests a difference in kind or order of being between her (or him) and the anguished admirer."[8] In the case of *Idyll* 3, we might go further and ask, with Hunter, whether "Amaryllis" even exists.[9] If

---

7. Konstan 1994, 169. For the same ideas applied to *Idyll* 3, see Isenberg and Konstan 1984, especially 303–304 (with a more explicit connection to Lacanian theory of subject formation). See also Goldhill 1991, 252, and especially Goldhill 1988, 88, in connection with Greek poetry in general as well as *Idyll* 11: "It is a constitutive factor in the rhetoric of desire that pursuit is precisely for the one who flees."

8. Konstan 1994, 168–169. See Konstan 2021 for an elaboration of the dynamics of eros in Theocritus, with particular emphasis on the way that idealization of the beloved entails diminishment of the lover's self-regard.

9. Hunter 1999, 109.

we assume that she does, we can put together an implied narrative of a lovely (χαρίεσσα) girl (or perhaps Nymph, since she lives in a cave) who used to peep out of her cave and invite a goatherd—her sweetheart (τὸν ἐρώτυλον)—inside but does so no longer (οὐκέτι, 3.6–7); who asked him to bring her apples (conventional love tokens) from a certain tree (3.10–11); but who got close enough to him (ἐγγύθεν) to see that he was ugly, snub-nosed, and with a jutting beard (3.8–9); and who now, repelled, refuses him entrance, so that all he can do is stand outside the cave with his tribute of apples and a promise of more tomorrow, wearing a wreath that he threatens to shred (3.21–23), and plead with her and sing to her, to no effect. In this case, we have a rustic version of the standard *kômos* situation, with the beloved's presence followed by absence and the arousal of desire.

Or, if "Amaryllis" is an illusion, this narrative of their past relationship is a coherent fiction. The goatherd animates this illusion by emphasizing her beauty (χαρίεσσα again) and her dark eyebrows (ὦ κυανόφρυ/νύμφα, 3.18–19), and especially by imagining her as the subject of sight (ἠνίδε, "look!" 3.10; θᾶσαι μάν, "come on and see!" 3.12; ὦ τὸ καλὸν ποθορεῦσα, "you with the beautiful glance," 3.18). We see how complete and systematic his illusion is. And that means that we appreciate all the more the power of desire to fill a void by creating a fiction that issues in a song set within a bucolic poem, and to constitute not only its own subject, as Konstan says, but also its object. We may laugh at the goatherd, but what does it matter if "Amaryllis" is his fantasy? He has filled his solitude (except for his goats) with an other, and he has engaged in the human activity of desiring, even if he finds Eros a "heavy god" (3.15) and even if the poem ends in an impasse.[10]

Somewhere between these extremes ("Amaryllis" as an actual Nymph or as pure figment of the goatherd's imagination) is the possibility, suggested by Gutzwiller, that "Amaryllis" is a statue.[11] In that case, τὸ πᾶν λίθος ("all stone,"

---

10. There is a parallel, it seems to me, in the story known from Stesichorus, Herodotus, and Euripides that for ten years the Akhaians and Trojans fought a war not over Helen herself but over an image (εἴδωλον) of her. This seems to have made no difference to the Trojan War itself. What kept the war going was the relation of mutual hostility between the two sides, fueled by Girardean "mimetic desire."

11. Gutzwiller 1991, 118–121. A parallel possibility is that the woman in the first scene on the cup in *Idyll* 1 is a statue—an idea already found in the scholia and well developed by Payne 2007, 29–31. There the statue would be an artifact represented on another artifact (the cup) set within a verbal description and not looked at during most of the poem by either the goatherd or Thyrsis. Similarly, in *Idyll* 3, the statue would be located within a cave that is set within a fictional landscape and would be animated by the goatherd's imagination. Both cases would be analogous to Theocritus's technique of framing and of embedded (sometimes multiply embedded) songs that will be discussed below. Cf. Payne's remark (2007, 64) on *Idyll* 3: "the cave is a cancelled *mise en abyme* of the poem itself; it figures the allure of fictional experience as the desire to enter a world available only through that experience."

Id. 3.18) would have a literal meaning as well as a metaphorical one ("hard-hearted"), and "you with the beautiful glance," which immediately precedes this phrase, could be an expression of aesthetic as well as erotic appreciation.[12] We would have a gesture to a story that resembles that of Pygmalion and an extreme illustration of the potential of the imagination to construct nature—here the element of stone—as sentient through its fiction-making, to do in its own way what Daedalus was said to do with his statues. For one reading this poem for the first time surely entertains the possibility, while reading, that "Amaryllis" will appear. At the same time, by the end of the poem, we have been able to take the measure of fiction and its limitations, because she never emerges.

The name "Amaryllis" occurs again in *Idyll* 4 (35–40), where Korydon recalls how Aigon dragged a bull by the hooves down from the mountain and gave it to "Amaryllis," and how the women screamed and "the cowherd" bellowed with laughter. Battos responds with an outburst of grief for the now dead "Amaryllis" (*Id.* 4.38–40, discussed in chapter 4). Whether or not the "Amaryllis" of *Idyll* 4 is literally the same person as the one of *Idyll* 3,[13] I would suggest that the name functions the same way in both poems: to mark absence. "Amaryllis" is, then, the signifier not necessarily of an actual person but of the missing object of desire whose absence provokes the song of longing or nostalgia;[14] that is why I have been enclosing the name in quotation marks. She is more of a poetic function than a person.[15]

One description of bucolic poetry is that it is about "herdsmen who sing." A more precise account would be that it is about "herdsmen who desire and for that reason sing." Even when love and song are alternatives to herding and seem

---

12. The scholia on line 18 give three explanations of "all stone": (1) gleaming white like a marble statue (a sense adopted by Prioux 2021, 390–391); (2) hard-hearted; and (3) capable of turning men to stone with her beauty, like a Gorgon.

13. The scholia consider her the same and identify the goatherd of *Idyll* 3 as Battos. The echo of *Id.* 3.6 in *Id.* 4.38 implies some sort of connection between the two poems, but there is no indication that *Idyll* 3 is set, like *Idyll* 4, near Kroton in southern Italy. Since "Amaryllis" figures in Korydon's anecdote about Aigon (*Id.* 3.36), she presumably was a real person, at least within the fiction of the poem. That does not affect my point about the similar function of her name in both poems.

14. Cf. Stanzel 1995, 30.

15. It is symptomatic of this that we are given no physical description other than two epithets: κυάνοφρυς, "dark-browed" (*Id.* 3.18), and χαρίεσσα, "lovely" (*Ids.* 3.6, 4.38). In Homer, the latter epithet can describe objects such as a temple or clothing, abstractions such as song, and the head, face, or forehead, but never the whole person. Even the name "Amaryllis," which suggests something like "Sparkles," points more toward her function as object of desire than toward individual identity. The name is borrowed by Longus and Vergil and becomes "almost an emblem of the bucolic world" (Hatzikosta 2008, 56).

The Poetics of Absence

to disrupt the bucolic world, as, for instance, in *Idylls* 3 and 11, they are basic to it. Such cases, in fact, assume an innocent world of wholeness (what I am going to call presence) that is now lost because it was invaded by desire and need and that is itself an object of longing. Thus, the bucolic world is always already alienated from itself. From this perspective, bucolic poetry seems a development of the Platonic insight that eros is always desire for what one does not have, that absence is the constitutive ground for desire (Pl. *Symp*. 199c3–206a12).[16] In fact, the goatherd of *Idyll* 3 sounds very much like Diotima's description of Eros in the *Symposium* (203c5–d3):

> ἅτε οὖν Πόρου καὶ Πενίας υἱὸς ὢν ὁ Ἔρως ἐν τοιαύτῃ τύχῃ καθέστηκεν. πρῶτον μὲν πένης ἀεί ἐστι, καὶ πολλοῦ δεῖ ἁπαλός καὶ καλός, οἷον οἱ πολλοὶ οἴονται, ἀλλὰ σκληρὸς καὶ αὐχμηρὸς καὶ ἀνυπόδητος καὶ ἄοικος, χαμαιπετὴς ἀεὶ ὢν καὶ ἄστρωτος, ἐπὶ θύραις καὶ ἐν ὁδοῖς ὑπαίθριος κοιμώμενος, τὴν τῆς μητρὸς φύσιν ἔχων, ἀεὶ ἐνδείᾳ σύνοικος.

As befits the son of Resourcefulness and Poverty, Eros exists in the following condition. First, he is always poor, and he is far from being delicate and beautiful, as the many think; but he is rough and parched, barefoot and homeless. He always sleeps on the ground and without bedding, lying in doorways and streets under the open sky, possessing his mother's nature, always a housemate of neediness.

Rough and no doubt dirty,[17] determined to sleep on the ground in front of "Amaryllis's" cave, the goatherd is not only a subject of desire but the very figure of Eros, of want and longing.[18] Because he is not named, and so given an individual identity, he seems no different from any other goatherd[19] and therefore seems to represent a type. That is to say again that absence and desire are basic to bucolic subjectivity.

---

16. This connection is also briefly made by Fantuzzi 2017, 331. On the relations of Theocritus's poetry to philosophical issues surrounding love raised by Plato, Aristotle, the Stoics, and the Epicureans, see Samson 2013. She organizes her discussion according to Diotima's description of types of lovers but does not discuss this passage.

17. For a fuller description of a goatherd (*Idyll* 3 gives almost no details), see *Id*. 7.13–19.

18. In her excellent chapter on "The Herdsman in Plato," Gutzwiller 1991, 78–79, discusses Socrates as a figure of Eros but not the Theocritean herdsman.

19. On the importance of not naming, as well as of names, see Kossaifi 2002, 357–358. Even in connection with the named Lykidas, *Id*. 7.13–14 suggests that there is a category of goatherds that is recognizable on sight: "his name was Lykidas, and he was a goatherd. No one seeing him would have mistaken him, since he looked just like a goatherd."

From one perspective, it may seem that love is antithetical to the values of the bucolic world because it is disruptive of that world's serenity.[20] In some ways, this is undeniable, but I would go further and say that absence and the desire it arouses are also constitutive of the bucolic world and that tranquility, which would involve humans seamlessly fitting into it, is an ideal never fully realized. This distinction seems important. Love, as an element of human culture, is one of the obstacles to humans merging with nature, as we have now seen in connection with *Idyll* 3. In chapter 1, I argued that the beginning of *Idyll* 1 shows in a different way that such merging, or fullness, can never be fully attained. So I do not see love in Theocritus's bucolic poems as disrupting an already existing, or an otherwise existing, peace so much as a condition of even existing in the bucolic world.

What would the fulfillment of desire be like? In Plato, it would ultimately be philosophical *noēsis*, but for bucolic poetry, it is harder to answer this question. But imagine if a fully embodied Amaryllis appeared at the entrance to her cave and exchanged gazes with the goatherd, if he could see (or see again) her beautiful glance (ὦ τὸ καλὸν ποθορεῦσα), and if they were not separated by the division between beauty and ugliness and were fully present to each other as lovers. More generally, we might imagine the full realization of the beauty and fertility of the natural world, and humans living in oneness with it and with one another. This is the condition that I will call "fullness" and "presence," and there are moments in the *Idylls* that at least gesture toward it and even envision it—but always in a distanced way that recognizes it as a not fully attainable ideal. And what would poetry be like in such a state? Would bucolic poetry be possible, if on its presuppositions it is desire aroused by absence and need that generates the energy of seeking and therefore of poetic creation? To put the point another way, according to the terms of *Idyll* 3, can the notion of an Amaryllis and a goatherd in love with each other strike us as anything but grotesque? Would we be interested in reading a poem that described it? But we are interested in the goatherd's song of need.

Idyll 12, in which an older man addresses the boy he loves after the latter has returned from absence, might seem to suggest that a poem can be written about presence as I have defined it; its first word is ἤλυθες ("you have come"), and the first nine lines describe the speaker's joy in terms that fit the relationship into nature at its most alluring. But line 10 introduces a wish and the consequences, including poetic immortality, that might flow from its fulfillment: "I wish the Erotes might breathe equally on both of us." The very utterance of the wish opens the possibility that the Erotes do not breathe on the boy as much as on the speaker, that if the boy left once he can do so again, and that he may not fully

---

20. Fantuzzi 2017.

share the lover's pleasure in their reunion. The speaker imagines the song that will be sung in the future about himself and the boy, which concludes (*Id.* 12.15–16):

ἦ ῥα τότ' ἦσαν
χρύσειοι πάλιν ἄνδρες, ὅτ' ἀντεφίλησ' ὁ φιληθείς.

Then indeed
men were of gold again, when the loved one loved in return.

Full and lasting reciprocity in love would mean a restoration of the Golden Age, and that is tantamount to admitting its impossibility. So the initial moment of fullness and presence is qualified by questions about the future—questions that are not canceled but only intensified by the self-fictionalizing fantasies in the lines that follow (*Id.* 12.12–21). As Diotima says, one can possess something good and still feel eros—desire for continued possession in the future.[21]

In what follows I will examine absence and presence and their interplay in other poems of Theocritus, principally but not only the bucolic poems.

Idyll 1: A Version of Bucolic Origins

If *Idyll* 1 is, as most scholars agree, "programmatic" for Theocritean bucolic poetry and deserves its initial position in the corpus;[22] if Daphnis represents the archetypal herdsman-singer; if his suffering and death from love represent the founding moment of bucolic poetry, so that "the sufferings of Daphnis" could be a condensed reference to its origins (*Id.* 7.72–77), the title of a song (*Id.* 1.19), or otherwise treated as proverbial (*Id.* 5.20), and the "bucolic song" that the Muses are asked to begin and then end in the refrains to Thyrsis's song embedded in *Idyll* 1 is *the* bucolic song; and if, therefore, in *Idyll* 1, bucolic poetry is constructing a history for itself; then the inaugural event of that poetry is a loss, and absence is the founding condition of bucolic.[23] Thyrsis is Daphnis's successor, and to the extent that his song is "programmatic," every bucolic song in some sense represents

---

21. Pl. *Symp.* 200b9–d10. For discussion of *Idyll* 12, see Payne 2007, 100–111.

22. Even if this position was not planned by Theocritus, ancient editors clearly thought that *Idyll* 1 belonged first. See Gutzwiller 1996. Gutzwiller 2006 has also suggested that *Idyll* 1 encapsulates the full range of meanings that βουκολεῖν ("to bucolicize") had acquired by Theocritus's time—an excellent way of appreciating how "foundational" for bucolic this poem is.

23. On the refrains, with their emphasis on the processes of beginning and ending, as expressions of the inaugural function of Daphnis's story for bucolic song, see also Billault 2006, 326, 328–329.

an attempt to overcome the loss of Daphnis, to restore that archetypal voice. But Daphnis's death can be read as the loss of the full presence of the bucolic world itself, a condition in which humans and animals share a sympathetic bond (the wild animals howl in the forest in grief for the dying Daphnis, and his cattle gather at his feet to mourn) and gods appear freely to mortals.

By implication, then, bucolic poetry would be an attempt to reconnect with the fullness of that world. Thyrsis claims that his voice is "sweet" (Θύρσιδος ἀδέα φωνά, *Id.* 1.65). The adjective is, of course, the first word of the poem, where it describes the whispering of the pine trees and seems programmatic for Theocritean bucolic.[24] Thyrsis then says that the goatherd's piping is also "sweet," and the goatherd says that Thyrsis's singing is "sweeter" than the sound of spring water running down a rock (*Id.* 1.1, 7–8). The echo of the poem's opening in line 65 places Thyrsis's song about Daphnis in close relation to the harmony of nature. But Thyrsis's song is fleeting; its three refrains emphasize beginning and then ending, and the middle one (lines 94–122) calls on the Muses to begin the song *again* (πάλιν). At the end, with a significant recurrence of the word "sweet," he anticipates further performances of his song when he promises the Muses that he will sing to them "more sweetly" (ἄδιον, *Id.* 1.145). The song lacks the permanence and continuity of the plashing water; it must end and has to begin again repeatedly. Thus, each song is at best an approximation; it can never succeed in realizing the fullness of nature or in restoring Daphnis's voice to full and lasting presence. Even if that were possible, in Idyll 1, it comes to us mediated by Thyrsis, whose own voice can only be recreated by someone else in performance or, through the medium of a written text, by a reader's imagination. Any attempt to recreate *the* song can only ever be repetition and replication, but this is what keeps bucolic song always "beginning again." Moments in which Theocritus's poems seem to grasp some of that fullness are rare and, as we shall see, always somehow qualified. More often the poems dwell on absence.

The situation that precipitates Daphnis's death also is one of absence. Priapos, who cannot see what all the fuss is about, asks him (*Id.* 1.82–85):

Δάφνι τάλαν, τί τὺ τάκεαι; ἁ δε τυ κώρα
πάσας ἀνὰ κράνας, πάντ' ἄλσεα ποσσὶ φορεῖται—
ἄρχετε βουκολικᾶς, Μοῖσαι φίλαι, ἄρχετ' ἀοιδᾶς.
ζατεῖσ[α] . . .

---

24. On this word as creating an aesthetic of sweetness and pleasure in bucolic poetry in opposition to Plato's criticisms of poetry and as an alternative to Callimachean aesthetics, see Sistakou 2021.

> Wretched Daphnis, why are you melting? The girl
> is running among all springs, all groves—
> Begin, dear Muses, begin the bucolic song—
> searching for you . . .

Whatever the exact circumstances—whether his and the girl's mutual love for some reason cannot be satisfied, or he is keeping himself aloof from her in order to keep a pledge of fidelity to a Nymph, or something else[25]—Daphnis is a victim of eros, and for some reason, he and the girl are irremediably absent from each other. That is, bucolic poetry's foundational story of Daphnis's absence from the bucolic world contains within it, evidently as its cause, another and parallel absence. The latter is emphasized by the heavy enjambment across the refrain of the participle ζατεῖσ[α] ("searching"), the only instance of such enjambment in Thyrsis's song. The Nymph is permanently frozen in a frenzy of movement across the enjambment, always searching (as is emphasized by the heavy stop after the participle) and never finding Daphnis—the condition of bucolic poetry itself. Judith Haber has suggested that the refrains in this song "[serve] to remove us from the events being portrayed, to foreground the formal qualities of the artist's performance, and to affirm the primacy of stasis and continuity over movement, disruption, and death."[26] In this case, interruption by the refrain creates a stasis of the girl's perpetual movement that replicates bucolic poetry's continual seeking for wholeness and fulfillment and its compulsion to keep "beginning again."

This textual effect imitates on the page or papyrus scroll the narrative's spatial enactment of the separation between the girl and Daphnis. This enactment takes place through the contrast between the woods where she runs and the open pastureland where he is wasting and between the frantic motion of her body and the immobility of his. Priapos's words imply a question similar to the one we raised in connection with the goatherd and the bee in *Idyll* 3: why cannot Daphnis and the girl simply get together? The answer is the same: because human sexuality is more complex than that of the animal world—a distinction that Priapos by his nature would never understand. This reminder of the separation between the human

---

25. For a helpful consideration of various possibilities, see Ogilvie 1962. If the girl is the same as the one named as Daphnis's love object in *Id.* 7.73, her name, Xenea, would stress her inaccessibility to him; she is "the stranger, the foreign, the alien." A new interpretation has been advanced by Anagnostou-Laoutides and Konstan 2008: Daphnis loves Aphrodite, whose now-abandoned consort he is in accordance with Near Eastern myth. Presumably, *Id.* 7.73 would reflect a different version of the Daphnis story. In this case, too, Daphnis desires what is inaccessible to him—a point explicitly made by the authors (2008, 522–523). The situation presupposed in Thyrsis's song is murky, but my point is the same whatever view one takes.

26. Haber 1994, 18.

and the bucolic world, which is sharpened by Priapos's subsequent words (*Id.* 1.85–88, discussed earlier), cuts against the notion of bucolic presence, in which humans fit harmoniously into nature and its conditions. Now we see that whereas the poem presents such fullness at the moment of its disappearance, it was an impossible ideal all along; its "loss" is a way of speaking about something we never had to begin with. Thus, even if we wish to see the story of Daphnis as a "mythic" expression of a lost harmonious presence, it seems that Theocritus is qualifying as an artificial construct what he is at the same time depicting as one of the founding presuppositions of bucolic as a poetic type.

In fact, it seems that when Daphnis is on the point of death, he is already in some sense outside the bucolic world. First in a succession of three gods, Hermes comes to him "from the mountain" (ἀπ' ὤρεος, *Id.* 1.77). The natural inference is that Daphnis is not there, and so, as John van Sickle suggests,[27] not in bucolic space if that is what "the mountain" designates here, as it seems to do everywhere else in the bucolic *Idylls*. It is difficult to tell where Daphnis is. He refers to having pastured his cattle "here" and having watered his bulls and cows "here" (*Id.* 1.120–21), so that he is still amid bucolic surroundings. Perhaps, then, just as the bucolic world is not literally on a mountain elsewhere, since the landscape seems to be in the foothills, "mountain" is used quasi-metaphorically here: the dying Daphnis no longer belongs to that world and is visited by divinities who do, Hermes, Priapos, and (by virtue of having been Adonis's lover) Aphrodite, who step out of it briefly.

Not only is Daphnis displaced, but the scene of his death also takes place amid another absence. The first words of the song proper, after a line identifying the singer, are these (*Id.* 1.66–69):

πᾷ ποκ' ἄρ' ἦσθ', ὅκα Δάφνις ἐτάκετο, πᾷ ποκα, Νύμφαι;
ἢ κατὰ Πηνειῶ καλὰ τέμπεα, ἢ κατὰ Πίνδω;
οὐ γὰρ δὴ ποταμοῖο μέγαν ῥόον εἴχετ' Ἀνάπω,
οὐδ' Αἴτνας σκοπιάν, οὐδ' Ἄκιδος ἱερὸν ὕδωρ.

> Where were you, when Daphnis was wasting, where, Nymphs?
> In the beautiful valleys of the Peneios or of Pindos?
> For indeed you were not present at the great stream of Anapos,
> nor on the peak of Aitna, nor at the holy water of Akis.

---

27. Van Sickle 1969, 137.

The Nymphs, rather than the Muses (at least in most cases), seem to be the inspiring patronesses of Theocritean bucolic.[28] Their absence would then signal the end of archetypal bucolic song as embodied by Daphnis, to which later herdsmen-singers such as Thyrsis can only look back as their model.[29] Or perhaps the idea is that the Nymphs could have saved Daphnis if they had been present (but how?), but their absence, especially if it is to avoid a death that they as divinities have foreseen, can be taken as a sign of indifference and so as another disjunction within the bucolic setting in Sicily.

And there is another absence that should surprise us. Just as Thyrsis addresses the Nymphs, Daphnis calls upon the absent Pan (*Id.* 1.123–130):

> ὦ Πὰν Πάν, εἴτ' ἐσσὶ κατ' ὤρεα μακρὰ Λυκαίω,
> εἴτε τύγ' ἀμφιπολεῖς μέγα Μαίναλον, ἔνθ' ἐπὶ νᾶσον
> τὰν Σικελάν, Ἑλίκας δὲ λίπε ῥίον αἰπύ τε σᾶμα
> τῆνο Λυκαονίδαο, τὸ καὶ μακάρεσσιν ἀγητόν.
>   λήγετε βουκολικᾶς, Μοῖσαι, ἴτε λήγετ' ἀοιδᾶς.
> ἔνθ' ὦναξ, καὶ τάνδε φέρευ πακτοῖο μελίπνουν
> ἐκ κηρῶ σύριγγα καλὸν περὶ χεῖλος ἑλικτάν·
> ἦ γὰρ ἐγὼν ὑπ' Ἔρωτος ἐς Ἄιδαν ἕλκομαι ἤδη.

> O Pan, Pan, whether you are on the huge mountain range of Lykaion,
> or if you frequent great Mainalos, come to the island
> of Sicily, leave the ridge of Helike and that high tomb
> of Lykaon's son there, wondered at by even the gods.
>   Cease, Muses, cease the bucolic song.
> Come, lord, and receive this *syrinx* honey-fragrant

---

28. Walker 1980, 42–43; Fantuzzi 2000, 145–147; 2004, 152–156. That Thyrsis invokes the Muses to begin and end the bucolic song Fantuzzi attributes to its subject, Daphnis, being a mythical as well as a bucolic figure, which would bring the song at least partly into the orbit of Homer and Hesiod. Line 141 can be read as reflecting Daphnis's simultaneous mythic and bucolic identities: Daphnis, as he dies, is described as "the man dear to the Muses, the man not hateful to the Nymphs." We might also see the line as an acknowledgment at once of bucolic's affinities with epic and, through the Nymphs, of its distance from most of epic in subject matter. More pointedly, we might see the Nymphs as rivals to the Muses as patronesses of bucolic poetry and in the process of displacing them. Displacement of the Muses could also be a questioning of traditional ideas of poetic inspiration that had been associated with orality in favor of textuality. Who needs the Muses when you have the Library? Cf. Berger 1984, 33, who suggests that *Idyll* 7 "shows that [bucolic poetry] finds both inspiration and art by moving into the city and toward the Library."

29. Or one could take Stanzel's approach (1995, 267): bucolic song is about herdsmen in love, but since Daphnis resists love, the Nymphs cannot help him. On this view, it is the archetypal singer's own character and choice that spell the end to fully authentic bucolic song.

> from hardened wax and with its lip beautifully fastened all around.
> For I am dragged by Eros to Hades now.

As in Thyrsis's invocation of the Nymphs, the list of places where the divinity might be focuses attention on Sicily, the "here" of the narrative, as a place from which he is absent. The epithets μακρά, μέγα, αἰπύ, and ἀγητόν ("huge," "great," "high," "wondered at") make those other places vivid to the mind's eye, and the imperatives ἔνθ(ε) and λίπε ("come," "leave") seek to overcome the distance between them and Sicily through language and to summon Pan's presence. The demonstrative τάνδε and the detailed description call particular attention to the *syrinx* as a significant object in this bucolic landscape that would forge a relationship between the dying Daphnis and Pan if the god were to come and receive it (the verb literally means "carry it off for your own"). All of this happens at the moment of loss, when Daphnis is being dragged to Hades "now"; the adverb gains emphasis by its placement at the end of its line and sentence, and the Muses, previously invoked to begin the bucolic song, are now for the first time asked to end it, so that the ending of the song is coordinated with Daphnis's death and perhaps re-enacts it. Pan's arrival would therefore mean some kind of continuity in the form of the *syrinx* amid that absence: a memorial and reminder of Daphnis, and presumably the survival of bucolic song after the death of the archetypal singer, even if in attenuated form—a survival now enacted by Thyrsis's singing.

So far there seems to be a positive meaning here for the genealogy of bucolic song. But the passage is peculiar from another perspective. Formally, with the εἴτε... εἴτε ("if... if") clauses, it follows the pattern of prayers to gods to appear, or at any rate to aid the speaker.[30] Instead, Daphnis summons Pan in order to give him a *syrinx*, and against the background of the Muses' gift of a staff or *skeptron* to Hesiod[31] and in the context of song, the gift of a significant object has the aura of a poetic investiture.[32] Here, however, the usual relationship is reversed, and it is a mortal who seems to be conferring the gift of song on a god—one who, in fact, is presented at the beginning of the poem as the *syrinx* player par excellence (*Id.* 1.3).[33] Are we to take seriously the implied claim that one type of bucolic music descends from a mortal through a god? Or should we understand it as part of

---

30. Cf., e.g., *Il.* 16.514–516; Aesch. *Eum.* 292–298.

31. Hes. *Theog.* 30–34; cf. *Id.* 7.128–129.

32. For this *syrinx* as a symbol of bucolic poetry, see Cairns 1984, 101. He suggests (107–108) that the passage has affinities with "the motif of dedicating the tools of one's trade to a god at the end of a career," but surely the Hesiodic model is also operative.

33. For other paradoxes at work in this passage, see Haber 1994, 16–17.

Daphnis's deathbed rhetoric, in which he seems to take self-dramatization a bit far (see below)? In support of the latter possibility is the fact that singing and *syrinx* playing are distinct—in fact, mutually exclusive—and that the opening of the poem seems to imply a distinction between Pan's activities and the singing that will take place (*Id.* 1.12–22).[34]

In fact, within Thyrsis's song, Pan never appears to claim the *syrinx*, so that we have, most unusually, an abortive *Dichterweihe*. We cannot look here for the genealogy of bucolic, and Pan remains part of the imagined bucolic world but not at its origin. We are left with Thyrsis's song as an attempt to reconnect with Daphnis's singing by celebrating his death. But even here the success of restoring that lost presence through song is not straightforward—a subject I would like to explore by drawing on Jonathan Culler's essay "Apostrophe."[35] Culler is concerned with post-Enlightenment English, French, and German lyric poetry, but his insights will transfer readily to Theocritean bucolic, in which, as Payne has shown, fictionalization is so prominent.[36]

Apostrophe, Culler observes, is peculiar because "it makes its point by troping not on the meaning of a word but on the circuit or situation of communication itself."[37] By its nature, it is founded on absence: it addresses someone who is not actually there, or inanimate physical surroundings, and seeks to summon them into presence. Thus,

> to apostrophize is to will a state of affairs, to attempt to call it into being by asking inanimate objects to bend themselves to your desire. In these terms the function of apostrophe would be to make the objects of the universe potentially responsive forces. . . . The apostrophizing poet identifies his universe as a world of sentient forces.[38]

By constituting the world or objects in it as a responsive subject, the apostrophizing speaker creates an "I–thou" relationship with his or her surroundings.

---

34. Cf. Walker 1980, 35: "In this section of *Idyll* 1 [lines 1–20] Theocritus is intent on defining a hierarchy of pastoral art forms, from simple piping to that recreation of ancient myth and legend which was one of the preoccupations of Alexandrian poetry."

35. Culler 1981. On various kinds of address in Theocritus (including, briefly, apostrophe) used to create the bucolic world and bring it to life for the reader—an approach compatible with mine—see Myers 2016.

36. Payne 2007.

37. Culler 1981, 135.

38. Culler 1981, 139.

In this very act, furthermore, the speaker at the same time constitutes him- or herself as a subject: "one who successfully invokes nature is one to whom nature might, in its turn, speak."[39] "To read apostrophe as a sign of fiction which knows its own fictive nature," therefore, "is to stress its optative character, its impossible imperatives."[40]

An excellent example of what Culler describes occurs when Daphnis, on the point of death, takes leave of his surroundings (*Id.* 1.115–121; this comes just before his invocation of Pan, quoted above):

> ὦ λύκοι, ὦ θῶες, ὦ ἀν' ὤρεα φωλάδες ἄρκτοι,
> χαίρεθ'· ὁ βουκόλος ὕμμιν ἐγὼ Δάφνις οὐκέτ' ἀν' ὕλαν,
> οὐκέτ' ἀνὰ δρυμώς, οὐκ ἄλσεα. χαῖρ', Ἀρέθοισα,
> καὶ ποταμοὶ τοὶ χεῖτε καλὸν κατὰ Θύβριδος ὕδωρ.
>   ἄρχετε βουκολικᾶς, Μοῖσαι, πάλιν ἄρχετ' ἀοιδᾶς.
> Δάφνις ἐγὼν ὅδε τῆνος ὁ τὰς βόας ὧδε νομεύων,
> Δάφνις ὁ τὼς ταύρως καὶ πόρτιας ὧδε ποτίσδων.

> O wolves, O jackals, O bears with lairs throughout the mountains,
> Farewell. I, Daphnis, the cowherd, am no longer present for you among
>   the forest,
> no longer among the thickets, or the groves. Farewell, Arethusa,
> and you rivers who pour your lovely water down from Thybris.
>   Begin, Muses, begin again the bucolic song.
> I whom you see here am that Daphnis, the one who herded cows here,
> Daphnis, who watered his bulls and calves here.

Before considering this passage in detail, it will be useful to discuss why it is not wholly satisfactory to call it an example of the "pathetic fallacy." Some scholars, in fact, have expressed skepticism that this phenomenon has much significance in Theocritus's poetry.[41] On the other hand, J. L. Buller[42] makes a strong case for its importance and argues that, although there are precursors in earlier poetry, it

---

39. Culler 1981, 142.

40. Culler 1981, 146.

41. For example, Dick 1968 argues that the "pathetic fallacy" is not essential to Theocritus's bucolic poems in the way it is to Vergil's *Eclogues*. Rosenmeyer 1969, 249, who says that "Theocritus . . . has little room for the pathetic fallacy," shows why it is necessary to be precise as to what we are talking about when we use the term.

42. Buller 1981.

makes its appearance in the form in which we know it in the Hellenistic period in tandem with certain other intellectual and cultural developments. His view, however, that the pathetic fallacy implies an actual unity between humanity and nature goes to my central point here. For example, he writes in connection with pseudo-Moschus's *Lament for Bion*, and particularly its first four lines, "there is nothing in the universe which does not grieve for Bion."[43] This claim overlooks the fact that all the verbs in that passage are imperatives urging natural elements and flora to mourn, not statements that they do so. At the end of his article, Buller makes the interesting point that the reason nature grieves at human death is that plants die and germinate again, whereas individual humans die absolutely. But that is to say that the "pathetic fallacy" is predicated on a gap between humans and nature that it only draws attention to by striving to overcome it. This is exactly the point I want to make. The advantage of doing so in terms of apostrophe is that the label "pathetic fallacy" too often blocks further examination of how passages like the one just quoted really work. Recognizing the rhetorical trope that underlies them brings out the fictive, wishful assumptions about the world that inform them. It also illuminates what they essentially have in common with invocations of gods, such as Daphnis's apostrophe of Pan.

What are the implications, then, when Daphnis addresses wild animals and natural features—the spring Arethusa and the rivers that pour down from Thybris (perhaps the mountain with rocky gorges above Syracuse)?[44] The first thing to notice is that the domesticated herd animals are not addressed in apostrophe here, even though they are earlier mentioned alongside wolves, jackals, and lions as mourning for Daphnis (*Id.* 1.71–75). There the herd animals were present at his feet, whereas the more distant untamed beasts could only be heard howling. Here Daphnis invokes wild animals and inanimate features of the natural world, both of which are separate from human culture, and seeks to make them present, to constitute them as feeling and responsive to him, and to put them into relation with himself. This "I–thou" relationship is indicated by the pathos-laden ὔμμιν ("for you") in line 116, which I have translated rather clumsily above in order to bring out this attempt at forging a connection whereby the animals and streams are expected to feel sorrow at the loss of Daphnis. Word order stresses this assumed connection: "for you" is enfolded between "the cowherd" and "I" (ὁ βουκόλος ὔμμιν ἐγώ). Daphnis's anaphoric use in line 115 of the particle ὤ, which was not used in spoken Greek in the Hellenistic period, seems also to claim a special relationship with the animals and may convey intense feeling as

---

43. Buller 1981, 36.

44. On Thybris, see Hunter 1999, 99.

well.[45] Right after these lines and the intervening refrain, Daphnis asserts his own identity and significance as a cowherd (that is, he constitutes himself as a bucolic subject), and he does so emphatically: the first four words of line 120 mean literally "Daphnis-I-this one here-that one [who]." In lines 120 and 121, Daphnis names himself for the third and fourth time out of five instances. In the other places, he speaks of himself in the third person; he "sees himself in a dramatic light."[46] Here he is claiming an identity as an "I," a subject.[47] The demonstrative ὅδε marks, as it often does, a person present physically or in one's thoughts. With it, Daphnis is claiming his presence to the animals and elements that he seeks to make present to himself (hence my translation, "whom you see"). The other demonstrative, τῆνος, will then mean "that one you know about," or "the famous one," and asserts Daphnis's place in the world he is leaving, which his addressees are assumed to know.[48]

These are all presuppositions underlying Daphnis's apostrophe and reflected in his language. Nature—even the untamed animals lurking in the wilds beyond the more gentle bucolic world—is constructed as sympathetic, as though there were a deep connection between it and humans. Notice, however, that the vision Daphnis assumes is a human-centered one that sees nature as an extension of the human. What if the natural world is actually indifferent? True, these same wild beasts howl as Daphnis lies dying, but that they do so in grief is a human inference. Then there is Daphnis's situation itself, caused by desire

---

45. See Williams 1973, 66, who classifies the line as a "hymnic formula" (i.e., one in which a mortal tries to establish a special connection with a god) and notes that it is the only certain case in genuine Theocritus of animals being addressed with ὦ.

46. A phrase I owe to T. S. Eliot 1960, 81: "The really fine rhetoric of Shakespeare occurs in situations where a character in the play *sees himself* in a dramatic light" (emphasis in original). The other instances are *Id.* 1.103, 113, and 135.

47. See Purchase's excellent treatment of Daphnis's self-naming and of the passage discussed here (2003–2005, 89). Daphnis's attempt at self-constitution fails, Purchase says, because he cannot bring his desires for dependence and autonomy into proper alignment (note especially his remark that Daphnis "swings between immersion and difference, between nature and Aphrodite, in his relationship with the external"). Purchase goes on to argue that Thyrsis is more successful, in virtue of his singing. We can see this difference, I would add, if we contrast Daphnis's ὕμμιν ἐγώ, addressed to the animals in farewell (line 116) with Thyrsis's ἐγὼ δ' ὕμμιν, addressed to the Muses with a promise of a "sweeter" song in the future (line 145): finality as opposed to continuity.

48. Hunter 1999, 99, comments on lines 120–121, "As Virgil saw (and made explicit), Daphnis here writes his own epitaph." An epitaph couched in the first person at least notionally addresses someone (a passerby at the tomb), and the dynamics are similar to those of apostrophe; so my reading of the lines is compatible with Hunter's (and Vergil's). The Vergilian passage is *Ecl.* 5.43–44, where Vergil both captures the flavor of Daphnis's self-assertion and does Theocritus one better: *Daphnis ego in silvis, hinc usque ad sidera notus.*

The Poetics of Absence

and absence. Priapos's rebuke (*Id.* 1.86–91), as we have seen, sets the complexity of culture off from the natural world's direct fulfillment of desire, so that humans are not finally one with nature, whatever unity Daphnis has enjoyed before now.

There is, in fact, a series of three apostrophes on Daphnis's part, from line 115 to line 136: to wild animals and streams, to Pan who does not appear, and finally to nature itself in optatives of wish (*Id.* 1.132–136; recall Culler's phrases about apostrophe: "its optative character, its impossible imperatives"):[49]

νῦν ἴα μὲν φορέοιτε βάτοι, φορέοιτε δ' ἄκανθαι,
ἁ δὲ καλὰ νάρκισσος ἐπ' ἀρκεύθοισι κομάσαι,
πάντα δ' ἄναλλα γένοιτο, καὶ ἁ πίτυς ὄχνας ἐνείκαι,
Δάφνις ἐπεὶ θνάσκει, καὶ τὰς κύνας ὤλαφος ἕλκοι,
κἠξ ὀρέων τοὶ σκῶπες ἀηδόσι γαρύσαιντο.

Now bring forth violets, you brambles, bring them forth, thornbushes,
and may the beautiful narcissus blossom on junipers,
let everything change, and let the pine tree bear pears,
since Daphnis dies, and let the stag harass the hounds,
and may the owls hoot from the mountain in competition with
    nightingales.

These are Daphnis's last words. He expects his absence in death to disorder nature, but in fact nothing happens.[50] Nature retains its lovely order and harmonious sounds, as the opening lines of this poem, set in the post-Daphnis world, make clear. The last line quoted may have poetological overtones, since nightingales are often a figure for skilled poets. Daphnis would then be envisioning a world in which inferior poets can compete on an equal footing with the pure-voiced

---

49. At least, the passage begins as a direct apostrophe, although the verbs then shift into the third person.

50. For a different view of these lines, see Gershenson 1974. As in other cultures, he argues, though nowhere else in Greco-Roman literature, a "topsy-turvy world" is a world of enhanced loveliness that is emblematic of death. Daphnis is thus inviting nature to join him in dying. A problem, I think, is that whereas the first two lines of the passage might be read as describing improvements to nature, it is hard to say the same about stags attacking hounds and owls hooting against nightingales. But if Gershenson is correct, that would not affect my point: nature does not, in fact, die with Daphnis, and he is not as central to it as he seems to expect. On either reading, as Gershenson says, Daphnis "pictures himself as Nature's Life. When he leaves all things can be subject to reversal, for he is no longer with them to give them life" (27), but nature remains itself without him.

singers of bucolic like himself.[51] But there is Thyrsis's song to show that poetry has not been altogether degraded, and the victory that he won with it over Khromis seems sufficiently memorable that his rival was a worthy competitor (*Id.* 1.23–24). Thyrsis's rebuke of the Nymphs falls into the same pattern as Daphnis's apostrophes. It also seeks to construct nature as responsive to human needs and desires, but it is unanswered. It, too, is paradigmatic, like the story of Daphnis's death: it shows bucolic poetry always striving to overcome the gap between humanity and nature that was opened up by the loss of Daphnis and never quite succeeding. As I argued in chapter 1, the spatial relations in the first part of *Idyll* 1 imply that the bucolic world inhabited by Daphnis's heirs, the goatherd and Thyrsis, is conditioned by the same interplay between identification with nature and distinctness from it. That is to say that there is a deep connection between the poem's frame and the song that is its center.

To say these things is not to deny that Daphnis's death really is a loss or that there are differences between conditions before and after that event. In other ways than I have mentioned, Daphnis represents a time of particular closeness between humans and nature. His herd animals evidently do mourn for him, and wherever the Nymphs and Pan might be, three divinities—Hermes, Priapos, and Aphrodite—do come to him in his last moments. But this is a world at the moment of its slipping away, a crisis that bucolic poetry represents as the moment of its own birth as a means of attempting to renew that lost presence and fullness. At the same time, it is a world already marked by absences, of Pan and the Nymphs. And we have seen how the series of Daphnis's apostrophes highlights—for the reader, at least—the fictionality of that world and of the whole notion of the presence of the human and natural orders to each other.[52] I do not mean *mere* fiction. As Wolfgang Iser argues, fictionality is important to human beings. It "provides the paradoxical (and perhaps, for this very reason, desirable) opportunity for human beings simultaneously to be in the midst of life and to overstep it." And "it presents the constitutive dividedness of human beings as the source of possible worlds within the world."[53] And so I am not arguing that fictionality undercuts bucolic fullness as an authentic object of

---

51. Cf., e.g., *Id.* 7.41, 47–48, *Id.* 5.136–137. On further implications of the line, see Hunter 1999, 103–104.

52. Miles 1977, 145, seems to come close to this point when he says, in connection with the opening of *Idyll* 1, "the herdsmen's relationship to the landscape, to their gods and to each other is largely a reflection of their own attitudes and their own perceptions."

53. Iser 1993, 79–86 (quotations from 83 and 84). This is the last section of a chapter titled "Renaissance Pastoralism as a Paradigm of Literary Fictionality." I think that Iser's ideas can also be applied to Theocritus, whom he discusses early in the chapter.

The Poetics of Absence

desire. Rather, the two coexist, and perhaps the former is even the ground for the latter.[54]

Fictionality raises the issue of the relation between poetry and the bucolic world, which we can address by asking one more question of *Idyll* 1: what makes Thyrsis's song especially good? As readers, we might want to give various answers, but the text emphasizes one: the quality of his voice. Right at the beginning of the song, when Thyrsis identifies himself and his place of origin, the one other thing he tells us about himself is the sweetness of his voice (*Id.* 1.65):

Θύρσις ὅδ' ὠξ Αἴτνας, καὶ Θύρσιδος ἀδέα φωνά.

I here am Thyrsis, the one from Aitna, and Thyrsis's voice is sweet.

This emphasis is, as we have seen, in keeping with the beginning of the poem, which describes the sweetness of natural sounds and the herdsmen's music. At the end, the grateful goatherd also mentions sweet things in his tribute to Thyrsis's singing (*Id.* 1.146–148):

πλῆρές τοι μέλιτος τὸ καλὸν στόμα, Θύρσι, γένοιτο,
πλῆρες δὲ σχαδόνων, καὶ ἀπ' Αἰγίλω ἰσχάδα τρώγοις
ἁδεῖαν, τέττιγος ἐπεὶ τύγα φέρτερον ᾄδεις.

Full of honey may your lovely mouth be, Thyrsis,
and full of honeycombs, and may you eat the fig from Aigilos,
the sweet fig, since you sing better than the cicada.

Honey was traditionally associated with eloquence and poetry.[55] To the extent that this usage is metaphorical, it gives a picture of the flow of beautiful speech

---

54. Here I am trying to get beyond the opposition between the "ironic" and "nostalgic" readings of Theocritus, as discussed by Berger 1984, who takes Miles 1977 and Segal 1981 as representative of these approaches, respectively. I find those labels rather misleading. Miles, for instance, acknowledges that Theocritus holds up the "ideal of innocence" to the reader but shows its inadequacy as a way of living or understanding the world. My own discussion of absence and presence goes in a different direction but fits well within his argument, although I would rather see the pulls toward the bucolic ideal and toward a recognition of the complexity of life as forming a tension or dialectic within the poems instead of a rejection of the former in favor of the latter. Kühn 1958, 74–79, interestingly, sees both as constituent elements of the poems, represented in *Idyll* 7 by the songs of Lykidas and Simikhidas, respectively, but the move he then makes into biographical speculation tends to obscure the value of his insight for our reading of Theocritus.

55. E.g., *Il.* 1.249: Nestor's voice flowed from his tongue sweeter than honey; Hes. *Theog.* 83–84: the Muses pour on the tongue of the *basileus* a sweet liquid (to be identified with honey,

as the sweet ooze of honey. In the present passage, there is a pleasing, if somewhat extravagant, reciprocity in the notion of the mouth filled with honey as a reward for the flowing out of honey-sweet song.[56] Emphasis on the mouth also works with honey to give a physical heft to the "sweet voice"—an effect that is set off by contrast with the "deep gullet" from which Herakles's inarticulate roars for the absent Hylas issue (*Id.* 13.58: ὅσον βαθὺς ἤρυγε λαιμός; the verb is indistinguishable in form from a possibly related word for "belch"). In the goatherd's compliment to Thyrsis, note especially "your *lovely* mouth"; the point is probably not so much Thyrsis's appearance, to which we are otherwise given no clue, as the beauty of his singing.

Elsewhere in the Theocritean corpus, the voice, honey, and the mouth also form an interrelated complex to describe the physical origin and the effect of beautiful song. I will discuss the case of Komatas in *Idyll* 7 below, but in the same poem, Simikhidas claims that he is the καπυρὸν στόμα, "pure (?) mouth," of the Muses. We do not do justice to the physical implications if we translate the noun as "mouthpiece"; the Muses literally sing through his mouth, he boasts. The meaning of the adjective is unknown. It is cognate with καπνός, "smoke," and may be associated with the breath, as the related verb καπύειν is (e.g., *Il.* 22.467); in that case, it, too, has a physical reference. The adjective also can mean "dry"[57] or can describe a piercing sound.[58] Possibly, then, it refers to the shrill voice of cicadas, themselves a common figure for poetry; the goatherd compliments Thyrsis by saying that he sings more sweetly than they do (*Id.* 1.148, quoted above). An epigram attributed to Theocritus (*A.P.* 9.437 = 4 Gow) has these lines (11–12):

ξουθαὶ δ' ἀδονίδες μινυρίσμασιν ἀνταχεῦσι
μέλπουσαι στόμασιν τὰν μελίγαρυν ὄπα.

West 1966, 183), and the words flow soothing (μείλιχα, perhaps associated by popular etymology with honey, μέλι). For the conceptual background, see Waszink 1974, 6–19, although he does not discuss Hellenistic poetry. On sweetness and honey in the Theocritean passages I have just mentioned here as linking Theocritus's poetry to that of Callimachus, see Cairns 1984, 93–95. Along similar lines, for the mouth filled with honey as a marker for "a light, delicate, refined style," see Worman 2015, 203–204; and on honey as a "synaesthetic symbol" that helps to create a Theocritean aesthetics of "sweetness," see Sistakou 2021, 330–336. I am interested in how those passages and others discussed below all show a marked emphasis on the physicality of the mouth, the voice, and its sweetness.

56. The last line of *Idyll* 3 (54) is a sarcastic parody of this image: the wolves will eat me here, and "may this be like sweet honey in your throat" (ὡς μέλι τοι γλυκὺ τοῦτο κατὰ βρόχθοιο γένοιτο).

57. It refers to a "parching" disease at *Id.* 2.85. On this meaning, see Allègre 1906, who discusses κραμβότατος at Ar. *Eq.* 539, for which the scholiast gives κάπυρος as a synonym.

58. See Chantraine 1999, 494. On the sense "clear," see Legrand 1907, especially 11, for the connection between this meaning and "dry."

And the quavering (?) nightingales in their warbling sing in response
pouring forth with their mouths their honey-toned voice.

Post-Theocritean bucolic picks up on this nexus of ideas, as in these lines (*Id.* 20.25–28):[59]

ὄμματά μοι γλαυκᾶς χαροπώτερα πολλὸν Ἀθάνας,
τὸ στόμα δ' αὖ πακτᾶς ἁπαλώτερον, ἐκ στομάτων δὲ
ἔρρεέ μοι φωνὰ γλυκερωτέρα ἢ μέλι κηρῶ.
ἁδὺ δέ μοι τὸ μέλισμα, καὶ ἢν σύριγγι μελίσδω...

My eyes flashed more brightly than those of gray-eyed Athena.
My mouth was softer than cream cheese, and from my mouth
my voice flowed sweeter than honey from the comb.
Sweet is my song, and if I play on the *syrinx*...

A wordplay associates honey (μέλι) with song (μέλισμα) and the act of singing (μελίσδειν), and this may also be drawn from Theocritus. We might hear a similar association in the first two lines of *Idyll* 1 (ἁδὺ... μελίσδεται), and it is unmistakable at *Id.* 7.89, in the fantasy of Komatas lying ἁδὺ μελισδόμενος ("sweetly singing"), just after he is said to have fed on the honeycomb; the word for "bees" is also brought into the sound play (*Id.* 7.84–85: καὶ τὺ <u>μελισσᾶν</u> / κηρία φερβόμενος).[60]

Why should bucolic poetry insist so emphatically on the quality and physical presence of the singing voice? Because we—the audience—never hear it. It always comes to us mediated in some way.[61] Let us consider again lines 115–121 of *Idyll* 1, quoted earlier as an example of apostrophe. This farewell to the animals and his surroundings and the dramatic self-presentation by Daphnis on the point of death seems intended to convey the effect of the last song of this archetypal

---

59. Cf. *Id.* 8.82–83, appropriately addressed to Daphnis: "Sweet [ἁδύ] is your mouth, Daphnis, and lovely is your voice. / Hearing you sing is better than licking honey."

60. Presumably, *Id.* 10.37 is a parody of the associations we have been examining: ἁ φωνὰ δὲ τρύχνος ("and your voice is a poppy"—or more accurately, it seems, "fleabane"). For possible implications, see Gow 1952, II, 203; Hunter 1999, 210. Their opposite is represented by *Id.* 25.74–75 (the old man's harsh voice when he threatens his dogs): τρηχὺ δὲ φωνῇ / ἠπείλει μάλα πᾶσιν. This phrase is all the more effective when we set it beside the normal bucolic idealization of the honeyed voice.

61. On this point and what follows, see Payne 2007, 46–48, especially 46: "the poem [*Id.*1] deconstructs its own illusion of primitive, oral song even as it produces it." For a different and equally illuminating account of the way Theocritus capitalizes on the shift from oral performance to writing, see Berger 1984, 26–28.

singer, very likely under the influence of Hellenistic euphonist theories. In line 115, the procession of omegas and alphas; the repeated –u- and –ou- sounds; the repetitions (or anaphora) of O ("O wolves, O jackals, O . . . bears," line 115), of "no longer" or "not" and "farewell" in lines 116–117; the name Daphnis beginning lines 120–121 and the end rhymes in those same lines (νομεύων, ποτίσδων, *nomeuōn, potisdōn*)—all these are effects that Hellenistic euphonic theorists considered essential to the beauty and the musicality of poetry from Homer onward.[62] Here this effect of musicality seems designed to bring us as close as possible to the sound of Daphnis's voice singing. But in fact we hear his song only as part of Thyrsis's performance. If we were tempted to think that we were being put into contact with that archetypal singing, we are reminded of the "now" of performance when one of the refrains that run through Thyrsis's song interrupts Daphnis's farewell (*Id.* 1.119):

ἄρχετε βουκολικᾶς, Μοῖσαι, πάλιν ἄρχετ' ἀοιδᾶς.

Begin, Muses, begin again the bucolic song.

Although this is the fourteenth occurrence of the refrain in Daphnis's song, it is especially significant in this context (and its recurrence for the fifteenth and last time at line 122, immediately after the passage we are discussing, drives home the effect). Not only does Thyrsis's voice break through what he represents as Daphnis's voice, but also the self-conscious naming of the type of song he is singing, bucolic, places him in a tradition (at least within this *Idyll*'s fiction; it is in fact in the process of creating a tradition for itself), and the emphatically repeated "begin," along with "again," locates his performance as the latest in a series of repetitions. The goatherd mentions "the sufferings of Daphnis" as a song Thyrsis is accustomed to singing and as the one with which he competed against Khromis the Libyan (*Id.* 1.19–20, 23–25), and Lykidas imagines Tityros singing of Daphnis's love for Xenea and his wasting away (*Id.* 7.72–77). Repeated performances of this theme, of course, keep Daphnis's story alive through generations and spread his fame.[63] But all the repetitions create an ever-growing distance from the authentic, original bucolic song (assuming that there was one). Thyrsis can only invoke the Muse to begin the bucolic song *again*.

---

62. Gutzwiller 2010, 346–354.

63. Kossaifi 2017, 44–46.

This question of keeping a song alive is raised at the end of the goatherd's speech asking Thyrsis to sing, immediately before he starts to do so (*Id.* 1.62–63):[64]

> πόταγ', ὠγαθέ· τὰν γὰρ ἀοιδὰν
> οὔ τί πᾳ εἰς Ἀίδαν γε τὸν ἐκλελάθοντα φυλάξεις.

> Come on, my good friend. For that song of yours—
> there is no way that you will carry it off to Hades that causes
>   forgetfulness and preserve it.

Hades causing forgetfulness means the death of song; its effect is the opposite of the life-affirming gift of the Muses, daughters of Memory. Note the complex layering in these lines. Thyrsis, whose death will bring forgetfulness of his song, is admonished to revive in his singing, while he lives, the memory of Daphnis, whose singing has already been stilled. It seems that the best he can do is keep Daphnis's story alive in some form and renew it, but he can only approximate that story and try without complete success to make contact with Daphnis. And where is Theocritus, where are we, in relation to Thyrsis's song? It seems legitimate to extrapolate from these lines difficult questions about a poetic tradition and the relation of each new generation of poets to the past—questions that clearly were of concern to Hellenistic poets.

What was the original, authoritative story of Daphnis? Was there ever one? As Theocritus and the erudite among his readers surely knew, Daphnis's story existed in several mutually irreconcilable versions.[65] There was no way to get to any original, "true" story. I suggest that it is in acknowledgment of this situation that Theocritus is—notoriously—vague about the nature and cause of Daphnis's erotic sufferings and also about the exact manner of his death. The existence of multiforms of a story might remind us of an oral poetic tradition, in which, within certain limits, a song is created anew in each performance and there is no single song, only songs. And perhaps Theocritus is deliberately suggesting that his poem, *Idyll* 1, has a place within such a tradition. But, however rooted in oral song traditions the story of Daphnis might ultimately have been, it was available to Theocritus through written texts. His poem fits at least as much into a literary tradition as into an oral tradition.

I am suggesting, then, that Theocritus is in the same position with regard to Daphnis's singing as Thyrsis is, but at one further remove: his is the latest in a

---

64. For helpful discussion of these lines, see Kyriakou 2018, 169–171.
65. These are conveniently summarized and discussed by Hunter 1999, 64–67.

chain of repetitions. And so the audience or reader cannot directly experience Daphnis's voice in its full presence; it comes to us as the voice of Thyrsis. But we do not actually hear that, either. Of course, if we take seriously the sweetness of Thyrsis's voice and its superiority to the sound of plashing water, aided by the euphonic effects described above, we might feel that we are getting at least an approximation of Daphnis's voice, although there is always an insurmountable difference. On the one hand, Naomi Kaloudis has recently pointed to Hellenistic euphonist theories to suggest that Theocritus tries to recreate something of the music of folk songs that lie behind bucolic poetry, and she uses *Idyll* 1 as a case study.[66] The many examples she discusses show that the poem as a whole, including Thyrsis's song, and not just Daphnis's farewell, strives for musical effects. So with assonance and other kinds of repetition, including refrains, we can come closer to the immediacy of Thyrsis's performance—but without ever actually getting there. For on the other hand, his song, like *Idyll* 1 as a whole and all the bucolics, is in dactylic hexameter, which is not a sung meter and which, evoking as it does the epic tradition, works together with the allusiveness and generic play of Alexandrian poetry to distance the poem from folk songs even while these are perhaps suggested. And of course, the poem was written and existed from the beginning in written form, so that it is a repetition just as Thyrsis's song is, even though Theocritus may have tried to preserve the fluidity of oral traditions through imprecision about the fundamentals of Daphnis's story. In these respects as in so many others, Theocritean poetry holds opposites in dynamic suspension.

Because Theocritus's poems were disseminated and received through writing, euphonic effects would have been all the more useful as a way to give the reader a greater sense of immediacy, however fictive. The written text, even if read aloud, would have been one more layer of mediation between the reader and Theocritus, who had to attempt to recreate the sweetness of Thyrsis's voice, while Thyrsis in turn tried to reproduce the sweetness of Daphnis's voice in the context of an archetypal bucolic world that was in the process of being lost. The regression of voices here resembles the one we will soon observe in *Idyll* 7. The issues here, however, should not be reduced to a straightforward opposition between orality and writing. Kaloudis argues that in the Hellenistic period, a newly strong book culture did not entirely supplant the earlier "song culture."[67] Although we lack certainty, we should always reckon with the possibility that the *Idylls* were

---

66. Kaloudis 2017.

67. Kaloudis 2017, 211–213, especially "A culture of sound still permeated the pages of this newly educated populace" (212) and "Alexandria's performance aesthetic had a profound literary dimension" (213).

performed before audiences, possibly at symposia or at public festivals, as well as being read in solitude. In a performance of *Idyll* 1, a performer (a professional actor? Theocritus himself?) imitated the voice of Thyrsis just as he had imitated the goatherd's voice, and Daphnis's voice, imitated by Thyrsis, came to the listeners twice removed. Did the listeners, helped by euphonic and other effects, though not by the mode of delivery, which was not singing but at most rhythmical chanting, succumb to the illusion? Or did the circumstance of performance remind them of the distance? We cannot be sure, of course, but it could fairly be asked whether the musical effects differed from those in earlier poetry and whether a performance of Theocritus would have been received differently from performances of earlier poetry.[68]

The answer to the first question is that there would have been no difference in the effects themselves; Hellenistic literary critics found them in texts from the whole range of the Greek tradition. But there was still something new as well: the very fact that, beginning (it seems) in the early third century BCE, euphony was being made the object of study and of theorizing. If, in fact, Theocritus was responding to euphonist theory and putting it into practice, as seems very likely,[69] then he self-consciously aimed at the effects of music and song as earlier poets evidently had not, and he did so in a context in which the presence of the voice was at issue and his poetry sought to recover it. This attempt in itself points to the problem and becomes part of the fabric of the poem.

My answer to the second question runs along similar lines. I do not have to claim that there was an essential difference in general between performances of Theocritus and those of earlier poetry in regard to audience reception. A great proportion of the Homeric epics consists of direct speech. The first time that Nestor speaks in the *Iliad*, the narrator introduces him by saying that "from his tongue the voice flowed sweeter than honey" (*Il.* 1.249) and then quotes him directly in a long speech in which he tries—unsuccessfully—to mediate the quarrel between Agamemnon and Akhilleus. The audience might well have tacitly accepted the fiction that they were hearing Nestor's voice and experiencing the power of its eloquence when in fact they were hearing the narrator quote him in direct speech (the performer might have changed delivery to imitate Nestor, of course, but that would only have reinforced the fiction). So, too, with Theocritus,

---

68. Questions, in fact, posed by a referee for Oxford University Press, whom I would like to thank.

69. In addition to Kaloudis 2017, see the excellent discussion of the intersection of this theory with Alexandrian poetry in Gutzwiller 2010, 351–354, which includes examples from Theocritus. That the influence of the theory can be traced in other poets as well makes it all the more likely that he responded to it.

except for one key point: his repeated insistence on the sweetness of the voice, which is much more sustained than in Homer. In one way, this might have promoted the fiction as in Homer, but it also pointed to the fact that the audience was not experiencing that sweetness directly. In a parallel way, they were hearing chanted hexameters and not an actual song in lyric meters, even though they were assured that Thyrsis was in fact singing. Significantly, when the Homeric poems incorporate an internal song such as the one about Ares and Aphrodite (*Od.* 8.266–367), they generally describe its contents in indirect speech, very likely because the hexameter cannot accommodate lyric.[70] Theocritus's emphasis on song and its sweetness lays bare the gap and stresses, rather than conceals, the artificiality of his poetry. It is a reflex of absence. If you are delivering the real goods, you do not have to keep insisting on their authenticity.

"Sweet" (ἁδύ), the first word of *Idyll* 1, sets the tone for this poem and, inasmuch as *Idyll* 1 is programmatic and exemplary, for the rest of Theocritean bucolic. This poetry gathers the elements of the bucolic world at its best into a unity of sensory experience for the humans in it: the sweet sounds of whispering pine, plashing water, singing and piping, and the harmony of song with the place of singing; the fragrance of the cup, covered with sweet wax and still smelling of the chisel (no rankness of goats and goatherds intrudes on this loveliness); the sweet taste of honeycomb and figs.[71] Using the powerful resources of his art, Theocritus comes so close to creating this world and inviting us into it. And yet Thyrsis and the goatherd do not enter the place of complete merging of human and natural sounds limned in the poem's opening lines but enjoy song in another place close to but not identical with it. And the listener or reader is treated to musical effects rather than music. There is always a gap, some kind of distance, that the poem acknowledges and tries to overcome without ever quite succeeding. And so the poem does not merely embody the dynamics of absence and desire. Absence and desire are its very essence, the ground of its being.

So the listener or reader, the poet, and the very text are in an analogous position to that of the characters within bucolic poetry: aware of the fullness of the bucolic world and even enjoying something like it at times, trying to come close to *the* song but writing, reading, and hearing only transcripts of songs, never fully attaining the object of desire. And it is this desire, aroused by the absence of the

---

70. An exception is the Sirens' song within Odysseus's internal narrative to the Phaiakians (*Od.* 12.184–191). Demodokos's song about Ares and Aphrodite (*Od.* 8.266–327) contains within it direct speech by various gods but is itself extended indirect speech, as the beginning and end make clear (*Od.* 8.268, 367).

71. Kossaifi 2017, 43–44. Cf. Daspet 2017, 111.

authentic bucolic world, which is always an imagined world, that keeps them—us—listening and reading.

Idyll 7: *Lykidas's Song*

Voice is very much at issue in *Idyll* 7, and especially in Lykidas's song (lines 52–89). If the difficulty of hearing the bucolic voice makes us experience the absence and desire that are basic to bucolic poetry in a poem with a mimetic frame, what happens in a poem structured on third-person narrative in which two songs are embedded, one of which imagines a song that only might take place and that in turn imagines another act of singing that cannot occur?

Lykidas's song is generated by desire for someone he does not possess: "scorching eros for him [Ageanax] is burning me up" (*Id.* 7.56). This is Lykidas's present state within the terms of his song, and everything he sings is a wish-fulfilling fantasy in response to his feeling. It is remarkable, then, that what he imagines is the opposite state: Ageanax's absence but his own freedom from desire that would make possible the enjoyment of leisure, comfort, food, drink, and song. The relation between the outer frame of his song and the internal narrative (if we ignore for the moment Tityros's further embedded song) is the opposite of that in *Idyll* 1: in the latter, a scene of enjoyment framing a narrative of suffering, and in *Idyll* 7, a situation of torment from desire leading to a (wished-for) scene of pleasure. Other bucolic figures sing about the torment of absence and loss, but Lykidas, who is the type of the goatherd-poet, sings of the contentment that will accompany Ageanax's absence in Mitylene. Is he then not typical after all? I will argue instead that Lykidas's imagined scene of peace is so contingent that its fulfillment is doubtful and that therefore Ageanax's absence will not free him from desire. So his song is finally about absence after all, even as it constructs a picture of presence.

Everything Lykidas describes depends on one premise, which is expressed in a conditional sentence, a rhetorical form that avoids guaranteeing fulfillment (*Id.* 7.52–56):

ἔσσεται Ἀγεάνακτι καλὸς πλόος ἐς Μιτυλήναν,
χὤταν ἐφ᾽ ἑσπερίοις Ἐρίφοις νότος ὑγρὰ διώκῃ
κύματα, χὠρίων ὅτ᾽ ἐπ᾽ ὠκεανῷ πόδας ἴσχει,
αἴ κα τὸν Λυκίδαν ὀπτεύμενον ἐξ Ἀφροδίτας
ῥύσηται· θερμὸς γὰρ ἔρως αὐτῷ με καταίθει.

Ageanax will have a fair voyage to Mitylene
both when, with the Kids appearing at evening, the south wind chases

the liquid waves, and when Orion holds his feet on the ocean,
if he rescues Lykidas, who is being roasted
by Aphrodite; for scorching desire for him is burning me.

How is Ageanax to rescue Lykidas—by gratifying his desire? If so, the condition Lykidas envisions for himself is one on the other side of desire, one matched, as Hunter says, by the calmness of the sea for Ageanax's voyage.[72] But perhaps Hunter is right to say that "the satisfaction of desire normally leads only to increased desire."[73] And yet the alternative interpretation, which Hunter adopts—that Ageanax's absence will tamp down Lykidas's desire—is even more unsatisfactory. It is hard to believe that such a tepid lover as Lykidas would turn out to be in that case is now being "roasted" by desire.[74] Perhaps the uncertainty is the point. Lykidas himself may not have thought through what form his—or anyone's—rescue from desire might take. The vagueness makes the possibility of rescue rather remote. The reference to the evening appearance of the Kids and the setting of Orion may support this suggestion, since the season designated in this way—late October and November—was notoriously stormy and the wrong time to undertake a sea voyage, a point underscored by the picture of the south wind chasing the waves. This is incongruously juxtaposed with καλὸς πλόος ("fair voyage") in the preceding line. An ancient reader would surely have been aware of the contradiction. The sentence can be read, then, as saying in effect that Ageanax is as likely to rescue Lykidas from desire as he is to have an easy late-autumn voyage.[75] The continuation of the sentence (lines 57–60) after the lines quoted above, which describe the halcyons calming the waves, may point in the same direction if the passage refers to halcyon days, which were believed to occur

---

72. Hunter 1999, 167.

73. Hunter 1999, 168.

74. A further possibility, that with the mention of the stormy season at sea Lykidas is subtly trying to keep Ageanax with him, involves the difficulty that the scene Lykidas goes on to describe, which is to take place on the day Ageanax reaches Mitylene (τῆνο κατ' ἆμαρ, line 63), will not occur if he stays. One could argue that for Lykidas, enjoying Ageanax's love would be better than that scene of solitary enjoyment. This would dovetail with my argument about the contingency of that scene, but it depends on some rather tenuous inferences. So does Stanzel's suggestion (1995, 273–274) that Lykidas is trying at once to remove any possible obstacles to Ageanax gratifying his desires by reminding him that the journey can be made later and to keep him from leaving by describing the attractions of staying.

75. An alternative is Hunter's explanation (1999, 168): "the point does not lie in chronological specificity: if Ageanax 'saves' Lykidas, he will have a fair voyage *whenever* he sails, even if he sails at the least propitious time of the year." This is possible, and I offer my own reading only as another possibility. It has the advantage of turning the obscurities of the passage to positive account.

at the winter solstice.[76] The blending of incompatible time markers adds to the impression of unreality surrounding this voyage. This unreality and the parallel vagueness about how Lykidas might be rescued from desire, then, point to that rescue as inconceivable—appropriately so, because bucolic poetry, according to its basic premise, cannot exist without restless desire.

Thus, the scene of post-desire contentment that Lykidas goes on to describe is contingent on an impossibility in the terms of bucolic poetry, and we have bucolic singing imagined as taking place outside its own essential conditions. Its contingency and unreality only affirm the strength of those conditions. But of course, in its own way, desire for the end of desire generates song. The contingency of this result is marked in other ways besides doubt that it can ever occur. Lykidas's vision of enjoyment is set in the future relative to the present time of his song, as the verb tenses of lines 64–72 show, and the two lines (61–62) that make the transition to the description of quiet festivity and recapitulate the preceding passage are couched as wishes, with verbs in the optative ("may Ageanax reach harbor safely").[77]

"On that day" of Ageanax's arrival (if it happens), Lykidas will, he imagines, lie wreathed by the fire drinking wine, munching beans, and listening to song in a rustic symposium[78] of one, undisturbed by unruly desires (*Id.* 7.69–70):

καὶ πίομαι μαλακῶς μεμναμένος Ἀγεάνακτος
αὐταῖς ἐν κυλίκεσσι καὶ ἐς τρύγα χεῖλος ἐρείδων.

And I will drink at ease, at ease remembering Ageanax
among the very wine cups and pressing my lip to the dregs.

The first line loops from the future (the tense of the verb) back to the present time of Lykidas's singing with the thought of remembering Ageanax. Lykidas foresees

---

76. The lines may just mean that halcyons calm the waves whenever they appear (Gow 1952, II, 147; Hunter 1999, 169), but I think they are more naturally taken as a description of the halcyon days.

77. I think it is unnecessary, and somewhat awkward, to assume with Hunter (1999, 170) that in these lines "Lykidas now imagines that Ageanax has 'got the message' and is indeed about to set sail." If we see their function as recapitulative and transitional, it is easy to supply "if he saves Lykidas from love" from the foregoing lines. That is, the wish is spoken on the assumption that Ageanax is willing to do so; then he deserves good wishes for his voyage. The shift from a "future more vivid" condition to optatives of wish suggests a little less certainty in the outcome.

78. On this passage as an example of Theocritus transferring an urban institution to a rustic setting and implicitly claiming it as a feature of the oral prehistory of bucolic song, see Pretagostini 2006, 63–65.

a time when Ageanax will no longer be present but will be the object of memory rather than of desire, and so an undisturbing memory; the significant μαλακῶς ("softly, at ease"), as Hunter says, "colors" both "I will drink" and "remembering" (and so I have translated it twice).[79] Even though Lykidas, in good sympotic style, will drink to his beloved, and although pressing the lips into the wine cup to the dregs suggests a kiss, the feeling is more commemorative than erotic. Elsewhere the symposium is the setting in which desire, usually for an absent beloved, bursts forth without restraint and is revealed for all to see; we might compare Delphis's distracted behavior at a drinking party in *Idyll* 2 (149–153).[80] In addition, this is a most unbucolic scene. The mention of a fire suggests that it takes place indoors, in contrast to the usual outdoor bucolic setting, and in cold weather, probably winter, a season that is usually ignored in bucolic poetry. It is as if bucolic poetry could accommodate a scene of ease and fullness resulting from the absence of desire only by departing from its own conventions and embracing those of sympotic lyric poetry.

But the singing that is to take place in this setting will be bucolic through and through. Two shepherds will play the *aulos*, and Tityros will sing the stories of two archetypal bucolic singers. The name "Tityros" indicates a rustic figure; it seems to be Doric for "satyr" or "he-goat." So he is a part of the bucolic world brought into this non-bucolic setting with his songs. This juxtaposition may imitate the original circumstances of reception of Theocritean bucolic, in which readers or listeners in an urban environment were invited to imagine a very different and distant world from their own. Like the audience of *Idyll* 7, Lykidas will be put in touch through song with a fictional world that contrasts with the circumstances he now enjoys. That Lykidas is himself a goatherd may be one of the ironies of the poem. To Simikhidas he represents the authentic bucolic world to which Simikhidas is trying to gain entry through his poetry (opinions of readers differ as to what success he has). But as we have seen, when Simikhidas meets him, Lykidas is oddly out of place: not in the mountains or pasturelands or with his goats but alone and on the road. And in his song he imagines himself in a rustic symposium that is the counterpart to the harvest festival in which Simikhidas participates at the end of the poem, which is not bucolic. Through his account of Tityros's song, Lykidas points beyond himself to what seems a more authentic version of "the bucolic." Notice how that bucolic world keeps receding.

---

79. Hunter 1999, 172.

80. Cf. *Id.* 14.18–49 and Callimachus *epigr.* 43, and note Hunter's observation (1999, 171) on φυλάσσων, *Id.* 7.64: "Poets treat the disintegration of a symposiast's garland as a sign that he is in love ... so the verb here may indicate Lykidas' release from passion."

If we identify this Tityros with the one mentioned in the opening lines of *Idyll* 3, an interesting contrast between the two poems emerges. That Tityros silently tended the animals "on the mountain" (*Id.* 3.2) while the goatherd (as we saw in chapter 1) stepped at least partly out of the bucolic world to deliver the rustic equivalent of the urban *kômos* at the mouth of a cave. Now Tityros will come forward to sing, also in a non-bucolic setting, but his themes will be bucolic; and Lykidas, the counterpart of the goatherd of *Idyll* 3, will be silent. Perhaps in *Idyll* 7 the singing that seeks to connect with bucolic fullness is imagined to happen in the absence of erotic desire, when that desire is redirected to the bucolic itself. In *Idyll* 3, where the goatherd has turned away from the bucolic world, this cannot happen. Furthermore, both Gow and Hunter remark that in *Idyll* 3, it is impossible to tell whether Tityros is goat or human.[81] The Tityros of *Idyll* 7 is obviously human, but his songs are to tell of a fuller merging of humanity and nature than *Idyll* 1 manages.

Tityros will first sing about how Daphnis loved Xenea, and how the mountain and the oaks on the banks of the Himeras River suffered and mourned for him as he melted like snow beneath the peaks of northern mountains or the Caucasus range (*Id.* 7.72–77). Embedded in the imagined scene of contentment by the fire is a contrasting story of absence and loss; the relation is the same as that between frame and embedded performance in *Idyll* 1 and the inverse of that between Lykidas's present state of desire and the fantasy enclosed in it. We have here a reprise also of the narrative of the origin of bucolic song told at greater length in *Idyll* 1. It is as if the gist of *Idyll* 1 (harmonious frame plus story of passion and loss) were further enclosed within the story of Lykidas's desire, so that Daphnis's story shows the tragic potential of longing and absence that in Lykidas's case is to be turned into its opposite if only Ageanax somehow rescues him from love (perhaps an impossibility). Tityros's song depicts Daphnis as fully integrated into the landscape so that the mountain and oak trees mourn for him, and so this story implies an imagined harmony and presence, even as these are being disrupted; the mountains associated with the snow to whose melting Daphnis's wasting away is likened are the cold spatial antithesis of the warm Sicilian setting.

Tityros will also sing about a goatherd shut in a chest whom the bees fed "because the Muse poured sweet nectar down into his mouth"—that is, he had a consummate poetic "gift" (*Id.* 7.78–82). Here is another story of presence involving another paradigmatic bucolic poet, one that involves not loss but the preservation of life and the collaboration of nature with the human that sets right an

---

81. Gow 1952, II, 65; Hunter 1999, 110–112. On the contrast between the silent Tityros of *Idyll* 3 and the singing Tityros of *Idyll* 4, see Segal 1981, 198.

injustice in the human world: the goatherd was closed in the box to die "because of the folly of his master [or the king]." Here for once is a tale of complete fulfillment in the bucolic world in which poetry has a central place; just as the Muses poured nectar into the goatherd's mouth, so the bees keep him alive by feeding him on flowers (or honey). But as in other examples discussed earlier, even as we are given this vision of presence, it is carefully distanced at the same time. It, along with the Daphnis song, is distanced from Lykidas because it is imagined as narrated in a song set within a scene sometime in the future that will only take place if Ageanax rescues Lykidas from desire in some unspecified way and has a safe voyage to Mitylene. It is distanced from the reader for the same reason, and additionally because it comes to us in indirect statement, so that we do not hear Tityros's voice even in fiction, much less those of the singers he tells about. In fact, it is not clear whose voice we do hear, because of the multiple frames. Lykidas's song, which projects Tityros's song, is set within Simikhidas's narrative of his encounter with the goatherd, which is in turn mediated for the audience by the poet Theocritus, in writing or by his own voice, in a scene of narration that may be distant from Kos, where *Idyll* 7 is set. How can we connect with the authentic bucolic world and hear *the* bucolic song in its full presence, experience with our own ears the sweetness of that voice? The answer to this fundamental question posed by Theocritean bucolic seems to be that we can do so only partially, through an act of imagination triggered by a fiction that goes out of its way to make us aware of its own fictionality even as we indulge it. In short, here again, Theocritean bucolic works by arousing our desire for something absent.[82]

This effect is heightened by what happens next. Immediately after the account of the goatherd fed by bees, the text breaks the anaphoric structure of Tityros's song (each narrative introduced by ᾀσεῖ, "he will sing") with an apostrophe to Komatas (*Id.* 7.83–89):[83]

---

82. Payne 2007, 126, makes the interesting point that the successive embedded passages grow progressively shorter in a process of "embedded miniaturization," at the end of which the voice of Komatas "is figured... only as a suggestive absence" (he sees the same process in the description of the cup in *Idyll* 1). Formally, then, the poem enacts the distancing and central absence I have been describing.

83. For my purposes, it does not matter much whether Komatas is the same as the goatherd of lines 78–82 or another figure. For what it is worth, I agree with Hunter (1999, 176) that the latter is more likely, for one thing because that is the best way of understanding καὶ τύ... καὶ τύ in line 84. The advantage of this view is that we then have a poetic succession, the goatherd and Komatas, into which the speaker seeks to insert himself, though at a distance.

ὦ μακαριστὲ Κομᾶτα, τὺ θην τάδε τερπνὰ πεπόνθεις·
καὶ τὺ κατεκλᾴσθης ἐς λάρνακα, καὶ τὺ μελισσᾶν
κηρία φερβόμενος ἔτος ὥριον ἐξεπόνασας.
αἴθ' ἐπ' ἐμεῦ ζωοῖς ἐναρίθμιος ὤφελες ἦμεν,
ὥς τοι ἐγὼν ἐνόμευον ἀν' ὤρεα τὰς καλὰς αἶγας
φωνᾶς εἰσαΐων, τὺ δ' ὑπὸ δρυσὶν ἢ ὑπὸ πεύκαις
ἁδὺ μελισδόμενος κατεκέκλισο, θεῖε Κομᾶτα.

O most blessed Komatas, you had experience of these pleasures.
You too were shut into a chest, you too, feeding on the bees'
honeycombs, toiled during the springtime of the year.
I wish that in my time you had been numbered among the living.
So that I would pasture your beautiful goats for you among the mountains,
listening to your voice, while you, beneath the oaks or beneath the pines,
reclined singing sweetly, divine Komatas.

The scene conjured up in the last three lines evokes Thyrsis's offer early in *Idyll* 1 (14) to pasture the goats while the goatherd plays the *syrinx* near a space of full bucolic presence where it seems for a moment possible to experience that fullness and its sounds—but only for a moment; the fear of Pan's anger at being awakened sends them to a less enchanted place where Thyrsis will sing.[84] Here the scene of Komatas's singing is similarly impossible. It can only be evoked through apostrophe, an attempt to make him present and responding to desire with song, as an unfulfilled fantasy.

The apostrophe is made emphatic by the occurrence of the vocative Κομᾶτα at both beginning and end, and the ring composition marks off the passage from the rest as a self-contained unit. These lines show the dynamics of apostrophe, as described by Culler, particularly well. They construct Komatas as someone who might respond and attempt to summon up presence from absence. They seek to put the speaker in relation to this consummate singer, whom the bees fed on honey and whose springtime labor of singing (ἐξεπόνασας) is echoed by Lykidas's labor (ἐξεπόνασα, line 51) in composing the song that enfolds this passage. But this attempt is offset by the unattainable wish in the last four lines, which both construct

---

84. Again, contrast *Idyll* 3, where Tityros's pasturing the speaker's goats allows him to distance himself from bucolic fullness in a vain search for Amaryllis's presence.

a fantasy of bucolic fulfillment[85] and, through their rhetorical form, recognize its impossibility.[86]

But whom are we to imagine speaking or singing these lines? Is it Tityros, whose voice breaks through Lykidas's indirect statement and suddenly becomes audible to us, though enclosed within frames that re-enact the chests in which the goatherd and Komatas were imprisoned? If so, Tityros tries to connect his own singing with theirs. The same is true if it is Lykidas, breaking through the frame, demolishing the distance created by his indirect statement, and responding in his own voice to what he imagines Tityros will sing. Even though line 90 makes it clear that Lykidas's speech continues until line 89, might we hear in the background Simikhidas, who is, after all, the narrator of all these embedded songs, trying to insert himself into a poetic type and its ethos to which his own relation is still not secure? And behind him, perhaps, Theocritus himself is making a metapoetic statement about his own bucolic ambitions. How can we tell, and why do we have to? I think that we should keep all these possibilities open at once and read as though they are all simultaneously true. They show us how all those involved in this poetic transaction, from Tityros at the center of these nested perspectives to the poet at the outside, are related in different ways to the always receding ideal that Komatas represents. Lykidas's song demands a multidimensional reading that asks us to adopt all these different viewpoints at once and to ask about our own participation in the bucolic ideal—our own desire provoked by its absence, our need for fictions and their paradoxical but comforting distance from reality.[87]

---

85. A small but telling detail is the imperfect ἐνόμευον in line 87, which refers to present time after an unfulfilled wish ("I would now be pasturing," Goodwin 1965, 333; the pluperfect κατεκέκλισο in line 89 would then refer to an act—of lying down—completed in present time (as the pluperfect can do in counterfactual conditional clauses with ἄν, Goodwin 1965, 410). So the scene is conjured up in the speaker's and the reader's minds as present, in a way much more vivid than the aorist could have achieved ("I would have pastured").

86. On Lykidas's song, see also Goldhill 1986, 38; 1991, 235–236, especially his comments on the "recession of voices" in it and his statement that "it is as if the instantiation of bucolic poetry in the programmatic poem [i.e., *Id.* 7] comes complete with a history of past pastoral, or as if an essential part of the 'bucolic muse' is the desire for what is *lost*" (emphasis in the original). Cf. also Haber 1994, 32–33: "But Lykidas secures Komatas' presence only by simultaneously acknowledging his absence; he unites his own time with that of his predecessor by recognizing the gulf that divides them." I would put more stress on the poem's acknowledgement of the final impossibility of Komatas's presence (with all that implies).

87. Many have wished to read Lykidas's song as showing the pangs of erotic desire subsumed into the aesthetic pleasures of song, e.g., Ott 1969, 149–153; Segal 1981, 140–143. Similar is Kühn 1958, 51–52, who, however, sees the wish about Komatas as tied to Lykidas's present situation: he would like Ageanax to play the same role toward him as he wishes he could have played for Komatas. The view that erotic desire is replaced by aesthetic satisfaction tends to ignore the

Idyll 6: Breaking the Frame

Framing and its porousness are prominently at issue also in *Idyll* 6, one of the most complex of Theocritus's poems.[88] The poem contains four discursive levels corresponding to three different temporal stages.[89] There is the song exchange between Daphnis and Damoitas, set at an indefinite time (ποκα, "once," *Id.* 6.2). Within that frame is a segment of the story of Polyphemos and Galateia, the subject of their songs, which presumably is assumed to have occurred before the time of their singing. Next, the narrator's address to Aratos means that the whole poem is addressed to him and implies a scene of narration later than the meeting between Daphnis and Damoitas. And finally there is the reader or audience and an even later time of narration than the others. Whoever this Aratos is, and whatever else may be implied by this address,[90] we as readers are witnessing a fragment of conversation between him and the narrator. The result is a further layer of separation between the reader and the scene of presence in which Daphnis and Damoitas narrate a story of the disrupted relationship between the Cyclops and the sea Nymph. As in *Idyll* 7, then, Theocritus puts a barrier between his audience and a scene of fullness, though not as elaborately or obtrusively.

Everything in the frame emphasizes mutuality and unity in the relationship between Daphnis and Damoitas and the similarity, stopping just short of complete identity, between them. They lead a single herd to "one place." Since Daphnis is

---

way Tityros's song is premised on Lykidas's love having *already* been calmed. But to the extent that it has some validity, it cannot be a complete account of Lykidas's song. The passage may show how we all need this healing function of song and what that experience might be like, but it simultaneously qualifies it as based on wish-fulfilling fantasy.

88. And I do think that *Idyll* 6 is by Theocritus, despite the interesting case made by Reed 2010 that this poem should be grouped with *Idylls* 8 and 9 as representing the post-Theocritean development of bucolic poetry. It seems to me equally possible that the innovations Reed finds in *Idyll* 6 were due to Theocritus himself and that the composers of the other two poems took their cue from them—a possibility that Reed also admits (2010, 249–250). The experimentation in narrative and other formal techniques on display in *Idyll* 6 seems to me characteristic of Theocritus, and this, in my view, tips the balance in favor of his authorship. Still, nothing I say here depends on who wrote it. It is a remarkable achievement whomever we have to thank for it.

89. See Cusset 2011, 44–46, who describes three levels, omitting the relation between Theocritus and the reader. See also Billault 2006, 20–21, who discusses these levels as "screens" that Theocritus erects between the story of Polyphemos and Galateia and the poem's audience but does not consider how those barriers are then crossed (see below). For a reading of *Idyll* 6 based on the complex combination of communication and discontinuity among these levels, see Foster 2016, 35–73.

90. See Bowie 1996, who suggests that the poem is an indirect declaration of love to Aratos by Theocritus.

explicitly called a cowherd, Damoitas is, too. This is unique in Theocritus's bucolics, where encounters regularly take place between different kinds of herdsmen.[91] Even formally, the complementarity between them is stressed: the ὁ μέν ... ὁ δέ in lines 2–3, referring to Daphnis and Damoitas, respectively, reverses the order of their names in line 1, in a chiastic arrangement that is picked up again in the double chiasmus of lines 42–44, which reflects the reciprocity in their exchange of gifts. Still, there is a slight difference between them. Daphnis's cheeks are covered with a golden fuzz, whereas Damoitas is half-bearded (lines 2–3), so that he is somewhat older. This distinction reduces the usual age difference between *erastês* and *erômenos* to almost nothing, but there is just enough of a gap to allow a love relationship between them and avoid, on the one hand, such thoroughgoing likeness that each would be completely loving an image of himself in the other and, on the other hand, so much difference that the relationship would be asymmetrical and vulnerable to problems.[92] With all this emphasis on complementarity, the last word of line 5 comes as a surprise: "First Daphnis began, since he first provoked a competition (ἔρισδεν)." When two herdsmen are together, they often sing, and when they trade songs or snatches of songs, they might compete for an agreed-on prize. The tone can range from the genial, as in the competitions envisioned at the beginning of *Idyll* 1 between the herdsmen and Pan and the Muses (where the divinities are already acknowledged as superior), to the mean-spirited, as in *Idyll* 5. The awarding of prizes in those poems establishes winner and loser and therefore a hierarchy. But the song exchange in *Idyll* 6 does no such thing. Daphnis and Damoitas exchange gifts on an equal basis, and the last line of the poem tells us that neither won, and both were undefeated. Whatever *eris* is built into the situation is reduced to almost nothing.[93]

Here, then, is another scene of what I have been calling bucolic presence: symmetry of desire, songs and kisses exchanged on an equal footing between two almost identical cowherds sitting by a spring in the heat of a summer midday (lines 3–4), although we should bear in mind that it is distanced from the reader and so has at least a slight air of unreality. The contrast with the situation depicted in the songs within this frame could not be stronger. For there the relationship,

---

91. Myers 2016, 23–25, with discussion of *Idyll* 6.

92. I agree with Hunter (1999, 249) that the relationship is erotic. For the contrary view, see Lawall 1967, 69–70 ("love of a spiritual, 'Platonic' temper").

93. For fuller discussion of the formal elements of a poetic agon in the framing sections and the minimalization of actual competition, see Ott 1969, 67–69. As will emerge in chapter 4, I am skeptical that a poetic agon was a constitutive element of Theocritus's bucolic, whatever may have been the case with his imitators.

instead of being grounded in the two parties' presence to each other, is constantly misfiring (*Id.* 6.17):

καὶ φεύγει φιλέοντα καὶ οὐ φιλέοντα διώκει.

And she flees you when you love her and when you don't love her she pursues you.

Again we have chiastic word order, but it reflects not the static symmetry of the relationship between Damoitas and Daphnis but the symmetry of, let us say, a swinging pendulum. Galateia, who in *Idyll* 11 did not respond to the desiring Cyclops's entreaties and appear to him, now seems to be on land and teasing him when he pretends not even to notice her. If he did respond to her, presumably she would run away. These are the familiar dynamics of desire in Theocritean bucolic; this perpetual being out of phase is what keeps desire alive.

What is not typical is the reciprocally fulfilled desire of Damoitas and Daphnis that is suggested by their exchange of kisses and pipes. But this idealized picture is not the whole story of Daphnis, if we understand this Daphnis, as I think we should, as the younger, happier version of the one who melts from love of Xenea (*Idyll* 7) or lies dying while a girl searches the woods for him (*Idyll* 1). Hans Bernsdorff has argued that within the inset story of Polyphemos and Galateia there are striking anticipations of Daphnis's fate, of which Daphnis cannot be aware, whereas the reader who makes the connection with the other *Idylls* can.[94] So *Idyll* 6 represents a carefree and innocent stage in Daphnis's life, before he falls victim to the complexities of mature (hetero-)sexuality. Alongside Bernsdorff's emphasis on Daphnis's tragic blindness, I would suggest that our awareness of what is to come colors our perception of this scene of bucolic presence. One could also sense something foreboding even here by applying Philip Purchase's Lacanian perspective on the Daphnis of *Idyll* 1.[95] There is not enough difference between Daphnis and Damoitas for Damoitas to be truly other to him, and so at this early stage there would be problems for Daphnis in autonomous subject formation (or more simply, here as well as in *Idyll* 1, he has not found the proper balance between autonomy and immersion). In any case, once again,

---

94. Bernsdorff 1994. Against this, Stanzel 1995, 41–42. The name seems more than a signifier of poetic talent (Legrand 1898, 151). If the cowherd Daphnis's ill-fated love was an item in the repertoire of bucolic song (*Id.* 7.72–77), the name inevitably would carry his story with it. On the different narrative levels on which Daphnis appears in *Idylls* 1, 6, and 7, see Payne 2007, 100.

95. Purchase 2003–2005.

Theocritus offers us a vision of plenitude, but the reader might well wonder about its reality or its stability.

Illusion and reality are, in fact, major themes of the poem, and their relation is built into its formal features, as we can see already in the first lines of Daphnis's song (*Id.* 6.6–7):

> βάλλει τοι, Πολύφαμε, τὸ ποίμνιον ἁ Γαλάτεια
> μάλοισιν.
>
> Galateia is pelting your flock, Polyphemos,
> with apples.

We might have expected the two songs to be third-person narrative (after all, Polyphemos must have lived long before Daphnis), but the vocative of the Cyclops's name signals a more dramatic form. We could suppose, as many do, that Daphnis is assuming the voice of an acquaintance and adviser of Polyphemos. That is a legitimate reading, but a stronger one is also available: Daphnis the singer is directly addressing a character within his song, and the boundary between two of the distinct discursive levels is being overcome.[96] Daphnis's song is not quite an apostrophe, but it works in the same way. The vocative assumes that Polyphemos will hear and respond; that is, it constructs this mythical and fictional figure (from Homer, Euripides, and Philoxenus) as a presence. It is in turn Daphnis, the fictional character in Theocritus's poem, who is breaking the frame. The outer frame holds, but our awareness of Daphnis's fictionality is heightened by the relation he constructs with Polyphemos. And so the sense of immediacy of contact with the pre-tragic bucolic world of this cowherd that the poem's first five lines may have tempted us with is blocked. Paradoxically, however, I would suggest that Polyphemos's presence is, at the same time and to some extent, summoned up for us through Daphnis's address to him, even though that address is playful or even mocking.

What happens after Daphnis finishes singing advances this process of making Polyphemos fictively present. Another vocative of Polyphemos's name (ὦ Πολύφαμε, *Id.* 6.19) rounds off Daphnis's song, as if to reinforce the effect of

---

96. On these two possible readings, see Cusset 2011, 78; Kyriakou 2018, 115. Examples of the first are Damon 1995, 122; Köhnken 1996, 177; Foster 2016, 47–50. Hunter 1999, 245–246, intriguingly suggests two other roles that Daphnis might be playing as a third-person observer: Eros or Odysseus. But I prefer to see Theocritus boldly experimenting with form. On the failure of the frame to enclose completely, see Goldhill 1991, 259–261.

his presence.[97] Then a transitional line in the narrator's voice (20) takes us back momentarily to third-person narrative and the present time of narration; this only makes more remarkable what happens when Damoitas begins to sing (*Id.* 6.21–22):

εἶδον, ναὶ τὸν Πᾶνα, τὸ ποίμνιον ἁνίκ' ἔβαλλε,
κοὔ μ' ἔλαθ(ε).

I saw, by Pan, when she was pelting the flock,
and she didn't evade my notice.

Polyphemos speaks. He answers Daphnis, in whose song he was a character, across the narrative frame.[98] Even though his voice comes to us through that of Damoitas, we can enjoy his fictive presence and his self-delusion: his failure to believe Telemos's prophecy about his blinding by Odysseus, his interpretation of Galateia's behavior (is she infatuated or just teasing him?), and his opinion of his good looks. Even though we remain at a skeptical (mocking or sympathetic?) distance from him, we are actually hearing a figure out of distant myth and the poetic tradition—or that is our illusion, if we give ourselves over to the fiction.

Galateia's presence is more elusive. In *Idyll* 11, Galateia never appears, and the boundary between land and sea separates her from Polyphemos. The situation there is the same as that in *Idyll* 3, and although we have Polyphemos's word for it that she came up on land to gather flowers with his mother (*Id.* 11.25–29), how reliable is he when he cannot tell the difference between dreams and reality (*Id.* 11.23–24)?[99] In *Idyll* 6 we have Daphnis's testimony that she is throwing apples at

---

97. This time, the vocative is preceded by ὦ, which seems to lend a condescending or mocking tone in keeping with the sentence in which it occurs (a comment on how the beautiful Galateia could be infatuated with the ugly Cyclops). Williams 1973, 64, sees the particle as just adding emphasis "to underline still further the force of the *sententia* within which it occurs," although he recognizes its possible ironic or teasing force in other Theocritean contexts. I think it can also have a similar overtone here as well as adding emphasis. In this way, it puts Daphnis into a relation to Polyphemos—one of superiority.

98. Cusset 2011, 122, comments that by adopting a viewpoint external to Polyphemos, Daphnis forces Damoitas into the more difficult task of adopting the Cyclops's perspective. This plays down the surprise of Damoitas ventriloquizing Polyphemos's voice, even though it is at the same time a very good maneuver in a song contest, though surely not Damoitas's only option. As Matthew Chaldekas points out to me, he could sing as Galateia. She would then be present, and *Idyll* 6 would be a very different poem.

99. Payne 2007, 76–77: while he dreams, "his unconscious mind is a veritable fiction machine." Cf. Cusset 2017, 228: "Elle [Galatée] n'est que l'effet du désir du Cyclope."

the Cyclops's flock—or is he making that up? And can we rely on Polyphemos's "I saw her"? How well does his single eye see? The point is not to decide whether or not Galateia exists. Her presence is evanescent, like that of the foam on the sea that Galateia perhaps represents if her name suggests the whiteness of milk (γάλα).[100]

For example, Daphnis describes how Galateia throws apples at Polyphemos's dog as well as at his sheep (*Id.* 6.9–14):

> πάλιν ἁδ', ἴδε, τὰν κύνα βάλλει,
> ἅ τοι τᾶν ὀίων ἕπεται σκοπός· ἁ δὲ βαΰσδει
> εἰς ἅλα δερκομένα, τὰ δέ νιν καλὰ κύματα φαίνει
> ἅσυχα καχλάζοντος ἐπ' αἰγιαλοῖο θέοισαν.
> φράζεο μὴ τᾶς παιδὸς ἐπὶ κνάμαισιν ὀρούσῃ
> ἐξ ἁλὸς ἐρχομένας, κατὰ δὲ χρόα καλὸν ἀμύξῃ.

> Look, there she goes again, she's pelting the dog
> that follows you as a guard of your sheep. And she [the dog] barks
> looking at the sea, but the beautiful waves show her
> running upon the softly plashing shore.
> Take heed lest she dart at the girl's shins
> as she [Galateia] emerges from the sea, and tear the beautiful skin.

In the first two lines, Galateia is (supposed to be) visible as she throws more apples, this time at the dog; the demonstrative and imperative (ἁδ' ἴδε, "look there!") stresses this. As the dog barks and looks toward the sea, we mentally follow its gaze. The second half of the third line ("the beautiful waves reveal her") seems at first to mean that Galateia can be seen among the waves (with the pronoun νιν referring to her), but as we read on into the fourth line, it becomes clear that it could also be the dog that is running on the shore, since "dog" is feminine and the participle θέοισαν ("running") could describe either it or Galateia. The last two lines tip the balance in favor of the dog, since Galateia is still in the water. (Is she actually emerging so that she is visible, or is the force of ἐρχομένας "when she emerges," so that she may not be? There is no way to tell.) But the possibility remains that it is Galateia running along the shore (she could be emerging so that the waves reveal her but close enough to the water's edge that she could be at least

---

100. Cusset 2017, 228–229, usefully links this evanescence to the contrasts in the poem between land and sea, solidity and fluidity, and male and female (I would add reality and illusion).

loosely said to be on the shore).[101] That is less likely, but I suggest that it remains in the reader's mind even as he or she pictures the dog barking at the waves and seeing only a reflection of itself. We might call this a "textual afterimage." Galateia seems to be present, but when you look, she is gone and perhaps was never there. You only see yourself.

What I am suggesting is that the text puts the reader or listener through the same experience the dog has: sensing Galateia's presence (why would the dog bark unless someone were there?) but following the narrative injunction to "look" (ἴδε) and seeing mirrored back our own perplexity. And there is another textual effect that also reproduces this strange absence amid presence. The name "Galateia" occurs only once in the poem, at the end of line 6, where she is throwing apples at the flock and seems most fully present.[102] But as Christophe Cusset points out, sounds from her name recur throughout the rest of the poem (for example, ἅλα, γαλάνα, and the many instances of καλός).[103] So the name disappears but retains a shadowy acoustic life; or we might say at the same time, it survives as *only* an echo.[104] Like her name, Galateia is as fugitive as the foam on the waves of the sea or the dry thistledown in summer to which the lines that follow those quoted above compare her.

In *Idyll* 6, the interplay of presence and absence is closely related to questions of illusion and reality, and mirroring plays an important role here. After all, the image in a mirror confirms the presence of the one who gazes into it, but how real is the image itself, and how trustworthy is the reflection? The situation of the dog looking at the waves and seeing not Galateia but itself is repeated in Damoitas's song, when Polyphemos recalls his gaze at his own image reflected in the sea (*Id.* 6.34–38):

καὶ γὰρ θην οὐδ' εἶδος ἔχω κακὸν ὥς με λέγοντι.
ἦ γὰρ πρᾶν ἐς πόντον ἐσέβλεπον, ἧς δὲ γαλάνα,

---

101. Gow 1952, II, 121; Dover 1971, 142; and Hunter 1999, 251, are all certain that the reference is to the dog. I would allow for more ambiguity, as does Cusset 2011, 98–99. The scholia understand the reference to be to Galateia, who thus sees her own reflection in the waves, but one scholion records a variant reading ῥαίνει ("spray") for φαίνει ("reveal"), which, it says, would imply the dog.

102. Notice that the article is used, so that the implication is "that Galateia whom you and I know, Polyphemos"; this is a small touch that gives her more substance and reality.

103. Cusset 2011, 80–81, who gives a complete list.

104. Cf. Cusset 2011, 81: "toutefois, si le nom est productif, on voit q'il n'a qu'une seule occurrence dans le text, comme s'il disparaissait aussitôt après avoir été nommé, tout en se répétant peu à peu à travers les noms qui lui font écho."

καὶ καλὰ μὲν τὰ γένεια, καλὰ δέ μευ ἁ μία κώρα,
ὡς παρ' ἐμὶν κέκριται, κατεφαίνετο, τῶν δέ τ' ὀδόντων
λευκοτέραν αὐγὰν Παρίας ὑπέφαινε λίθοιο.

You know, I don't have an ugly appearance as people say I do.
I was looking into the sea the other day—there was a calm—
and handsome appeared my beard, handsome my one eye,
so far as my judgment goes, and as for my teeth,
the sea reflected a gleam whiter than that of Parian marble.

The Cyclops looks into the sea, and like the dog he sees himself. But the possible presence of Galateia pervades the language of this passage. As commentators have seen, γαλάνα ("calm") evokes her name, as does the repeated καλά; Polyphemos sees his beautiful eyeball, κώρα, but the word also means "girl"; and as Cusset observes, the comparative λευκοτέρα occurs only one other time in Theocritus, at *Id.* 11.20, where Polyphemos is describing the beautiful appearance of Galateia.[105] Is Galateia, then, nothing more than the projection of the Cyclops's narcissistic self-regard?[106] We can at least say that, sea Nymph or illusion, by her elusiveness Galateia provokes desire that, instead of remaining directed at another, is frozen into a mirror-like self-contemplation. Commentators cite Plato, *Phaedrus* 255d, where the beloved without realizing it sees himself in the beloved "as in a mirror."[107] The allusion is, of course, ironical, since in Plato this is only one stage in the growth of love between two people, whereas Polyphemos seems fixated not on the Nymph but on his own eyeball (κώρα). But the relationship between Daphnis and Damoitas, who, as we have seen, are almost mirror images of each other, comes close to Plato's description. On the other hand, we have seen that this close resemblance may be problematic, and narcissism has seemed to some to be at the root of the older Daphnis's troubles in *Idyll* 1.[108] Polyphemos's self-contemplation, then, could be another way, in addition to those discussed by Bernsdorff, in which his story carries implications for Daphnis's later fate.

Polyphemos's state of solitary desire and its result in self-contemplation in *Idylls* 11 and 6 are set off by contrast with their Homeric models. In Book 1 of the

---

105. Hunter 1999, 257–258; Cusset 2011, 160–167.

106. Cusset 2011, 163–164, 166.

107. Hunter 1999, 258; and especially Cusset 2011, 159–160. The whole passage emphasizes seeing and the role of the eyes in the arousal of desire and love.

108. Zimmerman 1994; Purchase 2003–2005.

Iliad (348–351), after his quarrel with Agamemnon and the removal of Briseis, Akhilleus sits on the shore gazing over the sea and making many prayers to his mother, just as Polyphemos in *Idyll* 11 sits on a rock looking out to sea and singing, pleading with Galateia to come to him on land.[109] But Akhilleus's words get a response, and a sea Nymph emerges from the water onto dry land, Thetis, who happens to be Galateia's sister (*Il.* 18.45). In Book 5 of the *Odyssey* (81–86), Odysseus, having separated himself from a Nymph[110] as Polyphemos does in *Idyll* 6, sits weeping on the shore and looking out at the sea. But he is not looking at his own reflection in the water but longing for Penelope, and Hermes has just arrived to set in motion the events that will result in his reunion with her—reciprocal love, in sharp contrast to Polyphemos's solipsistic self-admiration.

Polyphemos's admiration of his own appearance contrasts strongly with his description in *Idyll* 11 (30–33) of those same, and other, facial features as ugly and as the reason Galateia shuns him. What makes a difference, clearly, is one's perspective and interpretation and perhaps also what one wants to see. That is the point of Polyphemos's qualification of his evaluation of his face: ὡς παρ' ἐμὶν κέκριται ("as it is judged in my opinion"). The phrase accentuates the distance between his perspective and that of readers, who evaluate those features very differently, especially if they have the description of them in *Idyll* 11 in mind; and as Hunter points out, they will know the use to which those gleaming teeth will be put.[111] Readers, that is, are in a position to take the measure of Polyphemos's delusion. For them, his self-admiration bears out Daphnis's comment on Galateia's supposed infatuation with him (*Id.* 6.18–19):

ἦ γὰρ ἔρωτι
πολλάκις ὦ Πολύφαμε, τὰ μὴ καλὰ καλὰ πέφανται.

Ah! for love [or by means of love]
frequently, Polyphemos, the not-beautiful appears beautiful.

Like Titania when she sees Bottom wearing the ass's head, Galateia is said to see ugliness and mistake it for beauty, as Polyphemos actually does. But for the

---

109. ἐς πόντον ὁρῶν (*Id.* 11.18) may echo ὁρόων ἐπὶ οἴνοπα πόντον (*Il.* 1.350, of Akhilleus). Cf. *Od.* 5.84: πόντον ἐπ' ἀτρύγετον δερκέσκετο (of Odysseus).

110. Kalypso is a daughter of Atlas in the *Odyssey* (1.52) but an Oceanid (and hence a sea Nymph) in Hesiod's *Theogony* (359).

111. Hunter 1999, 258.

reader, the line preserves the difference between the two: the side-by-side words for "beautiful" are not quite identical, because the first has a short alpha in the first syllable and the second has a long alpha. The latter tends to stand out because out of nine occurrences of this adjective in this short poem (only 46 lines), only one other has the first alpha long (line 14). The same variation in quantity in the word within a single line occurs elsewhere in Hellenistic poetry, but without such a sharp contrast or any particular effect.[112] So in *Idyll* 6, Daphnis and the reader of line 19 are in the position of dispassionate observers who see the spell to which Galateia (supposedly) succumbs when her desire transforms Polyphemos's ugliness to beauty.[113] Later, in Damoitas's song, Polyphemos similarly confuses illusion with reality (except that he really does it, whereas we cannot be sure about Galateia) when he admires his reflection in the sea (*Id*. 6.36):

καὶ καλὰ μὲν τὰ γένεια, καλὰ δέ μευ ἁ μία κώρα.

And beautiful was my beard, and beautiful my single eye.

The word for "beautiful," repeated in an emphatic anaphora, both times has the first alpha short. Now there is no skeptical interlocutor passing judgment and calling attention to the difference between ugliness and beauty; Polyphemos lives completely within his own delusion. In the same way, in a line that recalls *Id*. 6.19, Theocritus, stressing the accuracy of his and Nikias's appraisal of beauty, gives the syllable in question the same (short) quantity (*Id*. 13.3):

οὐχ ἁμῖν τὰ καλὰ πράτοις καλὰ φαίνεται ἦμεν.

We are not the first to whom beautiful things seem to be beautiful.

On a larger scale, the two songs of *Idyll* 6 together suggest how extensively our understanding of reality is shaped by our interpretation of appearances, and in fact, interpreting appearances is exactly what the reader is challenged to

---

112. See the examples cited by Cusset 2011, 118. *AP* 7.726.10 should actually not be included; both alphas are long. But there, too, the quantity may be effective: ἡ καλὴ καλῶς produces a heavy, dragged rhythm at the beginning of the last pentameter that adds emphasis. Cusset sees a contrast between appearance and reality in *Id*. 6.19, much as I do (I would say illusion and reality), but sees in it "the magic of art" as "thanks to love Polyphemos enters into the sphere of Galateia's beauty."

113. On line 19 and the sympotic background to *Idyll* 6 as a whole, including especially Plato's *Symposium*, see Acosta-Hughes 2006, 47–49.

do. It is not clear how we should understand the situation these songs describe. The uncertainty revolves not only around whether or not Galateia is real and present, although that is a major part of it. Let us suppose that she is fictive or at least not visible. Daphnis then is making up her pelting of the flocks and is perhaps teasing Polyphemos, who we know, from *Idyll* 11 and Philoxenus earlier, is in love with her. Polyphemos, with his emphatic εἶδον ("I saw her") at the beginning of his reply, is pretending in order to save face and then develops Daphnis's hints to explain his own behavior; perhaps he was just sitting and playing the *syrinx* (lines 8–9), without seeing Galateia because she was not there, but now he turns that behavior into a pretense of playing hard to get. This seems to me a viable reading, according to which Daphnis and Damoitas would be collaborating in creating a new episode in the story of Polyphemos's love for Galateia (and fictively summoning up Polyphemos's presence, as we have seen). Or suppose that Galateia exists and really is throwing apples. In that case, there are two other possibilities. She might really be in love with him now that he is aloof, and his stratagem, which is based on the dynamics of absence and desire, is paying off. After all, apples are conventionally love tokens. In that case, we might imagine a time when Polyphemos will respond to her and she will flee in turn. But how can we be sure that Galateia *is* infatuated with him and not instead teasing him without any thought of a relationship with someone so ugly (the apples could be just apples, convenient missiles)? In this case, Daphnis would be teasing him, encouraging him in the illusion from within which he speaks in Damoitas's song, and part of our pleasure in the poem derives from the gap between his delusion and our superior understanding.[114]

It is not necessary to choose among these different and mutually exclusive possibilities in order to enjoy the poem. What is remarkable, because it shows the power of fiction, is that the poem induces us to ask what, if anything, Galateia is "really" up to and what Polyphemos's "real" motives are—as if Daphnis actually is addressing the Cyclops and we hear his voice through that of Damoitas. In all the ways I have outlined, *Idyll* 6 puts to the test our understanding of the world and our ability to interpret it and leaves us uncertain how to locate the point at which that knowledge fails and illusion begins.

---

114. In any case, I take Polyphemos's studied indifference as a sign that he is still in love with Galateia, whom he still wants to come and "tend his bed" (*Id.* 6.32–33). I therefore would not agree with Hutchinson 1988, 184–185: "He treats Galatea so roughly not simply in order to win her but because he exults in his own freedom from ungovernable longing, and in Galatea's subjection to it."

Idyll *2: Desire in Town*

It is not only in the world of Theocritus's herdsmen that we find a close connection between absence and desire. *Idyll* 2 takes us into a town big enough to have a *palaistra*, if it is not a city. Here, too, however, the absence of the beloved generates, if not a song, a monologue by Simaitha that includes magic ritual and incantation followed by a long address to the moon, in which she narrates how she fell in love with Delphis, induced him to consummate that love, and now has been betrayed by him.[115] As Cusset has remarked, in contrast to the systematic absence of women in the bucolic poems, two of the urban *Idylls*, 2 and 15, are "saturated" with women's voices, and it is men who are mostly absent.[116]

Simaitha's situation, however, resembles those of Polyphemos and the goatherd in *Idylls* 11 and 3; her plight is the urban and feminine counterpart of theirs. In all three poems, although the speaker struggles in words to make the desired person present, that person never appears (and even the moon, which might be expected to be sympathetic, remains aloof and never responds to Simaitha). But Simaitha never addresses Delphis directly, whereas the direct addresses by Polyphemos and the goatherd at least suggest the possibility of a response. Delphis is always referred to in the third person; and even in the narrative of their lovemaking, although Simaitha quotes his disingenuous words to her, she never recounts any words that she may have spoken to him. As a result, Delphis seems more distant than he otherwise would, less likely to make an appearance, and this tells us something about his relationship with Simaitha: that it is definitively over, and that it was never a marriage of true minds. Polyphemos finds in song a φάρμακον ("drug" or "remedy") against love, although it seems doubtful that he succeeds in curing it.[117] Simaitha has recourse to magic, intended now to charm Delphis back into her love, now to harm him.[118] At the end of the poem, she puts these motives in some kind of order (*Id.* 2.159–162):

---

115. The refrains that run through the two parts of the poem may suggest song or incantation or both.

116. Cusset 2017, 229–230.

117. I think that the imperfect verb tenses at *Id.* 11.14, 18, and 80 and the ambiguity of both φάρμακον as either "remedy" or "poison" and ἐποίμαινεν as either "controlled" or "nurtured" in line 80 (see Goldhill 1988, 90–92; 1991, 254–255) suggest that the scene of his singing on the shore took place repeatedly—that is, that his desire was assuaged or at least controlled by song but then was aroused again and again, and it either found temporary relief in singing or (more in line with Goldhill) was indulged through song.

118. Gow 1952, II, 40, although he concludes that all the charms are intended to bring Delphis back and not to harm him. I think it is more vivid to see two contradictory but related impulses in Simaitha, love and desire for revenge.

νῦν μὲν τοῖς φίλτροις καταδήσομαι· αἰ δ' ἔτι κά με
λυπῇ, τὰν Ἀίδαο πύλαν, ναὶ Μοίρας, ἀράξει·
τοῖά οἱ ἐν κίστᾳ κακὰ φάρμακα φαμὶ φυλάσσειν,
Ἀσσυρίω, δέσποινα, παρὰ ξείνοιο μαθοῖσα.

Now I will bind him with my charms. But if he continues
to grieve me, he will knock, by the Fates, at Hades's gate.
Such drugs [φάρμακα] do I claim to keep for him in the chest,
which a foreigner from Assyria, mistress moon, taught me.

In contrast to the healing drugs of medicine, Simaitha chooses the sinister drugs that she associates with the "barbarian" world.[119] And whereas Polyphemos comes to some kind of accommodation with his feelings, either indulging them or calming them at least for the time being, it is not clear that Simaitha does. That depends on what she means when she says (*Id.* 2.164):

ἐγὼ δ' οἰσῶ τὸν ἐμὸν πόθον ὥσπερ ὑπέσταν.

But I will bear my desire as I have endured/undertaken it.

The question is the meaning of ὑπέσταν. Both Gow and Dover cite Euripides *Tro.* 414–415 for the meaning "undertook, incurred," and Dover explains: "Simaitha's point is: 'it was I, not you, mistress Moon, who fell in love; and I who will endure it, while you depart.'"[120] That is a conceivable meaning, though it requires some work to elicit it. Another possibility, still with this meaning of the verb, is "I will bear my desire in the same state as I was when I fell in love," that is, passionately. Gow, rejecting the Euripidean parallel, says, "the meaning however seems to be rather *as I have borne it hitherto* than *as I incurred it*."[121] That is, the verb can be taken to mean "I have endured." But she has not been bearing her desire with any kind of equanimity.[122] So rather than the resigned endurance that both Dover and Gow want to find here, on either meaning of the verb—"incurred" or

---

119. Drugs kept in a chest (κίστα) evoke Apollonius's Medea, who is one of the three sorceresses Simaitha mentions at *Id.* 2.15–16 as her role models. See *Arg.* 3.802, 808, 844; 4.25 (Apollonius's word for "chest" is φωριαμός). For another parallel with Apollonius, see Dover 1971, 97.

120. Dover 1971, 112.

121. Gow 1952, II, 63. *Id.* 1.93, which he cites, seems to me not much of a parallel.

122. Cf. Stanzel 1995, 225–228, who nevertheless sees Simaitha as having reached a certain clarity about her situation, though not full resignation.

"endured"—it seems more plausible to hear in Simaitha's words a desire for the absent Delphis that is doomed never to be satisfied or diminished, and this brings her closer to the goatherd at the end of *Idyll* 3 than to Polyphemos at the end of *Idyll* 11. As she has just said, either her magic of this night will bring Delphis back to her, or she will kill him with her drugs. On the other hand, the view that Gow and Dover adopt cannot be completely excluded. We simply cannot tell how this story will turn out.[123] *Idyll* 2 presents us with only part of the trajectory of Simaitha's passion. As a result, what the poem puts squarely at the center of attention is an irremediable absence, a hopeless desire (unless those magic charms work), and a vulnerable[124] woman's attempts to respond to them.

But Simaitha has already contrived to satisfy her desire for Delphis, so that we have a story of presence and fulfillment in the past framed within a situation of absence in the present, and Simaitha's situation now illustrates the Platonic idea that even when one satisfies desire, one still feels eros to possess the object of desire in the future. As usual in Theocritus, however, that picture of erstwhile presence is heavily qualified by a series of ironies and reversals.

It makes a great deal of difference that the speaker of this poem is a woman whereas the central figures of the two most closely comparable poems are male. The town setting perhaps facilitated this change, since women do not figure among Theocritus's herders. Instead of bucolic song, Simaitha deals in magic incantations and destructive drugs, which were especially associated with foreigners and women in Greek literature, if not in life.[125] Accordingly, in lines 15–16, Simaitha

---

123. I agree, therefore, with the excellent discussion of Segal 1985, 114–119, and with Goldhill 1991, 269–270 (with discussion of earlier views). Parry 1988, 48, also allows for complexity in this ending when he says, "the fire of her conflicting emotions seems more subdued than extinguished." For a different view of the ending, one based on careful consideration of changes in Simaitha's use of language in the course of the poem, see Griffiths 1979, 87–88. See also Klooster 2007, 104–105.

124. Simaitha is a woman living alone, though not a hetaira, who is well off enough to keep a slave (not necessarily affluent) and to hire a flute player but seems to be at the lower end of the social and economic scale. Delphis, who spends his time at the *palaistra* and symposia, probably occupies a significantly higher position. See Legrand 1898, 129–131; Gow 1952, II, 33; Dover 1971, 95–96; Burton 1995, 19. This mismatch helps explain why Simaitha is unrealistic to expect him to maintain a relationship with her and why he seems to take it for granted that he can enjoy her without a serious commitment.

125. The relation between Simaitha's witchcraft and her gender is a rich topic. As Gibbs-Wichrowska 1994, 255–256, suggests, the contrast between her magic and her ordinariness can be read either as trivializing the power of magic or as showing (from a male point of view) the explosive power latent even in "the girl next door." Parry's sensitive reading (1988) offers a Simaitha using the only resources for coping with intense desire that were open to Greek women in their powerlessness: the therapeutic effect of telling her story to the moon and magic as a parallel way of ritualizing and ordering her experience even if it has no effect on

refers to the φάρμακα ("potions," "drugs") of Kirke, Medea, and Perimede (again, contrast the φάρμακον, "medicine" or "cure," that the male Polyphemos found in song in *Idyll* 11, although the word can also mean "poison"). The fact that Simaitha is the initiator of the relationship with Delphis and so takes the active role entails various reversals. To the feminine space of Simaitha's house is opposed the *palaistra*, the setting of Delphis's homosocial relations with other young men, with its homoerotic associations. These associations are captured well by lines 124–125: καὶ γὰρ ἐλαφρός/καὶ καλὸς πάντεσσι μετ᾽ ἠιθέοισι καλεῦμαι ("for I am called *elaphros* and beautiful among all the youths"). Delphis is seeing himself as the object of attention in the context of his age-mates. If *elaphros* means "nimble," he fulfills the upper-class ideal of outstanding athletic ability and physical beauty expressed especially in the gymnasium. But it could also, among other things, mean "fickle"; in that case, the emphasis is on his role as lover or love object, again with homoerotic overtones but also with ominous implications for his relationship with Simaitha.[126]

Delphis is, in fact, ambiguous sexually. There is Simaitha's and her informant's uncertainty about whether he is now in love with a man or a woman (lines 44, 150). If a man, ἀνήρ in both lines would suggest that he has the role of *erômenos*; but his departure to cover the other person's house door with garlands would, if that person is male, put Delphis in the role of *erastês*. In that case, or if he is in love with a woman, he seems to have passed beyond the age when he is sexually attractive to men. And in fact, he has a beard (line 78), not the facial fuzz of the attractive boy. This uncertainty leads to a further possibility. The Philinos whom he tells Simaitha he beat in a foot race (line 115) could be, in the context, the famous Koan runner, or his name could be used to give a vague suggestion of athletic ability.[127] But there could also be at least a secondary association with the Philinos of *Idyll* 7 (line 121), the boy with whom Aratos is in love and whose charms are said, in an echo of Archilochus's invective against Neoboule, to be overripe (that is, he is getting too mature for a pederastic relationship). That description might also fit Delphis's time of life, and it is at least suggestive that allusions to Archilochus's

---

Delphis. Duncan's subtle interpretation (2001) depicts Theocritus using Simaitha's gender and magic to arouse in the male reader a "delicate combination of distancing and identification" that enchants him. Lambert (2002) takes a different approach: Simaitha's "bungled" ritual is a parody of magic in keeping with a depiction of her as banal, because the idea of a woman with initiative and agency was still not acceptable in Greek culture as late as the Hellenistic period.

126. On the ambiguity of this word, see Goldhill 1991, 266–268).

127. On this Philinos, see Gow 1952, II, 55. Note Gow's remark that "the name is common at Cos." Note also that Philinos is given the epithet χαρίεις ("charming," as Gow translates it), in keeping with the atmosphere of the gymnasium.

Cologne Epode are associated with both the Philinos of *Idyll* 7[128] and Delphis (see below).

When Simaitha first sets eyes on him, both she and Delphis are acting appropriately for their respective genders: she is going to a religious festival, conventionally one of the reasons deemed legitimate for women to leave the house, and he is coming with a male friend from the gymnasium (lines 76–80). But now the usual roles are reversed. She sees him; there is no indication that he also sees her. There is already a lack of mutuality that is especially pronounced, because in Greek culture the exchanged gaze could be erotic. Physically and emotionally stricken with love, she sends her slave to invite him to her house. He gains entrance easily. What is missing, as we saw in chapter 1, is the *kômos*, in which he would have played the active role and she would have been—at least for the moment—inaccessible. When Delphis himself tries to excuse its absence (*Id.* 2.118–122), we might hear in his words a certain uneasiness at his passive and her more aggressive role, as well as a need to cover up his tepid feelings. Just before this speech, he has glanced at her (no answering look from her, it seems) and then fixed his eyes on the ground (line 112: ἐπὶ χθονὸς ὄμματα πάξας). This phrase echoes *Iliad* 3.217 (ὑπαὶ δὲ ἴδεσκε κατὰ χθονὸς ὄμματα πήξας, "he kept looking down, fixing his eyes upon the ground"), which refers to Odysseus, that consummate manipulator of words—a sign to the reader that Delphis's speech is as artfully calculated as his.[129] But we might also think of Apollonius's Jason on his way to Hypsipyle, walking through the town with his eyes resolutely on the ground, oblivious of the Lemnian women crowding around him (*Arg.* 1.782–786). There, too, a male enters the intimate space of a woman, Hypsipyle's bedchamber, with clear overtones of sexual penetration, in a scene that also involves gender reversals.[130] Like Thyrsis with Simaitha, Jason will leave Hypsipyle after their affair, but only after telling her frankly that he cannot stay on Lemnos and receiving her assent.

---

128. See Henrichs 1980; Hunter 1999, 188.

129. On the Homeric echo and the tension between it and the allusions to Sappho in this passage, see Segal 1984, 203–204, 206. See also Goldhill 1991, 262–263. However, Delphis is not really a smooth trickster; as Legrand points out (1898, 118), there is a contrast between his flowery, banal love jargon and Simaitha's language of true passion. I would add that it says something about Simaitha or about the power of eros, or both, that she is taken in by his insincere speech.

130. Cf. also *Arg.* 3.1022–1023, where Jason and Medea both look shyly at the ground. It is tempting to read Delphis's lowered gaze as a feminine expression of modesty, and it is true that when Jason enters her bedroom, Hypsipyle gives him sidelong glances as she blushes (*Arg.* 1.790–791), but looking down is not a gesture characteristic of women only, as the example of Odysseus shows. It is not, however, "manly" (by Greek standards) in Apollonius; in addition to the other instances, see *Arg.* 3.422.

But any overtones of sexual penetration there may be when Delphis enters Simaitha's house are muted. Goaded, as he perhaps meant her to be, by Delphis's description of the effects of love, Simaitha takes the lead (*Id.* 2.138–139):

<u>ὡς ὁ μὲν εἶπεν</u>· ἐγὼ δέ νιν ἁ ταχυπειθεὶς
χειρὸς <u>ἐφαψαμένα μαλακῶν ἔκλιν</u>' ἐπὶ λέκτρων.

<u>So he spoke</u>; and I—credulous one—
<u>taking him by the hand laid</u> him upon the <u>soft</u> bedding.

Seldom in Greek poetry is there so frank a description of sexual intercourse as there is in these and the lines that follow, and never does the woman exert such mastery. The inversion of gender roles is all the more strongly marked because these lines echo the description of a similar moment in Archilochus's Cologne Epode, where it is the *male* speaker who is physically in control (fr. 196a.42–48 West):[131]

<u>τοσ]αῦτ' ἐφώνεον</u>· παρθένον δ' ἐν ἄνθε[σιν
τηλ]εθάεσσι <u>λαβὼν</u>
<u>ἔκλινα</u>· <u>μαλθακῆ</u> δ[έ μιν
χλαί]νῃ καλύψας, αὐχέν' ἀγκάλης ἔχω[ν,

****

μαζ]ῶν τε <u>χερσὶν</u> ἠπίως <u>ἐφηψάμην</u> . . .

<u>So many things I said</u>; and the girl—<u>taking hold of her</u>
    amid the flower blossoms
<u>I laid her down</u>. And covering her
with a <u>soft</u> cloak, holding her neck in the crook of my arm

****

I touched her breasts gently with my hands.

This inversion of gender roles (by Greek standards) is coordinate with the breaking down of distinctions between spaces considered proper to each gender.[132]

---

131. Perhaps because he concentrates on Archilochus as an invective poet in the Cologne Epode and on echoes of him as such in Simikhidas's song (*Id.* 7.120–124), Henrichs 1980 does not mention the equally striking allusion to the end of the epode in *Idyll* 2. As I pointed out earlier, the mention of Philinos at *Id.* 2.115 prepares for this allusion if it is a cross-reference to the Philinos of *Idyll* 7, where the echoes of Archilochus discussed by Henrichs occur.

132. See chapter 1.

In addition, Simaitha's story of events leading up to their affair inverts what seems to have been the conventional narrative pattern of irregular love affairs, of which we may take as representative Euphiletos's account of the beginning of his wife's adultery in the first speech of Lysias.[133] Eratosthenes saw Euphiletos's wife at her mother-in-law's funeral (like a religious festival, a legitimate occasion for a woman to appear in public); Simaitha saw Delphis as she was on her way to a festival of Artemis. Eratosthenes waylaid Euphiletos's slave woman as she was going to the marketplace (a typical errand for a female slave) and corrupted her into serving as his go-between with her mistress; Simaitha sent her slave woman to watch for Delphis at the *palaistra* and convey her invitation to her house.[134] So Simaitha takes on the seducer's role that in Lysias's narrative is played by the male Eratosthenes.

"We went all the way, and we both achieved our desire," says Simaitha (*Id.* 2.143: ἐπράχθη τὰ μέγιστα, καὶ ἐς πόθον ἤνθομες ἄμφω). But this moment of fulfillment has been contrived by means that are everywhere marked as reversing socially prescribed gender roles, and its irregularity reveals it as precarious, although Simaitha, the narrator, seems unaware of this. It is clear, furthermore, that Simaitha and Delphis have very different expectations of each other. And so it is no surprise that this past moment of presence is set within a monologue by Simaitha that is all about absence. Even the phrasing with which this consummation is described reflects its questionable reality. Literally, the second half of line 143 means "and we both arrived at our longing." As Dover comments, "πόθος is usually a state of longing and desire (as in 164)."[135] Rather than gloss over the strangeness of the phrase, as he does and as my initial translation does, we should appreciate the paradox. What does it mean to come to your longing? Can desire be desire when it is fulfilled? If, as many of Theocritus's poems seem to be telling us, absence, lack, and yearning are the conditions of human life, how do we manage our feelings? The goatherd of *Idyll* 3 and the Cyclops of *Idyll* 11 sing

---

133. Lysias 1.7–9. I want to stress that I am not claiming that Theocritus alludes to this speech (although there is no reason to rule that out, either) but comparing narrative patterns. I take the Lysias passage as representing the norm because it is more consistent with conventional Greek gender roles. After writing this, I saw that my point had been briefly anticipated by Hutchinson 1988, 157, and more fully by Segal 1985, 105n6.

134. There is a further parallel between the two stories in how the infidelity is revealed—another sign that we may be dealing with a typical story pattern. In Lysias, a woman who has had an affair with Eratosthenes and has been abandoned by him sends her slave woman to tell Euphiletos of his wife's affair (Lysias 1.15–17). In Theocritus, the mother of Simaitha's flute player visits her and in the course of gossip tells her that Delphis is in love (*Id.* 2.145–149).

135. Dover 1971, 110.

pleadingly to the Nymphs they love but get no response. Simaitha tells her desire to the moon, which she animates through an apostrophe that assumes the possibility of an answer. But the moon goes its way: "But you fare well, Mistress, and turn your colts toward the ocean. I will bear my longing [πόθον] as I undertook it" (lines 163–164). Simaitha, who came to her desire, is left in a state of yearning. How she will bear it—or if she will—is left uncertain.

Idyll *13: Herakles in Love*

Like the "urban mime" of *Idyll* 2, *Idyll* 13 is non-bucolic, but its depiction of absence and eros resembles that of the bucolic poems. As Hunter points out, Herakles wandering in frantic search for Hylas resembles the girl of *Idyll* 1 running through the forest in search of Daphnis, so that "Herakles' story has been assimilated to the archetypal bucolic story."[136] As I argued in chapter 2, however, I would put less emphasis on "the bucolicisation of epic"[137] or an opposition between the two forms than on the poem's demonstration of the power of eros through the interplay between presence and absence. I would read the similarity between the stories of Herakles and Daphnis as showing that heroes are just as susceptible to the problematics of eros as herdsmen are. From this point of view, the poem would seem to be constructing a *continuity* between epic and bucolic with, as we saw in chapter 2, an admixture of sympotic elegy and lyric.

Writing in the epic meter, Theocritus extends eros into heroic myth. That does not mean that he portrays eros as entirely compatible with heroism; the tension between them is what gives *Idyll* 13 its power and its delicately playful tone even as it portrays the magnitude of Herakles's grief at the loss of Hylas. That is not to say that there is a firm opposition between them, as modern scholars often assume. In fact, Theocritus had precedents in his linking of eros and the heroic. By the time he wrote, Aeschylus had depicted Akhilleus and Patroklos as lovers in his *Myrmidons*, and Phaedrus in Plato's *Symposium* (179e–180a) used Akhilleus as an example of someone spurred to deeds of excellence by his love for his *erastês*, so that he was willing to die on Patroklos's behalf. In this reinterpretation of Homer, eros becomes the very basis for heroic action. That will not work for Theocritus's Herakles, whose love for Hylas interrupts—for a time and not permanently—his participation in the Argonautic quest. But these examples show that by Theocritus's time, eros and heroism were not in principle mutually exclusive. An anti-heroic reading of *Idyll* 13 is not the only one possible.

---

136. Hunter 1999, 284.

137. Hunter 1999, 263.

As an example of the combination of the martial and the erotic, consider the passage in which Herakles, who withstood and killed the Nemean lion (*Id.* 13.6), is compared to a lion when he hurls himself through the woods, propelled by πόθος, "longing," for the vanished Hylas (*Id.* 13.62–65):

νεβροῦ φθεγξαμένας τις ἐν οὔρεσιν ὠμοφάγος λίς
ἐξ εὐνᾶς ἔσπευσεν ἑτοιμοτάταν ἐπὶ δαῖτα·
Ἡρακλέης τοιοῦτος ἐν ἀτρίπτοισιν ἀκάνθαις
παῖδα ποθῶν δεδόνητο, πολὺν δ'ἐπελάμβανε χῶρον.

When a fawn cries out in the mountains a raw-meat-eating lion
rushes from its lair toward a very ready meal.
Such was Herakles when among untrodden thorn bushes
he hurled himself in longing for the boy, and he covered much ground.

The lion slayer becomes lion-like; the conqueror of nature on behalf of civilization becomes like a beast in the untamed wilds. In addition, the cry of the fawn seems linked to Hylas's voice issuing faintly from the water immediately before this passage (the transmitted line 61 being spurious), so that Hylas is figured as the lion's (Herakles's) prey. The simile generally recalls a certain kind of battle simile in the *Iliad* that describes the ferocity of a warrior and the defenselessness of the opponent he is about to kill.[138] Though it makes no specific allusion, Theocritus's simile evokes the violence of the Homeric battlefield, but now to describe the extremity of desire. This reframing of the Homeric animal simile in an erotic context could, of course, be taken as a commentary on epic or as questioning "the relevance of the epic hero in a post-heroic era."[139] But it is equally possible, and I think more in keeping with the theme of the poem as announced in the opening lines, to say that it emphasizes the lover's subjection to the same ferocious compulsions as the epic warrior in the moment of battle fury and the hungry lion.

---

138. There are no exact parallels, but cf. *Il.* 3.23–26, 11.113–119, 16.756–758, and 22.189–192. There are also points of resemblance between this simile and the one at *Od.* 6.130–136, which itself draws on the kind of battle similes we see in the *Iliad*. Odysseus emerging from the thickets to meet Nausikaa and her slaves is compared to a hungry lion: "so Odysseus was about to mingle among the girls with beautiful tresses." His mature masculinity is sharply opposed to their sheltered virginity, and sexual tension is palpable. In *Idyll* 13's simile, there is not such a stark contrast between heroism and eros. For one thing, a heroic warrior is precisely what Herakles hopes to educate Hylas to be; for another, the Nymphs are the true threat to Hylas, not Herakles.

139. Mastronarde 1968, 275.

What facilitates this merging of warrior and lover is that the simile draws not only on epic but simultaneously on conventions of sympotic poetry; as Hunter points out, "the image of the lion and the fawn as a way of figuring the *erastês-erômenos* relationship is found at Theognis 949–50 and *PMG* 714, and is common in heterosexual contexts, where the point is often that the young fawn is exposed to danger because it is separated from its mother."[140] As Hunter's description suggests, the image has somewhat different implications depending on the erotic context, and Theocritus seems to combine them, just as he brings Herakles's pederastic desire into confrontation with the Nymphs' heterosexual eros. Hylas's role as the object of desire is the same in both. From the perspective of pederastic desire, Herakles is straightforwardly the lover engaged in erotic pursuit, but there is an important difference from the conventional situation. Usually the love object is assumed to be somehow within reach; but Hylas has disappeared, and Herakles does not know where he is. From the perspective of heterosexual desire, the simile involves ironic displacements and gender inversions. The role of predatory lion would suit the sexually aggressive Nymphs, and Herakles would more appropriately be the protective maternal figure. And Hylas is not simply in danger but already their prey. I suggest that the reuse of the image, with the evocation of the conventions of pederastic and heterosexual love poetry simultaneously, emphasizes that *Idyll* 13 portrays not the usual situation of erotic pursuit but the more intense longing provoked by loss and absence and that even so great a hero as Herakles fell victim to it.[141]

This is one kind of eros; the poem shows us another, leading up to it. Even before the voyage of the *Argo*, Herakles has been in love (*Id.* 13.5–9):

ἀλλὰ καὶ Ἀμφιτρύωνος ὁ χαλκεοκάρδιος υἱός,
ὅς τὸν λῖν ὑπέμεινε τὸν ἄγριον, ἤρατο παιδός,
τοῦ χαρίεντος Ὕλα, τοῦ τὰν πλοκαμίδα φορεῦντος,
καί νιν πάντ' ἐδίδασκε, πατὴρ ὡσεὶ φίλον υἱόν,
ὅσσα μαθὼν ἀγαθὸς καὶ ἀοίδιμος αὐτὸς ἔγεντο.

---

140. Hunter 1999, 284. Cf. Hunter's remarks on *Idyll* 13's relations with sympotic and lyric poetry as well as with epic (262).

141. For a very different reading of the simile that sees it as condemning Herakles's pederastic love for Hylas as "unworthy of the hero," see Mastronarde 1968, 277–278. Gutzwiller's interpretation (1981, 28) is along the same lines: the simile "transforms Heracles' martial aggressiveness into a lover's aggressiveness. Theocritus does not even allow Heracles a genuine concern for Hylas' safety but mocks him by implying a sexual motivation for his search." Where Gutzwiller sees an opposition between warrior and lover in this passage, I see a combination of roles that may seem incongruous, but is in fact Theocritus's innovation. The second sentence quoted assumes that a sexual motivation should open Herakles to ridicule, but is that consistent with the wider context of this poem? The other Argonauts taunt him at the end of the narrative for a different reason.

> But even the bronze-hearted son of Amphitryon,
> who withstood that savage lion, loved a boy,
> the charming Hylas, who wore his locks long,
> and as a father does his own son, he taught him all things
> that he himself learned in order to become noble and celebrated in song.

This is the pederastic ideal,[142] according to which the *erastés* instructs the *erómenos* so as to shape his character and physical abilities and produce him as a model of Greek manhood, "noble and celebrated in [epic] song" (the latter, of course, a catchword of epic poetry). Pederasty is not, of course, a Homeric institution but rather the subject of sympotic elegy and lyric poetry. But epic is also concerned with the father teaching his son the standards of manhood, just as Herakles here takes a quasi-paternal role, and this endeavor shares with pederasty (in its ideal form) the goal of passing on to younger generations traditional ideas of masculinity. Here once again, we see the poem constructing a line of continuity between itself and heroic epic with the help of sympotic poetry. Herakles's education of Hylas, in fact, recalls the education Herakles's mother Alkmene arranged for him (*Id.* 24.103–134). Herakles, *Idyll* 13 continues, was never apart from Hylas, morning, noon, or night, "so that the boy could be wrought with toil to his satisfaction" (*Id.* 13.14: ὡς αὐτῷ κατὰ θυμὸν ὁ παῖς πεπονᾱμένος εἴη)—like a poem (cf. *Id.* 7.51) or a work of art—and turn out to be "a true man" (*Id.* 13.15: ἐς ἀλαθινὸν ἄνδρ' ἀποβαίη).[143]

This is a very different kind of love from what we have seen elsewhere in Theocritus. The text names it as eros, but it is characterized not by absence but by the inseparability of Herakles and Hylas. But as with Simaitha in *Idyll* 2, and in a way accounted for by Plato, this fulfilled relationship leads to separation and fierce desire. The controlled, constructive love that promised to produce a traditional masculine hero for a new generation is first disrupted by the Nymphs'

---

142. Cf. Hunter 1996, 168–171; Miles 1977, 142. My own reading of the poem overlaps with Miles's. But although I agree that the poem has touches of "gentle humor," I am not so sure that they distance the reader from Herakles. The effect may just as well be gentle mockery of lovers, among whom the narrator includes himself and Nikias, and so self-mockery. See especially line 66, discussed below.

143. I am not ignoring the near-bathos in which the first two lines of the quotation end ("loved a boy") after the heroic buildup in what precedes. But again, is this mocking of Herakles and/ or pederasty, or is it—just as probably, I think—a demonstration of the power of love to subject even the greatest of heroes to itself? Hutchinson 1988, 195, well captures some of the complexity of this poem in his comment on ἀοίδιμος: "we think of this figure [Herakles] as the subject of high poetry; we think also, wryly, of the poem we are reading."

overwhelming desire for Hylas[144] and then replaced in Herakles by the passionate madness of the longing conditioned by separation and absence that is familiar from other *Idylls*. So turbulent is this version of eros that it disrupts even normal spatial relations, as we saw in chapter 2. The contrast between Herakles's bellow and Hylas's thin voice issuing from beneath the water at his feet (*Id.* 13.58–60) not only confuses the spatial sense of near and far, but especially because of the graphically physical description of Herakles's deep throat, which suggests his size and also, perhaps, his proverbial gluttony and therefore his larger-than-life qualities, there seems also to be a contrast between the mature man and the boy—one that very likely will now be permanent (*Id.* 13.48–49):

Νύμφαι μὲν σφετέροις ἐπὶ γούνασι κοῦρον ἔχοισαι
δακρυόεντ᾽ ἀγανοῖσι παρέψυχοντ᾽ ἐπέεσσιν.

The Nymphs held the weeping boy on their knees
and tried to calm him with gentle words.

This tableau—the last we see of Hylas—shows him, childlike, on the Nymphs' laps, tearfully resisting the Nymphs' attempts to soothe him, permanently cut off from Herakles's masculine guidance into maturity and instead surrounded, even dominated, by female figures. The Nymphs are now transformed from sexual predators to maternal figures. They may have achieved the object of their desire, but it does them little good. They will never have a sexually mature lover. In sharp contrast to the goal of Herakles's efforts, Hylas, it seems, will never become a man but will be immortalized as a boy (*Id.* 13.72, where κάλλιστος, "most beautiful," suggests a youth in accordance with κοῦρον in line 48).[145] Perhaps we should

---

144. This is described in strong terms (*Id.* 13.48–49): πασάων γὰρ ἔρως ἁπαλὰς φρένας ἐξεφόβησεν/Ἀργείῳ ἐπὶ παιδί ("for eros for the Argive boy turned in utter rout the tender minds of all [the Nymphs]"). The verb is a military/epic term, strengthened by a prefix: the domination of the Nymphs' minds by eros is like a victorious army turning the opposing army to panicked flight (Gow's "fluttered" misses this implication entirely). See van Erp Taalman Kip 1994, 163–164. There is an exact parallel at Aesch. *Pers.* 606 (ἐκφοβεῖ φρένας, "routs the mind"), where we may also hear military overtones (the Persian queen has just heard the news of the defeat at Salamis). But the use of the verb with "eros" as subject is surprising, especially in conjunction with the epithet "tender" describing the Nymphs' minds, and suggests the merging of warfare and love that this poem performs.

145. Segal 1981, 57–58, points in this direction without going quite so far, but I would not see this, as he does, as part of an irony directed at epic heroism. Another, widespread opinion is that through a liaison with the Nymphs, Hylas makes a transition to mature (hetero-)sexuality (e.g., Mastronarde 1968, 275). The text does not encourage this notion, although it does not give conclusive evidence for my view, either.

think of him as the heterosexual counterpart of Ganymede: forever pubescent. Such is the power of desire to disrupt human projects and goals. Even divinities, who have the power to satisfy their desires at whim, do not in this case get all that they presumably want. This poem's depiction of eros is disturbing. It shows to what extremes the overwhelming force of eros can drive mortals and immortals alike, how there is finally no way of controlling it, and how even in fulfillment there is still some unsatisfactory remnant, a restlessness that never can be stilled.

One reason I have been arguing against taking *Idyll* 13 merely as a commentary on or appropriation of the epic tradition and in favor of taking its depiction of eros seriously is the way the first four lines of the poem offer a particular perspective on the narrative that follows (*Id.* 13.1–4):

> οὐχ ἁμῖν τὸν Ἔρωτα μόνοις ἔτεχ', ὡς ἐδοκεῦμες,
> Νικία, ᾧτινι τοῦτο θεῶν ποκα τέκνον ἐγέντο·
> οὐχ ἁμῖν τὰ καλὰ πράτοις καλὰ φαίνεται ἦμεν,
> οἳ θνατοὶ πελόμεσθα, τὸ δ' αὔριον οὐκ ἐσορῶμες.

> Not for us alone, as we thought, did he beget Eros,
> Nikias, to whomever of the gods this child was born.
> We are not the first to whom beautiful things seem beautiful,
> we who are mortals and do not look upon tomorrow.

Although the first two lines might lead us to expect that both the speaker and Nikias are in love and that the idea that "we are not the first" is offered as consolation, the second couplet makes it clear that "we" are "all mortals."[146] "Not to us first," then, means that we are not the first generation to admire beauty. Herakles is then offered as an extreme example: "for *even* Amphitryon's bronze-hearted son ... loved a boy" (lines 5–6); that is, if anyone could have withstood eros, it should have been Herakles, but he could not. More than that, in good epic fashion,[147] a hero from the past is offered as a paradigm of behavior that should guide "us" in confronting present circumstances, much as, within the narrative, Herakles sought to train Hylas in traditional masculine virtues. But here, by contrast, the lesson is that, like Herakles, we are all at the mercy of a desire so passionate that it overthrows reason and restraint. In this sense, we might speak of the appropriation of epic to a new use in service of the poem's insistence on

---

146. Hunter 1999, 265.

147. Cf., e.g., *Il.* 9.524–528.

the universality of eros and what it drives us to do—something that, by implication, Homer left out. It is entirely in keeping with that theme, and not necessarily an "ironizing" of epic, that the poem also shows that eros and heroism go strangely together. In fact, as Hutchinson points out, if a rejection of traditional heroism were the point, it would be hard to explain why Herakles in the end gets to Colchis in this poem and in no other known version of the Argonautic story.[148] He therefore fulfills his heroic role, as he will continue to do until his apotheosis. At the same time, eros has left its mark on Herakles's heroic record: when he arrives, he has to endure the other Argonauts reproaching (or teasing?) him as a "ship deserter" (λιπoναύταν, *Id.* 13.73, something that Agamemnon dreaded becoming in Aeschylus *Ag.* 212: πῶς λιπόναυς γένωμαι;). But Herakles's walking a vast distance to get to Colchis shows his ultimate loyalty to the expedition.[149]

Thus, when the narrative voice intervenes with a comment on Herakles's crazed wanderings through the woods by exclaiming σχέτλιοι οἱ φιλέοντες ("lovers are hopelessly self-defeating"), he means "all of us." Not only do we mortals not look upon tomorrow, but our lives are also conditioned by lack and the desire it engenders, as Plato's Diotima tells us. *Idyll* 13, then, complements and supports the bucolic poems. It looks outside the bucolic world to the heroic tradition and reconstructs it[150] so as to align it with bucolic by including in it the same absence and longing that founded bucolic itself.

---

148. Hutchinson 1988, 194. I would not agree with his suggestion that the poem's last line playfully undercuts its beginning. Rather, the ending, I think, reinforces it.

149. My point is not affected if line 75 is part of the Argonauts' words to Herakles (as I prefer to think) rather than the narrator's conclusion to the story. The tone does not have to be condemnatory. The Argonauts could be using what is, after all, quite a feat of strength and endurance to tease a comrade they essentially admire for being so driven by eros—banter with a bit of a sting. For a good statement of the more usual view, see van Erp Taalman Kip 1994, 167–168.

150. I have in mind the fact that the story of Herakles and Hylas seems to have been of relatively recent date and enjoyed something of a vogue among Hellenistic poets. See Gow 1952, II, 231.

4

On the Margins of Bucolic

Poems Concerning Margins

The collection of Theocritus's poetry that we now have may seem at first bewilderingly miscellaneous, as it did for a long time to me. But although each poem can stand on its own and be grouped with some other poems into a particular type, it can also enrich our reading to consider certain poems in relation to others that belong to different types, as we have already seen in some cases. That is, we can often observe a loose and flexible coherence of theme and outlook that both gives the bucolic or encomiastic poems, for example, a distinct profile and, just as important, cuts across these categorical distinctions. One obvious commonality that has often been discussed is a concern with the making and functions of poetry itself. Another, as we have seen here, is the nature of desire, the interplay of absence and presence, and the creative artistic and other energies that are stimulated by desire for what is absent. Again, a spatial reading of Theocritus allows us to see that each category of poems constructs space in distinctive ways but also, in the end, that these spatial configurations are themselves interrelated. Whether or not we can sense here the traces of an original poetry book—and we will probably never know—it is surely legitimate to read the Theocritean corpus as a whole, as we now have it, including even some poems that are often thought spurious.

For many readers, bucolic poetry is most characteristic of Theocritus, and it has drawn the most scholarly attention. The central place often attributed to bucolic may be more than just a matter of reading fashions. We have seen how bucolic can be a strong presence in non-bucolic poems (*Idylls* 21, 16, and even 15), where it provides an idiom for describing certain places and settings. Such passages may reflect what I have called a bucolic sensibility, but they also represent the extension of the possibilities of bucolic into the world outside the charmed space of "the mountain." *Idyll* 16 even shows bucolic's possible political use in the vision it offers of the prosperous and harmonious state, which is cast in bucolic terms. Such moments do not dilute the distinctiveness of bucolic, but they do raise the question of its boundaries. Spatially, as we saw in chapter 1, the bucolic world is defined in significant part by its margins, but although it seems at times to be autonomous, it is not sealed off; the bucolic and non-bucolic worlds interpenetrate, as we have also observed. Boundaries, after all, are the locus of distinctions and of the creation of differences, but they are places of communication as well.

In this chapter, I consider three *Idylls* that, in one way or another, are concerned with those margins and help to define what is at stake in bucolic, its world, its way of life, and the values that inform them. One of the poems I have chosen is often thought not to be by Theocritus, but whatever its authorship, its presence adds something significant to the collection we now have.

Idyll 4: *The Waning of Bucolic*

Idyll 4 is always counted as among Theocritus's bucolic poems—appropriately so. It centers on herding and herdsmen (of sorts, at least), and the setting of the encounter between Korydon and Battos is evidently "the mountain" (*Id.* 4.46). But this bucolic space is in tension with Olympia; South Italy, the herdsmen's home, with mainland Greece; the local with the Panhellenic; and herding with athletics. The advantage seems to have gone to Olympia, which has attracted Aigon to compete in the games, leaving his cows in the care, such as it is, of Korydon. Like other Theocritean poems, then, *Idyll* 4 is informed by absence, of both Aigon and the dead Amaryllis. The key question I want to consider is whether those absences are productive of anything and, more generally, whether the bucolic world in this *Idyll* retains its integrity. My argument will be that *Idyll* 4 shows us that world suffering disintegration in important aspects, diminished though not destroyed. It is thus temporally marginal in relation to the other bucolic *Idylls*. If *Idyll* 1 represents the inauguration of bucolic and its construction of its own history in the death of Daphnis, with his heirs Thyrsis and the goatherd in possession of the bucolic world, *Idyll* 4 stands at or near the end of the cycle, with the bucolic world under stress and Battos and Korydon only questionably at home in it.

Idylls 4 and 5 seem to form a pair, since they are the only poems set in South Italy; I will have a suggestion to make about this location eventually. Not only does Korydon's attempt to drive the cows away from the olive shoots that they have started eating (*Id.* 4.44–46) have a parallel in Komatas's similar command to his goats (*Id.* 5.100–101), but both poems also end with images of unbridled sexuality. It is not clear whether Komatas succeeds in restraining his billy goat or, similarly, whether Korydon gets his cows away from the olive trees. *Idyll* 5 remains squarely within the bucolic world and can hardly be called "marginal" to it, but it does show an analogous tendency toward exploring limits in that, as I argued in chapter 1, it combines the highest and the lowest registers, descriptions of natural beauty with coarseness.

Idyll 4 has evoked a range of responses from critics. Some have taken the poem as central to defining Theocritean bucolic and as raising questions critical to its interpretation. Van Sickle has suggested that the two speakers of this "dramatic" poem, Battos and Korydon, represent types of poetry and that the tension between them reflects the artistic problems of the emerging bucolic genre.[1] Segal sees a wider set of tensions that are resolved in the end in a way that makes the poem typical of what bucolic (or pastoral) does for its readers. "The Fourth *Idyll*," he writes in the eloquent closing paragraph of his essay, "brings . . . a healing accord which runs beneath the antithetical structure. This accord might be termed moral in so far as it rests on the experience of an encompassing natural order and the mutual perception, by both figures, of the beauty and vitality of that order."[2] Gilbert Lawall considers the poem structured on an antithesis between sentimental yearning and physical desire, with the balance finally tilted toward the latter: Theocritus "is here attempting to define what it means to be human, and he does this in terms of the lower forms of human existence (herdsmen) and of animal behavior."[3] Haber's reading of the poem is more complex than these. She sees *Idyll* 4 as typical of pastoral poetry's constant need to measure itself against "the heroic," which it both can and cannot replace, so that we see at once the strength and the inadequacy of Korydon's claim to be a worthy substitute for the absent Aigon.[4]

On the other hand, Gutzwiller seems to have a sense of things not quite fitting in this poem. The basic structural pattern of the poem, she says, is "noncorrespondence because of nonequivalence." "What the poem is about, then," she continues, "is unequal conflict, conveyed contextually by the absence of the cowherd who competes at Olympia, structurally by the failure of the conversation between Battus and Corydon to develop agonistically, and thematically by the misdirection of conflicts to nonequivalents both within and without the herding

---

1. Van Sickle 1969.

2. Segal 1981, 85–106 (quotation from 106).

3. Lawall 1967, 50–51 (quotation from 51).

4. Haber 1994, 20–25. My own reading has points of contact with Haber's, although I am less concerned with bucolic's relations with "the heroic" (a term that in her usage seems a little too elastic, especially when applied to the old man who is described at the end of the poem).

world."[5] Thus, for example, she notes a lack of the harmony between humans and nature that is found in other poems. This she attributes to Battos and Korydon directing onto nature the aggressive tendencies that would more usually have found expression in equal competition between them—a situation that is correlated with, if not caused by, Aigon's absence.[6] Here Gutzwiller's reading is the opposite of Segal's.

I share Gutzwiller's sense that *Idyll* 4 is not typical of the other bucolic poems and that its dislocations are to be associated to a significant extent with Aigon's absence. But I think these dislocations are more far-reaching than she indicates. In developing my reading, I will be pursuing a line of interpretation also taken by Stephens, who treats *Idylls* 4 and 5 in a section of her book on Alexandrian poetry titled "The Failure of the Pastoral."[7] "The registers of heroic myth," she writes in connection with *Idyll* 4, "athletic achievement, and the timeless and apolitical *pleasance* are competing and discontinuous. Intrusion of the first two threatens the stability of the last."[8] This formulation accounts neatly for the way the harmony between human beings and between them and the natural world that Segal describes and that we have seen envisioned and wished for in some of the other idylls—what I have been calling presence and fulfillment—however self-consciously fictional, seems not even to be contemplated in *Idyll* 4.[9]

---

5. Gutzwiller 1991, 147. As she notes, part of her argument is briefly anticipated by Ott 1969, 46–47, who emphasizes the inequality of the partners to the conversation (which he calls an agon nevertheless). Ott finds other kinds of incongruity, especially in the lowly herdsmen's use of diction typical of "high" literary forms and their pretensions to artistry of song. This dissonance, he concludes, gives the poem a comic and ironic effect (56). Note also Kyriakou 2018, 32, on how *Idyll* 4 "projects an image of dislocation."

6. Gutzwiller 1991, 152.

7. Stephens 2018, 69–72. I had already drafted a version of this section when I saw Stephens's book and was pleased to see how well our readings dovetail. See her discussion for aspects of the poem that I omit, especially the threatened intrusion of heroic myth and the possible allusion at *Id.* 4.16 to an Aesopic fable about an ass and a cicada. Richer's recent argument (2017) that this poem systematically arouses and then frustrates the expectations the reader has gained from the other bucolic poems also implies *Idyll* 4's marginal position, although I would not go so far as to call it "an *Idyll* about nothing."

8. Stephens 2018, 71.

9. It is a mark of the richness and the fascinating elusiveness of Theocritus's poetry that van Sickle's (1969) attractive reading of *Idyll* 4 is the exact opposite of my own; he sees the poem as working out the conditions for the emergence of pastoral—*incrementum* (in the term he uses) as opposed to the devolution I see. I have toyed with the possibility that in *Idyll* 4 bucolic poetry symbolically charts its growth while containing within itself the seeds of its own decay—a dialectical inner structure that I find appealing. We might be able to trace this in Theocritus's bucolic poems taken as a group, but I doubt that it would be possible to do so within this poem. In order for this line of interpretation to succeed, it would be necessary to

The athlete (or trainer?) Milon has taken Aigon to Olympia, and the opening dialogue between Battos and Korydon revolves around whether the athletic pretensions of a cowherd are incongruous or not. Korydon takes Aigon's ambition at face value, but Battos's caustic comments at least raise the possibility that Aigon is out of his element at Olympia and that Korydon is hardly a fit judge of athletic potential. The accouterments Aigon has taken with him, a pickaxe and twenty sheep (*Id.* 4.10), encapsulate these two possibilities. They would have their uses in either context, so that Aigon might be acting as either an athlete or a rustic. But those uses are antithetical: digging the soil with a pickaxe as part of an athlete's strength training as opposed to productive labor in the countryside, and eating sheep as a source of protein but on a prodigious scale (as athletes were said to do) as opposed to the protecting and nurturing of flocks by shepherds. The two worlds seem opposed, and it is difficult to envision Aigon passing easily between them. That opposition appears more pointed if we consider what Battos says of Aigon in line 7: "and when did *he* set eyes on olive oil?" (Gow's translation). The reference to oil conjures up not only the sophisticated and higher-status environment of gymnasia (as with Delphis and his oil flask in *Idyll* 2)[10] but also the world of Panhellenic athletics associated with Olympia. This cultural processing and use of the olive contrasts sharply with the olive shoots growing naturally that are eaten by the cows later in the poem (lines 44–45).[11]

The diction describing Aigon's absence associates it with the finality of death (*Id.* 4.5):

αὐτὸς δ' ἐς τίν' ἄφαντος ὁ βουκόλος ᾤχετο χώραν;

To what place did the cowherd their master[12] go and vanish?

---

follow van Sickle in seeing Korydon as an effective cowherd and Battos's detached perspective on the bucolic world as without critical effect; Korydon's sample of what he sings as embodying the continued vitality of bucolic poetry (rather than as a reduced form of epinician); Korydon's attempts to shoo the cows away from the olive shoots as successful bucolic labor; and the old man's sexual activity at the end of the poem as signaling natural vitality rather than as a debasement of bucolic desire. All of these points would command agreement from other writers besides van Sickle, such as Walker 1980, 48–53; Segal 1981, 101; Vox 1985, 175–177, 178. I read the poem differently and lay out my arguments below.

10. Hunter 1999, 133.

11. A connection made with a different point by Segal 1981, 98–99.

12. My translation follows Gow's for αὐτός (see also Hunter 1999, 132), but the phrase can also mean "the cowherd *himself*," that is, the real cowherd as opposed to Korydon, whose competence is open to question.

The verb ᾤχετο by itself can suggest death, as in the English "he is gone,"[13] but the phrase ἄφαντος ᾤχετο has several precedents in Homer and tragedy.[14] I would suggest that there is a particular reference here to line 657 of Aeschylus's *Agamemnon*, which occurs in the messenger's description of the storm and the shipwreck of the Greek fleet returning from Troy. The ships, he says, crashing against each other in the gale,

ᾤχοντ' ἄφαντοι ποιμένος κακοῦ στρόβῳ.

are gone and vanished by the whirling of the evil shepherd.

Commentators generally ascribe a comic or ironical effect to the many allusions in *Idyll* 4 to "high" poetry, an effect created by the incongruity between the characters' rusticity and their high-flown language.[15] And there does seem to be an unusual concentration of such allusions in this poem. But whatever one wants to say about irony and the like, the gap between levels of diction and subject matter may also be a sign of the waning of bucolic, not only of the bucolic world but also of the bucolic poetry that is one with it, as though it can no longer find a language and style of its own. At the same time, we could say that the fact that Battos is the one alluding to Aeschylus suggests sarcasm on his part that fits with his skepticism about Aigon. Above all, none of these effects rules out the seriousness of the suggestion that Aigon's absence is permanent and that it is as catastrophic to the bucolic world as the storm and shipwreck were to the glory of Agamemnon's victory over Troy. Hunter suggestively comments that the overtone of death in line 5 connects Aigon to Daphnis: Aigon was drawn on by an eros for "an evil victory" (*Id.* 4.27), and so was Daphnis in a way (*Id.* 1.97–98).[16] But Aigon's lust, although it is for something he does not possess, is not of the bucolic kind. As Daphnis's death inaugurates the bucolic life and its poetry in the world he leaves, so Aigon's disappearance threatens to destroy them.

The oxymoron of the "evil shepherd" in the Aeschylean line is echoed by Battos's comment on the cows' longing for Aigon (*Id.* 4.13):

---

13. For οἴχεσθαι implying death as well as absence (or death as a particular form of absence), see, e.g., the opening line of Aeschylus's *Persians*. The verb re-echoes insistently with this overtone throughout the play (lines 13, 60, 178, 252, 546, 916).

14. For these, see Gow 1952, II, 78; Ott 1969, 50; Hunter 1999, 132–133.

15. See especially Ott 1969, 50–56.

16. See Hunter 1999, 131, 133.

> δείλαιαί γ' αὗται, τὸν βουκόλον ὡς κακὸν εὗρον.

> Poor things,[17] how they have found their cowherd to be evil.

"Evil cowherd" refers to Korydon and Aigon at once. As a reference to Aigon, it condemns his remissness (from the perspective of the bucolic world) in abandoning his herd. In Korydon's case, "evil" means "incompetent"; it comments on the cows' sorrowful lowing and their emaciation, which is described in the lines that follow.

As in other *Idylls*, absence provokes longing: the cows "yearn" (ποθεῦντι, *Id.* 4.12) for Aigon.[18] But in those other poems humans feel this emotion, and it is productive of song as an effort to overcome absence, to fill the gap. And, to continue with the analogy of Daphnis, his death stimulates commemorative song and herdsmen's attempts to reproduce his archetypal singing and to restore a lost bucolic fullness—in short, bucolic poetry itself. Here, instead, there is only the cows' mooing. We have only Korydon's word for it that they are giving voice to their longing for Aigon. They could just be hungry.[19] So much for the "pathetic fallacy" in this poem; at least Daphnis's cattle mourned at his feet (*Id.* 1.74–75).

Many scholars have remarked on sharp contrasts between the personalities of Battos and Korydon, although these have been evaluated in different ways.[20] Partly on the basis of the opposition between them, Gutzwiller has suggested that because of Korydon's obtuse literal-mindedness and failure to take the bait that Battos offers, they fail to get a proper agon or contest going of the sort that occurs in *Idyll* 5, animated by the mutual hostility between Lakon and Komatas, so that we end up with "an *agon* that is no *agon*."[21] In a similar vein, Hunter suggests that "the matching triplets of [lines 17–28] reinforce the sense of an *agon*" that never actually occurs.[22] Such a failure of a full-blown song contest to materialize

---

17. δείλαιαι, repeated emphatically by Korydon in the next line, is also in grand tragic style (Ott 1969, 51).

18. Lawall 1967, 43, notes the similarity here with the erotic situations in other *Idylls*.

19. Cf. Hunter 1999, 134, on line 12: "Subsequent verses and the pointed ambiguity of 13—is the βουκόλος Aigon or Korydon?—invite us rather to interpret the cattle's lowing as a sign of hunger."

20. See Ott 1969, 47–48; van Sickle 1969, 135–136; Lattimore 1973, 319–321; Walker 1980, 49; Segal 1981, 90–92; Vox 1985; Haber 1994, 20–22.

21. Gutzwiller 1991, 148–149. I would not join her in characterizing Battos as angry and hostile; he seems to me coolly (perhaps urbanely) cynical.

22. Hunter 1999, 130.

could be another symptom of decaying bucolic; but I would not rely on it heavily for my argument, although I would not rule it out, either. It does not seem clear that an agon is such a conventional feature of Theocritean bucolic that we should expect it here.[23] We should, on the other hand, expect some kind of song. But when Battos and Korydon get around to the subject of song as Theocritean herdsmen generally do, the resulting song exchange, within the context of the bucolic *Idylls*, is peculiar.

In lines 26–28, Battos laments, in effect, that because of Aigon's lust for "an evil victory," the cows will die of hunger, and "the *syrinx* that once you [Aigon] made for yourself is getting flecked with mildew" (translation based on Gow's). The issue, then, is not the musical superiority of one herdsman over another, as it is in *Idyll* 5, but the survival of music itself in the void that, according to Battos, Aigon has left behind him; and given the significance of the *syrinx*, that means the survival of *bucolic* music and therefore the integrity of the bucolic world itself. It was, we recall, a *syrinx* that the dying Daphnis wished to leave to Pan as a token of continuity, and although that effort was unsuccessful, his music survives in some form in the *syrinx* playing of the goatherd, whose piping is analogous to the whisper of the pine trees and second only to that of Pan (*Id.* 1.1–6). Even if we are to believe that Aigon was accomplished on the *syrinx*, can Korydon fill the same role as the goatherd of *Idyll* 1?

Korydon replies that the *syrinx* is not moldering, that he is putting it to good use, and that music is alive and well in the vicinity of Kroton (*Id.* 4.29–37):

οὐ τήνα γ', οὐ Νύμφας, ἐπεὶ ποτὶ Πῖσαν ἀφέρπων
δῶρον ἐμοί νιν ἔλειπεν· ἐγὼ δέ τις εἰμὶ μελικτάς,
κεὖ μὲν τὰ Γλαύκας ἀγκρούομαι, εὖ δὲ τὰ Πύρρω.
αἰνέω τάν τε Κρότωνα—"Καλὰ πόλις ἅ τε Ζάκυνθος…"—
καὶ τὸ ποταῷον τὸ Λακίνιον, ἇπερ ὁ πύκτας
Αἴγων ὀγδώκοντα μόνος κατεδαίσατο μάζας.

---

23. It seems an overstatement to call "a formal amoebean contest" "characteristic of most of Theocritus' bucolic idylls" (Kampakoglou 2014, 23; cf. Stanzel 2021, 346–347, who argues for a "dominant role" of contest poems in Theocritus). A competitive spirit may inform Theocritus's representations of poetry, and this may hint at poetic festivals as a performance context for his own poems, as in *Id.* 17.112–114 (Acosta-Hughes 2012c, 402–408), but that is not the same as claiming that formal song contests are a regular feature of the *Idylls*. In fact, agons occur in just two of Theocritus's genuine poems: *Idylls* 5 (highly competitive) and 6 (minimally competitive). The song exchange between Lykidas and Simikhidas in *Idyll* 7 could be considered mildly agonistic in that Simikhidas seems to be trying to prove himself to Lykidas (*Id.* 7.30–31; his actual rivalry is directed toward Asklepiades and Philitas, line 40), but to my mind it hardly counts. The one in *Idyll* 10 is not competitive but contrasts different types of song, and that poem is not bucolic anyway. For my purposes, it is enough to say that we expect some kind of bucolic song.

τηνεί καὶ τὸν ταῦρον ἀπ' ὤρεος ἄγε πιάξας
τᾶς ὁπλᾶς κἤδωκ' Ἀμαρυλλίδι, ταὶ δὲ γυναῖκες
μακρὸν ἀνάυσαν, χὠ βουκόλος ἐξεγέλασσεν.

No it isn't, no, by the Nymphs, because when he was leaving for Pisa
he left it to me as a gift. And I am something of a singer,
and skillfully I strike up the songs of Glauke, skillfully the songs of
    Pyrrhos.
And I praise both Kroton—"and a lovely city is Zakynthos..."—
And the Lakinian shrine to the east, where the boxer
Aigon by himself downed eighty loaves.
There too he brought the bull from the mountain grasping it
by the hoof, and gave it to Amaryllis, and the women
screamed loudly, and the cowherd laughed.

Critics often give a positive evaluation of Korydon's singing as he represents it. Steven Walker, for instance, calls the passage an "enthusiastic evocation of the joys of poetic creativity," and says that Korydon here turns out to be "very much the Theocritean herdsman-poet."[24] But attention to what it is that Korydon claims to sing will lead us to a different view.

To the extent that the gift of the *syrinx* by the departing Aigon was a gesture of investiture in bucolic song and full participation in the bucolic world, it has failed in that purpose. Whatever else is in Korydon's repertoire, it is not bucolic song. It includes "the drunken trifles of Glauke's Muses" (Γλαύκης μεμεθυσμένα παίγνια Μουσέων)[25] and the compositions of Pyrrhos—that is, the kind of salacious songs enjoyed in sophisticated urban settings such as the court at Alexandria but also by popular audiences.[26] Simikhidas may boast that their reputation has carried his songs "even, perhaps, to the throne of Zeus" (this is usually taken to mean "to the ears of Ptolemy," *Id.* 7.93), but his credentials as a bucolic poet are equally suspect. Urbane and sophisticated though the idylls of Theocritus really are, they present bucolic song as simple and in touch primarily with the energies of the natural world; thus, by implication, it is being contaminated by music from a very

---

24. Walker 1980, 50 and 52, respectively. Others take a more nuanced view but still fit Korydon into the bucolic ethos: Segal 1981, 91, 96; van Sickle 1969, 145; Vox 1985, 175–176.

25. From an epigram by Hedylos quoted by Athenaeus iv, 176d. On Hedylos, this epigram, Glauke, and the type of poetry she wrote, see Fraser 1972, I, 573–574.

26. For what is known or guessed about these two poets, see Gow 1952, II, 83–84; Hunter 1999, 136–137.

different cultural sphere. The incongruity is all the more vivid when we imagine the songs of Glauke and Pyrrhos accompanied by snatches of music played on the *syrinx*, the rustic instrument par excellence.[27]

Korydon gives us an idea of the contents of his other song, in praise of Kroton. According to the most reasonable punctuation and interpretation of line 32, the city is named, and then Korydon gives us a sample of his actual song, "and a lovely city is Zakynthos" (this may have been clear in performance, with a switch to singing here). This phrase would have been the beginning of a priamel that culminated in "but most lovely of all is Kroton."[28] The style is that of epinician, which often uses the priamel as a focusing device, often praises the victorious athlete's native city, and often mentions the place where the winning athletic feat occurred (here the temple of Hera at Lakinion near Kroton) as a transitional device to praise of the achievement itself.[29] Here the achievements are eating a prodigious number of loaves and dragging a bull from the mountain. Although epinician poetry suppresses it, in the popular view, gluttony was thought to be characteristic of athletes, and especially of the archetypal athlete Herakles, to whom Korydon likens Aigon in line 8.

Thus, when Korydon protests that Aigon's *syrinx* is not spotted with mildew and that he himself, its inheritor, is "something of a singer," we expect to hear a sample of bucolic song, but we get a debased form of epinician instead. We could consider it a parody that exposes epinician's presuppositions as parodies do: Herakles, founder of the Olympic games, was also, especially in his comic aspect, a prodigious glutton, and in this he is followed by Aigon. From this perspective, through the mention of Aigon's bolting down eighty loaves, bucolic would seem to be drawing epinician into itself, debasing it by contaminating it with comedy and so distinguishing itself from it. But that is only half the story. Even if in the form of parody, epinician invades bucolic and displaces it, just as Aigon drags the bull "down from the mountain" (*Id.* 4.35)—and so out of the bucolic world—in order to put it to non-bucolic uses. In the kind of antithetical reading recommended by Haber[30] for Theocritean bucolic and later pastoral, we can say that bucolic cannot appropriate

---

27. Van Sickle 1969, 142, although he sees Korydon as participating in the formation of a bucolic world, observes that "the poetry of Corydon is that of a new arrival." If Korydon in fact is not established in the countryside, that fits with my argument that there is no authentic herdsman to take care of Aigon's cattle.

28. Gow 1952, II, 84; Dover 1971, 124; Hunter 1999, 137. On the much-discussed textual and interpretive questions of line 32, see especially the thorough discussion of Kampakoglou 2014, 6–11, who favors Edmonds's καλὰν πόλιν ἅτε Ζάκυνθον.

29. See Hubbard 1998, 29–30, who does not ask why Theocritus represents a herder claiming to sing epinician.

30. Haber 1994.

epinician without transgressing the boundary between the two forms that it is trying to affirm. Bucolic poetry is "contaminated" by epinician's concern for the civic and communal (athletics, sacrifice, the shrine of Hera Lakinia) with which, in other idylls, it has nothing to do. More generally, Aigon's desire for athletic victory imports epinician values into the bucolic world even as he leaves it. Bucolic and epinician poetry carry with them their own characteristic outlooks and values; each is shorthand for a way of being in the world, and they are incompatible. Aigon incongruously combines them; in Korydon's paraphrase of his song, he is "the boxer" (ὁ πύκτας, line 33) but also the cowherd (ὁ βουκόλος, line 37) who laughs when the women shriek. But he has decided in favor of athletics and left the bucolic world crumbling. Or if the cowherd of line 37 is someone else, the owner of the bull Aigon has forcibly brought out of the mountain, he stands for a certain corruption of bucolic because he is amused at a use of the bull that objectifies the animal and is hard to reconcile with bucolic poetry's usual emphasis on the closeness between herders and their charges.[31]

Why does Aigon give the bull to Amaryllis? As a joking love token? In the bucolic world, apples (e.g., *Id.* 3.10–11) or birds (*Id.* 5.96–97, 133) serve this function, not herd animals.[32] They are the object of the herdsman's professional concern. But the setting, the famous shrine at Kroton to Hera Lakinia, suggests that the bull is ultimately for sacrifice. With only a few exceptions, the other *Idylls* make no mention of the cultural uses to which herd animals were put in ancient Greece. But in *Idyll* 4, there are specific references to eating their meat and sacrificing them: Aigon's taking twenty sheep to Olympia for provisions, the reference to bull sacrifice in lines 20–22, and most likely Aigon's purpose in dragging the bull to Hera's shrine. In the other *Idylls*, there is a passing reference to the tenderness of a kid's meat (*Id.* 1.6), and *Idyll* 5 mentions sacrifice, eating the meat, and animal skins (*Id.* 5.2, 11–12, 50–51, 56–57, 139–140). For the most part in the bucolic poems, the herdsman is the protector, not the consumer, of his animals.

---

31. For a different reading of this passage, see Kampakoglou 2014. He, too, sees a tension between bucolic and epinician but argues that it is resolved in favor of the former, that *Idyll* 4 "bucolicizes" epinician. He ends up in more or less the same place as van Sickle and Segal, with oppositions harmonized and bucolic values affirmed. On Kampakoglou's reading, the poem shows the commodiousness of bucolic, the way it can incorporate other genres (comedy as well as epinician). As with other poems, I think that there are issues that go beyond generic play, although that is important to this and other *Idylls*.

32. *Id.* 3.34–36 is a possible, but not certain, exception. Polyphemos is rearing eleven fawns and four bear cubs for Galateia (*Id.* 11.40–41), not herd animals. At *Id.* 5.98–99, Lakon announces his intention to give Kratidas the wool of a ewe for a cloak (that is, to be made into a cloak) when he shears it, not the sheepskin itself. Since this answers Komatas's reference to giving a girl a ring dove, the wool functions as a love token, but it is an animal product, not the animal itself.

This suppression of the more practical (and less gentle!) aspects of herding is an element of the idealizing picture of the bucolic world that these poems generally give. In *Idyll* 4, the roles given to sacrifice and eating are another sign of the dissolution, if not of bucolic life itself, then of the other poems' representation of it. It is, furthermore, interesting that almost all of the other such references cluster in *Idyll* 5, which is not shy about the grittier aspects of herding and, as we have seen, works with *Idyll* 4 in exploring the boundaries of the bucolic world.

Because of the way, in Theocritus, song condenses so much about its environment, Korydon's song and its affinities with epinician are a striking example of the decay of bucolic in *Idyll* 4. But now the mention of Amaryllis provokes three lines from Battos that seem (but only seem) squarely within the bucolic perspective and in the bucolic style (*Id.* 4.38–40):

ὦ χαρίεσσ' Ἀμαρυλλί, μόνας σέθεν οὐδὲ θανοίσας
λασεύμεσθ'· ὅσον αἶγες ἐμὶν φίλαι, ὅσσον ἀπέσβης.
αἰαῖ τῶ σκληρῶ μάλα δαίμονος ὅς με λελόγχει.

O lovely Amaryllis, even in death we shall not forget
you alone. As much as goats are dear to me, so [dear were
   you when] your life was quenched.
O the harsh daimon to whom I was allotted!

Here we have an absence that generates something like bucolic song, as the echo of *Id.* 3.6 in the first line quoted suggests, but it is actually an imitation. A love song such as the goatherd's in *Idyll* 3 or Polyphemos's in *Idyll* 11 is based on the hope that the Nymph it is addressed to may actually appear, even though we may have our doubts about her reality. Here Amaryllis is dead; what is the use of apostrophizing her? As Korydon, in his cliché-ridden attempt to console Battos, says somewhat tactlessly, "hopes are among the living" (or "while there's life there's hope," ἐλπίδες ἐν ζωοῖσιν, line 42). As with Aigon's cows, the longing based on absence is drained of productive energy, and Battos's lament becomes merely sentimental. And it is bad bucolic poetry, on the lips of someone who is ignorant of recent events concerning Aigon and Korydon, who displays citified resentment of a local deme (*Id.* 4.20–22, one of the references to sacrifice in the poem), and who needs to be told by Korydon not to come barefoot to "the mountain" if he does not want to get thorns in his feet,[33] and therefore seems an outsider to the

---

33. It may be true, as Hunter 1999, 142, suggests, that we should not assume that herders never went barefoot. But Korydon's phrasing, "when you come to the mountain," implies that Battos is not a habitué of this place.

bucolic world or someone who has only nodding acquaintance with it. Battos is often said to be a goatherd, but the only basis for the claim is line 39, in his lament.[34] What if he is, as Steven Lattimore suggests, only "playing at being a goatherd"?[35] With the tribute he pays Amaryllis in line 39, he seems to be trying to adopt the persona of the herdsman-singer as Simikhidas evidently does in *Idyll* 7—and with considerably less success. Line 39 fails miserably as a "pastoral analogy"; "I loved you as much as I love my goats" is not much of a tribute to Amaryllis, even if we grant that the expression reflects the bucolic value of closeness between humans and animals. Simikhidas does a better job (*Id.* 7.96–97):

Σιμιχίδᾳ μὲν Ἔρωτες ἐπέπταρον· ἦ γὰρ ὁ δειλός
τόσσον ἐρᾷ Μυρτοῦς ὅσον εἴαρος αἶγες ἔρανται.

The Erotes sneezed on Simikhidas. For the poor man
loves Myrtô as much as goats love the spring.

As goats love the spring, so Simikhidas loves Myrtô; she is then analogized to springtime, with all its implications of life and fertility. Battos might be trying to express sincere emotion using conventions that are under strain, or he might be pretending to have the emotion because bucolic characters are expected to, with the pretense showing through in his words. Either way, his attempt shows the emptying out of bucolic song. It functions somewhat in the way parody often does: its sentimentality and banal pretentiousness distance the reader and hold up for examination the speaker's diction and the rustic scale of values that he is trying to express. It is precisely in poetry that expresses the waning phase of the bucolic world that we might expect to find this kind of scrutiny of what is taken for granted during that world's flourishing.

So in this central passage of the poem (*Id.* 4.29–40), we have a degraded form of epinician imported into a bucolic context followed by an inept attempt at bucolic lament, both produced by two characters, neither of whom is a satisfactory bucolic figure. Now something else happens that occurs nowhere else in

---

34. See the (in my view) too credulous scholion on this line: ἐνταῦθα σαφὴς αἰπόλος ὢν ὁ Βάττος ("here it is clear that Battos is a goatherd"). Cf. Cairns 2017, 348.

35. Lattimore 1973, 324, with earlier bibliography that shows commentators' recognition that Battos does not quite fit the bucolic environment. I would not follow Lattimore in considering Battos a mask for Theocritus himself. Van Sickle 1969, 142n16, sees incongruity in Battos's resort to pastoral and comments that "displacement, hence incongruity of sentiment and of language, is the soul of the poem." I fully agree. Hutchinson 1988, 168, takes a very different view of Battos, namely that his words and attitudes are due to his having been Aigon's rival for Amaryllis's affections. It hardly needs saying that there is no basis for this in the text.

Theocritean bucolic. One of the suppositions of these poems is that the herdsmen have leisure to sing, and there are occasional nods to verisimilitude, as we have seen, in the notion that someone else might take over the job of herding for the duration of the song. But here talk of singing is interrupted, and for the only time in Theocritus, a herdsman has to do some work. Some of the cows have gone downhill and are eating the shoots of the olive trees, and Korydon has to drive them back uphill. This he tries to do, with much bustle and not much apparent success. He can only wish, impotently, that he had a curved club to beat the animals. And why does he not have one, since it seems to have been a standard part of a herdsman's equipment (*Id.* 7.18–19, 128)?[36] Its lack may be a sign of Korydon's inadequacy as a herdsman. As for Battos, all he can do is "gape" at one of the cows (line 53) after telling Korydon to throw things at the cows to force them back up the hill.[37] So he is not much use. We never do find out whether the cows obey Korydon, because the "work" is interrupted by the episode of the thorn in Battos's foot; his inexperience gets in the way of bucolic activity.

The poem ends with a discussion of the "little old man" (possibly Aigon's father, line 4), "hard at work," "grinding that dark-browed sweetie" (τήναν τὰν κυάνοφρυν ἐρωτίδα) beside the cattle pen (lines 58–63).[38] In this version of labor, desire is, for once, fulfilled, but in a debased way as the language describing it shows and as is also suggested by both the location and the fact that, as Hunter points out, the old man's "sweetie" is as likely to be animal as human.[39] The phrase used to describe her recalls the goatherd's language in his song of longing in *Idyll* 3, and the similarity underlines an essential contrast.[40] This direct, matter-of-fact satisfaction of desire is the antithesis of the recognition we have found in other poems of the complexity of human sexuality, which is manifested in energetic desire stimulated by lack and need, and again recalls *Idyll* 5.

---

36. See Gow 1952, II, 87–88, and the passages cited there.

37. Battos's ineffectiveness is, I take it, the point of χασμεύμενος rather than erotic attraction to the cow (Lawall 1967, 48–49).

38. Could ἠνήργει ("was hard at work") in line 61, aside from its crudity, be a sly allusion to Aristotle's definition of εὐδαιμονία, "happiness" or "well-being" (*Eth. Nic.* 10, 1177a12) as κατ' ἀρετὴν ἐνέργεια, "activity in accordance with virtue"?

39. Hunter 1999, 143. I have to disagree with Segal's (1981, 100–101) optimistic reading of this scene and of the end of the poem.

40. *Id.* 3.18–19, ὦ τὸ καλὸν ποθορεῦσα, τὸ πᾶν λίθος, ὦ κυάνοφρυ / νύμφα ("O you with beauty in your glance, all stone, O dark-browed nymph"); 3.7, τὸν ἐρωτύλον ("your sweetheart," the goatherd's hopeful description of himself). The similarities are merely noted by Gow and Hunter. But taken with the widely acknowledged echo of *Id.* 3.6 at 4.38, these similarities seem to underscore the significant differences between the two poems in their approaches to desire.

Within the framework of all the features that make *Idyll* 4 marginal in relation to Theocritus's more usual bucolics, an explanation can be sought of why it and *Idyll* 5 are set in South Italy, near Kroton and Sybaris/Thurii, respectively. This local specificity, although it is not extensive, is unusual in the bucolic *Idylls*, as we saw in chapter 1. Cities are a presence in *Idylls* 4 and 5. The contrast between the bucolics' usual vagueness about the herdsmen's status and the explicitly servile status of Lakon and Komatas in *Idyll* 5 works in a parallel way. Their masters live in the city and presumably exert control from there. *Idyll* 5 reveals the most earthy extreme of the bucolic world while still, in the embedded songs, retaining an appreciation of its beauties. *Idyll* 4 shows that world in the process of disenchantment.

But how can we explain the choice of South Italy in particular? Along with Stephens, I suggest that it adds to, and puts in a wider context, the atmosphere of disintegration that is palpable especially in *Idyll* 4.[41] Throughout the archaic period, Kroton was a thriving and powerful city, but its fortunes waned in the fourth century BCE. In the first quarter of the third century, it was sacked and occupied several times, a victim of the political and military turbulence that engulfed southern Italy.[42] Thurii, the successor of Sybaris, fared no better. These places provide a fitting backdrop for *Idylls* 4 and 5 as I have interpreted them. It is true that the landmarks mentioned in *Idyll* 4.17–24 construct a space lush with fodder for cattle, but with the possible exception of Latymnon (if that is a mountain), they imply lowland water meadows (as in *Idyll* 25). And for one reason or another, Aigon's cows are emaciated. This is not bucolic space, which as we have seen does not fare well in *Idyll* 4. The name of the man who took Aigon to Olympia, Milon (*Id.* 4.6), surely evokes the famous sixth-century BCE Krotonian athlete of that name. In stories about him, that Milon was credited with habitual copious eating and drinking and with carrying a four-year-old bull on his shoulders around the stadium at Olympia and then eating all of it

---

41. Stephens 2018, 70–71, on *Idyll* 4. About *Idyll* 5, she says, "the *Idyll* calls attention to the reduced circumstances of this region of Magna Graecia, and to the values that Theocritus invests in the rural landscape and its fruitfulness" (72). On the South Italian setting, see the more detailed discussion of Barigazzi 1974, 306–311. He sees it working in a positive way, because the mention of landmarks such as the Neaithos River would evoke in readers the memory of Kroton's past glories, especially its athletic renown. I emphasize instead its current desolate state (which Barigazzi uses only to date *Idyll* 4) and suggest that memories of the past, which I agree are alive in the poem, create a sad contrast with Kroton's (and Sybaris's) condition at the time of Theocritus's writing.

42. For details, see Gow 1952, II, 76–77; Barigazzi 1974, 310.

in one day.[43] Memories of Aigon in *Idyll* 4 show him miming the great Milon, but with a difference. Milon carried the bull around the stadium at Olympia in sight of all the audience—to Panhellenic acclaim, we might say. Outside of that context, Aigon's imitative display of strength seems gratuitous and pointless, and it is greeted not with admiring cheers but with women's shrieks. Taking the bull out of "the mountain" violates the integrity of the bucolic world. It may also be significant that Aigon merely drags the bull by the hooves rather than carrying it on his shoulders as Milon did. Aigon is a diminished and comic version of Milon, a would-be Milon, especially if we pay any attention at all to Battos's cynicism about his athletic pretensions (*Id.* 4.7, 9). The memory of Milon, which conjures up Kroton's glory in its heyday, serves only as a foil to the city's diminished state, which provides a civic analogy to the waning of the bucolic world in this poem.

Aigon truly, as Battos says, "is gone and vanished." His absence becomes a symbol for the disarray of bucolic. I would not, however, read *Idyll* 4 as cynical or destructive. It serves a positive purpose in relation to other bucolic *Idylls*. It sets in relief the foundational values of the bucolic world and bucolic poetry that those poems construct: that world's self-sufficiency and independence of the city and its forms of human society; song as the encapsulation of its values and as a means of striving toward a realization of the not-quite-attainable ideal of full bucolic presence; and the productive results of absence and eros as well as their frustrations. In addition, as Stephens has emphasized, the sorry state of Kroton may imply by contrast that the bucolic world can only flourish within a protective and well-ordered state ruled by an enlightened king—like Ptolemy![44] There is thus a link between this poem, where the crumbling of bucolic matches civic decay, and the vision, expressed in bucolic terms, of a restored Sicily in *Idyll* 16—a vision that, it is evidently hoped, will be fulfilled not so much by Hieron as by Ptolemy.

Idyll 10: The World of Labor

Work may be only occasional and not very effective in the bucolic world, but as soon as the focus shifts to the adjacent setting of agriculture, the emphasis is heavily on labor and its necessity. Work is what most sharply distinguishes between these two worlds, which otherwise communicate.[45] *Idyll* 10 consists of a dialogue

---

43. Athen. x, 412e–f. Hunter 1999, 138, also points to Theseus's dragging of the Marathonian bull and possible connections between *Idyll* 4 and Callimachus's *Hecale*.

44. Stephens 2018: 70, 82–83.

45. Cf. Walker 1980, 87: "The accent put on work is a sign that Theocritus has left the domain of the pastoral genre with this composition, however ingeniously it transposes pastoral themes

and song exchange between two reapers, so that in overall form it resembles the bucolic poems; but the formal resemblance, in my view, serves only to underscore the differences. Milon taxes Boukaios for his negligence in reaping, learns that Boukaios is in love with Bombyka, and after some teasing invites him to sing a love song to her in order to lighten his work. Milon then counters the love song with a work song that he attributes to the mythical agricultural hero Lityerses, and the poem ends with his saying that this is the kind of song that men working in full sun ought to be singing.

Boukaios's song, although not the most elegant composition, has clear affinities with those embedded in bucolic idylls. The apostrophe of Βομβύκα χαρίεσσα ("lovely Bombyka") that frames it (*Id.* 10.26, 36) harks back to the goatherd's ὦ χαρίεσσ' Ἀμαρυλλί in *Idyll* 3.6, and in good bucolic style Boukaios seeks to root his "madness" in the instinctual behavior of the natural world, including goats' preference for clover (*Id.* 10.30–31; cf. 5.128). *Idyll* 10 thus incorporates a bucolic-style song, but only to show how out of place it is away from "the mountain." Precisely to the extent that Boukaios is a character with bucolic tendencies, he is a failure as an agricultural laborer. According to Milon, love has no place in the scale of values of the agricultural world. It is a mere distraction in an environment conditioned by the necessity of work and the need for subsistence—the Hesiodic Age of Iron. For if Boukaios's song is fashioned in the manner of bucolic singing, Milon's song takes the *Works and Days* as its model.

The first two words of the poem, Milon's address to Boukaios, bring these worlds into confrontation: ἐργατίνα Βουκαῖε ("Boukaios the laborer"). The name "Boukaios" seems to mean "cowherd,"[46] and on the terms of Theocritean bucolic, the idea of a "cowherd laborer" is contradictory. If a cowherd is trying to reap, can the results be anything but unfortunate? Another incongruous juxtaposition occurs in line 4: Boukaios lags behind the line of reapers "as a ewe behind the flock, whose foot a thorn has pricked." One reading of this line might be

---

and motifs from the pastures to the cultivated fields." Here I want to examine that transposition and will argue that it serves to draw sharp distinctions. Hunt 2009, 391–394, is attentive to differences between this and the bucolic poems but includes *Idyll* 10 among them "on the basis of the similarity of their fictional worlds." He takes a carefully nuanced view, but in the end, it tends to obscure the contrast between the two worlds that I think *Idyll* 10 is drawing. For brief remarks about the unsentimental portrayal of work in this poem, see Scholten 2006, 76–78. She recognizes that the necessity of work leaves no room for love according to the poem but does not mention the contrast with the bucolic poems.

46. See Gow 1952, II, 193. For a somewhat different view of the juxtaposition, see Hunt 2009, 394–395. On the name, Hunter 1999, 201, comments, "Boukaios plays the 'Daphnis role'—the bucolic hero suffering from love." This is important. I would add only that the poem shows how out of place the "Daphnis role" is for a reaper.

that it "serves to remind (or perhaps to reassure us) that, though the immediate surroundings may be different, we have not entirely escaped from the landscape of the pastoral."[47] But to liken reapers to sheep is not entirely apt. The point of contact is that they form a group moving together docilely in the same direction and at the same speed. But the simile yokes two worlds that are distinct even if they are parts of the countryside, and I suggest that the dissimilarity within likeness here is a calculated effect. Right at the beginning of the poem, then, when the reader is not yet fully oriented to its themes and is only aware that Boukaios's lackadaisical reaping is a problem, there are signs that the setting is very different from that of the bucolic poems.

What do we learn about this different world as the poem progresses? The most obvious characteristic is that here work is what matters above all else, work that, at least at certain seasons such as the harvest, is hard and unremitting. The rhythm of work matches that of the year, but within that framework labor is measured by the day. In his song, Milon relays the Hesiodic-sounding[48] advice that at certain times of the year, reapers should begin work when the lark awakens and stop when it goes to sleep and should rest through the midday heat, but threshers should avoid rest even then (*Id.* 10.48–51). Just as Milon began his first speech with a significant vocative, Boukaios in his reply does the same (*Id.* 10.7):

Μίλων ὀψαμᾶτα, πέτρας ἀπόκομμ' ἀτεράμνω

Milon, reaper until late at night, chip of unyielding rock

A dedicated reaper, then, works until late in the evening. Boukaios's comparison of Milon to a piece of rock may imply insensitivity, in view of the question he goes on to ask: have you never been in love? But it also reflects the strength and endurance it takes to swing a scythe for many long hours. Reaping is harsh toil and not for those who stay awake all night tormented by love (*Id.* 10.10).

Another characteristic of *Idyll* 10 is its emphasis on food and drink, especially their scarcity.[49] In the bucolic poems, herdsmen never seem to lack milk, cheese, apples, and grapes. Outside of love, want is foreign to the bucolic world. But reapers such as Milon, it is implied, whether slaves or free wage earners, have to work

---

47. Whitehorne 1974, 34. The *landscape* of the pastoral is precisely what we have escaped, since, as we have seen, agricultural space is distinct from bucolic space.

48. There is no verbal echo here, but Hesiod also advises reapers to rise before dawn and work all day (*Op.* 571–581), a parallel noted also by Hunter 1999, 213.

49. On "eating and emaciation" in *Idyll* 10, see Grethlein 2012, 604–607. He makes this the basis for an ingenious metapoetic reading of the poem, to which I will return at the end of this section.

for mere subsistence. That is why love is a luxury and a dangerous distraction in his eyes. Milon expresses himself in pithy proverbial sayings that set his diction apart from Boukaios's and that reflect, or at least give the impression that they reflect, popular experience of the harshness of hardscrabble living. That only Milon speaks in proverbs and Boukaios does not is expressive of the difference between the two worlds and the outlook on life typical of each.[50] So in answer to Boukaios's question about whether he has ever lain awake at night because of love, Milon says, "it's a bad thing to give a dog a taste of guts" (χαλεπὸν χορίῳ κύνα γεῦσαι, *Id.* 10.11)—that is, it is bad to give someone not used to it an experience of luxury.[51] In the same vein, when Boukaios confesses that he has been in love for ten days, Milon responds acidly, "you're clearly draining off the [whole] storage jar, while I don't even have enough vinegar [that is, the sour wine left at the bottom of the jar]" (*Id.* 10.13). A work song might fittingly comment on the hard conditions of a life of toil as a way of uniting the group of laborers by appealing to their shared experience. This is how Milon ends his song, in lines addressed to his fellow reapers (*Id.* 10.52–55):

εὐκτὸς ὁ τῶ βατράχω, παῖδες, βίος· οὐ μελεδαίνει
τὸν τὸ πιεῖν ἐκχεῦντα· πάρεστι γὰρ ἄφθονον αὐτῷ.
κάλλιον, ὦ 'πιμελητὰ φιλάργυρε, τὸν φακὸν ἕψειν,
μὴ 'πιτάμῃς τὰν χεῖρα καταπρίων τὸ κύμινον.

    Pray for the frog's life, boys. He doesn't have to worry about
who is going to pour out his drink. There's water in plenty all around him.
    Overseer, you miser! Better to boil the beans,
so that you don't cut your fingers dicing up the cumin seeds.

A frog is better off than a laborer; he has plenty to drink. This takes up Milon's earlier complaint about having only the vinegar at the bottom of a wine jar and makes literal what was a metaphor (though one clearly drawn from experience). After scarcity of drink comes hunger. Since cumin seeds are very small, cutting them up (literally, "sawing them into bits") was a proverbial expression for stinginess, and the overseer is urged to stop stinting and cook soup for the workers

---

50. See now Palmieri 2021, 482–483.

51. The translation and interpretation are those given by Hunter 1999, 203. If χόριον means "skin" or "leather" without the meat, something attractive to the dog (Gow 1952, II, 195), the resulting meaning is the same. Or if leather is unpleasant to the dog, Milon is expressing disgust at the whole idea of being kept awake by love when he has to start work early in the morning.

instead.[52] This plea vividly conveys dependence for basic sustenance on another, who can at will be either generous or grudging, as the condition of a worker's life—dependence all the more complete if, as seems likely, Boukaios and Milon are slaves.[53] Milon's song, like Boukaios's, begins and ends with invocations, but the difference between the figures invoked underlines the sharp contrast between a love song and a work song. Boukaios calls upon the Muses and then Bombyka at the beginning and Bombyka again at the end. Milon begins by invoking Demeter as "bountiful in fruits, bountiful in grain" (Δάματερ πολύκαρπε, πολύσταχυ) and then asks her to make the crop both abundant and easy to harvest (εὔεργον)—plenty of food with less arduous work (*Id.* 10.42–43). And he ends, as we have just seen, with a plea to the overseer not to leave his workers hungry.

How is Boukaios's love portrayed in the poem? His language when he reveals his love to Milon is key (*Id.* 10.7–9):

BO. Μίλων ὀψαμᾶτα, πέτρας ἀπόκομμ' ἀτεράμνω,
     οὐδαμά τοι συνέβα ποθέσθαι τινὰ τῶν ἀπεόντων;

MI. οὐδαμά. τίς δὲ πόθος τῶν ἔκτοθεν ἐργάτᾳ ἀνδρί;

BO. Milon, reaper until late at night, chip of unyielding rock,
     Has it never happened to you to long for someone [or some things] among those that are absent?

MI. Never. What is longing for outside people [or things] to a laboring man?

"To desire someone who is absent" could be the motto for bucolic poetry. And, in good bucolic fashion, that desire generates a song, complete with apostrophes to Bombyka that try to summon up her presence. But whereas this dynamic is at home on "the mountain," Milon's reply shows that such desire is foreign to a

---

52. Hunter 1999, 213–214. As Hunter says, there is the further implication that the overseer should stop stinting on flavoring for the soup, cumin being extremely common and easy to obtain in the Mediterranean.

53. An indication of their status is that Bombyka is said to be "Polybotas's girl" (*Id.* 10.15), either his daughter or his slave. The name Polybotas ("possessor of many cattle") implies wealth, and if Bombyka was playing the pipes for reapers at Hippokion's farm, she is presumably of low status and so Polybotas's slave rather than his daughter. Boukaios must be of similar status. On the other hand, there is the exhortation in Milon's song to the sheaf binders to earn their wages (*Id.* 10.44–45), so they would be *thetes*. But there is no reason that slaves and wage laborers would not be at work in the same field, and sheaf binders might well be paid seasonal workers. In the end, there will have been little difference between slaves and *thetes* in regard to the precarious condition in which they lived.

context of work. He changes Boukaios's wording slightly and, rather than "those absent," speaks of "those outside," that is, those from outside the world of physical labor (Bombyka piping to reapers does not count as labor, though it helps ease it) or those people or things extraneous to the task at hand. By bringing to bear on it the perspective of one who must work to survive, he punctures the pathos-laden bucolic longing for the absent.

But there is a further implication in these lines. Boukaios's phrase could also mean "things that are absent" (τινα and the participle in this case being neuter plural and referring to things rather than people). Desire for what one does not have rather than being satisfied with what one does have was (outside Plato's *Symposium*) traditionally a dangerous compulsion in the eyes of the ancient Greeks, because it meant ambition for more than what one was given by *moira* or one's lot in life. Such desire led to a fall, often in the form of divine retribution. Milon's "those from outside" could then mean "those things outside the range of what one properly has" or, more specifically, "those things alien to what a laborer ought to want," that is, the necessity of work and sustenance at a subsistence level. In this light, Milon is, by the terms of traditional morality, prudent and thinks in the spirit of Hesiod's *Works and Days*. Boukaios is flighty on these terms, although not according to the presuppositions of the bucolic world, which seems exempt from the dangers traditional morality saw in loving what is absent. A number of passages in earlier literature speak of such desire in this way.[54] Thucydides, for example, ominously describes the Athenians, in their enthusiasm for attacking Syracuse and enlarging their empire, as δυσέρωτας ... τῶν ἀπόντων, "lusting disastrously after absent things." In the event, they suffered a catastrophic defeat. But since Milon is a Hesiodic figure, these lines from the *Works and Days* (365–367) may well be behind the Theocritean passage:

οἴκοι βέλτερον εἶναι, ἐπεὶ βλαβερὸν τὸ θύρηφιν.
ἐσθλὸν μὲν παρεόντος ἑλέσθαι, πῆμα δὲ θυμῷ
χρηΐζειν ἀπέοντος· ἅ σε φράζεσθαι ἄνωγα.

It is better to be in the house, since what is outside is harmful.
It is noble to take from what you have, but an affliction to the heart
to desire what is absent. I tell you to consider these things.

Just before these lines, Hesiod has been telling his brother to accumulate possessions bit by bit, and eventually they will amount to a lot; what is stored in the house never harmed anyone, whereas taking from someone is harmful. Milon's

---

54. See Hunter 1999, 202–203, for these passages, including the two I discuss.

"the things from outside," perhaps a distant echo of Hesiod's slightly different wording in the third line quoted, would imply "things we shouldn't desire because to do so is dangerous, or at least will make us discontented with what we do have."

Boukaios's words a few lines later, which scholars have often found puzzling, can also be interpreted in this light (*Id.* 10.14):

> τοιγὰρ τὰ πρὸ θυρᾶν μοι ἀπὸ σπόρω ἄσκαλα πάντα.

> [I am in love and] therefore everything in front of my door has been unhoed since the sowing.

The line has seemed to some to raise a problem of chronology in a poem that seems so realistic. It is now harvest season, and Boukaios has been in love for only ten days; hoeing should have occurred long before. But evidently some crops could be planted late, and the young shoots would need the earth loosened around them with the hoe.[55] The difficulty, which thus may not exist, has distracted attention from the line's implication. It may have a literal reference: Boukaios has a garden plot in front of his house. "In front of the door" means that the garden is an adjunct to his physical house and therefore, in Greek terms, is part of his *oikos* or household (such as it is). But the line may point beyond itself to an extended meaning, or it might be entirely metaphorical. In his desire for what is absent, Boukaios is neglecting what is at home, what legitimately belongs to him, contrary to Hesiod's advice. He fails to hoe and lags at reaping. His yearning for what is absent invites, if not divine punishment, then starvation. In this sense, the line has an interesting parallel in Polyphemos's advice to himself to give up Galateia, whom he cannot have: "milk the ewe that's near" (*Id.* 11.75: τὰν παρεοῖσαν ἄμελγε). That he naturally uses a bucolic figure whereas Boukaios uses one drawn from agriculture reflects the difference between the two worlds.

When Milon learns whom Boukaios is in love with, he responds that the gods see that people get what they wish for, and so Boukaios will sleep all night in the embrace of a praying mantis (*Id.* 10.17–18). Boukaios responds with his own piece of traditional morality, in a passage that is worth quoting in its entirety because it leads up to his song (*Id.* 10.19–23):

> BO. μωμᾶσθαί μ' ἀρχῇ τύ· τυφλὸς δ' οὐκ αὐτὸς ὁ Πλοῦτος,
> ἀλλὰ καὶ ὠφρόντιστος Ἔρως. Μὴ δὴ μέγα μυθεῦ.
> MI. οὐ μέγα μυθεῦμαι· τὺ μόνον κατάβαλλε τὸ λᾷον,

---

55. Whitehorne 1974, 35–38. On the supposed problem, see Gow 1952, II, 196.

καί τι κόρας φιλικὸν μέλος ἀμβάλευ. ἅδιον οὕτως
ἐργαξῇ. καὶ μὰν πρότερόν ποκα μουσικὸς ἦσθα.

BO. You're starting to make fun of me. Ploutos [Wealth] isn't the
only blind god,
but that careless Eros is too. Don't talk big.
MI. I'm not talking big. But you—just cut down the crop,
and strike up some love song for the girl. That way
you'll work more sweetly. Indeed, you used to be good at
music before.

"Talking big" for a Greek was to defy or ignore the gods and put oneself above them. Boukaios is answering Milon's "the god discovers the wrongdoer" (*Id.* 10.17) with another piece of traditional morality and accusing him of underestimating the might, and arbitrariness, of Eros as he claims that he himself is helpless in the god's power. Eros can be blind in two senses: he is indiscriminate in causing people to fall in love, and he blinds the lover to the beloved's imperfections (as, according to Milo, is the case with Boukaios). But Eros was rarely spoken of in antiquity as blind, although the lover's blindness was a commonplace.[56] So if Boukaios means to excuse himself as a victim of "blind circumstance" (as we say), his understanding of reality may be deficient. It is interesting also that he pairs Eros and Ploutos here, because he will do so again implicitly in his song, when he wishes for the wealth of Kroisos. It is as though the two gods have more in common than blindness, that they are intertwined: a person needs to be prosperous in order to afford being in love. And that has been Milon's point all along.

Milon responds by urging Boukaios to get to work, and in what seems a concession of sorts, he suggests that Boukaios sing a love song about Bombyka, for "that way you'll work more sweetly." He uses a key word in the bucolic ethos, its space, and its poetry. Against that background, to speak of *working* sweetly is a surprising oxymoron. More specifically, Milon's words recall Lakon's invitation to Komatas to join him in the *locus amoenus* where he is sitting: "you will sing more sweetly [ἅδιον ᾀσῇ] sitting here under the wild olive and these trees" (*Id.* 5.31–32).[57] The contrast between bucolic leisure and the necessity of work could not be sharper. Thus, the whole exchange between Milon and Boukaios leading

---

56. Gow 1952, II, 198–199; Hunter 1999, 205.

57. A parallel noted by Ott 1969, 61n181, and Hunt 2009, 397n17, but without comment on the incongruity when Milon uses the phrase. Hunt suggests that for Milon, work is sweet; in that case, we see the very different values of these two worlds. But Milon's song seems to depict work as necessary rather than pleasant.

up to Boukaios's song frames it as inappropriate to this setting. Love is not easily transported from an environment of leisure, where people can indulge longing for absent things, to the harsh reality of *Idyll* 10's Hesiodic world.

Critical opinions of Boukaios's song have ranged widely.[58] As he does so often, Theocritus makes a variety of very different responses available to his readers. One temptation is to smile at, or ridicule, a rustic's lack of sophistication and leave matters there. But I think we should recognize the depth of feeling in the song, even if, for example, his comparison of Bombyka's feet to knucklebones and her voice to fleabane shows him unable to find language adequate to express it.[59] Boukaios begins with an invocation to the Muses (*Id.* 10.24–25):

> Μοῖσαι Πιερίδες, συναείσετε τὰν ῥαδινάν μοι
> παῖδ'· ὧν γὰρ ἄψησθε, θεαί, καλὰ πάντα ποεῖτε.

> Pierian Muses, join me in singing the slender
> girl. For all that you touch, goddesses, you make beautiful.

The first two words echo, not with entire accuracy, the first two words of Hesiod's *Works and Days* (Μοῦσαι Πιερίηθεν), as though he were trying to fit his song into the agricultural context and produce a work song. But by the end of the line, with the word "slender," he has switched to Sappho as a model, and she remains a strong presence throughout the rest of the song.[60] Sappho, as the consummate poet of desire, fits right in with bucolic poetry but not with agricultural labor. What we see Boukaios doing in the song is attempting to reshape reality in accordance with his desire, as the goatherd seeks to do in *Idyll* 3, and he asks the Muses to help him do exactly this. The relative pronoun in the second line quoted ("whatever you touch") refers at once to his attempt at song and its subject, Bombyka. Milon has described her as ugly, but song will make her beautiful. That transformation begins in the next line: "Lovely Bombyka, they all call you Syrian, dried out, sunburnt,

---

58. Hunter 1996: "Deliberately bad poetry" (124), "a masterly text, but a poor love-song" (26); Whitehorne 1974: "not without art" (38), "a depth and fineness of texture that raise it far above the string of apophthegms that go to make up Milon's song" (39). Payne 2007, 75–76, takes the song seriously as bringing us closer to Boukaios's mind and imagination, as I would. Hunt 2009, 401–412, gives a detailed antithetical reading of Boukaios's and Milon's song, and his argument that the result is to lay bare the presuppositions of bucolic is close to my view.

59. This is essentially Payne's view (see note 58 above). In this sense, Boukaios resembles Battos lamenting Amaryllis in *Idyll* 4. But Battos's pretensions seem stronger because he is self-consciously trying to play a bucolic role, whereas Boukaios seems less artificial. A better comparison is with the goatherd of *Idyll* 3.

60. Lentini 1998; Acosta-Hughes 2006, 31–32, 51–52.

but I alone call you honey-hued." The violet and hyacinth, to which he goes on to compare her, are dark (a concession here to what "they say"), but they are most in demand for making wreaths. Even ugliness can be accounted beautiful if seen in the right way, or given the right analogy. As Daphnis sang in *Idyll* 6 (18–19), "to desire, ugly things have often seemed beautiful." In Boukaios, eros manifests itself in the same way. Poetry and song enable him to transform reality as love wishes, in a process not unlike Theocritus's own fiction-making in the bucolic *Idylls*.

Boukaios's reverie of being as rich as Kroisos (*Id.* 10.32–35), in sharp contrast to Milon's emphasis on neediness, works the same transformation. I say "reverie" because although he starts with an "unfulfilled wish" that implicitly recognizes its own impossibility ("If only it were possible for me [αἴθε μοι ἦς] to possess all that they say Kroisos once had"), Boukaios proceeds to elaborate on what he would do with that wealth, visualizing it in detail. Content outraces rhetorical form and becomes a fantasy. Both he and Bombyka, says Boukaios, would stand as solid gold statues dedicated to Aphrodite, Bombyka holding her pipes as a sign of her specialty,[61] or maybe a rose or an apple (both love tokens), he wearing new clothes and slippers. This urge to memorialize their love, to make something permanent of it, recalls that of the speaker of *Idyll* 12, who imagines the love between himself and the boy he is addressing as the subject of song for future ages, so that two hundred generations later, someone might bring him news in Acheron that it is still on everyone's lips (*Id.* 12.10–21). This passage, too, begins as a wish that is then elaborated into a detailed fantasy that is also doomed to remain just that, because of the boy's fickleness. Boukaios is no more tethered to reality. As Whitehorne points out, gold statues would have been familiar to readers in Alexandria; a number of them had figured prominently in Ptolemy Philadelphus's grand procession.[62] We might smile at this rustic with big-city, even royal, ambitions (or in Whitehorne's phrase, "the comic enormity of Bucaeus' ambitions"), but the size of the gap between fantasy and reality is also touching. It gives us a measure of the tribute Boukaios is paying to Bombyka and so of the depth of his feeling. It also, somewhat paradoxically, makes the reality of his situation all the more vivid. Boukaios the reaper is among the last people in the world likely to have new clothes and fancy footwear. And finally, Boukaios's fantasy—indeed, the whole song—is effective as an example of what the imagination can do even when it has little to work with.

---

61. The name "Bombyka" is evidently derived from the word for a type of flute (Gow 1952, II, 199), and Boukaios first identified her to Milon as "the girl who was piping for the reapers at Hippokion's farm the other day" (*Id.* 10.15–16). On the name, see Payne 2007, 88.

62. Whitehorne 1974, 44. He uses this fact as an indication that *Idyll* 10 "belongs to Theocritus' early days in Alexandria."

And yet a reaper indulging in this reverie would get very little work done. And so Milon, after praising Boukaios's musical ability (*not* the content of his song), sings his own work song as a corrective; *this* is the kind of singing that reapers need to get on with their work.[63] Once again, everything that Boukaios's song represents, which would be at home in the bucolic world, is out of place in a field that needs harvesting. Where Sappho is Boukaios's model, Milon offers Hesiod. Lityerses, to whom Milon attributes his song, was an archetypal heroic reaper, who is implicitly made the agricultural counterpart to Daphnis as inaugurator of a style of song repeated by his successors in this labor, so that he stands in the same relation to Milon as Daphnis does to herdsmen singers.[64] It is intriguing that Sositheus, a dramatist writing in Alexandria in the reign of Ptolemy Philadelphus and so a contemporary of Theocritus, wrote a satyr play called *Daphnis or Lityerses*, in which Daphnis, after a long search, found the girl he was in love with enslaved by Lityerses. Could this play also have opposed the bucolic and agricultural worlds, with Daphnis out of his element and needing to be rescued by Herakles?

It seems beside the point to consider this pair of songs a singing contest in which one party seeks to prove himself the better singer. More is at stake here: the question of which kind of song is appropriate to this context and which is not, and that means which outlook on life, which values and activities, belong in each of these rural spheres, the bucolic and the agricultural. A bucolic contest, on the other hand, revolves around which of two singers can better realize a single set of values that they both share. Milon's coda to his song in the final lines of the poem makes the issue of appropriateness clear (*Id.* 10.56–58):

ταῦτα χρὴ μοχθεῦντας ἐν ἁλίῳ ἄνδρας ἀείδειν,
τὸν δὲ τεόν, Βουκαῖε, πρέπει λιμηρὸν ἔρωτα
μυθίσδειν τᾷ ματρὶ κατ' εὐνὰν ὀρθρευοίσᾳ.

This is what men who work in the sun ought to sing.
As for your starveling love, Boukaios, it's the sort of thing
to tell your mother as she wakes up in bed in the morning.

---

63. On the contrast between the two songs and the different traditions that may have been behind each, see Pretagostini 2006, 55–57. The praise of Boukaios's music may or may not be ironic; the line that follows it (*Id.* 10.40) surely is, almost Socratically so: "alas for my beard, which I've grown in vain" (i.e., I've grown to manhood without *your* talent)—a witty preface to a song that is intended to replace Boukaios's song.

64. Hunt 2009: 402–403. The name "Lityerses" also offers an implicit rebuke to Boukaios. Lityerses challenged people to a reaping contest and killed them when they lost (he was eventually killed in turn by Herakles); Boukaios has been left behind by the other reapers. See Whitehorne 1974, 40.

These are fitting words on the lips of someone who has the name of the great Krotonian athlete.[65] The antitheses operative in the poem are all here: labor versus rest, subsistence versus starvation, outdoors (masculine) versus indoors (feminine), fully developed manliness versus excessive association with women, as though Boukaios were feminized by being in love. The Greeks associated tan skin, such as that of athletes, with masculinity, because men's activities kept them outside, and paleness with femininity, because women stayed in the house. In Euripides's *Bacchae* (457–459), the defensively masculine Pentheus taunts the effeminate Dionysos in this vein: "you have white skin by contrivance, not because of the sun's rays but by hunting Aphrodite in the shadows." There is something of the same attitude in Milon's final lines.[66]

In giving Milon the last word, Theocritus is not, I suggest, repudiating his bucolic poetry or conceding the superiority of Milon's values to those of Boukaios. He is showing that the worlds of herding and agricultural labor, though spatially close and conversant with each other, are in all other ways far apart. His method in *Idyll* 10 of making the differences clear—by incorporating a song with an essentially bucolic outlook in the mouth of a less than bucolic character into an environment where it is so out of place that it can seem ridiculous—may appear to put the bucolic at a disadvantage, but that very fact invites us as readers to put it, in our minds, back where it belongs, on "the mountain." The notion that *Idyll* 10 may have a metapoetic dimension—that Theocritus is defining his own bucolic poetry by contrasting it with what it is not—is strengthened by Jonas Grethlein's suggestion that the emphasis on food and thinness should be connected to the slenderness or λεπτότης (in various senses) that is a prominent part of the aesthetics of Hellenistic poetry and that the skinny Bombyka is thus a figure for that poetry.[67] Theocritus would then be suggesting that his brand of Hellenistic poetry, at least, should be associated with bucolic values and that the slender Muse is out of place in the workaday world but at home in a world of leisure, desire, and the imagination. At the same time, with the more comic aspects of Boukaios's song and Milon's strong advocacy of the necessity of work, *Idyll* 10 may contain an element of self-parody, an acknowledgment of the practical limitations of bucolic's efforts to remake reality.

---

65. Cf. Hunt 2009, 395.

66. Cf. Acosta-Hughes's excellent comment on these lines (2006, 33): "A part of Milon's criticism is of Bucaeus' personalization of song; his own song performance centers on public (and plural) male work experience, the immediately perceptible (rather than internalized sensation and imagination), and a natural world that is utilitarian rather than a field for erotic metaphor."

67. Grethlein 2012.

For that reason, I do not see in this poem a straightforward vindication of the bucolic or an unqualified claim of its superiority.[68] In the end, the two worlds comment on each other. If the gritty reality of subsistence labor emphasizes the fictive, impractical, wish-fulfilling nature of the bucolic, the comparison also works the other way by showing that the practical world of work precludes imagination and love. A concentration on work is necessary for survival and can be a positive value, as Hesiod shows, but it has to do without the leisure and appreciation of beauty that herdsmen enjoy. Herdsmen are surrounded by natural abundance, whereas reapers have barely what they need to survive. Nature may have its dangers (thorns, wolves that prey on goats), but herdsmen seek to be part of it; agricultural work intrinsically tames and exploits nature, though out of necessity, for survival. We can be grateful that we have *Idyll* 10 alongside the bucolic poems in the Theocritean corpus. Without it, they would seem sealed off within their own fictions, while they in turn, as exercises in the imaginative life, offset Milon's workaday utilitarianism, which is often, of necessity, our own approach to life. In the end, *Idyll* 10 helps us appreciate the bucolic poems all the more, while keeping us grounded in an awareness of their fictions.

Idyll *21: The Dream of a Fisherman*

Idyll 21 has come to us in two manuscripts, of the fourteenth and the fifteenth centuries CE, respectively, one of which attributes the poem to Theocritus. Since the Aldine edition (1495 CE), it has been included among the poems of Theocritus. The thinness of the manuscript tradition and a few unusual metrical and lexical features may point away from Theocritus as author, but these are not decisive. Theocritean authorship has had its defenders,[69] although most scholars think it was written by someone else. And because "inauthentic" has often come to mean "of low quality,"[70] little attention has been paid to the features that make *Idyll* 21 an interesting poem, although positive assessments have not been lacking.[71] Because it depends on only two manuscripts of the same family (the Laurentian) and perhaps because the poem was neglected even in antiquity, the text is in poor

---

68. At the end of his article, for instance, Grethlein 2012, 617, argues that Milon may have the last word but Theocritus outdoes him through the typically Hellenistic sophistication of his own poem: "It is . . . the ultimate refinement of Idyll 10 that it features an attack against refinement that seems to carry the day but, upon closer inspection, turns out to be subverted."

69. E.g., Campbell 1938; Giangrande 1977.

70. See Hunter 2008, 384–403, especially 394–395.

71. Kirstein 2007 is one. See his history of interpretations on 151–154. Because my views on this poem coincide so often with Kirstein's, I can keep my discussion short. Kirstein suggests

shape at many points. I follow Gow's text, but the reader should be aware that in a number of places, different readings would yield other meanings.[72]

For my purposes, the question of authenticity is not very important. The poem has affinities with Theocritus's bucolic *Idylls*, and Giuseppe Giangrande seems correct in saying that "whoever wrote the *Idyll*, if not Theocritus, was a Hellenistic poet who tried, not without success, to write in Theocritean style."[73] *Idyll* 21 concerns the life and outlook of lowly men—fishermen—who perform menial work and coexist with the herdsmen of the bucolic poems but are depicted as living a very different kind of life. To read this poem alongside those others, even if it originally was quite independent of them, is to gain a perspective on the bucolic world that has much in common with the one *Idyll* 10 offers.

After a narrative introduction, addressed to one Diophantos, that announces the theme of poverty and the worries it causes and describes the physical setting, the main part of *Idyll* 21 consists of a dialogue between two fishermen, Asphalion and his unnamed companion, who are lying awake at night. Asphalion has had a dream, which he asks his friend to interpret. In the dream, he caught a large fish made of gold and swore an oath that he would never again venture onto the sea but would stay on land and enjoy his new wealth. He feared that he had caught a fish dear to Poseidon or belonging to Amphitrite. Awake now and with no golden fish, he is afraid that if he returns to the sea, he will violate his oath. The companion tells him that the dream was deceptive and warns him to pursue fish of flesh and blood so that he does not die of "starvation and false dreams."

Although a fisherman on the shore about to cast his net is described in the Hesiodic *Shield of Herakles* (213–215), fishermen get little attention in Greek poetry until the Hellenistic period, when they appear in poetry and sculpture. These depictions are part of a new interest in representing humble people from daily life and their occupations, perhaps at least partly under the influence of Stoicism and Cynicism. In the case of fishermen, there may be an economic

---

that the poem might be by an imitator of Theocritus, if not Theocritus himself (215–216), and that seems possible to me, although not necessary. His further suggestion that it can be included in the bucolic genre, in the broad sense, seems to me to stretch the term "bucolic" beyond its usefulness for Theocritus. For the view that the poem was composed by an "emulator" of Theocritus and not a "slavish imitator" ("un emulatore e non un pedissequo imitatore di Teocrito"), see Belloni 2003, 286–297.

72. Gow accepts a number of emendations by others and produces a serviceable text. His approach seems preferable to Campbell's wholesale rewriting of the text (at one extreme) and (at the other extreme) Giangrande's often forced attempts to extract a satisfactory meaning from the transmitted text.

73. Giangrande 1977, 495.

reason as well: the importance of seafood in provisioning cities.[74] As we saw in chapter 1, fishermen are mentioned several times in Theocritus's bucolic *Idylls*, where they are peripheral to the bucolic world and help to define its limits. They inhabit the boundary between land, the place of herdsmen, and sea, and their work can either involve fishing from the shore, as with Olpis in *Id.* 3.26, or take them onto (and into) the water. Several of these passages, as well as a few from other poetry, will give us some context within which we can better imagine the fishermen in *Idyll* 21.

The description of the fisherman on the cup in *Idyll* 1 (39–44) emphasizes several key themes:

> τοῖς δὲ μετὰ γριπεύς τε γέρων πέτρα τε τέτυκται
> λεπράς, ἐφ' ᾇ σπεύδων μέγα δίκτυον ἐς βόλον ἕλκει
> ὁ πρέσβυς, κάμνοντι τὸ καρτερὸν ἀνδρὶ ἐοικώς.
> φαίης κεν γυίων νιν ὅσον σθένος ἐλλοπιεύειν,
> ὧδέ οἱ ᾠδήκαντι κατ' αὐχένα πάντοθεν ἶνες
> καὶ πολιῷ περ ἐόντι· τὸ δὲ σθένος ἄξιον ἄβας.

Next to them an aged fisherman and a rock are carved,
a rough rock, on which, laboring, he draws in a huge net for the cast,
the old man, looking like one straining mightily.
You would say that he is fishing to the limit of his limbs' strength
from the way that his sinews swell everywhere along his neck
gray-haired though he is. His strength would do credit to youth.

Scholars have often, and rightly, compared the fisherman described here with the one represented by a black marble statue in the Louvre, probably a Roman copy of a Hellenistic original.[75] The figure is notable for its dilated veins and (yes) the sinews standing out all around the neck, the muscular but aged body, and the worn facial features. The strength of both fishermen should not mislead us into thinking that these figures are in any way idealized—quite the opposite. Those muscles and those sinews popping out are graphic testimony to how arduous and physically demanding a fisherman's task was in antiquity.[76] Furthermore, three times in the lines quoted (and a fourth time in the line immediately following),

---

74. On fishermen in Hellenism, see Kirstein 2007, 184–203.

75. On this statue, see Pollitt 1986, 143.

76. The description of the fisherman on the cup seems to be the only basis for Scholten's claim (2006, 80–83) that Theocritus depicts labor as having the positive effect of strengthening the

the fisherman's age is stressed (note in particular the emphatically enjambed ὁ πρέσβυς in line 31). Fishermen are regularly old in Hellenistic poetry (including *Idyll* 21), surely in order to suggest a long lifetime of toil that has left its marks on the body and finally wears it down; in the line just after the quotation, the fisherman is referred to as "the sea-worn old man" (ἁλιτρύτοιο γέροντος).[77] And finally, the harshness of the fisherman's environment is implied by the ruggedness of the rock on which he stands, with the adjective λεπράς ("rough") also emphasized by enjambment. All the details in this description stand in sharp contrast to Theocritus's depiction of herdsmen, their leisure, and the lovely natural surroundings of the bucolic world, where you evidently would not find any harsh crags.

In *Idyll* 7, when Lykidas imagines a fair voyage for Ageanax, he envisions a calm at sea brought about by the halcyons, "who are most beloved of all birds to the green Nereids and all those whose catch comes from the sea" (*Id.* 7.59–60).[78] For this brief moment of calm, which is set against the reminders of the usual late-autumn storminess (*Id.* 7.53–54), the sea is gentle, the marine counterpart of bucolic peace. Storms and rough seas, of course, are what fishermen more often contend with.

The relation between land and sea and the hardships of fishermen are the subject of a fragment of Moschus (fr. 1 Gow). This poem postdates Theocritus by at least a century, but it gives a vivid idea of the way fishermen and their environment were thought of in the Hellenistic period. "When the wind falls gently upon the green sea," the fragment begins, "I am restless in my unhappy mind, land is no longer pleasing to me, and the great salt sea draws me much more to itself." But when a storm comes and the waves are wild, "I look toward earth and trees,"

γᾶ δέ μοι ἀσπαστά χἀ δάσκιος εὔαδεν ὕλα·
ἔνθα καὶ ἢν πνεύσῃ πόλυς ἄνεμος ἁ πίτυς ᾄδει.

---

body (cursory discussion of the passage on 75–76). I think the poet's emphasis there and in *Idylls* 10 and 21 is on its harshness instead.

77. Gow 1952, II, 10, very aptly cites Plato *Laws* 761D, πόνοις τετρυμένα γεωργικοῖς σώματα ("bodies worn out by the toils of farming").

78. ὅσοις τέ περ ἐξ ἁλὸς ἄγρα. A very similar phrase occurs in Theocritus fr. 3 Gow, ἐξ ἁλὸς ᾧ ζωή τὰ δὲ δίκτυα κείνῳ ἄροτρα, "one whose livelihood is from the sea, and his nets are his plow." Both phrases emphasize the fisherman's dependence on catching fish for life and survival. Cf. the description of the fishermen at *Id.* 21.6 as ἰχθύος ἀγρευτῆρες, "hunters of fish." The fragment concerns a goddess rewarding a sacrifice with a good catch and prosperity (ὄλβος)—a somewhat more realistic hope than Asphalion's dream in *Idyll* 21. The equation of nets with a plow draws a parallel between labor on land and labor at sea.

and land is welcome[79] to me, and the luxuriant wood delights me.
There, even if the wind blows strong, the pine tree sings.

The singing pine tree will, of course, recall the musical whisper of the pine in the opening lines of *Idyll* 1 and conjures up a bucolic place that blunts the force of weather and turns it benign, in the strongest possible contrast to the storm at sea. This pleasance leads to thoughts of fishermen, who have to be on the ocean:

ἦ κακὸν ὁ γριπεὺς ζώει βίον, ᾧ δόμος ἁ ναῦς,
καὶ πόνος ἐντὶ θάλασσα, καὶ ἰχθύες ἁ πλάνος ἄγρα.

Ah, miserable is the life a fisherman leads, whose ship is his house,
and the sea his toil, and fish his elusive prey.

The equation of ship and house only emphasizes the difference between them. The fisherman is not at home on the sea, which is only his place of toil as he labors for an uncertain livelihood. The speaker then differentiates himself from the fisherman, at least in his wishes:

αὐτὰρ ἐμοὶ γλυκὺς ὕπνος ὑπὸ πλατάνῳ βαθυφύλλῳ,
καὶ παγᾶς φιλέοιμι τὸν ἔγγυθεν ἆχον ἀκούειν
ἃ τέρπει ψοφέοισα τὸν ἄγρυπνον, οὐχὶ ταράσσει.

But as for me, may I have sweet sleep beneath the deep-leaved plane tree,
and may I be accustomed to hear the nearby sound of a spring
that delights with its plash the sleepless one, rather than disturbing him.

These lines, the last of the fragment, conjure up a vision of restful leisure in a lush natural setting; they look back to the mention of the pine tree's song, so that evocations of bucolic peace enfold the diametrically opposed picture of the fisherman's harsh life. If ἄγρυπνον, "sleepless," is the correct reading in the last line (it is Gow's very good emendation of the manuscripts' unmetrical ἀγροῖκον, "countryman"), we can contrast the man enjoying this peaceful setting with the fishermen of *Idyll* 21, who are wakeful because of their cares. The mention of sleep two lines earlier permits this in any case.

---

79. Likely an allusion to *Od.* 23.233–240 (which itself recalls 5.394–399), describing how welcome land is to shipwrecked sailors.

Writing in the early third century BCE, and so a little before Theocritus, Leonidas of Tarentum composed four epigrams on fishermen.[80] One, a grave epigram, indirectly suggests the hazards that fishermen had to face (*A.P.* 7.295):

> Θῆριν τὸν τριγέροντα, τὸν εὐάγρων ἀπὸ κύρτων
> ζῶντα, τὸν αἰθυίης πλείονα νηξάμενον,
> ἰχθυσιληϊστῆρα, σαγηνέα χηραμοδύτην,
> οὐχὶ πολυσκάλμου πλώτορα ναυτιλίης,
> ἔμπης οὔτ᾽ Ἀρκτοῦρος ἀπώλεσεν, οὔτε καταιγὶς
> ἤλασε τὰς πολλὰς τῶν ἐτέων δεκάδας·
> ἀλλ᾽ ἔθαν᾽ ἐν καλύβῃ σχοινίτιδι, λύχνος ὁποῖα,
> τῷ μακρῷ σβεσθεὶς ἐν χρόνῳ αὐτόματος.
> σῆμα δὲ τοῦτ᾽ οὐ παῖδες ἐφήρμοσαν, οὐδ᾽ ὁμόλεκτρος,
> ἀλλὰ συνεργατίνης ἰχθυβόλων θίασος.

> Theris, the old, old man, who from traps good for catching fish
> earned his livelihood, who swam more than the shearwater,
> fish plunderer, seiner, diver into crevices,
> no sailor on a many-oared ship—
> nevertheless Arktouros's stormy setting did not kill him, nor did the tempest
> hound to death his many decades.
> But he died in his reed hut, extinguished like a lamp
> of his own accord, from sheer length of years.
> This tomb—no children built it, nor wife,
> but the brotherhood of his fellow workers, net casters after fish.

A great deal about Theris's life is packed into these lines. In the piling up of epithets in the first four lines, we get an impression of the various activities that his profession demanded and, by implication, of their hazards: setting underwater traps and seine nets; diving into crevices for octopus, shrimp, and shellfish; spending more time in (or on) the sea than a shearwater, a marine bird that flies close to the surface of the water and dives for fish and shellfish and so an excellent parallel to a fisherman. He did not sail on a large ("many-oared") ship but, by implication, on a skiff (like that of the fishermen in *Idyll* 21), and so was exposed to storms and rough seas. But despite the dangers and the harshness of his work

---

80. For discussion of these in relation to *Idyll* 21, see Kirstein 2007, 168–175. One of these epigrams, *A.P.* 6.4, concerns a fisherman with the same name as the addressee of *Idyll* 21, Diophantos. The two texts may be related, although the name is a common one.

(ἔμπης, "nevertheless," in line 5 is a key word), storms and shipwreck did not kill him, but he died a natural death of old age. There is perhaps a sense of achievement here, as if he were very skilled at his work, and so survived that way, or at least fortunate—for a fisherman. Materially, he seems to have lived at a basic level of survival, in a reed hut (recall "his ship is his house" in the Moschus fragment) and with no family, but within a network of other fishermen who clearly looked out for one another. The fishermen in *Idyll* 21 also live in a wattled hut, with only one another to depend on.[81]

All of these passages are consistent in depicting the fisherman's life as one of unremitting labor and poverty, and the one by Moschus explicitly contrasts it with bucolic ease and pleasure. *Idyll* 21 fits easily into this context, although it has some different emphases and offers more explicit detail, especially in the opening lines. The first word of the poem is, in fact, "poverty," and fishermen are then used—naturally, given their depiction in other texts—to illustrate its effects (*Id.* 21.1–3):

> Ἀ πενία, Διόφαντε, μόνα τὰς τέχνας ἐγείρει·
> αὕτα τῶ μόχθοιο διδάσκαλος, οὐδὲ γὰρ εὕδειν
> ἀνδράσιν ἐργατίναισι κακαὶ παρέχοντι μέριμναι.

> Poverty, Diophantos, alone stimulates the crafts;
> she is a teacher of toil, because for laboring men
> evil anxieties do not allow even sleep.

Gow finds in these lines little connection between the various concepts of poverty, skills or crafts, toil, and anxieties,[82] but I think they form a coherent and significant complex. Poverty stimulates crafts in the sense that it forces people to devise the means of survival, in this case techniques for catching fish, such as diving, traps, and nets, and also strength. It is thus the teacher of toil in a concrete sense but also of the suffering that accompanies it (the word μόχθος, like the English "toil," can encompass this intangible meaning as well). This latter meaning passes easily into the "anxieties" that keep poor people awake at night, so that γάρ, "for" or "because," is in place, and there is an effective contrast between ἐγείρει, "stimulates" but literally "arouses" (often from sleep), at the end of the first line and εὕδειν, "[not even] to sleep," at the end of the second. Unlike the other passages we looked at, which concentrated on fishermen's material conditions,

---

81. For other similarities between this epigram and *Idyll* 21, see Kirstein 2007, 172–173.

82. Gow 1952, II, 370–371.

this poem from the beginning shows an interest in the psychological effects of poverty, one that leads directly to Asphalion's wish-fulfilling dream of sudden riches and release from the grinding necessity of toil. *Idyll* 21 is thus not about fishermen for their own sake; it uses them to prove a larger point about poverty and its effects.[83]

It is in service of that theme that we now get a detailed description of the hut where the fishermen have lain down to sleep and of their possessions, almost all of which—except for the mats on which they lie, their clothes, and their felt caps—have to do with their work. "Near them lay their hands' struggles" (τὰ ταῖν χειροῖν ἀθλήματα, that is, "the instruments of their hands' struggles," *Id.* 21.8–9). There follows a list of fishing implements, all seen not as neutral parts of their surroundings but as intimately connected with labor; even in sleep, these men are not separated from their tools, and these tools are all they have. Οὗτος τοῖς ἁλιεῦσιν ὁ πᾶς πόνος,[84] οὗτος ὁ πλοῦτος, "this was their entire [means of] labor, this their wealth" (*Id.* 21.14). Their object-world signifies only work, and it is all the riches they have. The next lines seem to talk about what they lack, and, in fact, do not need precisely because they are poor (*Id.* 21.15–18):

> οὐ κλεῖδ', οὐχὶ θύραν ἔχον, οὐ κύνα· πάντα περισσὰ
> ταῦτ' ἐδόκει τήνοις· ἁ γὰρ πενία σφας ἐτήρει.
> οὐδεὶς δ' ἐν μέσσῳ γείτων πέλεν, ἁ δὲ παρ' αὐτᾷ
> θλιβομέναν καλύβᾳ τραφερὰν προσέναχε θάλασσα.

> They had no key, no door, no dog; all these things seemed
> superfluous to those men, for poverty protected them.
> No neighbor was nearby, and beside the hut itself
> the sea slid toward the hemmed-in dry land.

---

83. My reading of *Idyll* 21 is the diametric opposite of Belloni's (2003). He sees the poem as a celebration of labor and poverty as an ideal way of life. Much of his argument hinges on his interpretation of the phrase φίλος πόνος ("accustomed toil," *Id.* 21.20), which he relates to ideas of labor held by Stoics and other philosophical systems (289–293). The context is a problem for any such connection, which is in any case difficult to prove. "Accustomed toil" is what wakes the fishermen up, and wakefulness has been said in lines 2–3 to be caused by "evil cares" (κακαὶ μέριμναι). The epithet shows that this is not the philosophical wakefulness that Belloni wishes to claim that it is.

84. I would retain the manuscripts' πόνος because it fits with τὰ ταῖν χειροῖν ἀθλήματα in line 9 as I have interpreted it; cf. also καὶ πόνος ἐντὶ θάλασσα, "the sea is his [source of] toil" in Moschus fr. 1.10, quoted earlier. The word also drives home the connection of these objects with labor. Gow prints the emendation πόρος, "resource, revenue," which is both unnecessary and redundant with πλοῦτος. My explanation of πόνος is more or less consistent with that of Giangrande 1977, 503 ("source of work"), although his explanation obscures the significance that I think the phrase has.

This is the text that Gow prints, which incorporates a number of emendations intended to fix a very corrupt transmitted text. Key, door, dog, poverty protecting them, and dry land are all imported into it by these conjectures. There are problems with the reconstruction, but if it is anywhere near correct—and the text of the manuscripts is very difficult, if not impossible, to interpret[85]—the lines make a good contribution to the context. The list of the men's few possessions, only those necessary for work, is followed by what they do not have: a key, a door, and a watchdog, which are all unnecessary because they have nothing worth stealing. And anyway, there are no neighbors (this, at least, is in the manuscripts); this emphasizes their solitude. The hut itself is right beside the water, either on a spit of land, as Gow suggests, or on a narrow beach, the slight margin squeezed between sea and land. This physical detail stresses how constricted their life is and how vulnerable. And it bears out the spatial significance of fishermen as discussed in chapter 1: they inhabit the boundary between sea and dry land that marks one of the defining limits of the bucolic world, and they cross that boundary and enter the sea, as herdsmen such as Polyphemos cannot do and as the goatherd of *Idyll* 3 contemplates doing, but only to commit suicide for love. The manuscript text in these last two lines does make sense and has pretty much the same effect, except that the hemmed-in dry land is lost and the misery of the hut is stressed instead: "the sea slid gently ashore beside the hut itself, which was oppressed by poverty."[86]

The dialogue that follows this scene-setting description by the narrator needs little comment, except for lines 39–41, the beginning of Asphalion's account of his dream. He fell asleep, he says, in the late afternoon, "after our labors at sea"[87]— a sign of the exacting nature of their work. He adds that they had eaten their evening meal early, and that "we spared our stomachs." I take the phrase to be a grimly ironical way of saying that they had little to eat.

---

85. Giangrande 1977, 502–510, but some of his explanations seem far-fetched and problematical, at least to me, especially in lines 15–16. The repetition of πάντα, presumably for emphasis, has little point. More seriously, οὐδεὶς δ' οὐ χύθραν εἶχε ought to mean that everyone had a pot, not that neither fisherman did, as Giangrande understands the phrase (when a negative is *preceded* by a compound negative, both negatives retain their force; "no one did not" means "everyone did").

86. πενίᾳ δὲ παρ' αὐτάν/θλιβομέναν καλύβαν τρυφερὸν προσέναχε θάλασσα. The only change here from the manuscripts is dative πενίᾳ for the nominative. This version of the line yields an interesting contrast between the gentleness, almost daintiness, of the sea sliding ashore (τρυφερόν) and the grinding effects of poverty.

87. Reading ἐπ' for the manuscripts' ἐν, despite the ingenious argument of Giangrande 1977, 514–515.

Asphalion asks his companion to interpret his dream, because he has seen favorable things; evidently, he expects that the dream signifies good fortune in the future and assumes that it cannot have been literally true. So it needs a skilled interpreter. The companion, in keeping with his grounding in the harsh realities of the world, takes a matter-of-fact approach, saying in effect that the best dream interpreter is common sense (*Id.* 21.32–33).[88] And in his response to the dream, his common sense punctures the fantasy of unlooked-for riches (*Id.* 21.63–67):

> μὴ σύγε, μὴ τρέσσῃς· οὐκ ὤμοσας· οὐδὲ γὰρ ἰχθὺν
> χρύσεον ὡς ἴδες εἷλες, ἴσα δ' ἦν ψεύδεσιν ὄψις.
> εἰ δ' ὕπαρ οὐ κνώσσων τὰ πελώρια ταῦτα ματεύσεις,
> ἐλπὶς τῶν ὕπνων· ζάτει τὸν σάρκινον ἰχθύν,
> μὴ σὺ θάνῃς λιμῷ καὶ τοῖς χρυσοῖσιν ὀνείροις.

> Oh, no, don't you be afraid. You didn't swear an oath. For you didn't
> catch any golden fish as you thought you did. The dream was as good as
>   a lie.
> If you're going to seek out marvels like this when you're awake and not
>   slumbering,
> your hope is as good as your dream.[89] Go after fish of flesh and blood,
> so that you don't die of starvation and those golden dreams.

Poverty allows no room for hope of anything better. As the companion tells Asphalion, and as the poem's opening lines say, all a poor man can do is work. He has the role of *Idyll* 10's Milon to Asphalion's Boukaios.

We are a long way from a world in which a goatherd can leave his flock in the care of a friend (or a he-goat), stand outside a cave, and serenade an Amaryllis who may not even exist, indulging the hope that she will come to him.

The poems we have considered in this chapter depict spaces that are marginal to the bucolic world and characters within them whose activities and outlook are conditioned by those spaces. These *Idylls* are related to the bucolic poetry, and shed light on its world and its values, in different ways.

---

88. For a different view of the passage—that Asphalion claims to be a skilled dream interpreter but that his companion, despite lacking that skill, induces him to tell his dream anyway—see Giangrande 1973, 79–81.

89. I take τῶν ὕπνων as a defining genitive: "[you have] a hope consisting of dreams." Hope was, for the Greeks, a slippery and unreliable thing. For the sense "your dreams sound hopeful," see Giangrande 1973, 82. That hardly fits the context.

Idyll 4 is still more or less in that world and, like other bucolic poems, is conditioned by an absence; but the situation is not a spur to creativity but causes stasis, or worse. Amaryllis is dead, but grief for her produces only an inept gesture toward bucolic song. The satisfaction of desire takes the form of the little old man's lechery by the cattle fold. Neither Battos nor Korydon seems up to the task of carrying on the bucolic life, and Battos may not belong to it at all. In keeping with the setting in South Italy, which was in disarray when the poem was written, *Idyll* 4 shows us the bucolic world in the process of decay. It thus constructs a fictional chronological limit that balances *Idyll* 1's construction of the origin of bucolic poetry in Daphnis's death, and it acts as a foil to the vitality of the bucolic world that is depicted in the other poems.

The other two poems discussed in this chapter concentrate on the realities of labor. *Idyll* 10 moves out of bucolic space, with its leisure for singing songs of desire, and into the neighboring agricultural world that is conditioned by the necessity of labor, where only a work song is appropriate. It imports some bucolic conventions into the world of work, but only to show how out of place they are there—but also, by implication, how in place they are in the world constructed by the bucolic *Idylls*. *Idyll* 21 shows the life of the fishermen who are only casually mentioned a few times in the bucolic poems as inhabiting the edges of both their world and the land. Whoever wrote it, the poem bears similarities to *Idyll* 10. It, too, depicts a category of people for whom work is the defining condition of life; they are "laboring men" (ἀνδράσιν ἐργατίναισι, *Id.* 21.3), just as Boukaios is "laborer Boukaios" (ἐργατίνα Βουκαῖε, *Id.* 10.1). But now the emphasis is on grinding poverty and life materially reduced to the basics. As in *Idyll* 10, one character's aspirational fantasy of something beyond work is punctured by the other's reminder of their actual conditions, and the last lines of the poem make explicit the danger they face—starvation—that is only implied by Milon's emphasis on lack of food and drink.

These poems can fruitfully be seen in relation to the bucolic *Idylls*, and the bucolic *Idylls* likewise can be read against them. They shed light on the limitations of the bucolic vision of life even as they help us appreciate it by contrast, and they act as a check on the urge that the bucolic poems might arouse to indulge nostalgia for a prettified version of the natural world and a simple life within it. On the other hand, they help show how the fictionality of the bucolic poems is precisely their point. We would starve to death if we spent all our time indulging in a bucolic daydream, but a life that by necessity makes no room for the imagination, they show, is impoverished. Such, these poems about labor remind us, is the condition of much of the world.

5
Conclusion

HOW IS IT possible to gather together the various strands of suggested meanings in these richly complex poems?

We can make a start by recalling how the space of the Ptolemaic empire as it is constructed in *Idyll* 17 encompasses the bucolic, urban, and, I would say, indirectly even the mythological spaces that other poems represent. The bucolic poems build a world with clearly defined margins that seems largely self-contained and autonomous. But it is located, in *Idyll* 15, within the empire as part of its economic system, with the wool of sheep on Samian hillsides transformed into the coverlets for the couch of Aphrodite and Adonis. In the same way, Praxinoa buys wool, spins it, and weaves it into the dress that Gorgo admires. Urban space similarly fits into this larger spatial system. The centripetal force that Alexandria exerts on the movement of people and goods is depicted from within it in *Idyll* 15 and from outside, from somewhere else in the empire, in the town in which Aiskhinas and Thyonikhos converse, in *Idyll* 14. The town or city in which Simaitha lives has a distinctively Greek *palaistra*, but Delphis is a Myndian. These small touches are a reminder of the multicultural conditions of the Ptolemaic world, and Simaitha might be living in either Greece or Asia Minor. The bucolic *Idyll* 1 similarly refers to Thyrsis's victory in a singing contest over the Libyan Khromis (line 24). The mythological *Idylls* depict spaces as they existed long before the empire, and the relationship may seem more tenuous. But the links are there, in the importance of both the Dioskouroi and Herakles in the Ptolemies' self-presentation. The connection becomes explicit in the vignette of Alexander, Ptolemy Soter, and the latter's tipsy putative ancestor Herakles, together on Olympos at the beginning of *Idyll* 17. This picture represents the fulfillment of Teiresias's prophecy of Herakles's apotheosis in *Idyll* 24, and that poem also seems to look ahead, in the manner of *aitia* familiar from Callimachus and Apollonius, through its apparent reference to the story of Philadelphus's exposure as an infant in a bronze shield and by the way Herakles is given the education of a Ptolemaic prince, as many have pointed out. Within this context, it might not be too much of a stretch to suggest that some aspects of space in the mythological poems—the dangerous spring and the undifferentiated wild space Herakles rushes through in *Idyll* 13, Amykos's more benign spring that needs to be claimed for Greek values of hospitality in *Idyll* 22, even the house that cannot keep the malevolent serpents out in *Idyll* 24—represent primitive conditions that some readers, at least, might compare with the order brought by Greek culture, especially under imperial rule. In similar fashion, as Stephens has suggested, the vision of a restored Sicily in *Idyll* 16 is a paradigm of the flourishing of nature and society brought about by a good ruler, such as Ptolemy is supposed to be or—it is hoped—might become.[1]

From this angle, the Theocritean collection as a whole might be considered homage to an autocratic patron.[2] But this is only part of what these poems could be said to be about. In tandem with this implicit depiction of empire, the poetry speaks to the experiences of Greeks under the new conditions of mobility: deracination, issues of interethnic relations, and questions of place and placelessness. The bucolic poems in particular address these matters, in an indirect but suggestive way; and if I give pride of place to them in what follows, it is because what I have called a "bucolic sensibility" pervades a number of the non-bucolic poems, so that the bucolic *Idylls* are somehow central.

In various ways that I will discuss, Theocritus's poetry involves the relation of self to other, a question that, as I suggested in chapters 1 and 4, the bucolic *Idylls* raise spatially by defining the margins of the bucolic world and showing how the boundaries both define differences (such as the contrast between herdsmen's leisure and agricultural labor) and are permeable. This seems a particular case of a more general Hellenistic interest in boundaries and their instability, as seen, for example, in the figure of Pan, who combines human and animal. In an earlier publication,[3] I argued that in the case of Apollonius's *Argonautika*, this interest reflects questions about relations between Greeks and non-Greeks that were of particular importance to Greeks living in Alexandria and elsewhere in the extensive areas now under Greek rule after Alexander's conquests. We might see

---

1. As the example of Pindar shows, telling an autocratic patron that he possesses certain virtues can be as much a way of admonishing him to display them as it is of describing his actual character.

2. Homage but not necessarily straightforward praise or flattery. Murray 2008 has argued that these things were required by later forms of patronage but that Ptolemaic patronage followed the archaic pattern with its sympotic features. This suggestion would neatly account for the mixture of humor and seriousness that gives such a distinctive tone to the treatments, in *Idylls* 13, 17, and 24, of the alleged Ptolemaic forebear Herakles.

3. Thalmann 2011.

the same anxieties manifested more indirectly in the function of boundaries in Theocritus's bucolic poems; that would not be surprising in view of the obvious relation between these two poets. In addition, I also suggested in chapter 1 of this book that the bucolic poems raise the question of being in and out of place—a broader issue that includes interethnic relations. We can also appreciate how the attractions of the bucolic world that they hold out to the reader might include a desire to be fully "in place" that can never be entirely satisfied. That is, being "in place" in nature in the *Idylls*' terms would be a paradigm for being at home socially, culturally, and in respect to interethnic relations in a world filled with movement and displacement. That the representation of a fictional world would offer the reader a vantage point for thinking about actual issues encountered in daily life is in the very nature of a heterotopia.

In addition to this very important function—which may help account for why Theocritus created bucolic poetry at this historical and cultural juncture—the *Idylls* offer the reader attractions that have to do more generally with the relations between self and other and between readers and fictional worlds (here the inspiration of Payne should be obvious). If we consider the bucolic *Idylls* from the perspective of space, we find that Theocritus builds up a picture of a setting impressionistically by means of relatively few details that recur here and there throughout the poems: springs and meadows, certain shrubs and trees, bees, herd and wild animals, herders, and so on. This space can be located in the physical world through indirect clues such as botany, as the maquis or a typical Greek hillside in the Aegean basin and the eastern Mediterranean, as Lindsell argues. And some *Idylls* are explicitly set in Sicily and South Italy. Two of these, *Idylls* 4 and 5, mention nearby cities. But even there we have few indications of where in the landscape the bucolic world is to be located. Instead, Theocritus consistently sets the bucolic world vaguely on τὸ ὄρος, "the mountain." We get a little more definition through references to places and activities at the boundaries of the bucolic world: the extremities beyond it, with thickets and brambles as opposed to pasturage and wild rather than herd animals; agricultural fields and orchards; and the seashore, the haunt of fishermen. Poems set in the latter two areas draw a clear contrast between the hard labor that must occur there and herdsmen's leisure, which is so pervasive that only once (*Idyll* 4) are herdsmen shown having to do any work at all—and they seem ineffectual at it.

Then what do they do, and what is at the center of these clearly demarcated if sometimes porous boundaries? The bucolic world does not constitute an absent center, entirely. The *Idylls* explore the extremes of this world, from the idealizing to the base, and there are nods toward mimetic realism, as in the reminders of how goatherds smell. Theocritus's bucolic world refers to a real-life counterpart;

there were herdsmen who pastured their animals on hillside vegetation much like what he describes. But he gives us a stylized version of this world and of herdsmen's activities. The bucolic world is therefore a fictional space, and it is entirely in keeping with its character—in fact, constitutive of it—that within this space Theocritus's herdsmen do not labor but sing, and what they sing of is absence, loss, and yearning. In this world, what is not there is at least as significant as what is. Even the very act of their singing is a sign of absence. It descends from, and without attaining it seeks to recapture, the singing of such herdsman archetypes as Daphnis and Komatas. And the erotic longing their songs express is an attempt to connect with what is absent and summon it into presence—beautiful Nymphs, of course, but also, as we see in Lykidas's song in *Idyll* 7, the fullness of an idealized bucolic world itself. Such lovely visions of full presence as the poems offer us are never more than momentarily successful, held alluringly before us but kept at a distance, embedded within nesting songs and so always receding, or viewed through the lens of human culture that keeps the natural world at least somewhat apart. Even at the beginning of *Idyll* 1, whose opening lines offer an alluring picture of a place in which humans and the natural landscape might be fully present to one another, we find, when we attend to the deictics in the passage, that it is inaccessible to the goatherd and Thyrsis.

If the bucolic world is elusive in these ways, so is Theocritean poetry itself. Again and again, we have found passages that can be interpreted in more than one way and in which it seems best to keep the various possibilities open. One potential meaning jostles with others, and readings can take several different paths at once. Even on this small scale, the poetry resists interpretive closure. As a whole, a given *Idyll* will create an impression of constructing a complete world in language and at the same time call attention to its own fiction-making. As readers, we are in the same position as Theocritus's herdsmen-singers. The bucolic *Idylls* arouse in us the same desire for something absent, a world apart from (let us say) urban Alexandria, draw us into their fictions, and then remind us of those fictions' constructed quality. The effect is not necessarily the kind of frustration that the goatherd feels at the end of *Idyll* 3 and that has him contemplating his own death, devoured by wolves. More often, I think, we return to the poems with desire to grasp their world, desire for a meaning, aroused again, and again not fully satisfied—just as Polyphemos seems to have sat again and again on the shore singing in an always vain attempt to summon up Galateia, seeking to "shepherd"—nurture or control—his love. And can we be sure that *Idyll* 3's goatherd will not be back at the mouth of the cave on another occasion, trying to summon up Amaryllis's presence? If we as readers are allowed to enter the bucolic world vicariously, it is largely through sharing the herdsmen's desire for what they, and we, cannot have. This is paradoxical: we grasp something of this world by not being allowed to possess it. But if we attained this object of the desire the poems arouse in us, we would stop reading.

Those passages in which the "bucolic sensibility" surfaces in non-bucolic poems work roughly in the same way. In *Idyll* 16, the bucolic mode in which the picture of wished-for peace is cast, together with the optative verbs in the description, leaves the fulfillment of that utopian vision uncertain even as it helps arouse the reader's desire for it. *Idyll* 15 also puts the bucolic to a political use. Just as the reference to the Samian shepherd who is proud of having contributed his wool for the coverlets used in the tableau of Aphrodite and Adonis explicitly assigns the bucolic world to a place within the Ptolemaic empire, that bucolic tableau is enfolded within the Alexandrian royal palace, as though to signal that the bucolic has a function within the city, and perhaps by implication that its poetry can be of use to urban readers. This lush and peaceful scene of union between divine lovers contrasts sharply with, and helps to characterize, the bustle of the city streets and the noise and the jostling of the crowds at the palace doorway, as well as the housewives' discontent with their husbands. But the tableau shows the goddess's futile embrace of her dying lover, and the scene of bucolic presence that it represents is fleeting. Adonis returns from the dead briefly once a year. Tomorrow the women will bathe his image and lament him in preparation for another year of his absence. And the sight of his image provokes in Praxinoa nothing else but yearning: ὁ τριφίλητος Ἄδωνις, ὁ κἠν Ἀχέροντι φιληθείς ("the thrice-loved Adonis, Adonis loved even in Akheron," *Id.* 15.86). Because the festival and this elaborate spectacle are part of royal display, we see the dynamics of bucolic desire for what is absent harnessed to Ptolemaic self-legitimation, just as this poem, likely produced under Philadelphus's patronage, adds to his cultural capital as it seeks, perhaps, to capture the reader's desire for the dying god and joy at his return, contrived under royal sponsorship.

A bucolic scene figures prominently in the first narrative part of *Idyll* 22 as the setting in which the Dioskouroi encounter Amykos. It is tempting to see here a confrontation between bucolic and epic or hymnic poetry, and there does seem at first to be a lack of fit in this scene. But as the examples of Polyphemos and the low mimetic register of *Idyll* 5 show, the grotesque as embodied by Amykos is not necessarily foreign to bucolic poetry. What is incongruous from the point of view of bucolic is the violence that results from this meeting at a spring. It is offset by another feature of the narrative that is unexpected, this time from the perspective of epic: the peaceful resolution to the conflict, whereby Polydeukes spares Amykos and Amykos promises never again to be hostile to strangers. Presumably, Amykos can continue to enjoy his beautiful natural surroundings unmolested but will share them with guests according to the Greek norms of hospitality. Bucolic is thus part of an idealizing solution to the epic problem of competition, violence, and destruction arising from notions of honor that depicts violence as a means of achieving peace. Such a resolution is, by epic standards, very difficult if not impossible to attain.[4] Even out of its usual context, then, bucolic remains a mode for expressing what is elusive, the object of ungratified desire—in this case, resolution of a stubborn "real-world" problem.

Other poems that do not incorporate bucolic elements still share with the bucolic *Idylls* an interest in the nature and power of eros. In *Idyll* 2, Simaitha recounts an episode of desire fulfilled, but that is in the past. In the poem's present, she is driven by desire for the absent Delphis, and the intensity of her feeling is conveyed by her resort to magic either to lure him back or to harm him, even to cause his death. By the end of the poem, she seems to have reached a pause of some sort, but we have no way of knowing whether she has tamed her desire or will again be overwhelmed by it. *Idyll* 13 (to which, I have argued, bucolic is not central) takes the all-pervasive power of eros as its theme and uses Herakles as an extreme example of how it can make people act in ways that are uncharacteristic of them (in Herakles's case, his abandonment, for a time, of the Argonautic expedition). Among Ptolemy's virtues, in addition to kindliness, culture, and a "sweet" disposition, is that he is ἐρωτικός, devoted to eros (*Id.* 14.62). In these poems, eros may not trigger the reader's desire for an elusive world, but it is still a central preoccupation.

Theocritus's poetry is remarkable for its verbal and narrative experimentation and its reworking of earlier texts, singly and in surprising combinations. But besides the pleasure of these formal elements, what else is in it for the reader? I have said that the bucolic poems arouse readers' desire for a fictional world because it is out of their reach. Why should that be important? Why should readers, then or now, care about herdsmen and their erotic frustrations? Why might we not, by comparison with, say, epic or tragic poetry, find these poems trivial? Some readers do respond in just that way, but why are others drawn to the poems? Various answers have emerged singly in the preceding chapters, where I have drawn on the insights of writers such as Charles Segal, Harry Berger, Mark Payne, and Susan Stephens. I shall try to bring those answers together here.

One of the recurring themes of Segal's essays on Theocritus is that the poetry, with its use of fundamental images such as water, draws us close to nature and simplicity. This may well be a strong source of its appeal to urban readers in ancient Alexandria or today. We have seen a number of passages in the poems

---

4. One might think of the ending of the *Odyssey* as an exception, but there it takes Athena's intervention to restore peace to Ithaka after Odysseus's slaughter of the suitors and when he is on the point of wreaking further bloodshed. The contrived nature of this ending marks it as utopian.

that seem to idealize nature, images of full bucolic presence. But at the same time as the poems offer this vision, they limit the temptation to lapse into mere nostalgia. They balance it with reminders of gritty realities underlying country life; *Idyll* 5 is a good example of a poem that contains both the lofty and the base and holds them in a kind of dialectic. Through framing and other distancing devices, they hold the ideal out of reach, and they depict it through a complex and allusive poetics. This is William Empson's "putting the complex into the simple,"[5] of course, but what it means is that the reader cannot put off his or her sophistication and plunge into simplicity. Humans can never be fully a part of nature. The artfulness of Theocritus's poetry is that it at once tempts us into nostalgia and makes us aware that it is a trap. It works through the dynamics of eros, arousing desire for what we know we cannot have. Desire can be pleasurable as well as painful, and as *Idyll* 13 suggests, it is a condition of being human.

Following the lead of Payne, I have also emphasized the importance of the imagination, both in the poems' own world-building and in the way they provoke the reader's own imagination. When the *Idylls* show us characters in the grip of eros and indulging in fantasies of fulfillment and when they call attention to their own fictionality, they are telling us that they are exercises in imagination as they invite us to join in their fictions. *Idyll* 10, on my reading at least, implicitly designates the bucolic world as the place of eros and imagination, which the world of labor cannot afford without risk of starvation, and *Idyll* 21, even if it is not by Theocritus, similarly opposes wish-fulfilling dreams to labor, which is the necessary condition of the fisherman's world. These poems set in relief the impracticality of the bucolic, but they also show the harshness of subsistence conditions and by implication the richness of what the bucolic world and its poetry offer, even if that is almost parodied in Boukaios's song. By offering a perspective on bucolic poetry from the margin in *Idyll* 10, Theocritus suggests both the rewards of bucolic poetry and its limits. In this way, Theocritus seems to put another check on any tendency to use the bucolic poems for mere escapism.

Payne's own treatment of these poems as fictions is much too sophisticated to succumb to this latter danger, although he sees them as offering readers access to a world removed from "actuality," self-sufficient and alluring. When herdsmen sing or listen to bucolic songs, this arouses readers' desire to enter the bucolic world and, through imaginative "self-projection," to become one with its inhabitants: "being bucolic means becoming bucolic: merging the self with an imagined counterpart is one of the attractions of this world."[6] For Payne, too, then, desire

---

5. Empson 1974, 22.

6. Payne 2007, 17.

is fundamental, but I see it working in a somewhat different way. Although he acknowledges here and there moments of frustrated desire in characters and readers, he seems to understand them as successfully entering this other world in imagination, whereas I see the poems as offering the reader entry into it as an object of desire but constantly deferring its fulfillment. So the singers in the "monologue poems" "[tell] stories in which they fashion an imaginative escape from the desire that led them to sing in the first place."[7] In *Idyll* 11, he says, Polyphemos constructs in imagination a world that takes the place of Galateia's presence.[8] I am less sure of Polyphemos's success and have suggested above that he both controls and feeds his desire; the double meaning of ἐποίμαινεν, "shepherded," at *Id.* 11.80 precisely models for a character within the poem the reader's experience of desire. In a similar way, Payne sees the imagined song of Tityros in *Idyll* 7 as a form of "therapy" for Lykidas: the longing it arouses in him for an idealized version of his own world "displaces his grief over his lover's departure."[9] This is an attractive way to understand the relation between Lykidas's love for Ageanax and the song he imagines Tityros would sing, but it seems to me hard to square with the admittedly enigmatic lines 52–56 of *Idyll* 7, together with τῆνο κατ' ἆμαρ ("on that day") in line 63, which suggest that Lykidas's rustic symposium and Tityros's singing are to occur, if they ever do, after Ageanax has "rescued" Lykidas from love (however that is supposed to happen). Still, Payne's approach to the bucolic *Idylls* as fictions in the sense he gives that term goes a long way toward explaining the complex ways in which Theocritus offers us "the pleasures of the imaginary" (the title of one of Payne's chapters).[10]

Another approach to the question of what these poems offer readers is to say that it cultivates in them what Martha Nussbaum calls "the narrative imagination," which she sees as a major function of literature in general.[11] Literary fictions, she says, extend our understanding beyond the limits of our selves and our experience, especially as that is shaped by our position in society, and help us to understand what it is to be someone very different from us and to develop

---

7. Payne 2007, 93.

8. Payne 2007, 79.

9. Payne 2007, 125.

10. In an important recent article, Yukai Li 2019 has extended the views of Payne and the art theorist Michael Fried to propose a sophisticated model of "absorption-distraction" and desire to account for the ways that Theocritean characters can never fully "become bucolic" and the reader can never fully enter the bucolic world. This is congenial to my own readings of Theocritus and might underlie some of the features of the poems that I have pointed to. I regret that the article appeared too late for me to take it into account in the body of this book.

11. Nussbaum 1997, 85–112.

"compassion" for others. This view, like Payne's, involves a kind of imaginative projection, but rather than resulting in a merging with another world, this sympathetic understanding is based on an awareness of differences between ourselves and others. Another difference is that the effects of this understanding are carried over into our daily lives in society. In the case of Theocritus, urban readers, many of them elite and highly educated, would be put in touch with the natural environment and would evolve a fellow feeling, but not identification, with lowly herders and sympathize with their pleasures and pains. What would connect these readers and fictional characters would be a shared experience of eros for what they cannot have. That the poems often treat characters with humor and irony is no obstacle for this view. It helps maintain a necessary distance from the characters and their world, which the reader cannot fully enter.

On the other hand, one could see the use of imagination in Theocritus's bucolics in the opposite way, as Charles Isenberg and David Konstan do, as arousing on the part of urban elite readers "a patronizing sympathy for lovesickness in the humble."[12] This reading stresses the effect of all those elements in the poems that create distance between their audience and their characters. It takes full account of the difference in class and economic position between those at Ptolemy's court (let us say, but the readership was surely wider, eventually if not at first) and those at the bottom of society and sees it as a gulf not fully bridged by any sympathy the reader might feel, which would be condescending. It may be a point in its favor that Nussbaum, who is very aware of the differences of ethnicity, class, and gender between groups but argues that the narrative imagination can promote mutual understanding and sympathy, writes with her eye on liberal democracy and draws especially on Greek tragedy, a product of democratic Athens, whereas in a monarchy such as the Ptolemaic empire, hierarchies may have been more pronounced. I should add that "patronizing sympathy" would not rule out the poems' arousal of eros in their readers as I have described it.

The texts are open to any of these responses, and I suspect that many readers would have felt a complicated mixture of several. Their horizons would have been extended by the poems, and they would have gained some understanding of what it was like to be a victim of frustrated desire at the bottom of society; they would also be made acutely aware of the attractions of a world for which a characteristic adjective was "sweet" and be drawn toward it. At the same time, they would never have forgotten their own higher standing and the more complex lives they led even while attracted to simplicity. Consider again Polyphemos of *Idyll* 11. We are entertained by the incongruity of a Cyclops's love for a beautiful Nymph and by

---

12. Isenberg and Konstan 1984, 302–303.

his delusion that he has a chance with her. We might read his song to her with a sense of cognitive superiority, especially since some of his own words foreshadow (to us, not to him) what will happen to him at Odysseus's hands. He seems so immersed in the bucolic ethos that he is unaware that she might be unmoved by the attractions of his life in a cave on land. And yet that very absorption exercises a powerful pull on the reader in ways that Payne discusses: according to the bucolic scale of values, his life is attractive. And the narrator tells us (*Id.* 11.10–11) that he loved not with tokens but with ὀρθαῖς μανίαις—"upright/genuine/true madness." His perspective may be limited, and he may use the bucolic idiom because it is all that he knows, but the depth and sincerity of his passion come through as well. Much the same might be said about the goatherd in *Idyll* 3. Perhaps the terms "patronizing" and "compassion" are too polarized to capture the complicated responses that Theocritus's poetry potentially calls forth.[13]

Like all good literature, but in their own ways, Theocritus's poems test our willingness and ability to extend our horizons beyond our customary cultural and social worlds. They challenge us to give ourselves over to their complexity and imagine various places and modes of being: herdsmen and other rural types, different trees and shrubs, wild and domesticated animals, cities, Alexandrian housewives, men and women from myth and their physical environments, authoritarian rulers. Whether we read with sympathy, condescension, or other feelings depends on us and on what we bring to the poetry in the way of our experiences and preconceptions. The poems have the power to make us think about our assumptions concerning nature and human society, their relation to each other, and all that fills them. Whether or not to avail ourselves of these possibilities is up to each of us. This book has been intended to give some idea, if only an approximation, of the worlds Theocritus constructed for his ancient readers and for us.

---

13. Some (probably) Hellenistic sculpture, with its realism bordering sometimes on the grotesque, poses similar questions. Seeing an image of a drunk old woman or a straining fisherman, does a viewer feel a sense of superiority or sympathetic interest in common people and the difficulties of their lives? See Pollitt 1986, 142–146.

References

Acosta-Hughes, Benjamin. 2006. "Bucolic Singers of the Short Song: Lyric and Elegiac Resonances in Theocritus' Bucolic *Idylls*." In Fantuzzi and Papanghelis, 25–52.

Acosta-Hughes, Benjamin. 2012a. "Miniaturizing the Huge: Hercules on a Small Scale (Theocritus *Idylls* 13 and 24)." In *Brill's Companion to Greek and Latin Epyllion and Its Reception*, edited by Manuel Baumbach and Silvio Bär, 245–257. Leiden: Brill.

Acosta-Hughes, Benjamin. 2012b. "Les Dioscures dans la poésie Alexandrine: Caractère et symbolique." In *Mythe et pouvoir à l'époque hellénistique*, edited by C. Cusset, N. Le Meur-Weissman, and F. Levin, 155–169. Leuven: Peeters.

Acosta-Hughes, Benjamin. 2012c. "'Nor When a Man Goes to Dionysus' Holy Contests'" (Theocritus 17.112): Outlines of Theatrical Performance in Theocritus." In *Theater outside Athens: Drama in Greek Sicily and South Italy*, edited by Kathryn Bosher, 391–408. Cambridge: Cambridge University Press.

Alcock, Susan. 1993. *Graecia Capta: The Landscapes of Roman Greece*. Cambridge: Cambridge University Press.

Allègre, F. 1906. "Aristophane *Chevaliers*, 537–540." *REG* 19: 299–303.

Alpers, Paul. 1996. *What Is Pastoral?* Chicago: University of Chicago Press.

Anagnostou-Laoutides, Eva, and David Konstan. 2008. "Daphnis and Aphrodite: A Love Affair in Theocritus *Idyll* 1." *AJP* 129: 497–527.

Andrews, N. E. 1996. "Narrative and Allusion in Theocritus Idyll 2." In Harder, Regtuit, and Wakker, 21–53.

Austin, Norman. 1967. "Idyll 16: Theocritus and Simonides." *TAPA* 98: 1–21.

Bakhtin, M. M. 1981. *The Dialogic Imagination: Four Essays by M. M. Bakhtin*. Austin: University of Texas Press.

Bakker, Egbert. 2013. *The Meaning of Meat and the Structure of the* Odyssey. Cambridge: Cambridge University Press.

Barigazzi, Adelmo. 1974. "Per l'interpretazione e la datazione del carme IV de Teocrito." *RFIC* 102: 301–311.

Bell, Malcolm. 2011. "Agrarian Policy, Bucolic Poetry, and Figurative Art in Early Hellenistic Sicily." In *Krise und Wandel: Süditalien im 4. und 3. Jahrhundert v. Chr.: Internationaler Kongress anlässlich des 65 Geburtstages von Dieter Mertens*, edited by Richard Neudecker, 193–211. Wiesbaden: Reichert.

Belloni, Luigi. 2003. "'Povertà' e 'ricchezza' nel *Corpus Theocriteum* in margine al testo degli ΑΛΙΕΙΣ." In *L'officina ellenistica: Poesia dotta e popolare in Grecia e a Roma*, edited by Luigi Belloni, Lia de Finis, and Gabriella Moretti, 269–300. Trento: Università degli studi di Trento.

Berger, Harry. 1984. "The Origins of Bucolic Representation: Disenchantment and Revision in Theocritus' Seventh *Idyll*." *CA* 3: 1–39.

Bernsdorff, Hans. 1994. "Polyphem und Daphnis: Zu Theokrits sechstem Idyll." *Philologus* 138: 38–51.

Bernsdorff, Hans. 2006. "The Idea of Bucolic in the Imitators of Theocritus, 3rd–1st Century BC." In Fantuzzi and Papanghelis, 167–207.

Billault, Alain. 2006. "Théocrite et Polyphème: Remarques sur les *Idylles* XI et VI." In *Palimpsestes epiques: Récritures et interferences generiques*, edited by Dominique Boutet and Camille Esmein-Sarrazin, 13–23. Paris: Presses de l'Université de Paris–Sorbonne.

Borgogno, Alberto. 2002. "Spazio, tempo e azione nelle *Talisie* di Teocrito." *GIF* 54: 13–27.

Bowie, E. L. 1985. "Theocritus' Seventh *Idyll*, Philetas and Longus." *CQ* 35: 67–91.

Bowie, E. L. 1996. "Frame and Framed in Theocritus' Poems 6 and 7." In Harder, Regtuit, and Wakker, 91–100.

Buller, J. L. 1981. "The Pathetic Fallacy in Hellenistic Pastoral." *Ramus* 10: 35–52.

Burton, Joan. 1992. "The Function of the Symposium Theme in Theocritus' *Idyll* 14." *GRBS* 33: 227–245.

Burton, Joan. 1995. *Theocritus's Urban Mimes*. Berkeley: University of California Press.

Cairns, Francis. 1984. "Theocritus' First Idyll: The Literary Programme." *WS* 97: 89–113.

Cairns, Francis. 2017. "Battus and Corydon in Theocritus *Idyll* 4." In Cusset, Kossaifi, and Poignault, 347–358.

Calame, Claude. 2005. *Masks of Authority: Fiction and Pragmatics in Ancient Greek Poetics*. Ithaca, NY: Cornell University Press.

Campbell, Archibald. 1938. "The Restitution of 'The Golden Fish' ('[Theocritus]' XXI)." *Annals of Archaeology and Anthropology* 25: 24–44.

Campbell, Malcolm. 1974. "Three Notes on Alexandrine Poetry." *Hermes* 102: 38–46.

Chaniotis, Angelos. 1995. "Problems of 'Pastoralism' and 'Transhumance' in Classical and Hellenistic Crete." *Orbis Terrarum* 1: 39–89.

Chantraine, Pierre. 1999. *Dictionnaire étymologique de la langue grecque*. 2nd ed. Paris: Klincksieck.

Chriyaa, Abdelouahid. 2004. "The Use of Shrubs in Livestock Feeding in Low Rainfall Areas." *Land Use, Land Cover and Soil Sciences*, edited by Willy H. Verheye in

Encyclopedia of Life Support Systems (EOLSS), Developed under the Auspices of UNESCO, 1–20. Eolss Publishers, Paris, France [http://www.eolss.net].

Clayman, Dee L. 2021. "Rulers and Patrons in Theocritus." In Kyriakou, Sistakou, and Rengakos, 559–583.

Crane, Gregory. 1988. "Realism in the Fifth Idyll of Theocritus." *TAPA* 118: 107–122.

Culler, Jonathan. 1981. "Apostrophe." In Jonathan Culler, *The Pursuit of Signs: Semiotics, Literature, Deconstruction*, 135–154. Ithaca, NY: Cornell University Press.

Cusset, Christophe. 1999. "L'enfance perdue d'Héraclès: L'image du héros au service de l'autre." *BAGB*: 191–210.

Cusset, Christophe. 2011. *Cyclopodie: Édition critique et commentée de l'*Idylle *VI de Théocrite*. Lyon: Maison de l'Orient et de la Méditerranée.

Cusset, Christophe. 2017. "Les voix féminines dans les *Idylles* de Théocrite." In Cusset, Kossaifi, and Poignault, 221–241.

Cusset, Christophe. 2021. "Θεόκριτος Κωμῳδοποιός: Comic Patterns and Structures in Theocritus' Bucolic Poems (with a Supplement on Tragic Patterns)." In Kyriakou, Sistakou, and Rengakos, 271–297.

Cusset, Christophe, Christine Kossaifi, and Rémy Poignault, eds. 2017. *Présence de Théocrite*. Clermont-Ferrand: Centre de Recherches A. Piganiol–Présence de l'Antiquité.

Damon, Cynthia. 1995. "Narrative and Mimesis in the 'Idylls' of Theocritus." *QUCC* n.s. 51: 101–123.

Daspet, Françoise. 2017. "Les lieux de chant dans les *Idylles* pastorals de Théocrite." In Cusset, Kossaifi, and Poignault, 91–115.

Davidson, John. 2000. "Alkmene: Mother of a Child Prodigy." *Scholia* 9: 2–11.

Davies, Malcolm. 1995. "Theocritus' *Adoniazusae*." *G&R* 42: 152–158.

De Certeau, Michel. 1984. *The Practice of Everyday Life*. Berkeley: University of California Press.

Dick, Bernard. 1968. "Ancient Pastoral and the Pathetic Fallacy." *Comparative Literature* 20: 27–44.

Doležel, Lubomír. 1988. "Mimesis and Possible Worlds." *Poetics Today* 9: 475–496.

Dover, K. J. 1971. *Theocritus: Select Poems*. London: Bristol Classical Press.

Duncan, Anne. 2001. "Spellbinding Performance: Poet as Witch in Theocritus' Second *Idyll* and Apollonius' *Argonautica*." *Helios* 28: 43–56.

Edquist, Harriet. 1975. "Aspects of Theocritean Otium." *Ramus* 4: 101–114.

Effe, Bernd. 1978. "Die Destruktion der Tradition: Theokrits mythologische Gedichte." *RhM* n.f. 121: 48–77.

Eliot, T. S. 1960. *The Sacred Wood: Essays on Poetry and Criticism*. London: Methuen.

Elliger, Einfried. 1975. *Die Darstellung der Landschaft in der griechischen Dichtung*. Berlin: De Gruyter.

Empson, William. 1974. *Some Versions of Pastoral*. Reprint of 1935 ed. New York: New Directions.

Fantuzzi, Marco. 2000. "Theocritus and the Demythologizing of Poetry." In *Matrices of Genre: Authors, Canons, and Society*, edited by Mary Depew and Dirk Obbink, 135–151. Cambridge, MA: Harvard University Press.

Fantuzzi, Marco. 2004. "Theocritus and the Bucolic Genre." In *Tradition and Innovation in Hellenistic Poetry*, edited by Marco Fantuzzi and Richard Hunter, 133–190. Cambridge: Cambridge University Press.

Fantuzzi, Marco. 2017. "Theocritus' Shepherdly Eros." In Cusset, Kossaifi, and Poignault, 331–346.

Fantuzzi, Marco, and Theodore Papanghelis, eds. 2006. *Brill's Companion to Greek and Latin Pastoral*. Leiden: Brill.

Foster, J. Andrew. 2006. "Arsinoe II as Epic Queen: Encomiastic Allusion in Theocritus, Idyll 15." *TAPA* 136: 133–148.

Foster, J. Andrew. 2016. *Reading Voices: Five Studies in Theocritus' Narrating Techniques*. Lang Classical Studies 21. New York: Peter Lang.

Foucault, Michel. 1986. "Of Other Spaces." *Diacritics* 16: 22–27.

Frangeskou, Vassiliki. 1996. "Theocritus' 'Idyll' 1: An Unusual Bucolic Agon." *Hermathena* 161: 23–42.

Fraser, P. M. 1972. *Ptolemaic Alexandria*. Oxford: Clarendon Press.

Gershenson, Daniel. 1974. "Theocritus *Idyll* 1 and the Reversal of Nature." *SCI* 1: 24–28.

Giangrande, Giuseppe. 1973. "Hellenistic Fountains and Fishermen." *Eranos* 71: 68–83.

Giangrande, Giuseppe. 1977. "Textual Problems in Theocritus' *Idyll* 21." *AC* 46: 495–522.

Gibbs-Wichrowska, Laura. 1994. "The Witch and the Wife: A Comparative Study of Theocritus, *Idyll* 2, Simonides, *Idyll* 15, and *Fatal Attraction*." In *Women in Ancient Societies: An Illusion of the Night*, edited by Léonie J. Archer, Susan Fischler, and Maria Wyke, 252–268. London: Macmillan.

Goldhill, Simon. 1986. "Framing and Polyphony: Readings in Hellenistic Poetry." *PCPhS* 32: 25–52.

Goldhill, Simon. 1988. "Desire and the Figure of Fun: Glossing Theocritus 11." In *Post-Structuralist Classics*, edited by Andrew Benjamin, 79–105. London: Routledge.

Goldhill, Simon. 1991. *The Poet's Voice: Essays on Poetics and Greek Literature*. Cambridge: Cambridge University Press.

González, José. 2010. "Theokritos' *Idyll* 16: The χάριτες and Civic Poetry." *HSCP* 105: 65–116.

Goodwin, William. 1965. *Syntax of the Moods and Tenses of the Greek Verb*. London: Macmillan.

Gow, A. S. F. 1942a. "Theocritus, *Idyll* XXIV: Stars and Doors." *CQ* 36: 104–110.

Gow, A. S. F. 1942b. "The Twenty-Second Idyll of Theocritus." *CR* 56: 11–18.

Gow, A. S. F. 1952. *Theocritus*. 2nd ed. Cambridge: Cambridge University Press.

Grethlein, Jonas. 2012. "A Slim Girl and the Fat of the Land in Theocritus, *Id.* 10." *CQ* 62: 603–617.

Griffiths, Alan. 1996. "Customising Theocritus: Poems 13 and 24." In Harder, Regtuit, and Wakker, 101–118.
Griffiths, Frederick. 1976. "Theocritus' Silent Dioscuri." *GRBS* 17: 353–367.
Griffiths, Frederick. 1979. *Theocritus at Court*. Leiden: Brill.
Griffiths, Frederick. 1981. "Home Before Lunch: The Emancipated Woman in Theocritus." In *Reflections of Women in Antiquity*, edited by Helene Foley, 247–273. New York: Gordon and Breach.
Griffiths, Frederick. 2021. "Theocritus' Intercultural Poetics." In Kyriakou, Sistakou, and Rengakos, 584–603.
Gutzwiller, Kathryn. 1981. *Studies in the Hellenistic Epyllion*. Meisenheim: Anton Hain.
Gutzwiller, Kathryn. 1983. "Charites or Hieron: Theocritus' *Idyll* 16." *RhM* n.f. 126: 212–238.
Gutzwiller, Kathryn. 1991. *Theocritus' Pastoral Analogies: The Formation of a Genre*. Madison: University of Wisconsin Press.
Gutzwiller, Kathryn. 1996. "The Evidence for Theocritean Poetry Books." In Harder, Regtuit, and Wakker, 119–148.
Gutzwiller, Kathryn. 2006. "The Bucolic Problem." *CP* 101: 380–404.
Gutzwiller, Kathryn. 2010. "Literary Criticism." In *A Companion to Hellenistic Literature*, edited by J. J. Clauss and M. Cuypers, 337–365. Malden, MA: Wiley-Blackwell.
Haber, Judith. 1994. *Pastoral and the Poetics of Self-Contradiction: Theocritus to Marvell*. Cambridge: Cambridge University Press.
Halperin, David. 1983. *Before Pastoral: Theocritus and the Ancient Tradition of Bucolic Poetry*. New Haven, CT: Yale University Press.
Hans, Linda-Maria. 1985. "Theokrits XVI. Idylle und die Politik Hierons II. von Syrakus." *Historia* 34: 117–125.
Harder, M. A., R. F. Regtuit, and G. C. Wakker, eds. 1996. *Theocritus*. Hellenistica Groningana 2. Groningen: Egbert Forsten.
Harder, M. A., R. F. Regtuit, and G. C. Wakker, eds. 2014. *Hellenistic Poetry in Context*. Hellenistica Groningana 20. Leuven: Peeters.
Harvey, David. 2006. "Space as a Keyword." In *David Harvey: A Critical Reader*, edited by Noel Castree and Derek Gregory, 270–293. Oxford: Blackwell.
Hatzikosta, Styliani. 2008. "Personal Names in Theocritus: A Form of Arte Allusiva." *Tyche* 23: 47–78.
Henrichs, Albert. 1980. "Riper Than a Pear: Parian Invective in Theokritos." *ZPE* 39: 7–27.
Hinge, George. 2009. "Language and Race: Theocritus and the Koine Identity of Ptolemaic Egypt." In *Alexandria: A Cultural and Religious Melting Pot*, edited by George Hinge and Jens Krasilnikoff, 66–79. Aarhus: Aarhus University Press.
Hubbard, Thomas. 1998. *The Pipes of Pan: Intertextuality and Literary Filiation in the Pastoral Tradition from Theocritus to Milton*. Ann Arbor: University of Michigan Press.

Hunt, Jeffrey. 2009. "Bucolic Experimentation in Theocritus' Idyll 10." *GRBS* 49: 391–412.

Hunter, Richard. 1996. *Theocritus and the Archaeology of Greek Poetry*. Cambridge: Cambridge University Press.

Hunter, Richard. 1999. *Theocritus: A Selection*. Cambridge: Cambridge University Press.

Hunter, Richard. 2003. *Theocritus: Encomium of Ptolemy Philadelphus*. Berkeley: University of California Press.

Hunter, Richard. 2008. *On Coming After: Studies in Post-Classical Greek Literature and Its Reception*, Part I: *Hellenistic Poetry and Its Reception*. Berlin: De Gruyter.

Hunter, Richard. 2021. "Theocritus and the Bucolic Homer." In Kyriakou, Sistakou, and Rengakos, 223–241.

Hutchinson, G. O. 1988. *Hellenistic Poetry*. Oxford: Clarendon Press.

Isager, Signe, and Jens Erik Skydsgaard. 1992. *Ancient Greek Agriculture: An Introduction*. London: Routledge.

Isenberg, Charles, and David Konstan. 1984. "Pastoral Desire: The Third Idyll of Theocritus." *Dalhousie Review* 64: 302–315.

Iser, Wolfgang. 1993. *The Fictive and the Imaginary: Charting Literary Anthropology*. Baltimore: Johns Hopkins University Press.

Jones, Frederick. 2011. *Virgil's Garden: The Nature of Bucolic Space*. London: Bristol Classical Press.

Kaloudis, Naomi. 2017. "Daphnis' Folksong: The Euphonist's Effect on the Creation of a Textual Performance." In *Voice and Voices in Antiquity*, edited by Niall W. Slater, 208–230. Leiden: Brill.

Kampakoglou, Alexandros. 2014. "Cowherd or Athlete: Aegon's Ambiguous Status and the Erotics of Genre in Theocritus *Idyll* 4." *Phoenix* 68: 1–26.

Kampakoglou, Alexandros. 2021. "Pan's Pipes: Lyric Echoes and Contexts in Theocritus." In Kyriakou, Sistakou, and Rengakos, 242–270.

Kirstein, Robert. 2007. *Junge Hirten und alte Fischer: Die Gedichte 27, 20 und 21 des Corpus Theocriteum*. Texte und Kommentare 29. Berlin: De Gruyter.

Kloft, Hans. 1989. *Imagination und Realität: Überlegungen zur Wirtschaftsstruktur des Romans Daphnis und Chloe*. Groningen Colloquia on the Novel II. Groningen: Egbert Forsten.

Klooster, J. J. H. 2007. "Theocritus." In *Time in Ancient Greek Literature: Studies in Ancient Greek Narrative*, Vol. 2, edited by Irene J. F. de Jong, 97–111. Leiden: Brill.

Klooster, J. J. H. 2012. "Theocritus." In *Space in Ancient Greek Literature: Studies in Ancient Greek Narrative*, Vol. 3, edited by Irene J. F. de Jong, 99–117. Leiden: Brill.

Köhnken, A. 1996. "Theokrits Polyphemgedichte." In Harder, Regtuit, and Wakker, 171–186.

Konstan, David. 1994. *Sexual Symmetry: Love in the Ancient Novel and Related Genres*. Princeton, NJ: Princeton University Press.

Konstan, David. 2021. "*Eros* and the Pastoral." In Kyriakou, Sistakou, and Rengakos, 517–533.
Kossaifi, Christine. 2002. "L'onomastique bucolique dans les *Idylles* de Théocrite: Un poète face aux names." *REA* 104: 349–361.
Kossaifi, Christine. 2017. "La houlette de Mnémosyne: Écouter et transmettre le chant dans les *Idylles bucoliques* de Théocrite." In Cusset, Kossaifi, and Poignault, 41–62.
Krevans, Nita. 2006. "Is There Urban Pastoral? The Case of Theocritus' *Id.* 15." In Fantuzzi and Papanghelis, 119–146.
Kühn, Josef-Hans. 1958. "Die Thalysien Theokrits (id. 7)." *Hermes* 86: 40–79.
Kurke, Leslie. 1999. *Coins, Bodies, Games, and Gold: The Politics of Meaning in Archaic Greece*. Princeton, NJ: Princeton University Press.
Kurz, André. 1991. "Idylle 22 de Théocrite: Quelques réflexions à propos d'une conjecture de Wilamowitz (v. 170)." *MH* 48: 237–247.
Kwapisz, Jan. 2021. "'Linking Together Rushes and Stalks of Asphodel': The Forms of Theocritean Poetry." In Kyriakou, Sistakou, and Rengakos, 105–127.
Kyriakou, Poulheria. 2004. "ΚΛΕΟΣ and Poetry in Simonides Fr. 11 W² and Theocritus, Idyll 16." *RhM* n.f. 147: 221–246.
Kyriakou, Poulheria. 2018. *Theocritus and His Native Muse: A Syracusan among Many*. Trends in Classics supp. 71. Berlin: De Gruyter.
Kyriakou, Poulheria. 2021. "Women in Theocritus." In Kyriakou, Sistakou, and Rengakos, 626–647.
Kyriakou, Poulheria, Evina Sistakou, and Antonios Rengakos, eds. 2021. *Brill's Companion to Theocritus*. Leiden: Brill.
Lambert, Michael. 2001. "Gender and Religion in Theocritus, *Idyll* 15: Prattling Tourists at the *Adonia*." *AC* 44: 87–103.
Lambert, Michael. 2002. "Desperate Simaetha: Gender and Power in Theocritus, *Idyll* 2." *AC* 45: 71–88.
Lattimore, Steven. 1973. "Battus in Theocritus' Fourth *Idyll*." *GRBS* 14: 319–324.
Laursen, Simon. 1992. "Theocritus' Hymn to the Dioscuri: Unity and Intention." *C&M* 43: 71–95.
Lawall, Gilbert. 1967. *Theocritus' Coan Pastorals: A Poetry Book*. Washington, DC: Center for Hellenic Studies.
Lefebvre, Henri. 1991. *The Production of Space*. Translated by Donald Nicholson-Smith. Oxford: Blackwell.
Legrand, Ph.-E. 1898. *Étude sur Théocrite*. Paris: Libraire des Écoles Françaises d'Athènes et de Rome.
Legrand, Ph.-E. 1907. "ΚΑΠΥΡΟΣ." *REG* 20: 10–17.
Leigh, Matthew. 2016. "Vergil's Second *Eclogue* and the Class Struggle." *CP* 111: 406–433.
Lentini, Giuseppe. 1998. "Amore 'fuori luogo': Presenze saffiche et esiodee nell'idillio 10 di Teocrito." *SCO* 46: 903–907.

Levi, Peter. 1993. "People in a Landscape: Theokritos." In *Hellenistic History and Culture*, edited by Peter Green, 111–137. Berkeley: University of California Press.

Li, Yukai. 2019. "The Distraction of Pastoral and Theocritus' Painted World." *CP* 114: 383–405.

Lindsell, Alice. 1937. "Was Theocritus a Botanist?" *G&R* 6: 78–93.

Looijenga, André. 2014. "The Spear and the Ideology of Kingship in Hellenistic Poetry." In Harder, Regtuit, and Wakker, 217–245.

Massey, Doreen. 2005. *For Space*. London: Sage.

Mastronarde, Donald. 1968. "Theocritus' Idyll 13: Love and the Hero." *TAPA* 99: 273–290.

Matthews, V. J. 1985. "Disembarking from the Argo: Theocritus 13.32–34 and 22.30–33." *LCM* 10: 68–69.

Miles, Gary. 1977. "Characterization and the Ideal of Innocence in Theocritus' Idylls." *Ramus* 6: 139–164.

Moulton, Carroll. 1973. "Theocritus and the Dioscuri." *GRBS* 14: 41–47.

Murray, Jackie. 2014. "Anchored in Time: The Date in Apollonius' *Argonautica*." In Harder, Regtuit, and Wakker, 247–283.

Murray, Oswyn. 2008. "Ptolemaic Royal Patronage." In *Ptolemy II Philadelphus and His World*, edited by P. R. McKechnie and P. Guillaume. Leiden: Brill.

Myers, Tobias. 2016. "O Poimen: Addresses and the Creation of the Theocritean Bucolic Milieu." *CP* 111: 19–31.

Nevett, Lisa. 1999. *House and Society in the Ancient Greek World*. Cambridge: Cambridge University Press.

Nisetich, Frank J. 1980. *Pindar's Victory Songs*. Baltimore: Johns Hopkins University Press.

Noel, Anne-Sophie, and Myrtille Remond. 2017. "Des femmes très matérielles? Objets, féminité et performance dans l'*Idylle xv* de Théocrite." *Bulletin* 2: 76–113.

Nussbaum, Martha. 1997. *Cultivating Humanity: A Classical Defense of Reform in Liberal Education*. Cambridge, MA: Harvard University Press.

Ogilvie, R. M. 1962. "The Song of Thyrsis." *JHS* 82: 106–110.

Ott, Ulrich. 1969. *Die Kunst des Gegensatzes in Theokrits Hirtengedichten*. Spudasmata XXII. Hildesheim: Georg Olms.

Palmieri, Viola. 2021. "Theocritus and the Rural World." In Kyriakou, Sistakou, and Rengakos, 473–493.

Papadopoulou, Maria. 2017. "Poems from the World of Wool: Dress and Identity in Theocritus' *Idylls*." In Cusset, Kossaifi, and Poignault, 163–179.

Parry, Hugh. 1988. "Magic and the Songstress: Theocritus Idyll 2." *ICS* 13: 43–55.

Pausch, Dennis. 2011. "Lebst Du noch oder schreibst Du schon? Ptolemaios II und die Dichtung in Theokrits 14. Idyll." *A&A* 57: 18–38.

Payne, Mark. 2007. *Theocritus and the Invention of Fiction*. Cambridge: Cambridge University Press.

Pollitt, J. J. 1986. *Art in the Hellenistic Age*. Cambridge: Cambridge University Press.

Pretagostini, Roberto. 2006. "How Bucolic Are Theocritus' Bucolic Singers?" In Fantuzzi and Papanghelis, 53–73.

Prioux, Éveline. 2021. "Theocritus and the Visual Arts." In Kyriakou, Sistakou, and Rengakos, 387–427.

Purchase, Philip. 2003–2005. "The Life of Objects: Bounds of Creativity in Theocritus' First Idyll." *Ramus* 32: 85–101.

Reed, Joseph. 2000. "Arsinoe's Adonis and the Poetics of Ptolemaic Imperialism." *TAPA* 130: 319–351.

Reed, Joseph. 2010. "*Idyll* 6 and the Development of Bucolic after Theocritus." In *A Companion to Hellenistic Literature*, edited by James Clauss and Martin Cuypers, 238–250. Chichester, UK: Wiley-Blackwell.

Richer, Hamidou. 2017. "La IVe Idylle de Théocrite: Est-elle une 'Idylle sur rien'?" In Cusset, Kossaifi, and Poignault, 117–130.

Rinkevich, Thomas. 1977. "Theokritos' Fifth Idyll: The Education of Lakon." *Arethusa* 10: 295–305.

Rosenmeyer, Thomas. 1969. *The Green Cabinet: Theocritus and the European Pastoral Lyric*. Berkeley: University of California Press.

Samson, Lindsay Grant. 2013. "The Philosophy of Desire in Theocritus' *Idylls*." PhD diss., University of Iowa.

Scholl, Reinhold. 1989. "L'esclavage chez Théocrite." *Index* 17: 19–28.

Scholten, Helga. 2006. "Die kulturelle Bewertung körperlicher Arbeit in den Gedichten Theokrits." In *Arbeit in der Antike, in Judentum und Christentum*, edited by Detlev Dormeyer, Folker Siegert, and J. Cornelis de Vos, 66–85. Berlin: LIT Verlag.

Seeck, Gustav. 1975. "Dichterisches Technik in Theokrits Thalusien und die Theorie der Hirtendichtung." In *Dôrêma Hans Diller zum 70. Geburtstag: Dauer und Überleben des antiken Geistes*, edited by K. Vourveris and A. Skiadas, 195–209. Athens: Griechische Humanistische Gesellschaft.

Segal, Charles. 1981. *Poetry and Myth in Ancient Pastoral: Essays on Theocritus and Virgil*. Princeton, NJ: Princeton University Press.

Segal, Charles. 1984. "Underreading and Intertextuality: Sappho, Simaetha, and Odysseus in Theocritus' Second Idyll." *Arethusa* 17: 201–209.

Segal, Charles. 1985. "Time and Imagination in Theocritus' Second *Idyll*." *CA* 4: 103–119.

Selden, Daniel. 1998. "Alibis." *CA* 17: 289–412.

Sens, Alexander. 1992. "Theocritus, Homer, and the Dioscuri: *Idyll* 22.137–223." *TAPA* 122: 335–350.

Sens, Alexander. 1994. "Hellenistic Reference in the Proem of Theocritus, *Idyll* 22." *CQ* 44: 66–74.

Sens, Alexander. 1997. *Theocritus: Dioscuri (Idyll 22). Hypomnemata* 114. Göttingen: Vandenhoeck & Ruprecht.

Sens, Alexander. 2021. "Theocritus' Hymns and 'Epyllia': Poems 13, 22, 24, 26." In Kyriakou, Sistakou, and Rengakos, 176–197.

Sistakou, Evina. 2021. "The Sweet Pleasures of Theocritus' *Idylls*: A Study in the Aesthetics of ἁδύτης." In Kyriakou, Sistakou, and Rengakos, 324–345.

Skinner, Marilyn. 2001. "Ladies' Day at the Art Institute." In *Making Silence Speak: Women's Voices in Greek Literature and Society*, edited by André Lardinois and Laura McClure, 201–222. Princeton, NJ: Princeton University Press.

Stanzel, Karl-Heinz. 1995. *Liebende Hirten: Theokrits Bukolik und die alexandrinische Poesie*. Stuttgart: B. G. Teubner.

Stanzel, Karl-Heinz. 2021. "Theocritus' Contest Poems." In Kyriakou, Sistakou, and Rengakos, 346–363.

Stephens, Susan. 2003. *Seeing Double: Intercultural Poetics in Ptolemaic Alexandria*. Berkeley: University of California Press.

Stephens, Susan. 2006. "Ptolemaic Pastoral." In Fantuzzi and Papanghelis, 91–117.

Stephens, Susan. 2018. *The Poets of Alexandria*. London: I.B. Tauris.

Stern, Jacob. 1974. "Theocritus' *Idyll* 24." *AJP* 95: 348–361.

Stern, Jacob. 1975. "Theocritus' *Idyll* 14." *GRBS* 16: 51–58.

Strootman, Rolf. 2014. "The Dawning of a Golden Age: Images of Peace and Abundance in Alexandrian Court Poetry in Relation to Ptolemaic Imperial Ideology." In Harder, Regtuit, and Wakker, 323–339.

Thalmann, William. 1998. *The Swineherd and the Bow: Representations of Class in the Odyssey*. Ithaca, NY: Cornell University Press.

Thalmann, William. 2011. *Apollonius of Rhodes and the Spaces of Hellenism*. New York: Oxford University Press.

Thomas, Richard. 1996. "Genre through Intertextuality: Theocritus to Virgil and Propertius." In Harder, Regtuit, and Wakker, 227–246.

Tilley, Christopher. 1994. *A Phenomenology of Landscape: Places, Paths and Monuments*. Oxford: Berg.

Tuan, Yi-Fu. 1977. *Space and Place: The Perspective of Experience*. Minneapolis: University of Minnesota Press.

Van Erp Taalman Kip, Maria. 1994. "Intertextuality and Theocritus 13." In *Modern Critical Theory and Theocritus 13*, edited by Irene J. F. de Jong and J. P. Sullivan, 153–169. *Mnemosyne* suppl. 130. Leiden: Brill.

Van Sickle, John. 1969. "The Fourth Pastoral Poems of Virgil and Theocritus." *Atti e memorie* ser. 3: 129–148.

Vox, Onofrio. 1985. "Il contrasto di Batto e Coridone nell'idyllio IV di Teocrito." *MD* 15: 173–178.

Walker, Steven. 1980. *Theocritus*. Boston: Twayne.

Waszink, Jan. 1974. *Biene und Honig als Symbol des Dichters und der Dichtung in der griechisch-römischen Antike*. Rheinish-Westfälische Akademie der Wissenschaften. Opladen: Westdeutscher Verlag.

West, M. L. 1966. *Hesiod* Theogony. Oxford: Clarendon Press.

White, Heather. 1979. *Studies in Theocritus and Other Hellenistic Poets*. Amsterdam: J. C. Gieben.

Whitehorne, John. 1974. "The Reapers: Theocritus 'Idyll' 10." *Journal of the Australasian Universities Modern Language Association* 41: 30–49.

Whitehorne, John. 1995. "Women's Work in Theocritus, Idyll 15." *Hermes* 123: 63–75.

Williams, Frederick. 1973. "Ω in Theocritus." *Eranos* 71: 52–67.

Worman, Nancy. 2015. *Landscape and the Spaces of Metaphor in Ancient Literary Theory and Criticism*. Cambridge: Cambridge University Press.

Zimmerman, Clayton. 1994. *The Pastoral Narcissus: A Study of the First Idyll of Theocritus*. Lanham, MD: Rowman & Littlefield.

Index of Passages Cited

For the benefit of digital users, indexed terms that span two pages (e.g., 52–53) may, on occasion, appear on only one of those pages.

Aeschylus
Ag. 13, 60, 178, 252, 546, 916: 159n.13
Ag. 212: 152–53
Ag. 657: 159
Eum. 292–298: 106n.30
Pers. 606: 151n.144

Apollonius of Rhodes
Argonautika
1.782–786: 144
1.790–791: 144n.130
2.4: 58n.35
2.8: 55–56
3.422: 144n.130
3. 802, 808, 844: 141n.119
3.1022–1023: 144n.130
4.25: 141n.119
4.26–42: 42–43n.116
4.866–879: 71–72

Archilochus
fr. 196a.42–48W: 145

Aristophanes
Aves
240, 620: 15

Aristotle
Eth. Nic. 10, 1177a12

Athenaeus
176d: 162n.25
412e-f: 169n.43
476f–477e: 10n.26

Callimachus
Epigr. 22: 45
Epigr. 43: 124n.80

Diodorus Siculus
16.83.1: 67

Euripides
Bacchae
457–459: 180
Troades
414–415: 141–42

Herodotus
1.31.3: 69n.66
4.172: 64n.56

Hesiod
[*Shield of Herakles*]
213–215: 182–83
Theogony
23: 13n.37
30–34: 106n.31
83–84: 113–14n.55
359: 137n.110

Hesiod (*cont.*)
Works and Days
 1: 177–78
 182: 87n.102
 225–247: 81–82
 235: 87n.102
 365–367: 174–75
 571–581: 171n.48

Homer
Iliad
 1.249: 64n.55, 119–20
 1.348–351: 136–37
 2.763–767: 91n.116
 3.23–26: 148n.138
 3.90: 42–43n.116
 3.217: 144
 11.113–119: 148n.138
 16.514–516: 106n.30
 16.756–758: 148n.138
 18.45: 136–37
 18.54–60: 71–72
 22.189–192: 148n.138
 22.467: 114
 23.653–699: 57
Odyssey
 3.120–125: 87n.102
 5.63–75: 50
 5.81–86: 136–37
 5.394–399: 185n.79
 6.130–136: 148n.138
 8.266–367: 119–20
 8.573: 56n.27
 9.20: 78–79
 9.107: 78–79
 9.107–111: 58–59
 9.259: 56n.27
 9.346: 10n.26
 9.447–460: 58–59
 10.223: 39
 11.225–30: 69n.66
 12.184–191: 120n.70
 12.285: 56n.27
 14.78: 10n.26
 15.382: 56n.27
 16.52: 10n.26
 17.204–253: 57
 18.90–99: 60n.38
 19.33–40: 64–65
 19.107–114: 81–82
 20.98–121: 64–65
 22.481–482, 493–494: 68n.64
 23.233–240: 185n.79
Homeric Hymn to Demeter
 275–280: 71

Leonidas of Tarentum
 A. P. 7.295: 186–87

Lysias
 1.7–9: 145–46
 1.15–17: 146n.134

Moschus
 Fr. 1 Gow: 184–85
 Fr. 1.10 Gow: 188n.84
 Lament for Bion: 108–9

Pindar
 N. 1.41: 67
 N. 1.60–61: 68
 N. 1.62–72: 68
 N. 10.65–68: 61–62
 O. 7.1–4, 7–9: 76–78

Plato
Phaedrus
 230b: 64n.56
 255d: 136–37
Symposium
 179e–180a: 147
 200b9–200d10: 101n.21
 203c5–203d3: 98–99

Simonides
 PMG 543.8–20: 66–67

Theocritus
Epigr. 4
    7: 56n.28
    11–12: 114–15

Fr. 3 Gow
    C4P152 n78

Idyll 1
    1.1: 102
    1.1–2: 5
    1.1–6: 161
    1.1–23: 25–27
    1.3: 106–7
    1.6: 164–65
    1.7–8: 5, 56, 102
    1.12–23: 19, 107
    1.14: 127
    1.19: 101–2
    1.19–20: 116
    1.23–24: 111–12
    1.23–25: 116
    1.27: 10n.26
    1.39–44: 183–84
    1.45: 183–84
    1.45–54: 9–10
    1.57–58: 9–10
    1.62–63: 117
    1.65: 102, 113
    1.66–69: 12–13, 104–5
    1.68: 10–11
    1.71–75: 12, 109–10
    1.74–75: 160
    1.77: 104
    1.82–85: 102–4
    1.85–88: 95–96, 103–4
    1.86–91: 110–11
    1.94–122: 102
    1.97–98: 159
    1.105: 39–40
    1.106: 49–50
    1.106–107: 25n.66
    1.115–121: 12, 108–11, 115–16
    1.115–136: 111
    1.120–121: 104
    1.122, C3P138
    1.123–126: 12–13
    1.123–130: 105–7
    1.131–132: 25n.66
    1.132–136: 5–6, 111–12
    1.143: 10n.26
    1.145: 102, 110n.47
    1.146–148: 113–14
    1.148: 114
    1.149: 10n.26
    1.151–152: 26–27

Idyll 2
    2.15–16: 141n.119, 142–43
    2.35: 40n.109
    2.44: 143–44
    2.56–60: 42–43
    2.76: 41–42
    2.76–80: 144
    2.78: 143–44
    2.83–85: 41–42
    2.86: 41–42
    2.91–92: 41–42
    2.101: 42–43n.116
    2.104–106: 42–43
    2.112: 144
    2.115: 143–44, 145n.131
    2.118–122: 42–43, 144
    2.124–125: 142–43
    2.124–128: 42–43
    2.136–138: 42–43
    2.138–139: 145–46
    2.143: 146–47
    2.145–149: 146n.134
    2.149–153: 123–24
    2.150: 143–44
    2.151–153: 42
    2.156: 42
    2.159–162: 140–41
    2.160: 42–43

Theocritus (*cont.*)
  2.163–164: 146–47
  2.164: 141–42

Idyll 3
  3.2: 6–7, 13n.36, 125
  3.6: 6–7, 98n.13, 165–66, 167n.40, 170
  3.6–7: 96–97
  3.7: 167n.40
  3.8–9: 96–97
  3.10: 97
  3.10–11: 6–7, 9–10, 96–97, 164–65
  3.12: 97
  3.12–14: 94–96
  3.15: 97
  3.18: 97–98, 98n.15
  3.18–19: 97, 167n.40
  3.21–23: 96–97
  3.23: 50n.12
  3.25–26: 6–7
  3.26: 182–83
  3.29: 94
  3.31: 16
  3.34–36: 164n.32
  3.35–36: 16
  3.36: 98n.13
  3.38: 6–7
  3.39–40: 6–7
  3.46: 39–40

Idyll 4
  4.4: 16, 167
  4.5: 158–59
  4.6: 168–69
  4.7: 158, 168–69
  4.8: 163
  4.9: 168–69
  4.10: 158
  4.12: 160
  4.13: 159–60
  4.16: 157n.7
  4.17–19: 13–14
  4.17–25: 5, 168–69
  4.20–22: 164–66
  4.21: 11–12
  4.23–25: 13–14
  4.26–28: 161
  4.27: 159
  4.29–37: 161–64
  4.29–40: 166–67
  4.32: 11–12, 163
  4.33: 163–64
  4.35: 163–64
  4.35–40: 98
  4.37: C4P46
  4.38: 98n.13, 98n.15, 167n.40
  4.39: 165–66
  4.42: 165–66
  4.44–45: 158
  4.44–46: 13, 155–56
  4.53: 166–67
  4.56: 13, 155
  4.56–57: 12–13, 13n.36
  4.57: 12
  4.58–63: 167

Idyll 5
  5.1–4: 16–18
  5.2: 164–65
  5.3–7: 18
  5.5: 16
  5.8: 16
  5.10: 16n.49
  5.11–12: 164–65
  5.20: 25n.66, 101–2
  5.31–32: 176–77
  5.31–34: 19
  5.34: 49–50
  5.36–37: 18
  5.38–40: 165–66
  5.41–42: 18, 95–96
  5.43: 19–20n.59
  5.45: 20, 49–50
  5.45–46: 25n.66
  5.45–49: 19
  5.50–51: 164–65
  5.51–52: 24–25

Index of Passages Cited

5.52: 28n.73
5.56–57: 164–65
5.60: 17–18
5.61: 20
5.62: 11–12
5.63–65: 11–12
5.66: 11–12
5.67: 17–18
5.72–73: 16
5.78: 11–12
5.78–79: 11–12
5.80–81: 25n.66
5.88–89: 9–10
5.96–97: 164–65
5.98–99: 164n.32
5.100: 20
5.100–101: 155–56
5.101: 25n.66
5.104: 56n.28
5.108–115: 9–10
5.111: 80n.90
5.117: 20
5.118: 19–20n.59
5.120–123: 21–24
5.128: 170
5.133: 164–65
5.136: 17–18
5.136–137: 112n.51
5.139–40: 164–65
5.141: 18
5.142–144: 17–18
5.147–150: 25n.66

Idyll 6
6.1–4: 17–18
6.2: 129
6.2–3: 129–30
6.3: 6–7
6.3–4: 130–31
6.6–7: 9–10, 132
6.7: 95n.6
6.8–9: 138–39
6.9–14: 134–35

6.10–12: 7
6.14: 137–38
6.17: 130–31
6.18–19: 137–38, 177–78
6.19: 132–33
6.21–22: 132–33
6.32–33: 139n.114
6.33: 49n.10
6.34–38: 135–36
6.36: 137–38
6.40: 16
6.42: 18
6.42–44: 129–30
6.42–46: 17–18
6.43: 18
6.45: 6–7, 18

Idyll 7
7.10: 41–42
7.10–11: 28–29
7.13–14: 30–31, 99n.17
7.13–19: 27–28, 99n.17
7.18–19: 166–67
7.21–23: 28–29
7.30–31: 161n.23
7.32–34: 9
7.35: 18n.53
7.37: 114
7.40: 161n.23
7.41: 112n.51
7.47–48: 112n.51
7.51: 13n.36, 27–28, 127–28, 150
7.52–56: 121–23, 198–99
7.53–54: 184
7.56: 121
7.57–60: 122–23
7.59–60: 184
7.60: 7
7.60–61: 29–30
7.61–62: 123
7.63: 198–99
7.64–72: 123
7.67: 49–50

Theocritus (*cont.*)
   7.67–68: 29–30
   7.68: 50n.12
   7.69–70: 123–24
   7. 72–77: 101–2, 116, 125, 131n.94
   7.73: 103n.25
   7.76–77: 12–13, 29–30
   7.78–79: 29–30
   7.78–82: 125–26
   7.78–85: 56, 79
   7.82–89: 24–25, 126–28
   7.84–85: 115
   7.88: 56n.28
   7.89: 115
   7.91–93: xviiin.13
   7.91–95: 13n.37
   7.92: 13n.36, 27–28
   7.93: 162–63
   7.96–97: 165–66
   7.103–114: 27–28
   7.111–114: 12–13
   7.120–124: 145n.131
   7.121: 143–44
   7.122–125: 27–28
   7.123–126: 27–28
   7.128: 166–67
   7.128–129: 106n.31
   7.131–157: 4–5, 32
   7.132–134: 29–30
   7.133: 49n.10
   7. 155–158: 27–28
[*Idyll* 8]
   [8].2: 13n.36
[*Idyll* 9]
   [9]. 7–13: 15
   [9].15–21: 15n.47
Idyll 10
   10.1: 191
   10.1–2: 170–71
   10.4: 170–71
   10.7: 171
   10.7–9: 173–74
   10.10: 171
   10.11: 171–72
   10.13: 171–72
   10.14: 175
   10.15: 173n.53
   10.15–16: 178n.61
   10.16–17: 9
   10.17: 176
   10.17–18: 175
   10.19–23: 175–76
   10.24–25: 177–78
   10.26: 170, 177–78
   10.30–31: 170
   10.32–35: 178
   10.36: 170
   10.40: 179n.63
   10.42–43: 172–73
   10.44–45: 173n.53
   10.48–51: 80n.89, 171
   10.52–55: 171–73
   10.56–58: 179–80
Idyll 11
   11.7: 11n.29
   11.10–11: 200–1
   11. 13–16: 7
   11.14: 140n.117
   11.17–18: 7
   11.18: 140n.117
   11.20: 136
   11.23–24: 133–34
   11.25–29: 133–34
   11.30–33: 137
   11.34–49: xviiin.13
   11.40–41: 164n.32
   11.45: 56n.28
   11.54–60: 7
   11.75: 175
   11.77–78: 16
   11.80: 140n.117, 198–99
Idyll 12
   12.10: 100–1
   12.10–21: 178

Index of Passages Cited

12.13–14: 38–39n.103
12.15–16: 100–1
Idyll 13
  13.1–4: 101–53
  13.3: 138
  13.5–6: 152–53
  13.5–9: 149–51
  13.6: 148
  13.8–9: 21
  13.14: 150
  13.15: C3P318
  13.19–24: 45–47
  13.23: 48
  13.25: xvii
  13.25–26: 53
  13.25–31: 46–47
  13.26: 56
  13.30–31: 49–50
  13.32: 50–51
  13.32–35: 49, 55
  13.35: 56n.27
  13.37: 56
  13.37–38: 50–51
  13.39–42: 50
  13.39–45: 49
  13.40: 50
  13.43–45: 50
  13.48–49: 150–52, 151n.144
  13.49: 50
  13.53–54: 50–51
  13.58: 113–14
  13.58–60: 150–51
  13.59–60: 50–51
  13.62–65: 148–49
  13.62–67: 50–51
  13.66: 150n.142, 153
  13.72: 151–52
  13.72–75: 47–48
  13.73: 152–53
  13.75: 48
Idyll 14
  14.6–7: 89–90

14.8: 89n.112
14.12: 91n.116
14.14: 90
14.18–19: 124n.80
14.20–21: 89n.112
14.23: 89n.112
14.31: 89n.112
14.41: 89n.112
14.53–54: 90–91
14.55: 90–91
14.62: 197
14.63–65: 91–92
Idyll 15
15.1: 33n.87
15.4–7: 35
15.6: 35n.93
15.7: 35
15.18–20: 33–34
15.24: 33–34
15.34–37: 36–37
15.34–38: 33–34
15.43: 33n.87
15.45: 38
15.46–50: 33–34, 38, 39–40
15.51–52: 35, 38
15.57: 37
15.61–62: 39
15.73: 38, 39
15.77: 33n.87
15.79: 39
15.80: 33–34
15.80–86: 33–34
15.86: 196
15.87–88: 38
15.87–95: 39–40
15.106–108: 39–40
15.106–111: 38
15.118–122: 39–40
15.125: 33–34
15.126–127: 35–37, 85
15.136–137: 39–40

Theocritus (*cont.*)
Idyll 16
  16.2: 75–76
  16.5–65: 73
  16.6–12: 75–76
  16.22–23: 75–76, 86
  16.27–28: 76–77
  16.29: 86
  16.30–34: 86
  16.31–33: 84–85
  16.34–35: 84–85
  16.34–39: 81
  16.38: 58–59
  16.40–47: 82
  16.48–57: 86
  16.51–53: 78–79
  16.66–100: 73
  16.73: 73
  16.88–97: 79–82
  16.95: 59n.36
  16.98–100: 78–79, 81, 82
  16.101–103: 82–83
  16.103: 87
  16.104–109: 83–84
Idyll 17
  17.16–33: 73n.71
  17.56–57: 87
  17.77–94: 87–88
  17.96: 86
  17.97: 88–89
  17.106–116: 86
  17.112–114: 161n.23
  17.118–120: 86
[*Id.* 20]
  [20].25–28: 115
Idyll 21
  21.1–3: 187–88
  21.2–3: 188n.83
  21.3: 191
  21.6: 184n.78
  21.8–9: 188
  21.14: 188

  21.15–18: 188–89
  21.20: 188n.83
  21.32–33: 190
  21.39–41: 189
  21.63–67: 190
Idyll 22
  22.27–29: 53–54
  22.30–33: 55
  22.34–36: 55–56
  22.37–43: 56
  22.44: 58–59
  22.54–74: 61–62
  22.75–79: 59–60
  22.105–106: 59
  22.131–134: 60
  22.145–180: 61
  22.170–180: 62n.45
  22.199–200: 61–62
  22.214–222: 61–62
Idyll 24
  24.5: 65–66
  24.7–8: 66
  24.10: 65–66
  24.11–12: 73n.71
  24.13–16: 67
  24.17–20: 67
  24.21: 69–70
  24.41: 68
  24.46: 64–65
  24.47–53: 64–65
  24.49: 65n.57
  24.54–56: 64–65
  24.73: 70, 71
  24.75–80: 68–69
  24.79–85: 67–68
  24.81–83: 68
  24.95: 67–68
  24.96: 67–68
  24.103–104: 69–70, 71–72
  24.103–134: 150
  24.105: 73n.71
  24.134: 68

Idyll 25
   25.7–33: 8–9
   25.13–17: 13–14
   25.33: 9
   25.36: 9
   25.45: 9
   25.153: 9
   25.157–158: 8n.22
   25.173: 70

Thucydides
   6.13.1: 174

Vergil
   Ecl. 5.43–44: 110n.48

Subject Index

For the benefit of digital users, indexed terms that span two pages (e.g., 52–53) may, on occasion, appear on only one of those pages.

absence, 93–101
  bucolic vs. agricultural responses to, 173–74
  as constituting bucolic song, 96, 194–95
  as fundamental for bucolic, 93, 101–2
  Idylls generated by, xiii
  in *Id.* 1, 101–21
  in *Id.* 2, 140–47
  in *Id.* 4, 160, 169
  in *Id.* 6, 115, 129–39
  in *Id.* 7, 121–28
  in *Id.* 13, 147–53
  as presupposed by *kômos*, 94
  and readers, 195–96
  tragic potential of, 125
  of voice, 119–20
  See also eros
Acosta-Hughes, Benjamin, 44n.1
Adonis
  festival of, 33–34, 36, 39–40, 196
agon. *See* competition
agricultural world
  vs. bucolic world, 9–10, 20–21, 27–28, 169–81
  eros alien to, 170, 173–74, 176–77
  linguistic characteristics of, 171–72
  scarcity of food and drink in, 171–73
  work song in, 171–73, 179–80
  See also bucolic world; labor
Akhilleus, 71–72, 73, 87n.102, 136–37, 147
Alexandria
  centripetal force of, 36–37, 38, 88–89, 91–92, 192–93
  centripetal force of royal palace in, 35–36
  as city of immigrants, 92
  ethnic diversity of, 32–33
  ethnic identity in, 31–32, 33–34
  as imperial center, 89–90
  interethnic relations in, 33–34, 38, 60–61, 193–94
  as microcosm of Ptolemaic empire, 33–34
  as spatial system, 33–34
  See also Ptolemaic empire
Alpers, Paul, 3, 16–17
Anagnostou-Laoutides, Eva, 103n.25
Andrews, N. E., 42–43n.116
Apollonius of Rhodes, xvi–xvii, 1, 44–45, 46–47, 70, 71–72, 192–93
  Theocritus's relation to, xvii, 48–49, 54–56, 58–59, 60, 144, 193–94
apostrophe, 107–12, 127–28, 132, 146–47
Archilochus
  Cologne Epode, 145
  poetic investiture of, 30–31

Arsinoe, 36, 38, 72–73
athletics
    Aigon's pretensions to (*Id.* 4), 158, 168–69
    and gluttony, 163–64
    vs. herding, 155, 158
    as subject of epinician, 163–64
Augeias, farm of, 7–9, 10, 16, 49–50, 80
aulos, 9, 18
Austin, Norman, 74–75

Bacchylides, 73–74, 78n.84
Barigazzi, Adelmo, 168n.41
bees, 125–26, 129–30
Belloni, Luigi, 188n.83
Berenike, 72–73, 88–89
Berger, Harry, 113n.54, 197
Bernsdorff, Hans, 131–32
Borgogno, Alberto, 29–30
boundaries
    between bucolic and agricultural space, 7–8, 11–12
    between bucolic and untamed space, 12
    between human and divine, 50–51, 67–68
    between inside and outside, 6–7, 42–43, 65, 67
    between land and sea, 7, 133–34, 182–83, 189
    of earth, 79
    fluidity of, xiv, 31–33, 39–40, 89–90, 91–92, 132, 154–55, 193–94
    reassertion of, 67–68
    territorial, 67–68
    See also houses; margins; space
bucolic
    definitions of, xviii
    grotesque accommodated by, 59, 196–97
    ideology of, 84–85
    in *Id.* 16, 80–71
    in *Id.* 22, 56–61
    and Ptolemaic self-legitimation, 196
    within Ptolemaic palace, 39–40, 196
    readers' responses to, 197–201
    sensibility, 53
bucolic sensibility, xiii–xiv, 53, 154–55, 193, 196
bucolic song
    as attempt to restore lost presence, 102, 107, 112–13
    as attempt to recover Daphnis's singing, 101–2
    of Boukaios (*Id.* 10), 170
    vs. epinician, 163–65
    vs. urbane songs, 162–63
    waning of (*Id.* 4), 159, 165–66
    vs. work song, 172–73, 177–80
bucolic world
    and cities, 10–12, 36–37, 168, 196
    defined by margins, 7, 154–55, 182–83, 189, 190, 193–94
    disintegration of (*Id.* 4), 155–69, 191
    extremes encompassed by, 21–24
    foundational values of, 169
    and interethnic relations, 60–61
    lost wholeness of, 98–99
    sacrifice elided in, 164–65
    stylization of, xiii, 5–7, 194–95
    work exceptional in, 166–67
    See also absence; agricultural world; eros; leisure; mountain
Buller, J. L., 108–9
Burton, Joan, 32–33, 39, 42–43n.116

Callimachus, xvi–xvii, 1, 38–39n.103, 44n.1, 74–75, 113–14n.55, 192–93
de Certeau, Michel, 33–34
Chaniotis, Angelos, 14–15
cicadas, 114
class
    in *Id.* 2, 142n.124
    and readers' responses, 199–200

Subject Index

Clayman, Dee, 74–75
colonization, 53, 60–61
comedy, 57
competition
    poetic, 17–18, 129–30, 160–61, 179
    masculine, 19, 21–24, 53, 60, 61–62, 196–97
crete, 14–15
Culler, Jonathan, 107–8, 111, 127–28
cup (*Id.* 1), 9–10, 97n.11, 120, 183–84
Cusset, Christophe, 7n.17, 133n.98, 135

Danae, 66, 70, 73n.71
Daphnis
    as archetypal bucolic singer
    death of, 26–27
    death of, as founding bucolic, 101–2
    Rescue of, by Herakles, 179
    story of, 103, 117, 125, 131–32
Davies, Malcolm, 34n.90
deictics, 19, 25, 194–95
Demeter, xv–xvi, 71–72, 172–73
desire. *See* eros
Dover, K. J., 90, 141–42
Duncan, Anne, 142–43n.125

Edquist, Harriet, 7–8n.21
Elliger, Einfried, 49
Empson, William, 84–85, 197–98
enclosures
    in *Id.* 7, 29–30, 125, 128
    in *Id.* 16, 75–76, 79, 83
    in *Id.* 24, 65–67, 70
    See also frames
encomium
    Idyll 16 and, 73–75
epic poetry
    Theocritus's relation to, xviii–, 39, 44–45, 49, 51–53, 57–60, 62–64, 147, 150, 151n.144, 152–53, 196–97
epinician, 163–65

Epyllion, 44–45
eros, 93–101
    for bucolic world, 125
    as constituted by absence, 99, 131, 136, 141–42, 149, 169
    as constituting bucolic world and song, 100, 123–24, 198
    dangers of, 174
    debasement of (*Id.* 4), 167
    and fiction-making, 97, 98
    fulfillment of, 100–1, 146–47, 150–51
    and heroism, 147, 152–53
    and leisure, 176–77
    of Lykidas, 122–23
    Plato's view of, 98–99
    and possession, 101
    power of, 48–49, 147, 151–53, 197
    of readers, xiii, 120–21, 125–26, 128, 195–96, 198–99
    reality reshaped by, 137–38, 177–78
    at symposium, 123–24
    See also absence
eros (god), 99, 176
ethnic identity
    fluidity of, 31–32, 89–90
euphonist theory, 115–16, 119

fantasy, 2, 97, 100–1, 115, 121, 125, 127–28, 128–29n.87, 178, 190, 191, 198
Fantuzzi, Marco, 105n.28
fictionality, 30–32, 112–13, 125–26, 132, 133, 138–39, 177–78, 181, 191, 194–96
    and apostrophe, 107–8
    See also eros; fantasy; imagination
fishermen
    in bucolic *Idylls*, 182–84
    in Greek poetry, 182–83
    hard labor of, 183–84, 186–87, 191
    in Hellenistic poetry outside Theocritus, 184–87

fishermen (*cont.*)
    in Hellenistic sculpture, 183–84, 201n.13
    Poverty of, 187–90
    tools of, 188
    See also labor; poverty
Foucault, Michel, xiv–xv
frames, 21–24, 27–28, 48, 111–12, 121, 125–26, 128, 129, 130–31, 132, 133, 194–95, 197–98
    See also enclosures

gender
    in *Id.* 2, 41–43, 140, 142–43, 145–46
    in *Id.* 14, 89n.112, 90–91
    in *Id.* 15, 33–34
    in *Id.* 24, 68–73
    and paleness vs. tan, 180
    roles of, inverted, 50–51, 144, 145–47, 149
    spatial expression of, 38, 41–43, 68
    See also houses; space; wool and textile production
genre, xviii–xix, 51–53, 57–58, 64
Gershenson, Daniel, 111n.50
Giangrande, Giuseppe, 182, 189n.85
Gibbs-Wichrowska, Laura, 142–43n.125
Glauke, 162–63
González, José, 74–75
Gow, A. S. F., 37, 65, 78–79, 141–42, 181–82, 189
Graces (Χάριτες), 75–76, 78–79
Grethlein, Jonas, 180
Griffiths, Frederick, 34n.90, 61–62, 73–74, 75
Gutzwiller, Kathryn, xviii, 25–26, 44n.1, 73–74, 84–85, 97–98, 149n.141, 156–57, 160–61

Haber, Judith, 103, 156, 163–64
Halperin, David xix, 52
Harvey, David, 2, 25

Herakles
    alleged ancestor of Ptolemies, 63–64, 73n.71, 88, 192–93
    apotheosis of, 67–68, 70, 73n.71, 192–93
    Daphnis rescued by, 179
    education of, 68, 73n.71, 150, 192–93
    gluttony of, 150–51, 163
    gullet of, 113–14
    heroic and comic potential of, 64
    importance of, in Theocritus, 63–64
    Olympic games founded by, 163–64
    paternity of, 65–66, 69–70
    and pederasty, 21, 149–50
    subject to eros
heroism. *See* epic poetry
Hesiod
    poetic investiture of, 30–31, 106–7
    presence of, in *Id.* 10, 170, 174–75, 176–78, 179
    and work, 181
heterotopia, xiv–xv, 3–4n.8, 31–32, 87–88, 193–94
Hieron II of Syracuse, 73, 81, 83n.95, 85–86
Hinge, George, 38–39n.103
Hipponax, 74–75
honey, 113–15, 125–26, 127–28
hospitality, 54, 60–62, 76–78, 196–97
houses
    and gender, 42–43, 68, 142–43
    in *Id.* 2, 41
    in *Id.* 16, 75–78
    as setting for *Id.* 24, 63–66, 67–68
    See also gender; space
Hunt, Jeffrey, 169–70n.45
Hunter, Richard, 96–97, 123–24, 147, 149, 159
Hutchinson, G. O., 152–53

Idylls
    categories of, xii–xiii, xix
    defined, xi

loose coherence of, xiv
as poetic corpus, xv–xvi
relations between, 39–40
Spatial system constructed by, 3–4, 36–37, 59, 192–93
illusion, 132, 133, 135, 137, 138–39, 177–78, 200–1
imagination, 21–24, 125–26, 178, 180–81, 191, 198
See also fantasy; fictionality
Isenberg, Charles, 200
Iser, Wolfgang, 112–13

Jones, Frederick, 7n.20

Kaloudis, Naomi, 117–19
Kampakoglou, Alexandros, 164n.31
Kirke, 39
Kirstein, Robert, 181–82n.71
Klooster, Jacqueline, 3–4n.8
Kômos, 42–43, 93, 97, 144
space in, 94
Konstan, David, 96–97, 103n.25, 200
Krevans, Nita, 39–40
Kroton, 11–12, 85, 161, 163, 164–65, 168–69
Kühn, Josef-Hans, 113n.54
Kwapisz, Jan, 91–92
Kyriakou, Poulheria, 72n.70, 74–75

labor
agricultural, 169–81, 191
of fishermen, 183–88, 191
Lambert, Michael, 34n.90, 142–43n.125
Laursen, Simon, 62n.46
Lawall, Gilbert, 156
Lefebvre, Henri, 1–2
leisure
bucolic, 5, 43, 58–59
and eros, xiv–xv, 121, 176–77
vs. labor, xiii, 7–8, 9n.24, 29–30, 32, 80n.90, 85, 166–67, 169–81, 183–84, 185, 191, 193–94, 198

vs. mobility, 80
See also bucolic world; eros
Li, Yukai, 199n.10
Lindsell, Alice, 5–6, 194
Lityerses, 179
Looijenga, André, 87
lyric poetry, 63–64, 149, 150
Lysias, 145–46

magic, 41–42, 140, 141–43, 197
margins
and boundaries, 31–32
bucolic world defined by, 7, 154–91
Massey, Doreen, 38
Mastronarde, Donald, 49
mercenaries, 90–91
meter, 137–38
Miles, Gary, 113n.54
Milon (athlete), 168–69
Miletos, 36
mirror, 135, 136
mobility, 34–35
and ethnic identity, 38, 89–90
idylls as response to, xiv, 31–33, 193
within city, 33–34
See also Alexandria; mercenaries; place; space
mountain, the
bucolic world designated by, xiii, 13–14, 27–28, 55–56, 104, 173–74, 180
Muses, 105, 117

names
of Amaryllis, 98
of Bombyka, 178n.61
of Boukaios, 170–71
of Daphnis, 131–32
of Galateia, 133–34, 135
of Komatas, 24–25
of Lityerses, 179n.64
of Milon, 168–69, 180
of Philinos, 143–44

names (*cont.*)
   of τηλέφιλον, 94
   of Tityros, 7n.18, 124
narcissism, 136
narrative imagination, 199–200
nature
   bucolic vs. agricultural attitudes to, 181
   human culture's relation to, 25–27, 31–32, 95–96, 108–9, 120, 148, 194–95, 197, 201
Nussbaum, Martha, 199–200
Nymphs
   absence of, from Daphnis's death, 105, 111–12
   in *Id.* 13, 48–49, 50–51, 149, 151–52
   as inspirers of bucolic song, 105

Odysseus
   encounter of, with Melanthios, 57
   fame of, 78–79
   gazes over sea, 137
   house purified by, 68n.64
   and Iros, 60n.38
   and Kirke, 39
   as manipulator of words, 144
   and Nausikaa, 148n.138
   as paradigm of return, 78–79
   as πολυμήχανος, 67
   and Polyphemos, 58–59, 133
   Praise by, of Penelope, 81–82
   visit of, to the dead, 69
   wanderings of, 55–56
Olympia
   vs. bucolic world, 12–13, 155
   as Panhellenic center, 158
orality, 117–19

palaistra, 41, 142–43, 142n.124
Pan
   in *Id.* 1, 25–26, 105–6, 193–94
Papadopoulou, Maria, 36–37
paraclausithyron, 42–43n.116
Parry, Hugh, 142–43n.125
pastas, 64–65
pathetic fallacy, 108–9
patronage, 75, 77–78, 82, 85–86, 91–92, 193n.2
Pausch, Dennis, 89n.111
Payne, Mark, 26–27, 194, 197, 198–201
pederasty, 18, 19–20, 21, 129–30, 143–44, 149–50
penestai, 81, 84
performance, 118–19
Perseus, 66, 70, 73n.71
Philoxenus, 58–59, 132, 138–39
Pindar, 44–45, 61, 63–64, 65n.59, 67, 68, 69–70, 73–74, 76–79, 83, 193n.1
place
   and placelessness, 28–29, 30–31, 90, 92, 193–94
   places aligned by movement, 33–34, 41, 43
   relations between places, 50–51, 55
   as spatial concept, 38
   See also houses; space
Ploutos, 176
poet
   and autocratic rulers, 84, 87–88
   social role of, 75–76, 82, 86
poverty, 187–88, 190, 191
presence, 98–99, 100, 101–2, 103–4, 125–28, 129, 130–31, 135, 157, 169, 194–95
Ptolemaic empire
   basis of wealth of, 36
   Egypt within, 37
   multiculturalism in, 192–93
   spatial configuration of, 88–89, 192–93
   See also Alexandria
Ptolemy I Soter, 73n.71, 88–89
Ptolemy II Philadelphus
   as apex of empire, 36
   birth of, 88–89
   claims of, to legitimacy, 69–70
   devotion of, to eros, 197

effects of authority of, 38
generosity of, 86, 88–89
grand procession of, 178
as hoped-for good king, 85–86, 169, 192–93
as protector of Egypt, 87–88
sister-marriage of, 73n.71
as "spearman," 87
Purchase, Philip, 110n.47, 131–32
Pyrrhos, 162–63

reciprocity
in *Id.* 1, 17–18
in *Id.* 6, 129–30
in *Id.* 16, 77–78
in *Id.* 17, 86
Reed, Joseph, 129n.88
road
encounters on, 28–29, 32–34, 40
fluidity of identities on, 30–31

sacrifice, animal, 163–65
Sappho, 177–78, 179
Samos, 36
Scholten, Helga, 169–70n.45
Segal, Charles, 3n.7, 45, 113n.54, 156, 157, 197
Sens, Alexander, 52, 54n.24, 62n.46
sexuality
animal vs. human, 95–96, 103–4, 167
of Delphis (*Id.* 2), 143–44
Simonides, 44–45, 66–67, 70, 81
Sistakou, Evina, 26–27
Skinner, Marilyn, 34n.90
slavery, 8–9, 14–15, 16, 21–24, 41, 64–65, 85, 145–46, 171–74
Sositheus, 179
South Italy
as setting for *Ids.* 4 and 5, 155–56, 168–69
space
and absence, xiii, 45

bucolic, 4–32, 43, 55–56
confusion of (*Id.* 13), 50–51
elision of, 46–47, 53, 54
encomiastic, 73–92
in Fiction, xii, 1–3
and gender, 68, 69–70, 143–44, 145–46
hierarchies expressed by, 35–36, 38
and human culture, 3, 20
in masculine competition, 19, 20
mythological, 44–73
Relational, 2, 25, 38
Relative, 2–3, 25, 26–27, 35
Representations of, 1–2
of representation, 2, 15
as subsumed within Ptolemaic empire, 192–93
in urban mimes, 32–43
See also Bucolic world; houses; place; space-time
space-time, 75, 80, 88–89
spear
as imperial symbol, 87
springs, 5, 6–7, 16–18, 25, 45, 130–31, 194
in *Id.* 13, 49, 50–51, 192–93
in *Id.* 22, 53, 55–56, 192–93, 196–97
Stanzel, Karl-Heinz, 105n.29
Stephens, Susan, 85–86, 157, 168–69, 192–93, 197
Stern, Jacob, 67–68
Sybaris, 11–12, 16, 85, 168–69
symposium, 21, 42–43, 123–24, 142n.124
and Greek identity, 89–90
in *Id.* 14, 90–91
syrinx, 9n.24, 18, 106, 161, 162–63

Theocritus
in Alexandria (?), xvi–
and contemporary culture, 83
life, xvi–xvii
works, xi
Thetis, 71–72, 136–37
Thomas, Richard, 57–58

Thurii, 11–12, 16, 168–69
time
  agricultural, 80, 171
  bucolic, 56, 80
  of day, 28–29, 80n.89
  linear, 33–34
  markers of, 53, 56, 80, 81, 123
  mythic, 25
  narrative, 129, 132–33
  and relative space, 35
  ritual, 33–34
  telescoping of (*Id.* 13), 48
  See also space-time
transhumance, 14–15

Van Sickle, John, 156, 157–58n.9
voice, 102, 113–20, 121, 125–26, 128
  See also voice

Walker, Steven, 162, 169–70n.45
Whitehorn, John, 33–34, 170–71, 178
wool and textile production, 33–34, 36–37
  and gender, 33–34, 36–37
  See also gender
world-building, 1–2, 20–21
Worman, Nancy, 3–4n.8, 28n.75